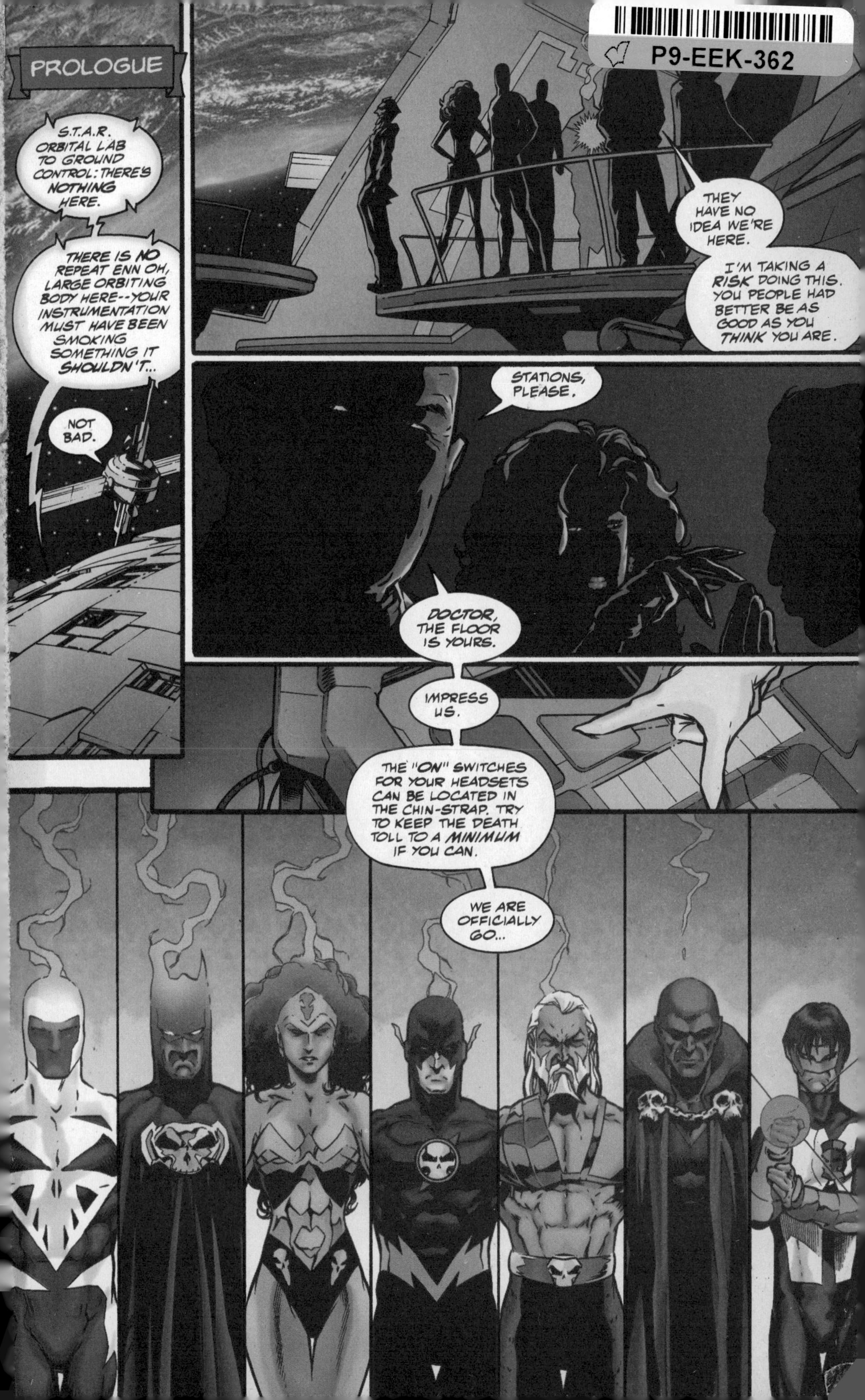
PROLOGUE
S.T.A.R. ORBITAL LAB TO GROUND CONTROL: THERE'S NOTHING HERE.
THERE IS NO REPEAT ENN OH, LARGE ORBITING BODY HERE--YOUR INSTRUMENTATION MUST HAVE BEEN SMOKING SOMETHING IT SHOULDN'T...
NOT BAD.
THEY HAVE NO IDEA WE'RE HERE.
I'M TAKING A RISK DOING THIS. YOU PEOPLE HAD BETTER BE AS GOOD AS YOU THINK YOU ARE.
STATIONS, PLEASE.
DOCTOR, THE FLOOR IS YOURS.
IMPRESS US.
THE "ON" SWITCHES FOR YOUR HEADSETS CAN BE LOCATED IN THE CHIN-STRAP. TRY TO KEEP THE DEATH TOLL TO A MINIMUM IF YOU CAN.
WE ARE OFFICIALLY GO...

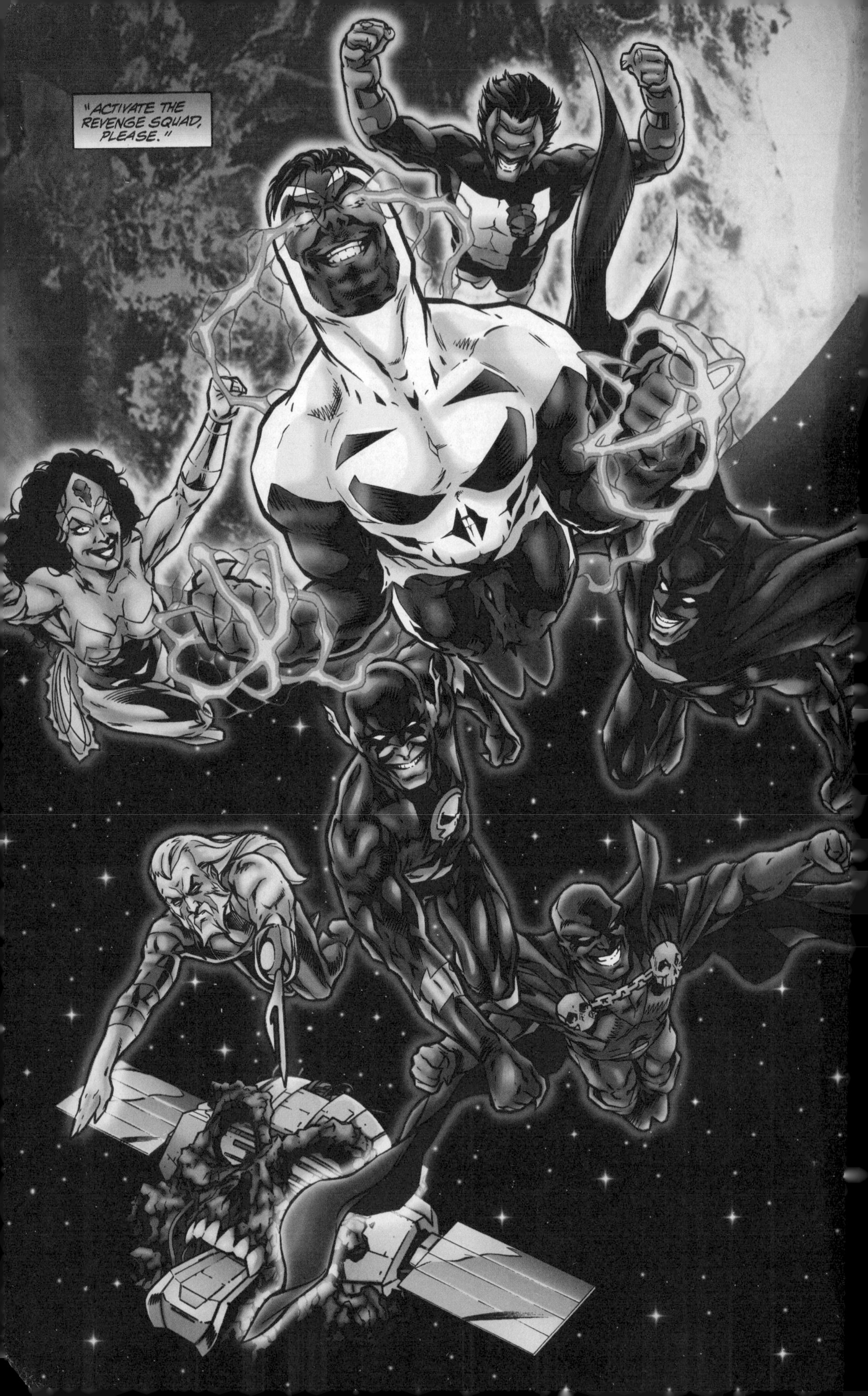
"ACTIVATE THE REVENGE SQUAD, PLEASE."

JLA
ROCK OF AGES

GrantMorrisoN
Writer

HowardPorteR
GaryFranK   OscarJimenez   GregLanD
Pencillers

JohnDell
BobMcLeod   ChipWallace
Inkers

PatGarrahY
Colorist

KenLopeZ
Letterer

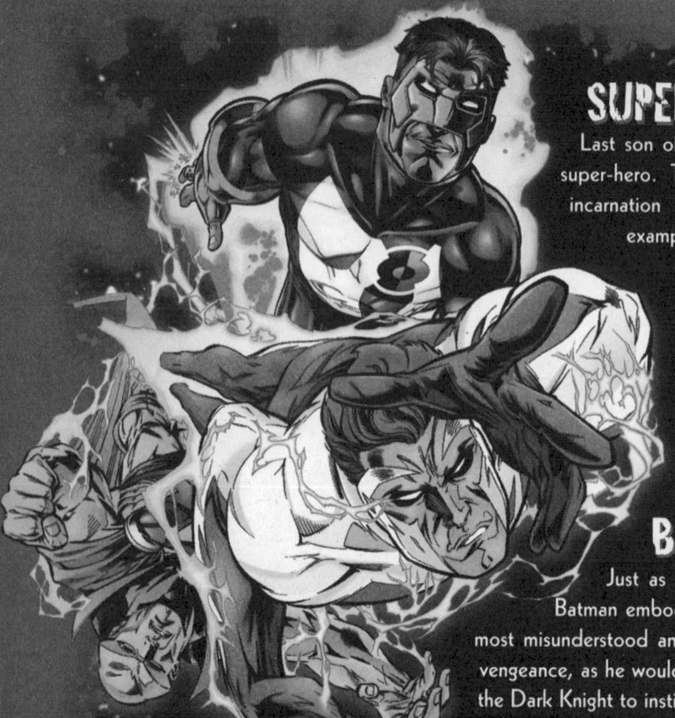

SUPERMAN

Last son of the planet Krypton, Superman is the world's super-hero. The guiding force behind the formation of t incarnation of the Justice League, Superman has becc example all metahumans on Earth strive to equal changed his adopted planet forever by existence. His powers transformed by still- events, Superman is now able to become pure energy. His special containment suit car energy to create a variety of effects, includi jection and manipulation of electromag control over his molecular density and fly at electrifying speeds.

BATMAN

Just as Superman is the perfection all superhumans Batman embodies everything Man can ever hope to be. P most misunderstood and complex figure of his day, Batman is no vengeance, as he would have us believe, but by a desire to use the the Dark Knight to instill fear in his opponents and ensure that others w experience the tragedy that has shaped his life. Using his keen a body honed to physical perfection and a vast arsenal of technological an resources, Batman wages a personal war with crime on its own shadowy terrain.

WONDER WOMAN

Daughter of Queen Hippolyta of the island nation Themyscira, Wonder Woman was chosen above all Amazon sisters to enter Man's World as their ambassador. Trained in the arts of war since childhood, and g by the gods of Olympus with great strength and the power of flight, Wonder Woman uses her talents to de the ideal of peace she holds dear. One of the cornerstones of the new League, Diana recently died in at the hands of the demon Neron.

THE FLASH

His name is Wally West — and he is the Fastest Man Alive. The third in a long tradition of super-speedsters Flash has been a very public super-hero for almost his entire life, unlike many of his teammates. Originally kn as Kid Flash, Wally became the only former sidekick to fulfill the job's unspoken duty when he took over the F identity. By tapping into an extradimensional "speed force," the Flash is able to reach velocities that appro speed of light itself. His link to the speed force also enables him to "lend" additional velocity to objects a in motion and vibrate through solid objects, but not without causing them to explode.

GREEN LANTERN

One of the youngest members of the team, Green Lantern makes up for what he lacks in experience wit unmatched enthusiasm. Regarded by the other members as a major player, Kyle Rayner is relatively inse knowing that he was chosen to be Green Lantern through a twist of fate, rather than by being carefully selected. G Lantern's power ring, the most powerful weapon in the universe, is able to create solid light images which c shaped to take any form he can imagine — and imagination is an ability that Kyle has in abundance.

AQUAMAN

Born of an Atlantean queen and an ancient wizard, King of the Seas and sworn protector of almost three-q of the Earth, Aquaman's name is known — and often feared — both above and below the waves. Quiet, serious as the tides, all his teammates gladly give Aquaman the respect he demands. A lifetime spent withstan the intense pressures of the deep have made him incredibly strong and amazingly fast both in water and on lan Unlike other Atlanteans, he alone possesses the power to telepathically communicate with sea creatures. The hoo that replaces his lost left hand can be fired like a harpoon when necessary and is cybernetically controlled.

...IN J'ONZZ, THE MANHUNTER FROM MARS

...hrough time and space from his native Mars by Earth science, J'onn J'onzz was left stranded on a strange ...ld. Possibly the most highly regarded by his JLA peers, he has been a founding member of every ...n of the team. An intensely silent figure, as is common among telepaths, his loyalty to his adopted home ...d challenge and his determination to overcome any obstacle is unmatched. Among his many inhuman ...re the powers of flight, super-strength, super-speed, Martian vision and the natural Martian ability to alter ...l shape and density.

...N ARROW

...known son of the original Green Arrow, Connor Hawke the complete antithesis to his volatile, ...father. An earnest young man with a mature and thoughtful nature, Green Arrow was recently ... the JLA by Green Lantern in a bid to enlarge the team roster. Incorrectly perceived as the League's ...er, Green Arrow is far more than a guy with a bow and arrow. An expert in martial arts and a skilled ... able to single-handedly defeat one of the team's oldest and deadliest foes, the Key.

...K, THE ULTIMATE MAN

...member of the Justice League, Aztek was asked to join based on the ringing endorsements of Superman, ...d Green Lantern. Prepared since childhood by the secretive and single-minded Q Foundation to be a ... Aztek is more comfortable trying to live up to his mentors' high expectations than he is dealing with the ...asks of day-to-day life. Aztek's armored costume gives him enhanced strength, the powers of flight and ... X-ray and infrared vision and a variety of other abilities — all of which are controlled by the Helmet ...zalcoatl.

...E INJUSTICE GANG

...s the new Justice League was formed in response to the growing threat of super-villains, ...justice Gang was created by Lex Luthor as a counterreaction. ... current membership is made up of...

... LUTHOR — the super-intelligent leader of the Injustice Gang ... commands through fear and intimidation

... JOKER — a deadly and unpredictable psychopath ...finds humor in the pain and suffering of others

...CE — a cunning enchantress whose stunning ... and beauty belies her ancient origins

...E MIRROR MASTER — a merce-...whose mirror-based technology is at the ...ce of the highest bidder

...EAN MASTER — half-brother of ...man and the sorcerous scourge of the seas

...TOR LIGHT — the master of light ...s forms who uses bravado to mask his ... cowardice

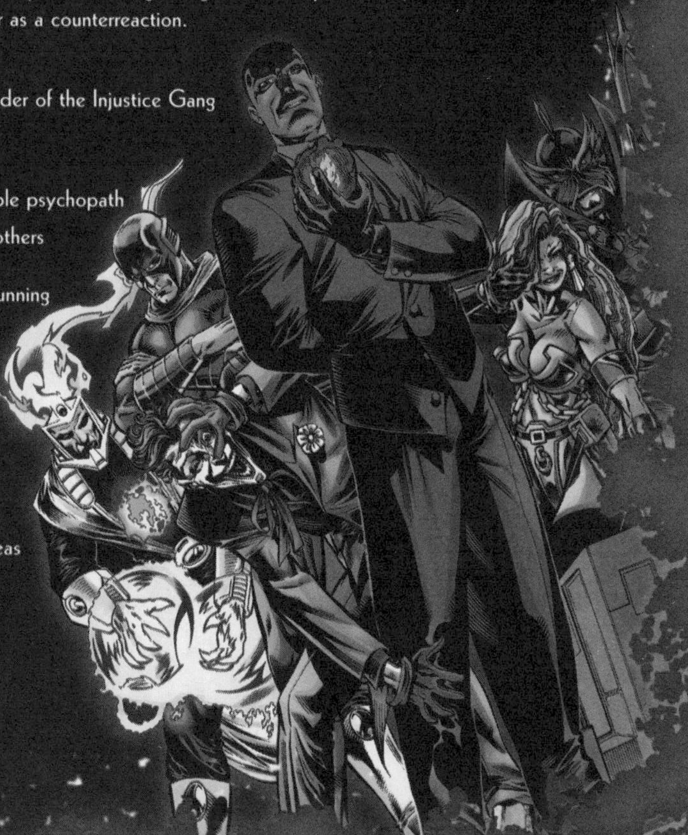

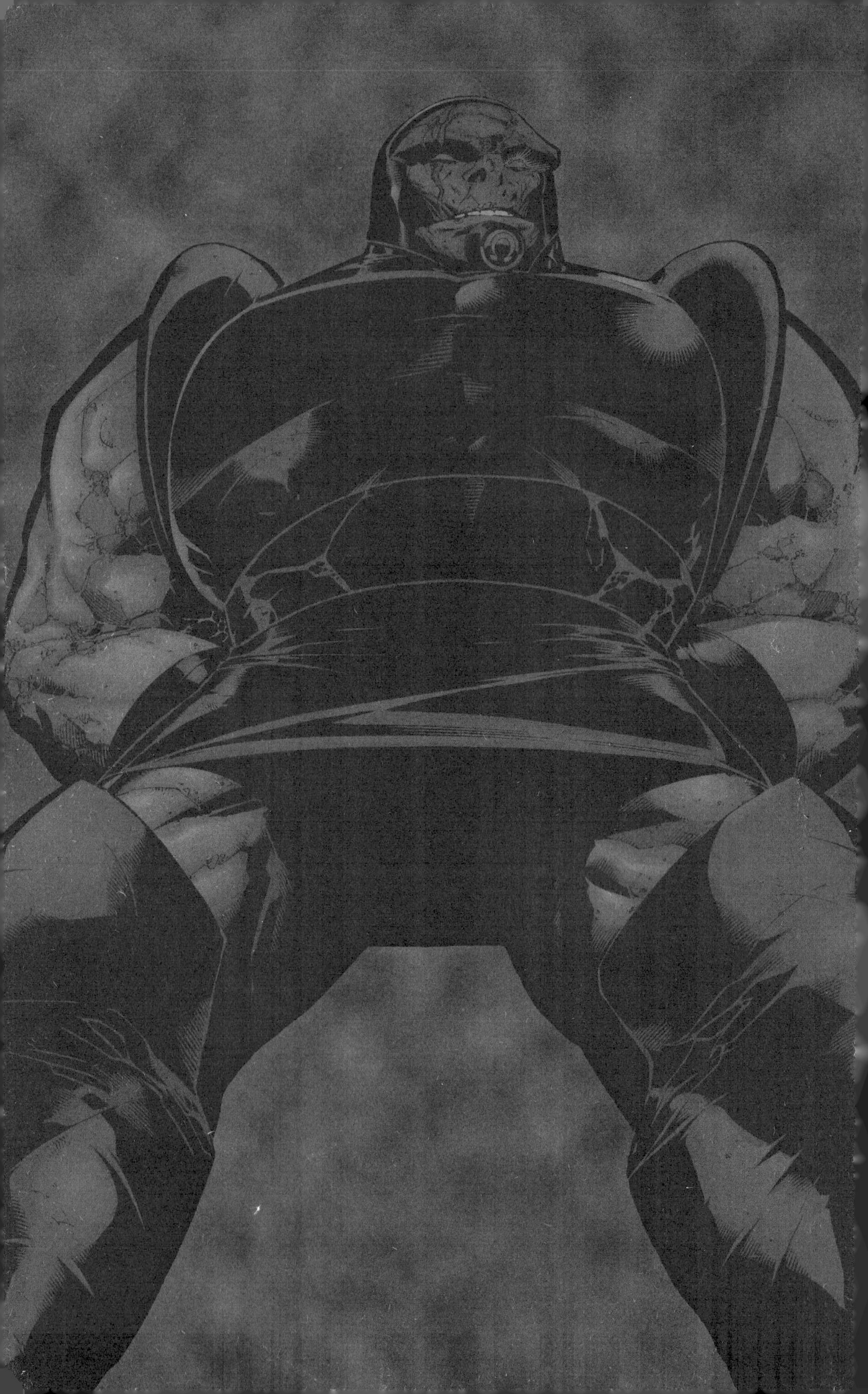

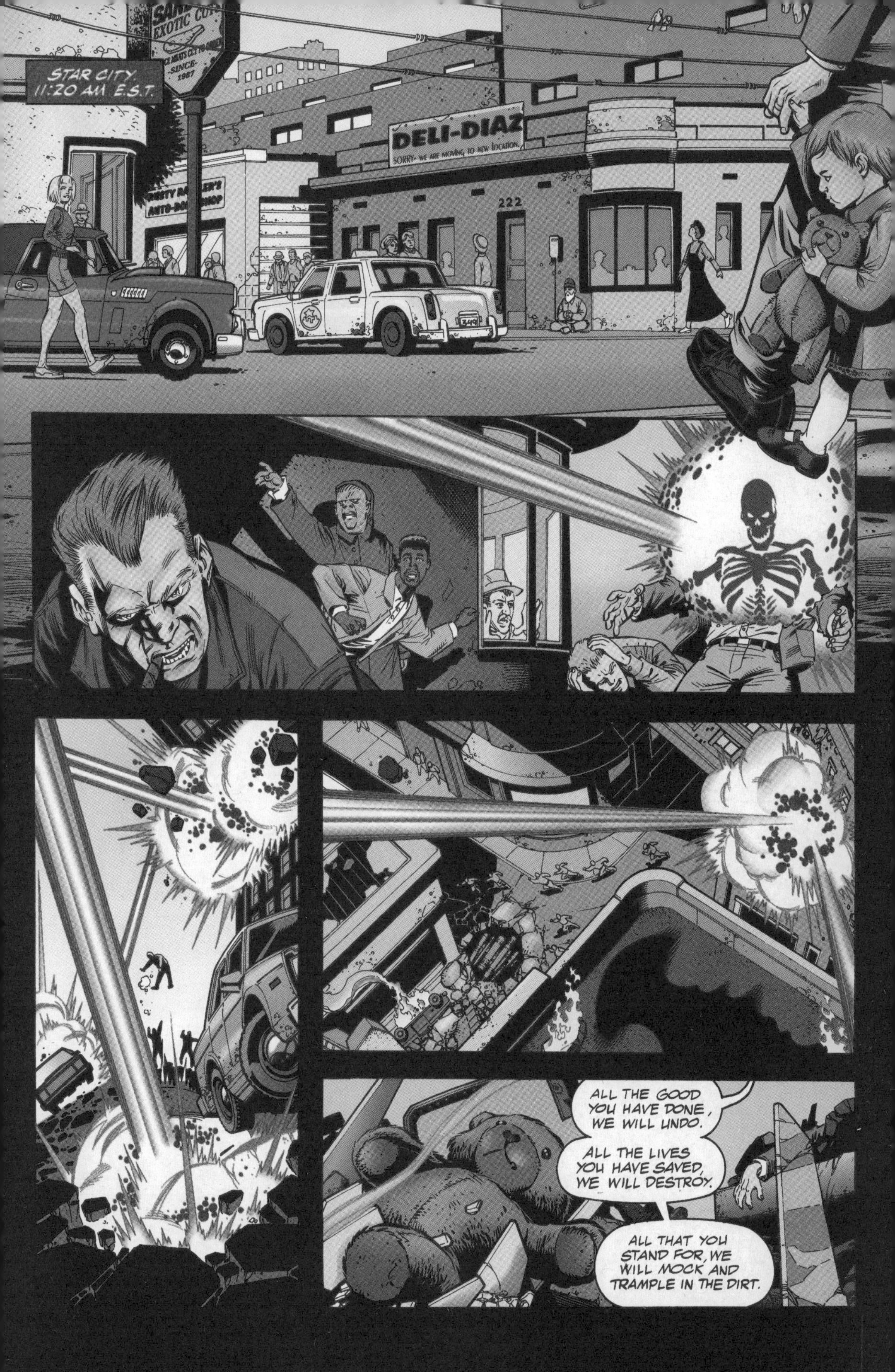
STAR CITY.
11:20 AM E.S.T.
-SINCE-
1987
DELI-DIAZ
SORRY- WE ARE MOVING TO NEW LOCATION.
222
ALL THE GOOD YOU HAVE DONE, WE WILL UNDO.
ALL THE LIVES YOU HAVE SAVED, WE WILL DESTROY.
ALL THAT YOU STAND FOR, WE WILL MOCK AND TRAMPLE IN THE DIRT.

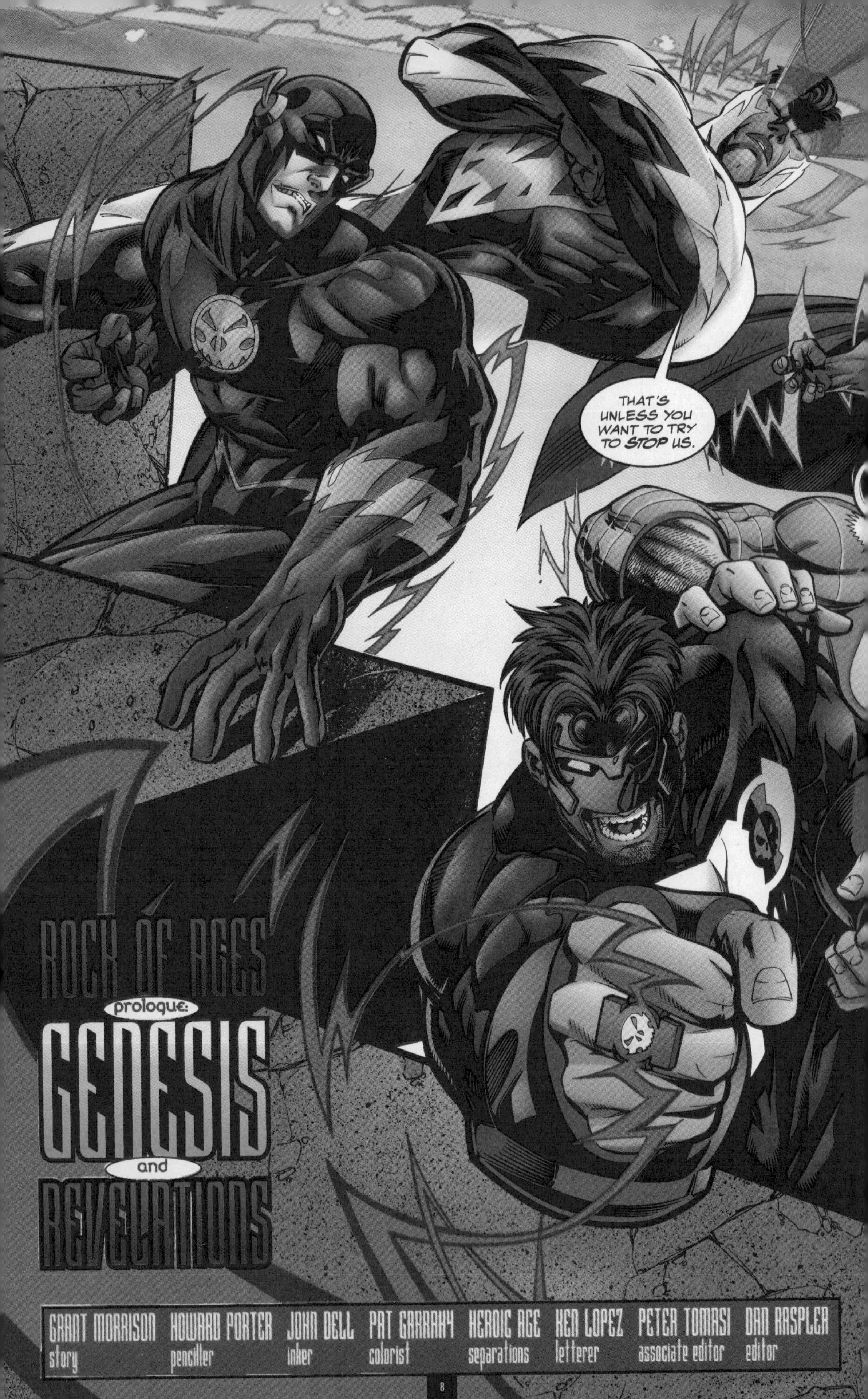

THAT'S UNLESS YOU WANT TO TRY TO STOP US.
ROCK OF AGES
prologue:
GENESIS
and
REVELATIONS
GRANT MORRISON story
HOWARD PORTER penciller
JOHN DELL inker
PAT GARRAHY colorist
HEROIC AGE separations
KEN LOPEZ letterer
PETER TOMASI associate editor
DAN RASPLER editor

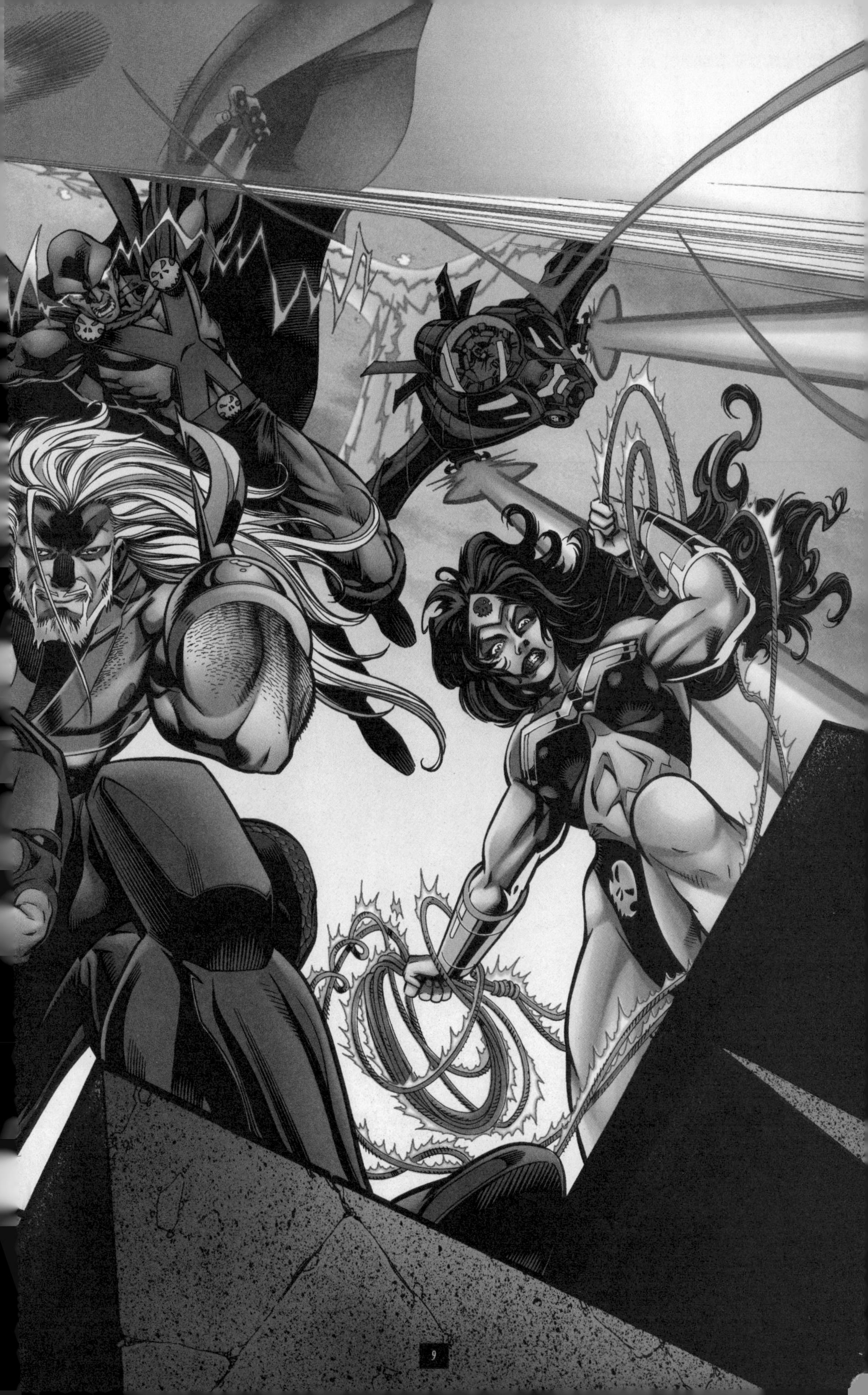

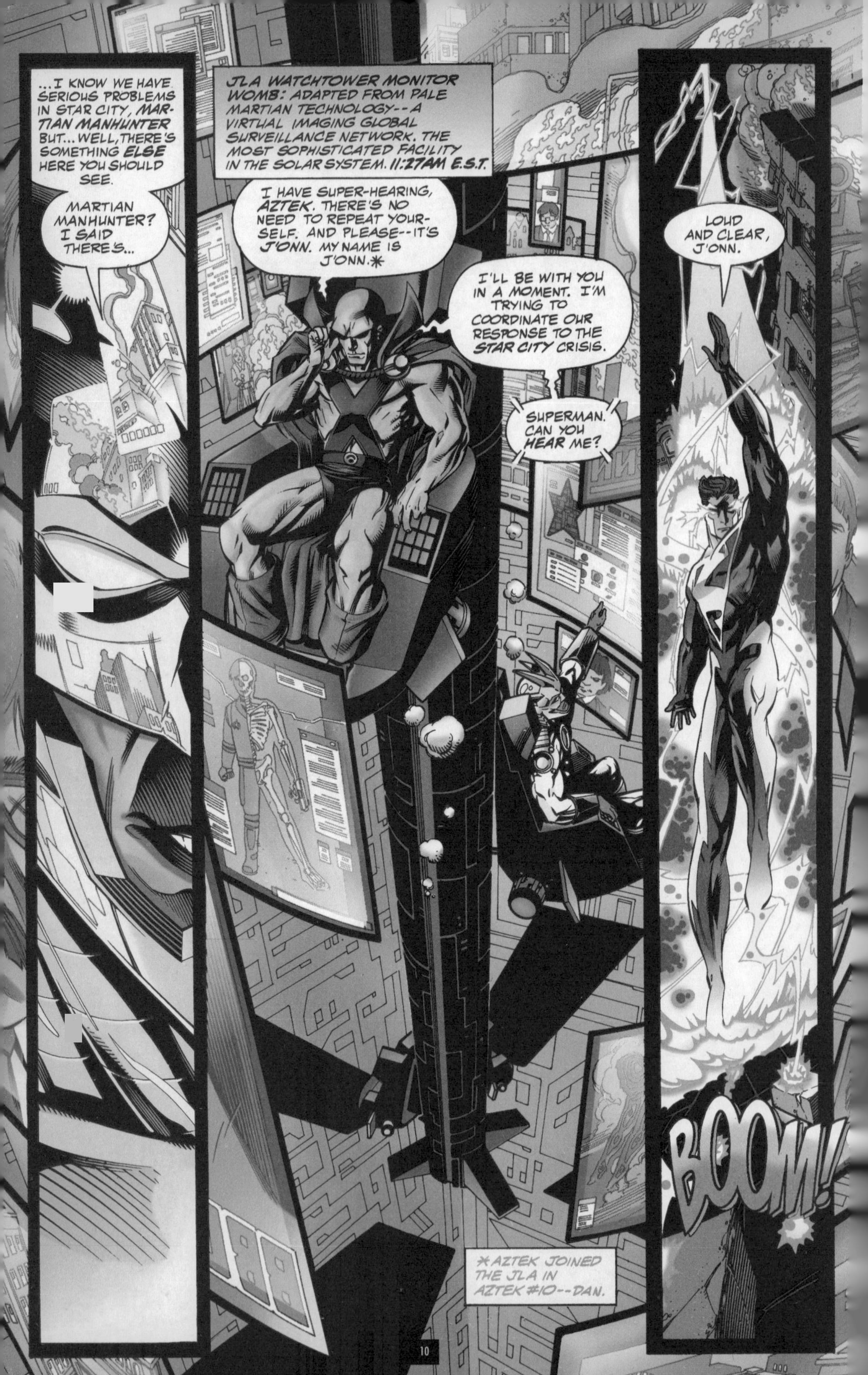

...I KNOW WE HAVE SERIOUS PROBLEMS IN STAR CITY, MARTIAN MANHUNTER BUT... WELL, THERE'S SOMETHING ELSE HERE YOU SHOULD SEE.
MARTIAN MANHUNTER? I SAID THERE'S...
JLA WATCHTOWER MONITOR WOMB: ADAPTED FROM PALE MARTIAN TECHNOLOGY-- A VIRTUAL IMAGING GLOBAL SURVEILLANCE NETWORK. THE MOST SOPHISTICATED FACILITY IN THE SOLAR SYSTEM. 11:27AM E.S.T.
I HAVE SUPER-HEARING, AZTEK. THERE'S NO NEED TO REPEAT YOURSELF. AND PLEASE--IT'S J'ONN. MY NAME IS J'ONN.*
I'LL BE WITH YOU IN A MOMENT. I'M TRYING TO COORDINATE OUR RESPONSE TO THE STAR CITY CRISIS.
SUPERMAN. CAN YOU HEAR ME?
LOUD AND CLEAR, J'ONN.
BOOM!!
*AZTEK JOINED THE JLA IN AZTEK #10--DAN.

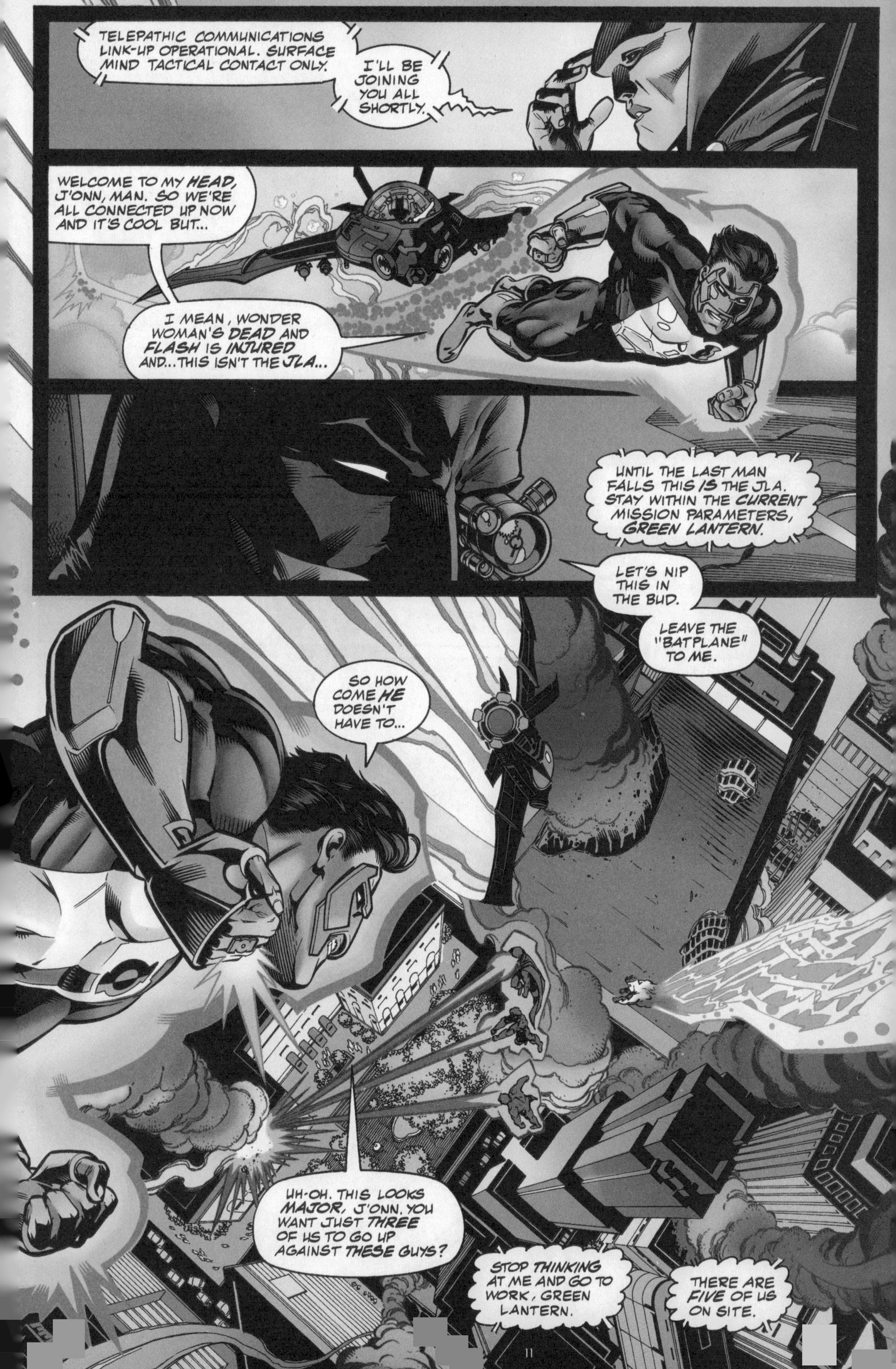
TELEPATHIC COMMUNICATIONS LINK-UP OPERATIONAL. SURFACE MIND TACTICAL CONTACT ONLY.
I'LL BE JOINING YOU ALL SHORTLY.
WELCOME TO MY HEAD, J'ONN, MAN. SO WE'RE ALL CONNECTED UP NOW AND IT'S COOL BUT...
I MEAN, WONDER WOMAN'S DEAD AND FLASH IS INJURED AND... THIS ISN'T THE JLA...
UNTIL THE LAST MAN FALLS THIS IS THE JLA. STAY WITHIN THE CURRENT MISSION PARAMETERS, GREEN LANTERN.
LET'S NIP THIS IN THE BUD.
LEAVE THE "BATPLANE" TO ME.
SO HOW COME HE DOESN'T HAVE TO...
UH-OH. THIS LOOKS MAJOR, J'ONN. YOU WANT JUST THREE OF US TO GO UP AGAINST THESE GUYS?
STOP THINKING AT ME AND GO TO WORK, GREEN LANTERN.
THERE ARE FIVE OF US ON SITE.

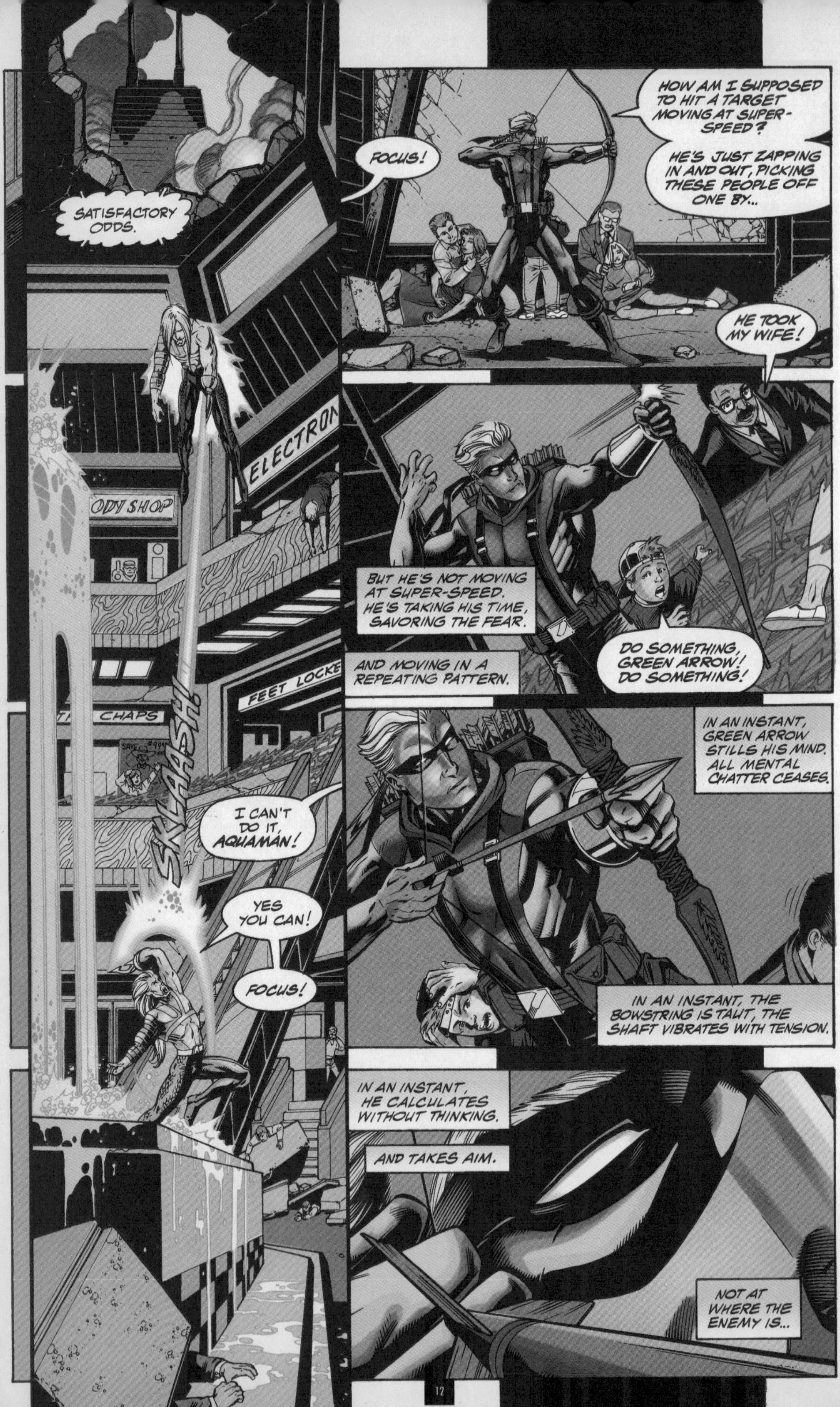
SATISFACTORY ODDS.
ELECTRON
ODY SHOP
FEET LOCKE
CHAPS
SKLAASH!
I CAN'T DO IT, AQUAMAN!
YES YOU CAN!
FOCUS!
HOW AM I SUPPOSED TO HIT A TARGET MOVING AT SUPER-SPEED?
HE'S JUST ZAPPING IN AND OUT, PICKING THESE PEOPLE OFF ONE BY...
FOCUS!
HE TOOK MY WIFE!
BUT HE'S NOT MOVING AT SUPER-SPEED. HE'S TAKING HIS TIME, SAVORING THE FEAR.
AND MOVING IN A REPEATING PATTERN.
DO SOMETHING, GREEN ARROW! DO SOMETHING!
IN AN INSTANT, GREEN ARROW STILLS HIS MIND. ALL MENTAL CHATTER CEASES.
IN AN INSTANT, THE BOWSTRING IS TAUT, THE SHAFT VIBRATES WITH TENSION.
IN AN INSTANT, HE CALCULATES WITHOUT THINKING.
AND TAKES AIM.
NOT AT WHERE THE ENEMY IS...

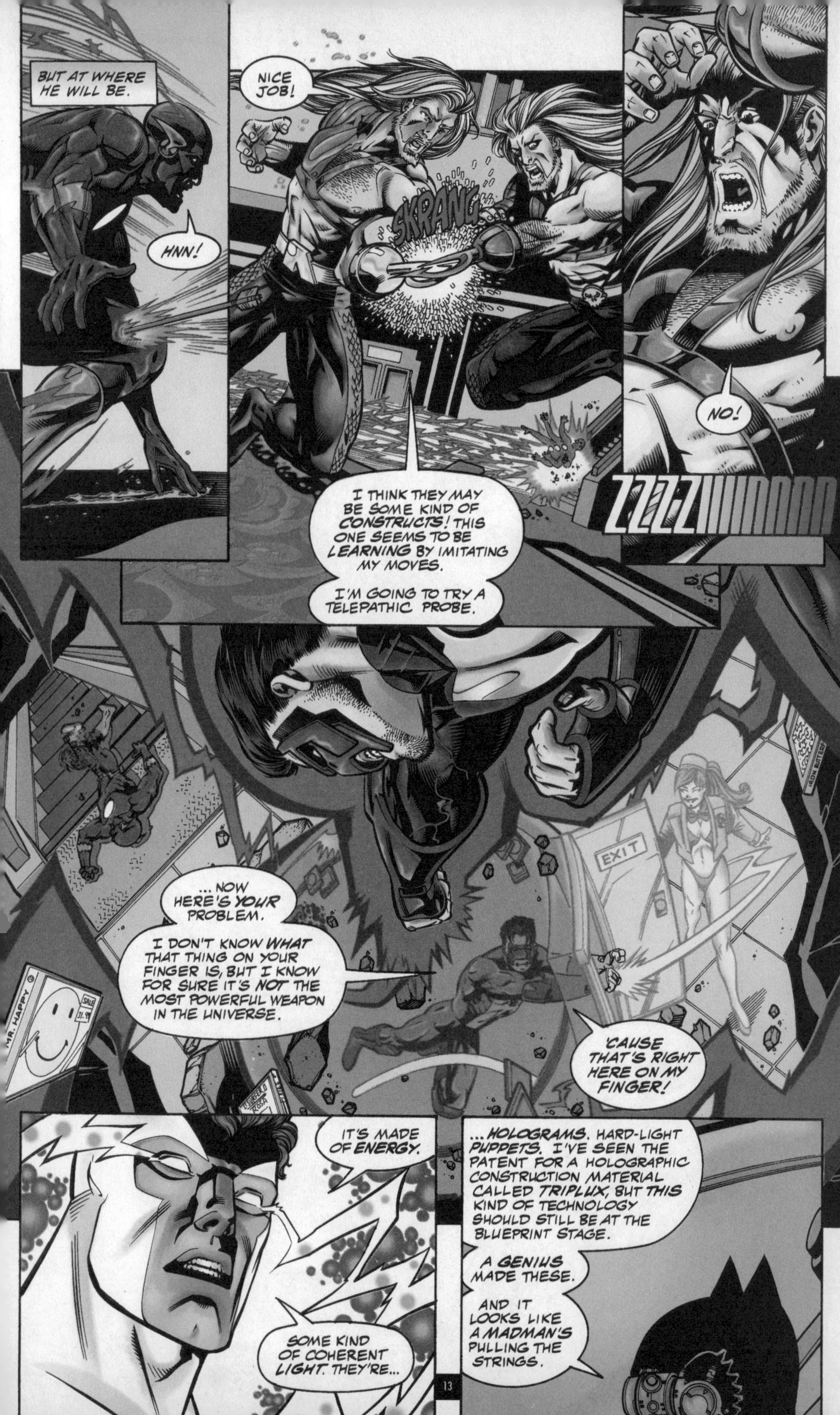

BUT AT WHERE HE WILL BE.
HNN!
NICE JOB!
SKRANG
NO!
ZZZZIIIINNNNN
I THINK THEY MAY BE SOME KIND OF CONSTRUCTS! THIS ONE SEEMS TO BE LEARNING BY IMITATING MY MOVES.
I'M GOING TO TRY A TELEPATHIC PROBE.
EXIT
...NOW HERE'S YOUR PROBLEM.
I DON'T KNOW WHAT THAT THING ON YOUR FINGER IS, BUT I KNOW FOR SURE IT'S NOT THE MOST POWERFUL WEAPON IN THE UNIVERSE.
MR. HAPPY
SALE
'CAUSE THAT'S RIGHT HERE ON MY FINGER!
IT'S MADE OF ENERGY.
SOME KIND OF COHERENT LIGHT. THEY'RE...
...HOLOGRAMS. HARD-LIGHT PUPPETS. I'VE SEEN THE PATENT FOR A HOLOGRAPHIC CONSTRUCTION MATERIAL CALLED TRIPLUX, BUT THIS KIND OF TECHNOLOGY SHOULD STILL BE AT THE BLUEPRINT STAGE.
A GENIUS MADE THESE.
AND IT LOOKS LIKE A MADMAN'S PULLING THE STRINGS.

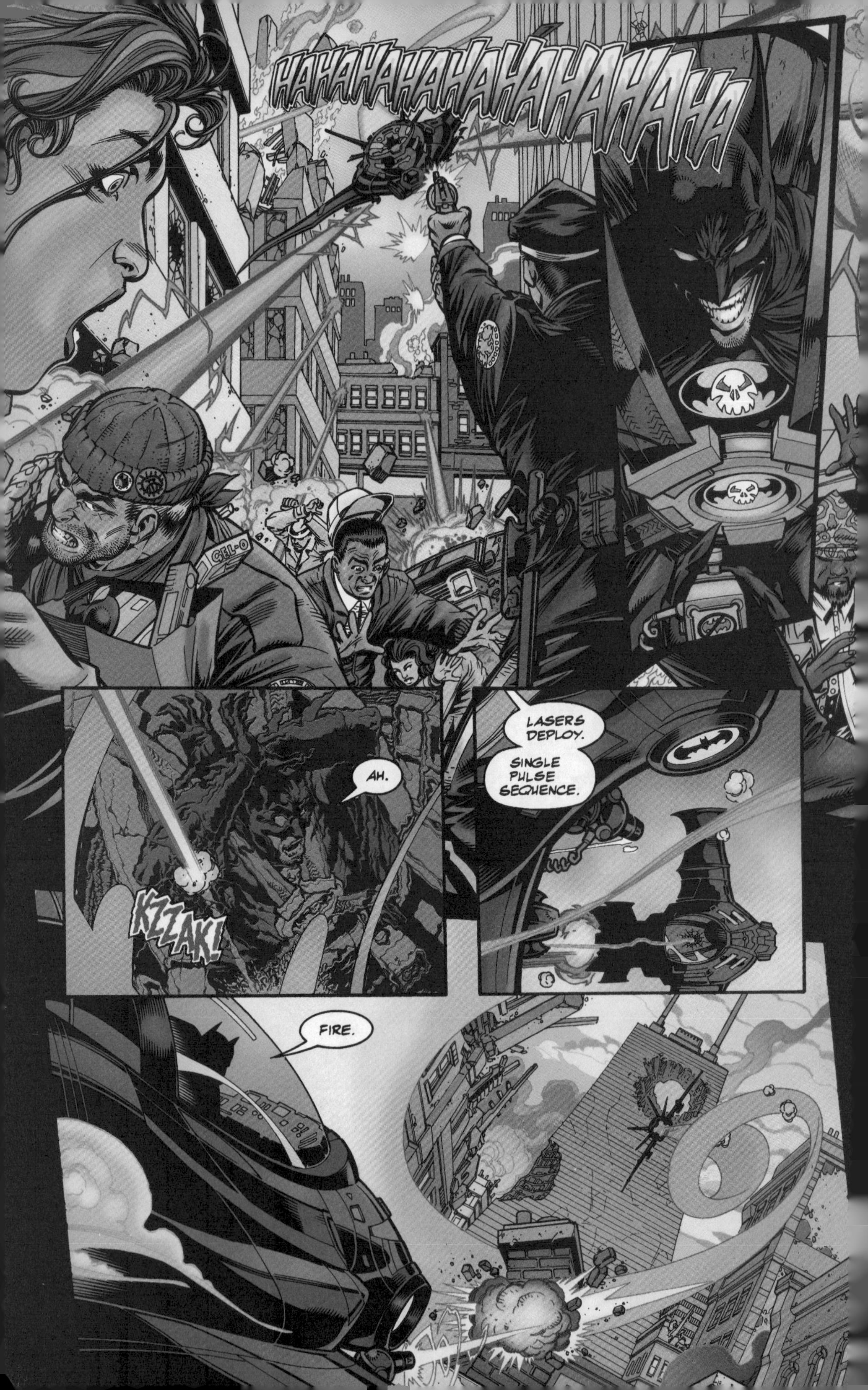
HAHAHAHAHAHAHAHAHAHAHA
GEL-O
AH.
KZZAK!
LASERS DEPLOY.
SINGLE PULSE SEQUENCE.
FIRE.

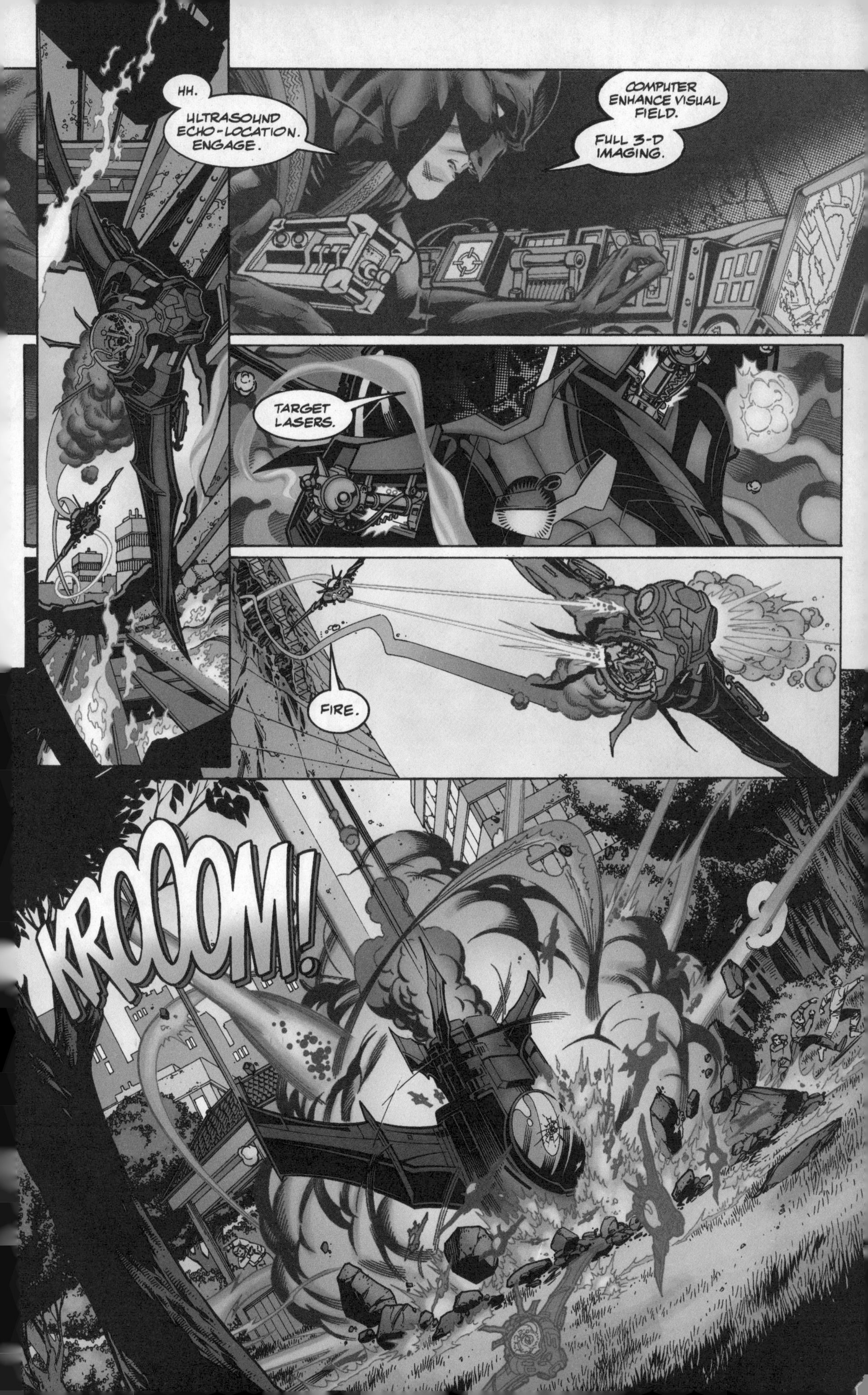
HH.
ULTRASOUND ECHO-LOCATION. ENGAGE.
COMPUTER ENHANCE VISUAL FIELD.
FULL 3-D IMAGING.
TARGET LASERS.
FIRE.
KROOOM!

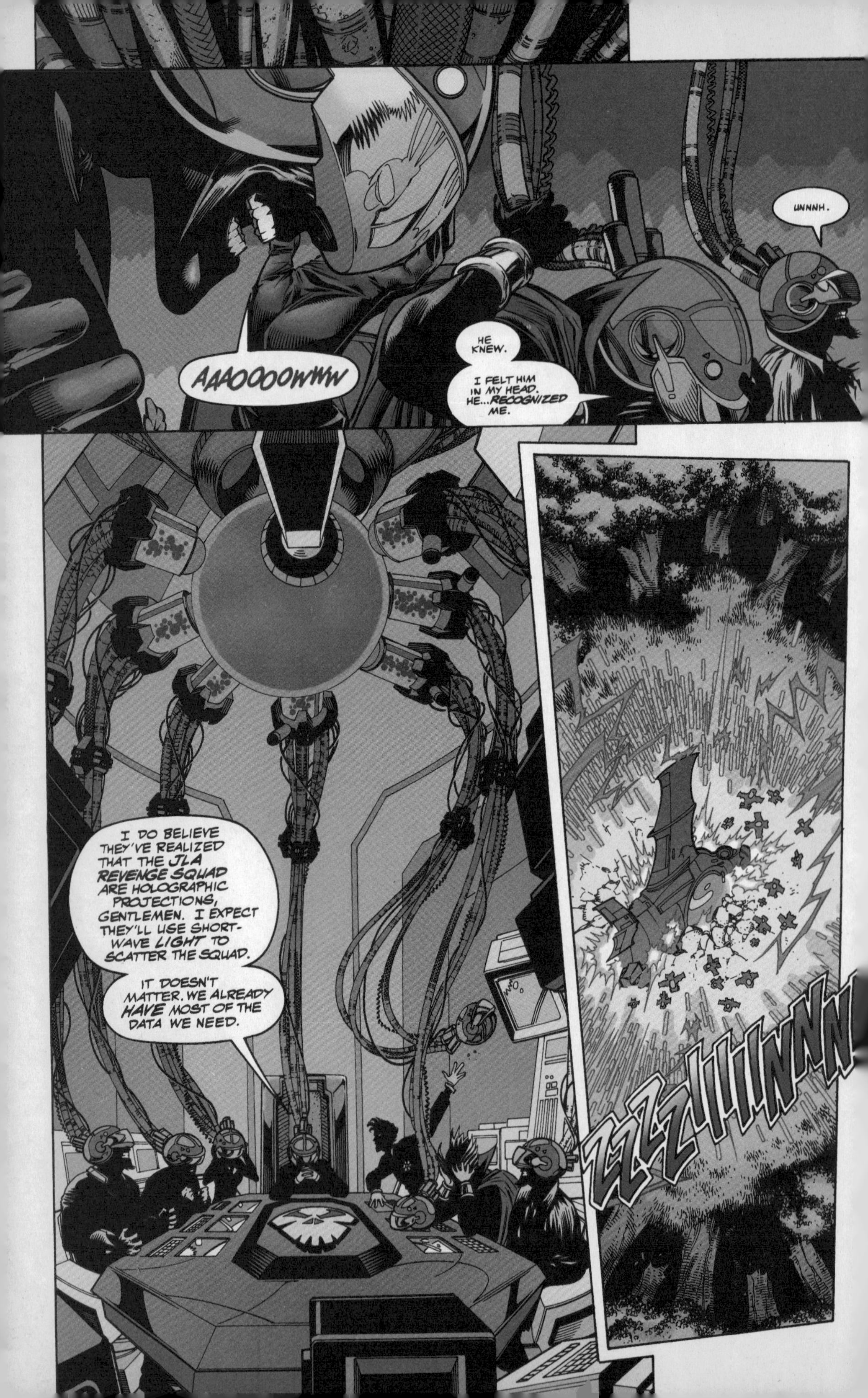

AAAOOOWWW
HE KNEW.
I FELT HIM IN MY HEAD. HE...RECOGNIZED ME.
UNNNH.
I DO BELIEVE THEY'VE REALIZED THAT THE JLA REVENGE SQUAD ARE HOLOGRAPHIC PROJECTIONS, GENTLEMEN. I EXPECT THEY'LL USE SHORT-WAVE LIGHT TO SCATTER THE SQUAD.
IT DOESN'T MATTER. WE ALREADY HAVE MOST OF THE DATA WE NEED.
ZZZIIIINNNN

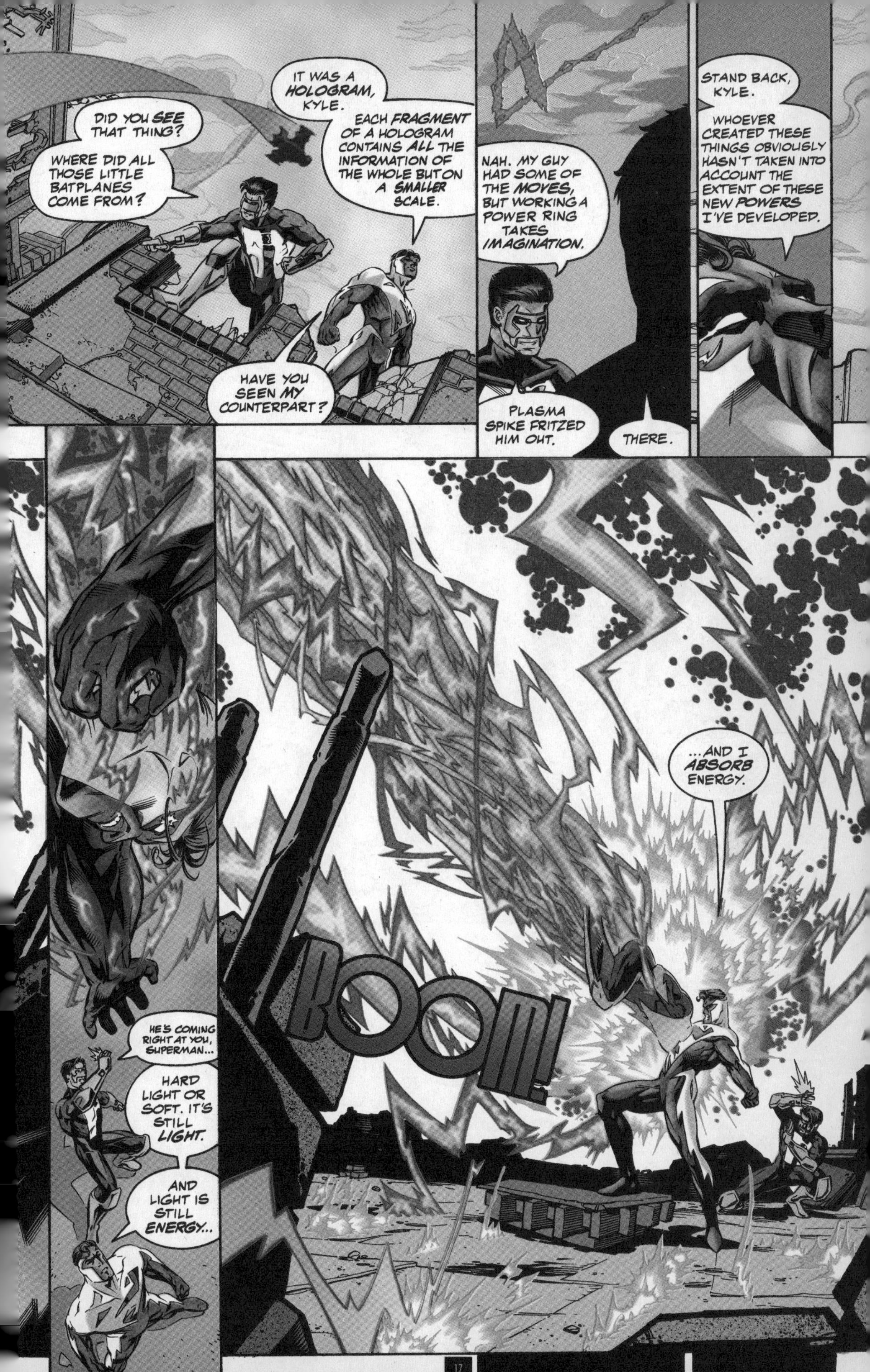
DID YOU SEE THAT THING?
WHERE DID ALL THOSE LITTLE BATPLANES COME FROM?
IT WAS A HOLOGRAM, KYLE.
EACH FRAGMENT OF A HOLOGRAM CONTAINS ALL THE INFORMATION OF THE WHOLE BUT ON A SMALLER SCALE.
HAVE YOU SEEN MY COUNTERPART?
NAH. MY GUY HAD SOME OF THE MOVES, BUT WORKING A POWER RING TAKES IMAGINATION.
PLASMA SPIKE FRITZED HIM OUT.
THERE.
STAND BACK, KYLE.
WHOEVER CREATED THESE THINGS OBVIOUSLY HASN'T TAKEN INTO ACCOUNT THE EXTENT OF THESE NEW POWERS I'VE DEVELOPED.
HE'S COMING RIGHT AT YOU, SUPERMAN...
HARD LIGHT OR SOFT. IT'S STILL LIGHT.
AND LIGHT IS STILL ENERGY...
...AND I ABSORB ENERGY.
BOOM!

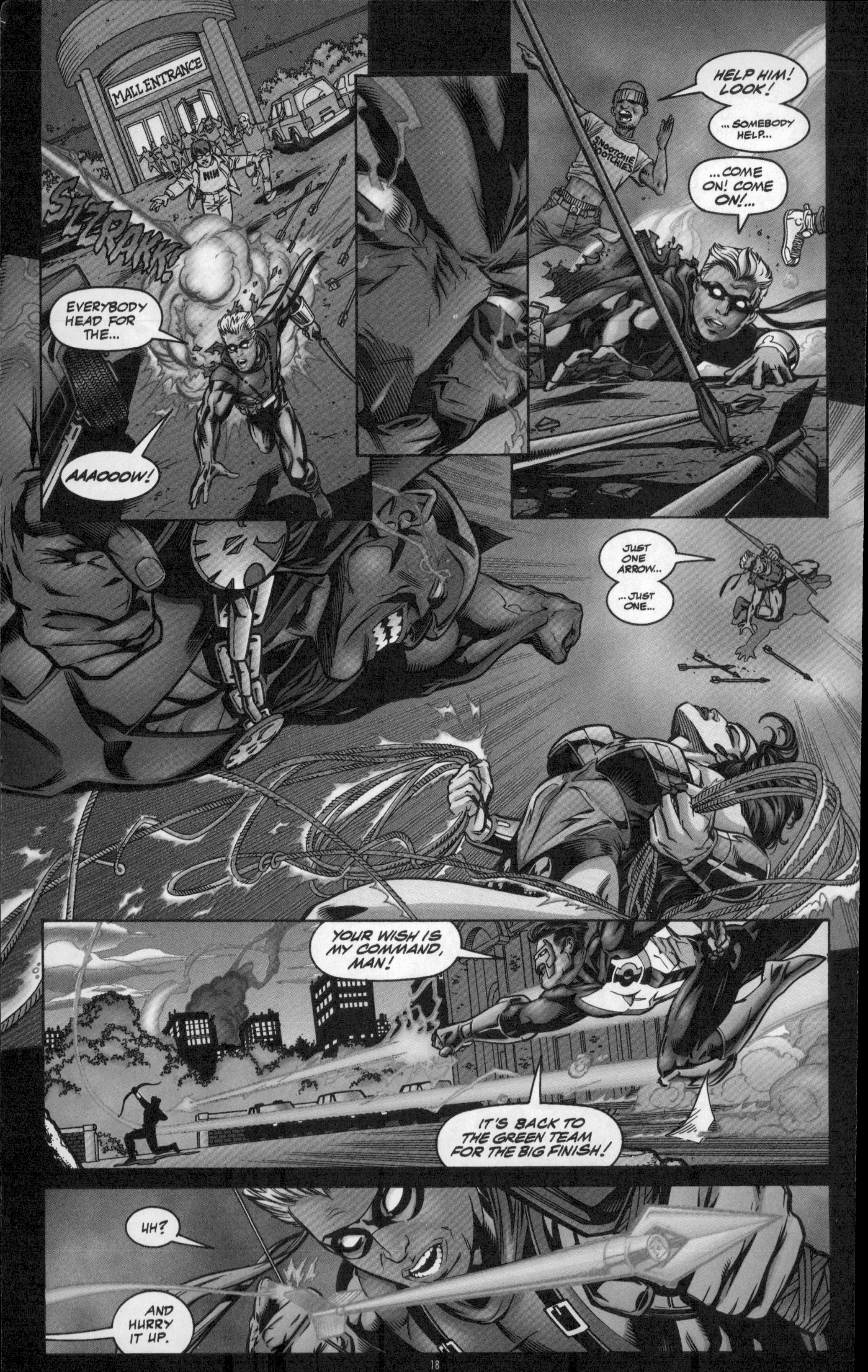
MALL ENTRANCE
SZZRAKK!
EVERYBODY HEAD FOR THE...
AAAOOOW!
HELP HIM! LOOK!
...SOMEBODY HELP...
...COME ON! COME ON!...
JUST ONE ARROW...
...JUST ONE...
YOUR WISH IS MY COMMAND, MAN!
IT'S BACK TO THE GREEN TEAM FOR THE BIG FINISH!
UH?
AND HURRY IT UP.

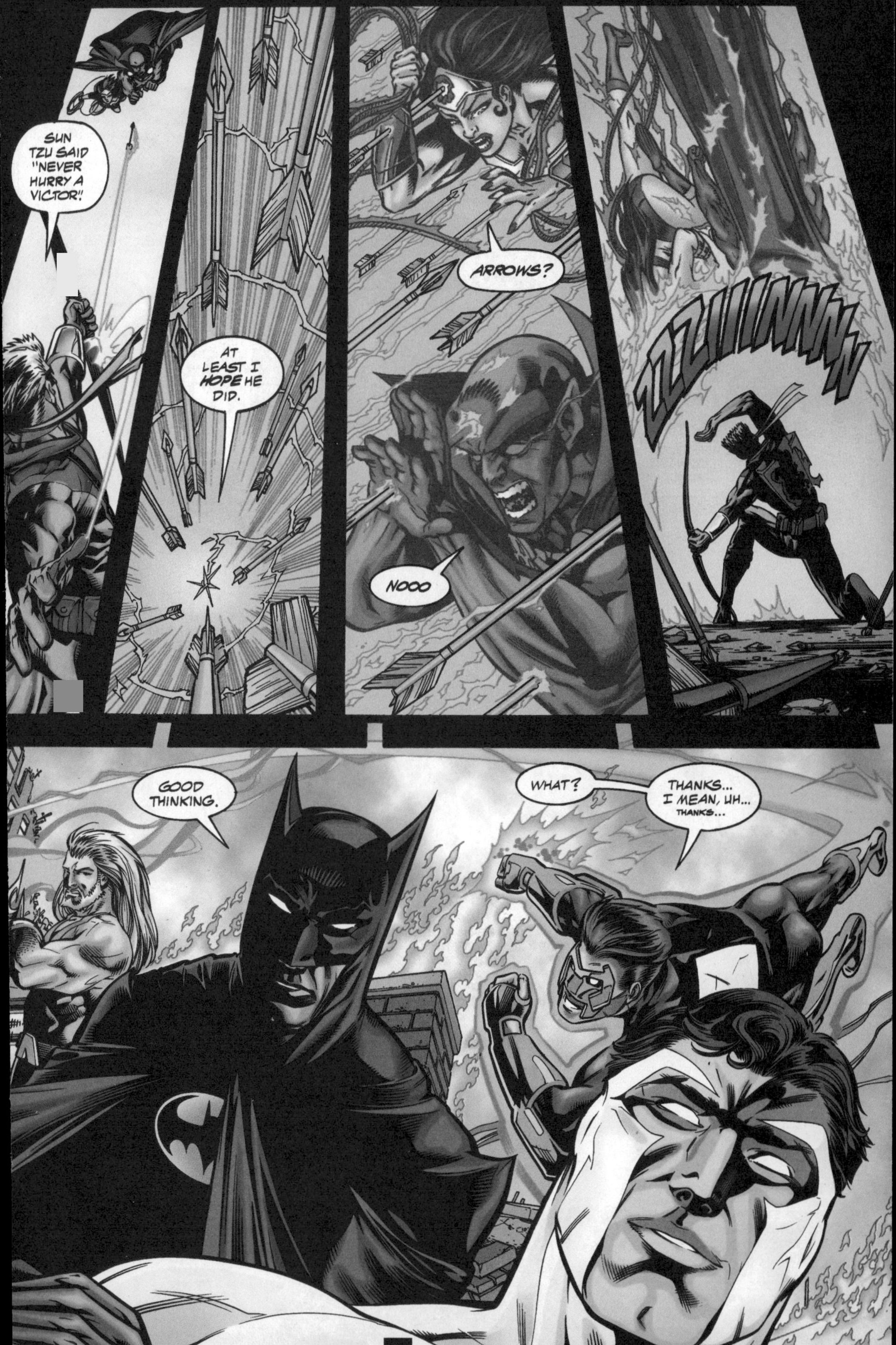
SUN TZU SAID "NEVER HURRY A VICTOR."
AT LEAST I HOPE HE DID.
ARROWS?
NOOO
ZZZIIIIINNNN
GOOD THINKING.
WHAT?
THANKS... I MEAN, UH... THANKS...

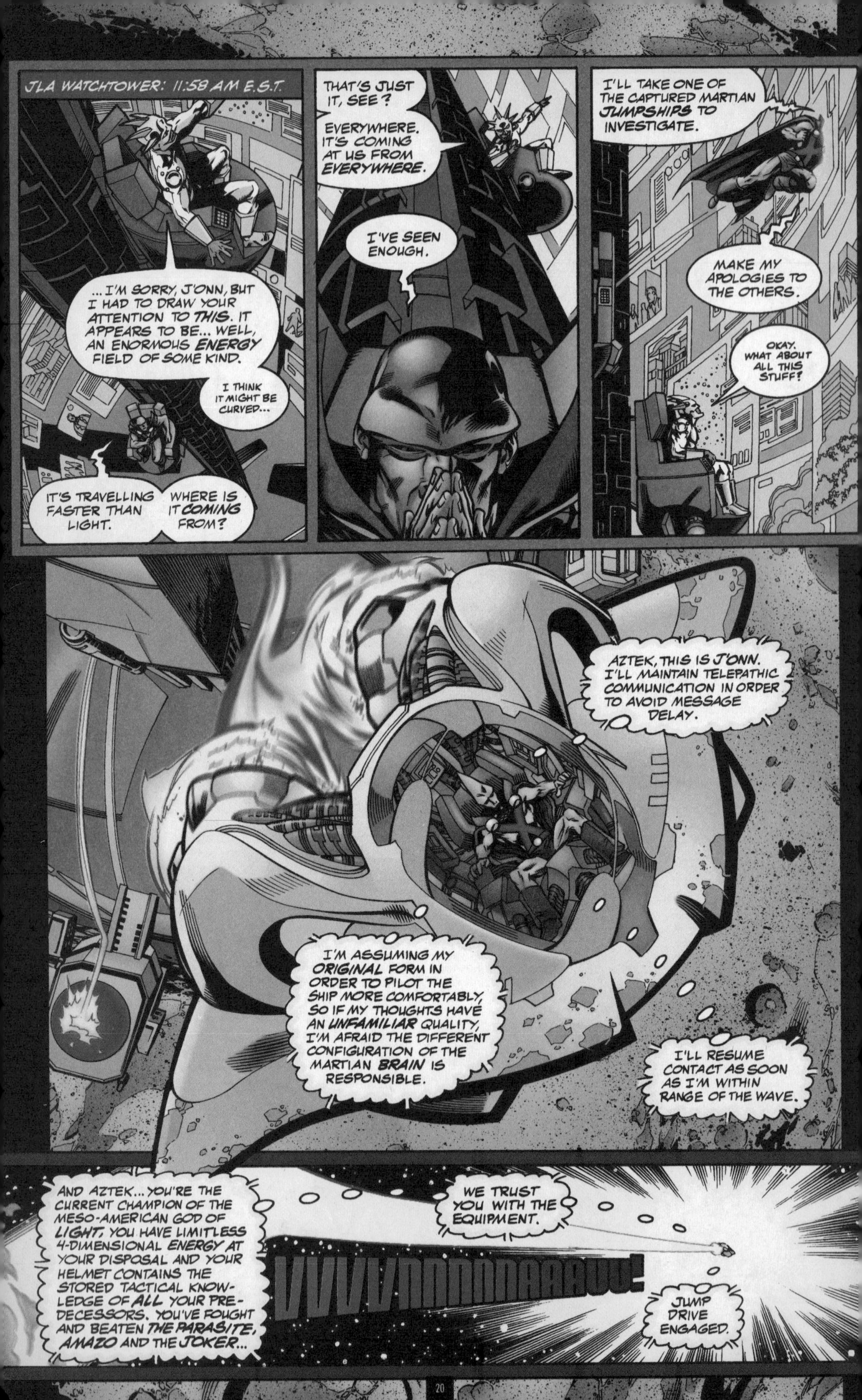
JLA WATCHTOWER: 11:58 AM E.S.T.
...I'M SORRY, J'ONN, BUT I HAD TO DRAW YOUR ATTENTION TO THIS. IT APPEARS TO BE... WELL, AN ENORMOUS ENERGY FIELD OF SOME KIND.
I THINK IT MIGHT BE CURVED...
IT'S TRAVELLING FASTER THAN LIGHT.
WHERE IS IT COMING FROM?
THAT'S JUST IT, SEE?
EVERYWHERE. IT'S COMING AT US FROM EVERYWHERE.
I'VE SEEN ENOUGH.
I'LL TAKE ONE OF THE CAPTURED MARTIAN JUMPSHIPS TO INVESTIGATE.
MAKE MY APOLOGIES TO THE OTHERS.
OKAY. WHAT ABOUT ALL THIS STUFF?
AZTEK, THIS IS J'ONN. I'LL MAINTAIN TELEPATHIC COMMUNICATION IN ORDER TO AVOID MESSAGE DELAY.
I'M ASSUMING MY ORIGINAL FORM IN ORDER TO PILOT THE SHIP MORE COMFORTABLY, SO IF MY THOUGHTS HAVE AN UNFAMILIAR QUALITY, I'M AFRAID THE DIFFERENT CONFIGURATION OF THE MARTIAN BRAIN IS RESPONSIBLE.
I'LL RESUME CONTACT AS SOON AS I'M WITHIN RANGE OF THE WAVE.
AND AZTEK... YOU'RE THE CURRENT CHAMPION OF THE MESO-AMERICAN GOD OF LIGHT, YOU HAVE LIMITLESS 4-DIMENSIONAL ENERGY AT YOUR DISPOSAL AND YOUR HELMET CONTAINS THE STORED TACTICAL KNOW-LEDGE OF ALL YOUR PRE-DECESSORS. YOU'VE FOUGHT AND BEATEN THE PARASITE, AMAZO AND THE JOKER...
WE TRUST YOU WITH THE EQUIPMENT.
VVVVNNNNNAAAUU!
JUMP DRIVE ENGAGED.

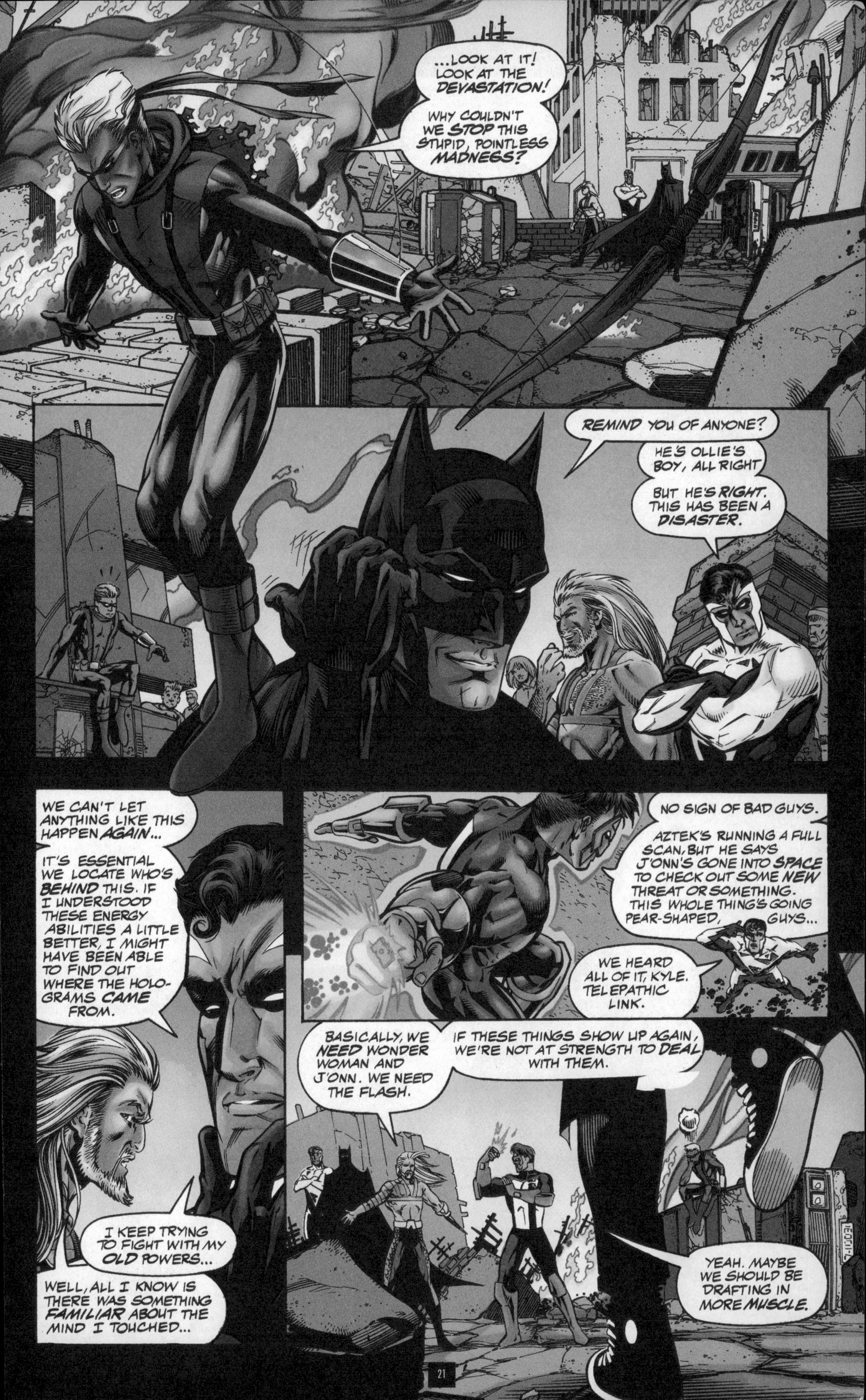
...LOOK AT IT! LOOK AT THE DEVASTATION!
WHY COULDN'T WE STOP THIS STUPID, POINTLESS MADNESS?
REMIND YOU OF ANYONE?
HE'S OLLIE'S BOY, ALL RIGHT
BUT HE'S RIGHT. THIS HAS BEEN A DISASTER.
WE CAN'T LET ANYTHING LIKE THIS HAPPEN AGAIN...
IT'S ESSENTIAL WE LOCATE WHO'S BEHIND THIS. IF I UNDERSTOOD THESE ENERGY ABILITIES A LITTLE BETTER, I MIGHT HAVE BEEN ABLE TO FIND OUT WHERE THE HOLOGRAMS CAME FROM.
I KEEP TRYING TO FIGHT WITH MY OLD POWERS...
WELL, ALL I KNOW IS THERE WAS SOMETHING FAMILIAR ABOUT THE MIND I TOUCHED...
NO SIGN OF BAD GUYS.
AZTEK'S RUNNING A FULL SCAN, BUT HE SAYS J'ONN'S GONE INTO SPACE TO CHECK OUT SOME NEW THREAT OR SOMETHING. THIS WHOLE THING'S GOING PEAR-SHAPED, GUYS...
WE HEARD ALL OF IT, KYLE. TELEPATHIC LINK.
BASICALLY, WE NEED WONDER WOMAN AND J'ONN. WE NEED THE FLASH.
IF THESE THINGS SHOW UP AGAIN, WE'RE NOT AT STRENGTH TO DEAL WITH THEM.
YEAH. MAYBE WE SHOULD BE DRAFTING IN MORE MUSCLE.

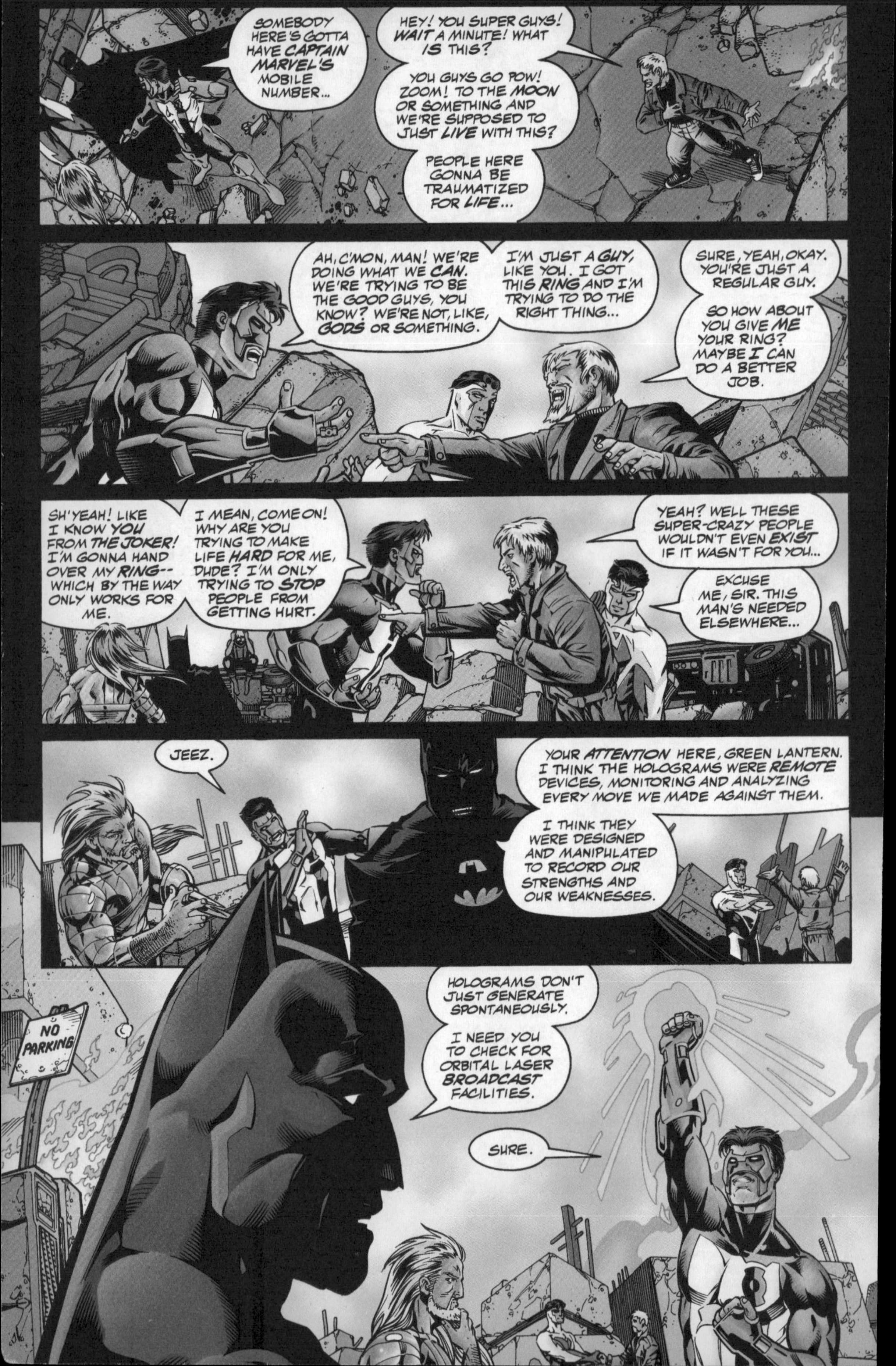
SOMEBODY HERE'S GOTTA HAVE CAPTAIN MARVEL'S MOBILE NUMBER...
HEY! YOU SUPER GUYS! WAIT A MINUTE! WHAT IS THIS?
YOU GUYS GO POW! ZOOM! TO THE MOON OR SOMETHING AND WE'RE SUPPOSED TO JUST LIVE WITH THIS?
PEOPLE HERE GONNA BE TRAUMATIZED FOR LIFE...
AH, C'MON, MAN! WE'RE DOING WHAT WE CAN. WE'RE TRYING TO BE THE GOOD GUYS, YOU KNOW? WE'RE NOT, LIKE, GODS OR SOMETHING.
I'M JUST A GUY, LIKE YOU. I GOT THIS RING AND I'M TRYING TO DO THE RIGHT THING...
SURE, YEAH, OKAY. YOU'RE JUST A REGULAR GUY.
SO HOW ABOUT YOU GIVE ME YOUR RING? MAYBE I CAN DO A BETTER JOB.
SH'YEAH! LIKE I KNOW YOU FROM THE JOKER! I'M GONNA HAND OVER MY RING-- WHICH BY THE WAY ONLY WORKS FOR ME.
I MEAN, COME ON! WHY ARE YOU TRYING TO MAKE LIFE HARD FOR ME, DUDE? I'M ONLY TRYING TO STOP PEOPLE FROM GETTING HURT.
YEAH? WELL THESE SUPER-CRAZY PEOPLE WOULDN'T EVEN EXIST IF IT WASN'T FOR YOU...
EXCUSE ME, SIR. THIS MAN'S NEEDED ELSEWHERE...
JEEZ.
YOUR ATTENTION HERE, GREEN LANTERN. I THINK THE HOLOGRAMS WERE REMOTE DEVICES, MONITORING AND ANALYZING EVERY MOVE WE MADE AGAINST THEM.
I THINK THEY WERE DESIGNED AND MANIPULATED TO RECORD OUR STRENGTHS AND OUR WEAKNESSES.
NO PARKING
HOLOGRAMS DON'T JUST GENERATE SPONTANEOUSLY.
I NEED YOU TO CHECK FOR ORBITAL LASER BROADCAST FACILITIES.
SURE.

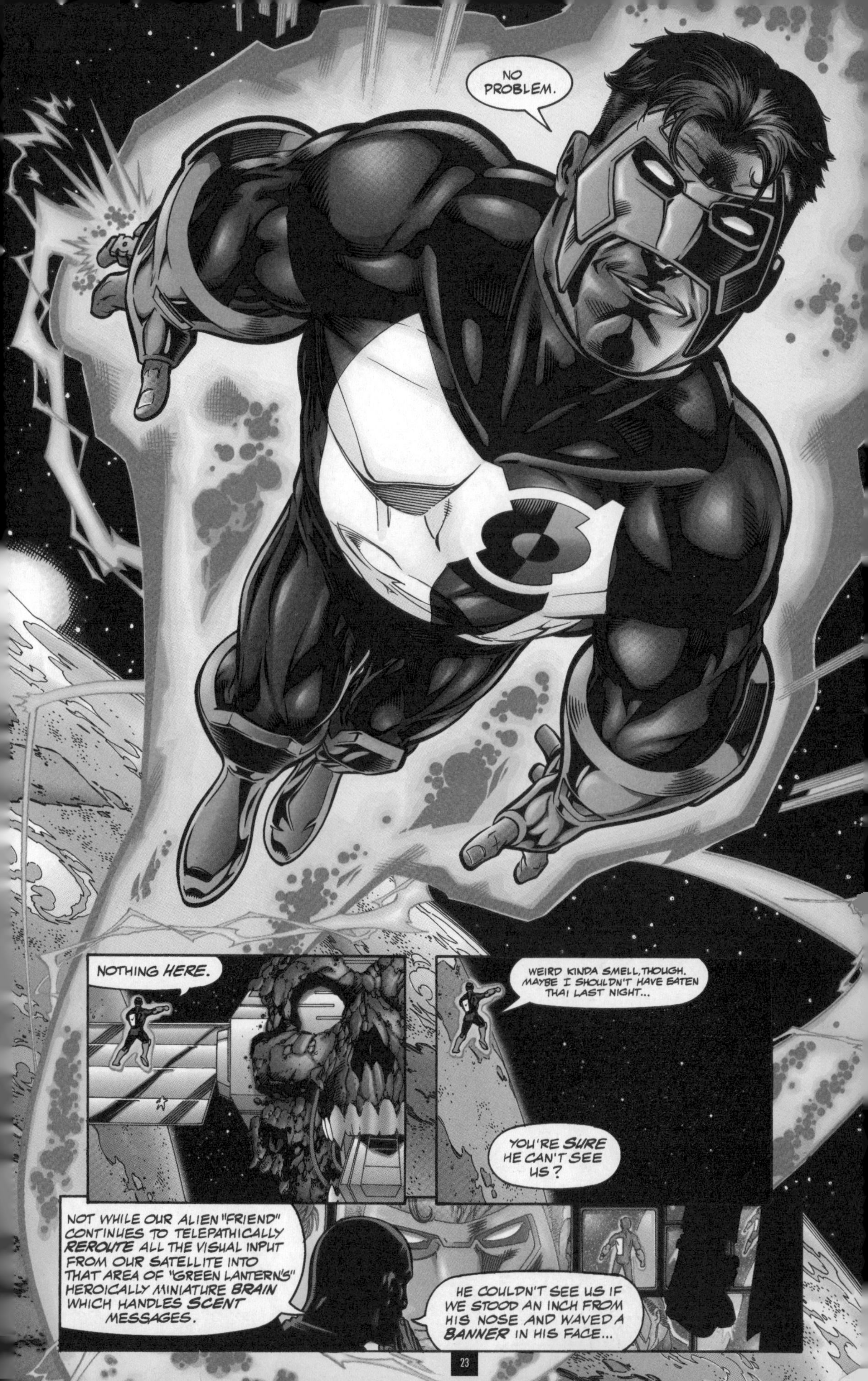
NO PROBLEM.
NOTHING HERE.
WEIRD KINDA SMELL, THOUGH. MAYBE I SHOULDN'T HAVE EATEN THAI LAST NIGHT...
YOU'RE SURE HE CAN'T SEE US?
NOT WHILE OUR ALIEN "FRIEND" CONTINUES TO TELEPATHICALLY REROUTE ALL THE VISUAL INPUT FROM OUR SATELLITE INTO THAT AREA OF "GREEN LANTERN'S" HEROICALLY MINIATURE BRAIN WHICH HANDLES SCENT MESSAGES.
HE COULDN'T SEE US IF WE STOOD AN INCH FROM HIS NOSE AND WAVED A BANNER IN HIS FACE...

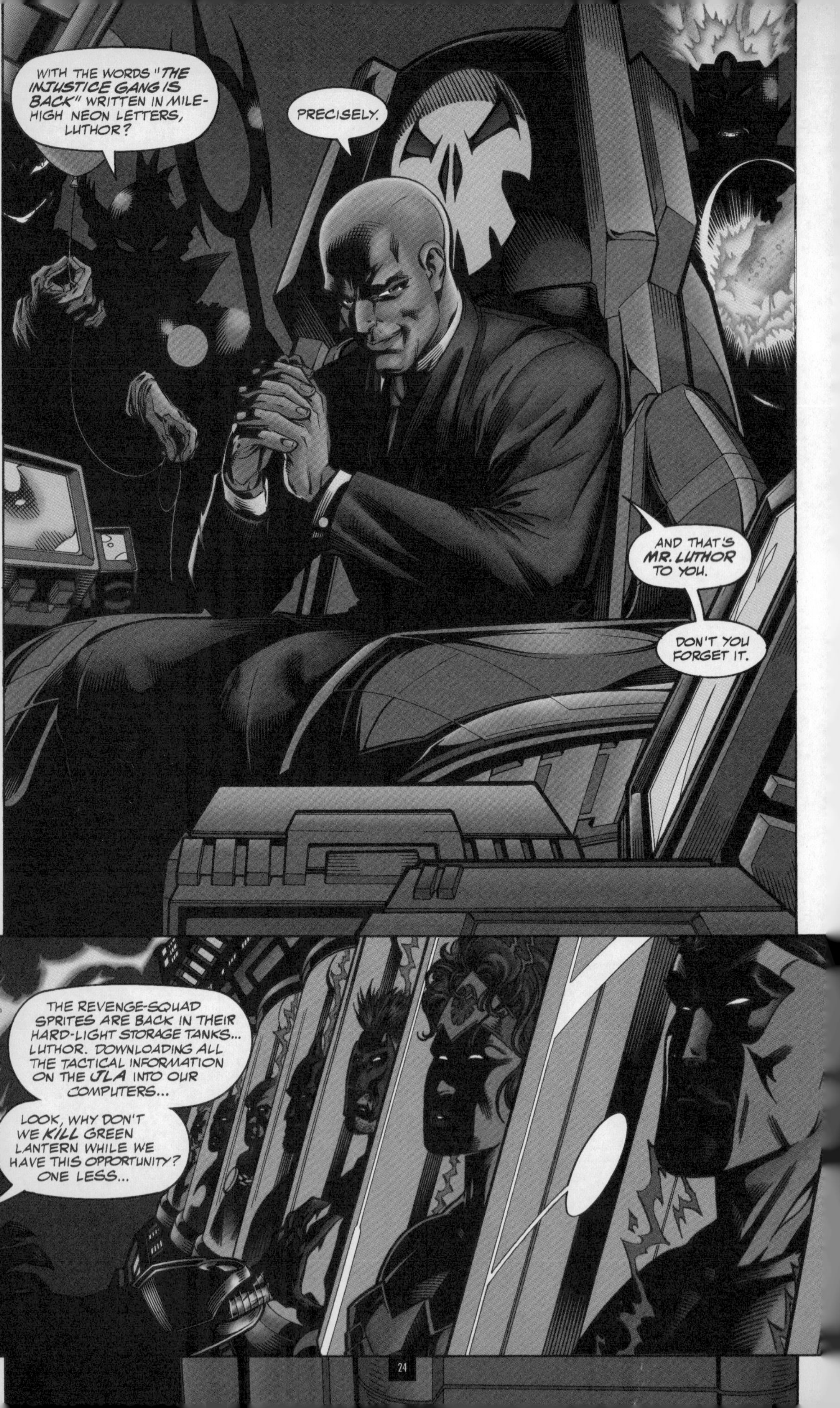
WITH THE WORDS "THE INJUSTICE GANG IS BACK" WRITTEN IN MILE-HIGH NEON LETTERS, LUTHOR?
PRECISELY.
AND THAT'S MR. LUTHOR TO YOU.
DON'T YOU FORGET IT.
THE REVENGE-SQUAD SPRITES ARE BACK IN THEIR HARD-LIGHT STORAGE TANKS... LUTHOR. DOWNLOADING ALL THE TACTICAL INFORMATION ON THE JLA INTO OUR COMPUTERS...
LOOK, WHY DON'T WE KILL GREEN LANTERN WHILE WE HAVE THIS OPPORTUNITY? ONE LESS...

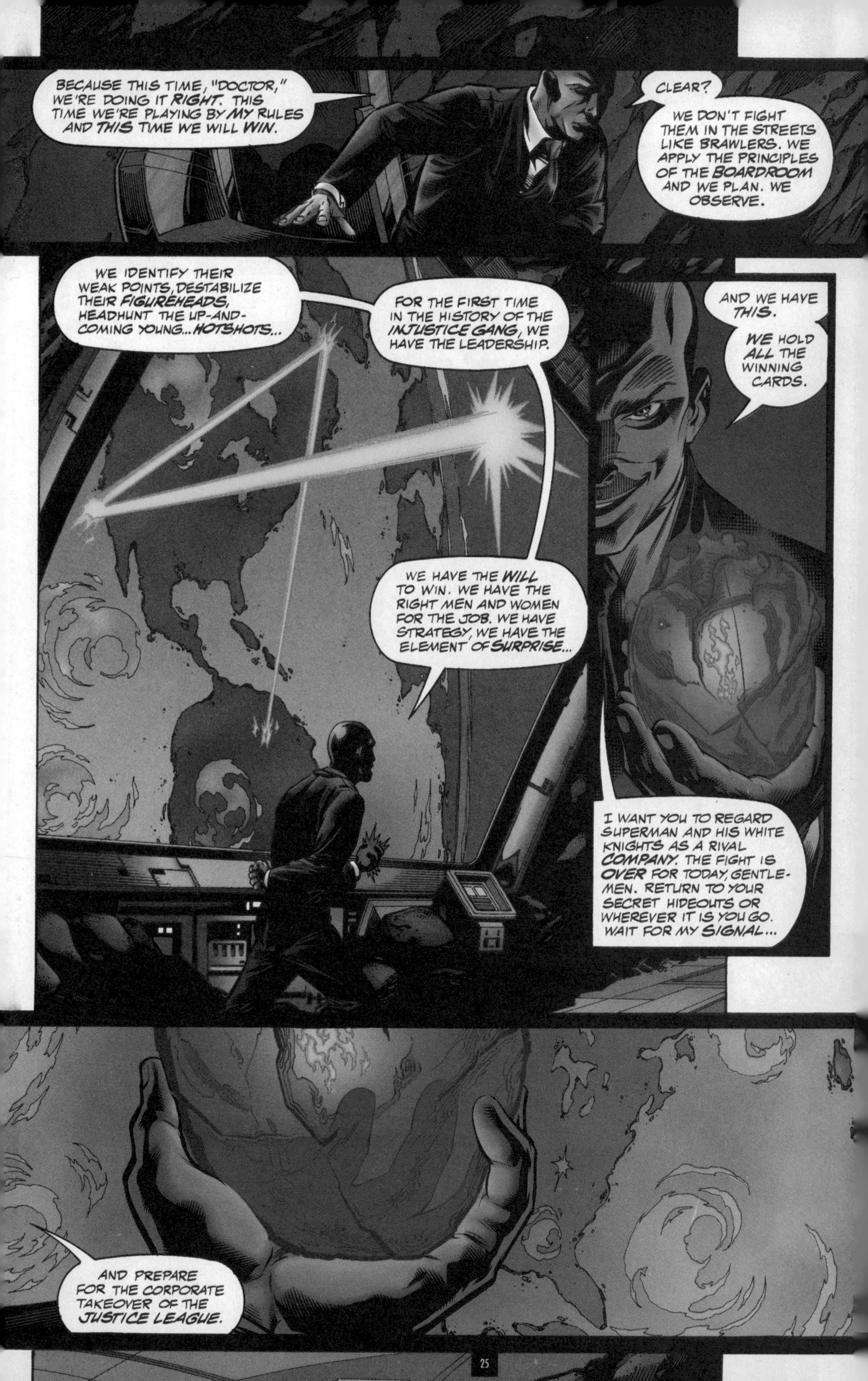
BECAUSE THIS TIME, "DOCTOR," WE'RE DOING IT RIGHT. THIS TIME WE'RE PLAYING BY MY RULES AND THIS TIME WE WILL WIN.
CLEAR?
WE DON'T FIGHT THEM IN THE STREETS LIKE BRAWLERS. WE APPLY THE PRINCIPLES OF THE BOARDROOM AND WE PLAN. WE OBSERVE.
WE IDENTIFY THEIR WEAK POINTS, DESTABILIZE THEIR FIGUREHEADS, HEADHUNT THE UP-AND-COMING YOUNG...HOTSHOTS...
FOR THE FIRST TIME IN THE HISTORY OF THE INJUSTICE GANG, WE HAVE THE LEADERSHIP.
WE HAVE THE WILL TO WIN. WE HAVE THE RIGHT MEN AND WOMEN FOR THE JOB. WE HAVE STRATEGY, WE HAVE THE ELEMENT OF SURPRISE...
AND WE HAVE THIS.
WE HOLD ALL THE WINNING CARDS.
I WANT YOU TO REGARD SUPERMAN AND HIS WHITE KNIGHTS AS A RIVAL COMPANY. THE FIGHT IS OVER FOR TODAY, GENTLEMEN. RETURN TO YOUR SECRET HIDEOUTS OR WHEREVER IT IS YOU GO. WAIT FOR MY SIGNAL...
AND PREPARE FOR THE CORPORATE TAKEOVER OF THE JUSTICE LEAGUE.

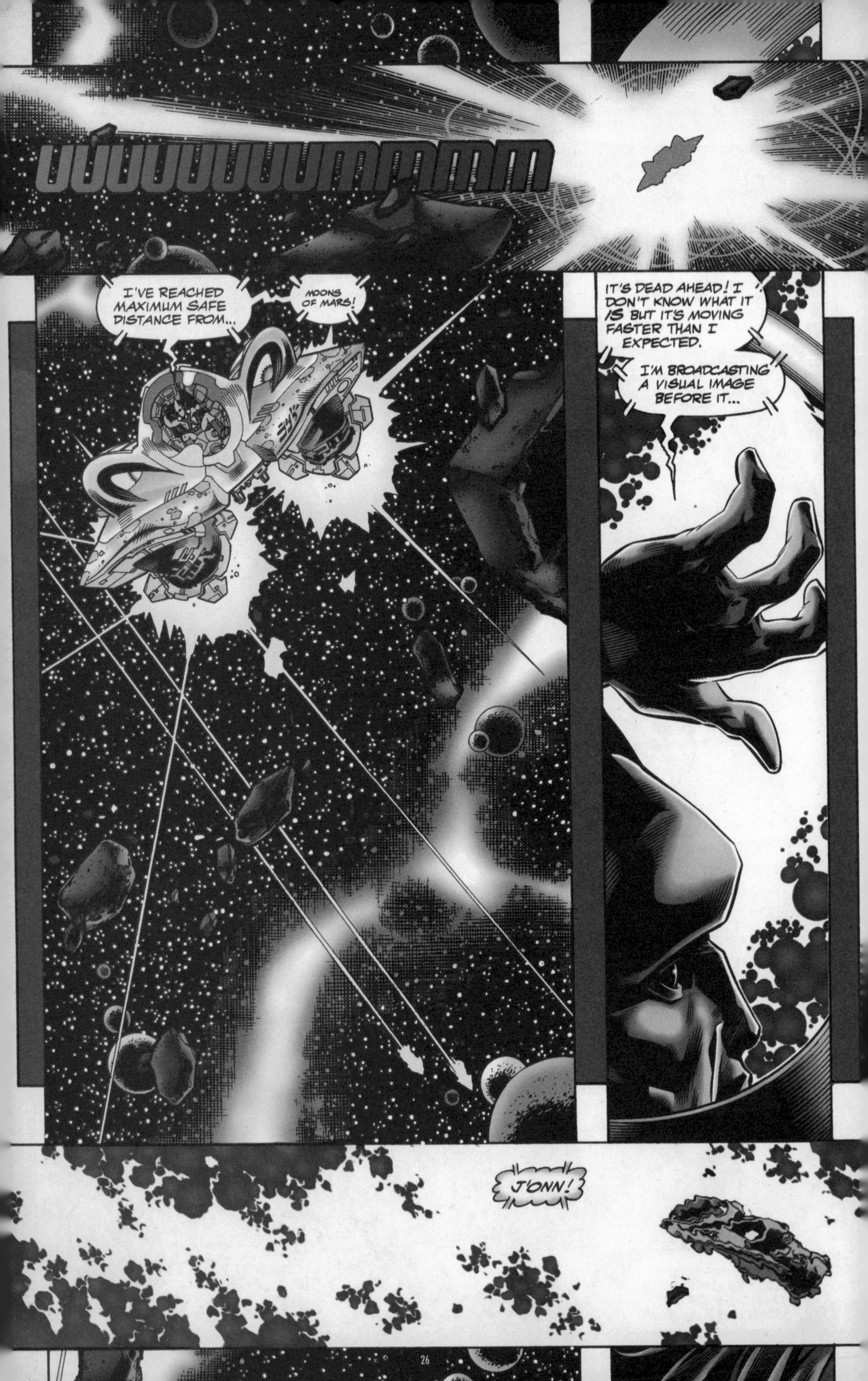
UUUUUUUUUMMMMM
I'VE REACHED MAXIMUM SAFE DISTANCE FROM...
MOONS OF MARS!
IT'S DEAD AHEAD! I DON'T KNOW WHAT IT IS BUT IT'S MOVING FASTER THAN I EXPECTED.
I'M BROADCASTING A VISUAL IMAGE BEFORE IT...
J'ONN!

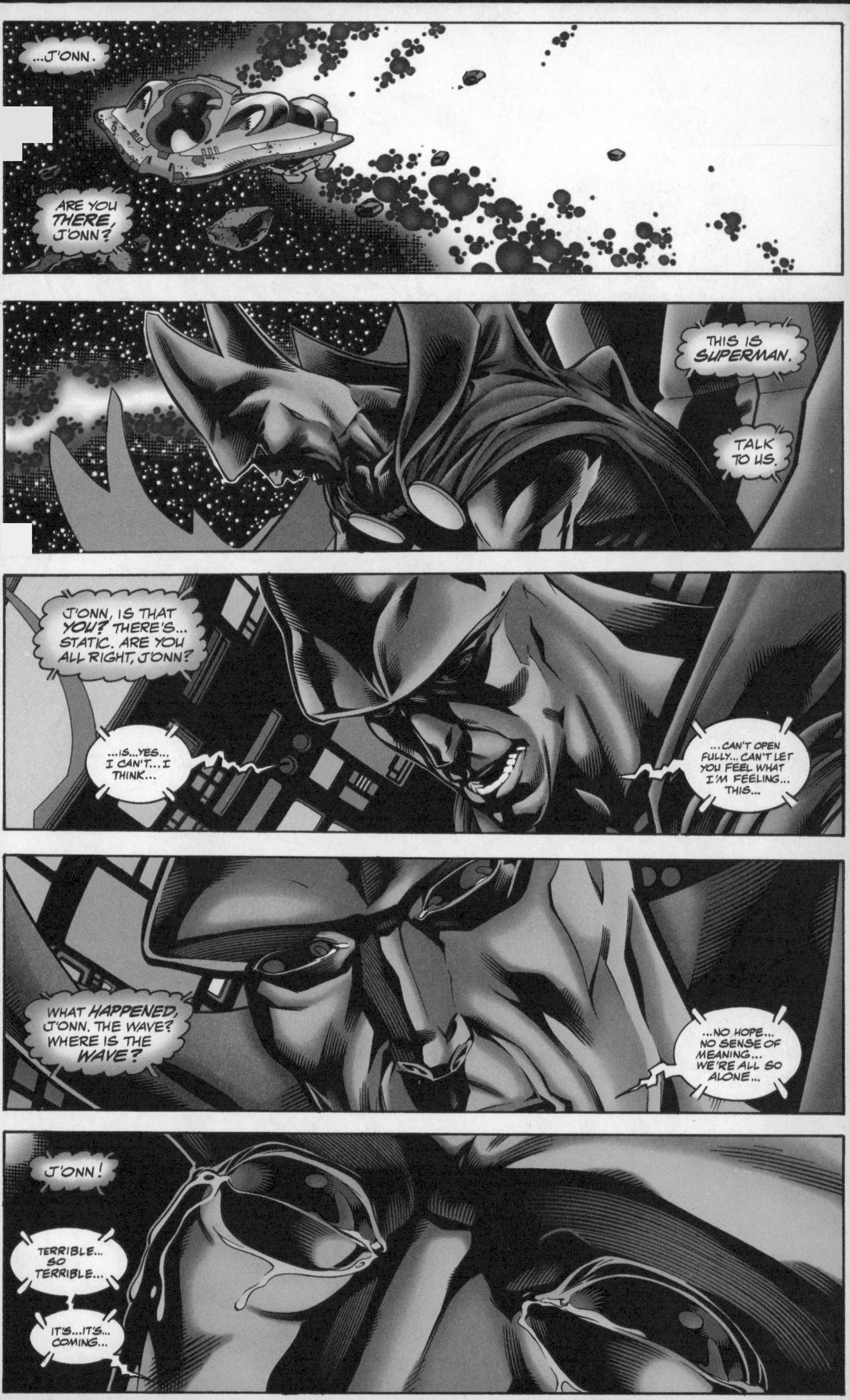
...J'ONN.
ARE YOU THERE, J'ONN?
THIS IS SUPERMAN.
TALK TO US.
J'ONN, IS THAT YOU? THERE'S... STATIC. ARE YOU ALL RIGHT, J'ONN?
...IS...YES... I CAN'T...I THINK...
...CAN'T OPEN FULLY...CAN'T LET YOU FEEL WHAT I'M FEELING... THIS...
WHAT HAPPENED, J'ONN. THE WAVE? WHERE IS THE WAVE?
...NO HOPE... NO SENSE OF MEANING... WE'RE ALL SO ALONE...
J'ONN!
TERRIBLE... SO TERRIBLE...
IT'S...IT'S... COMING...

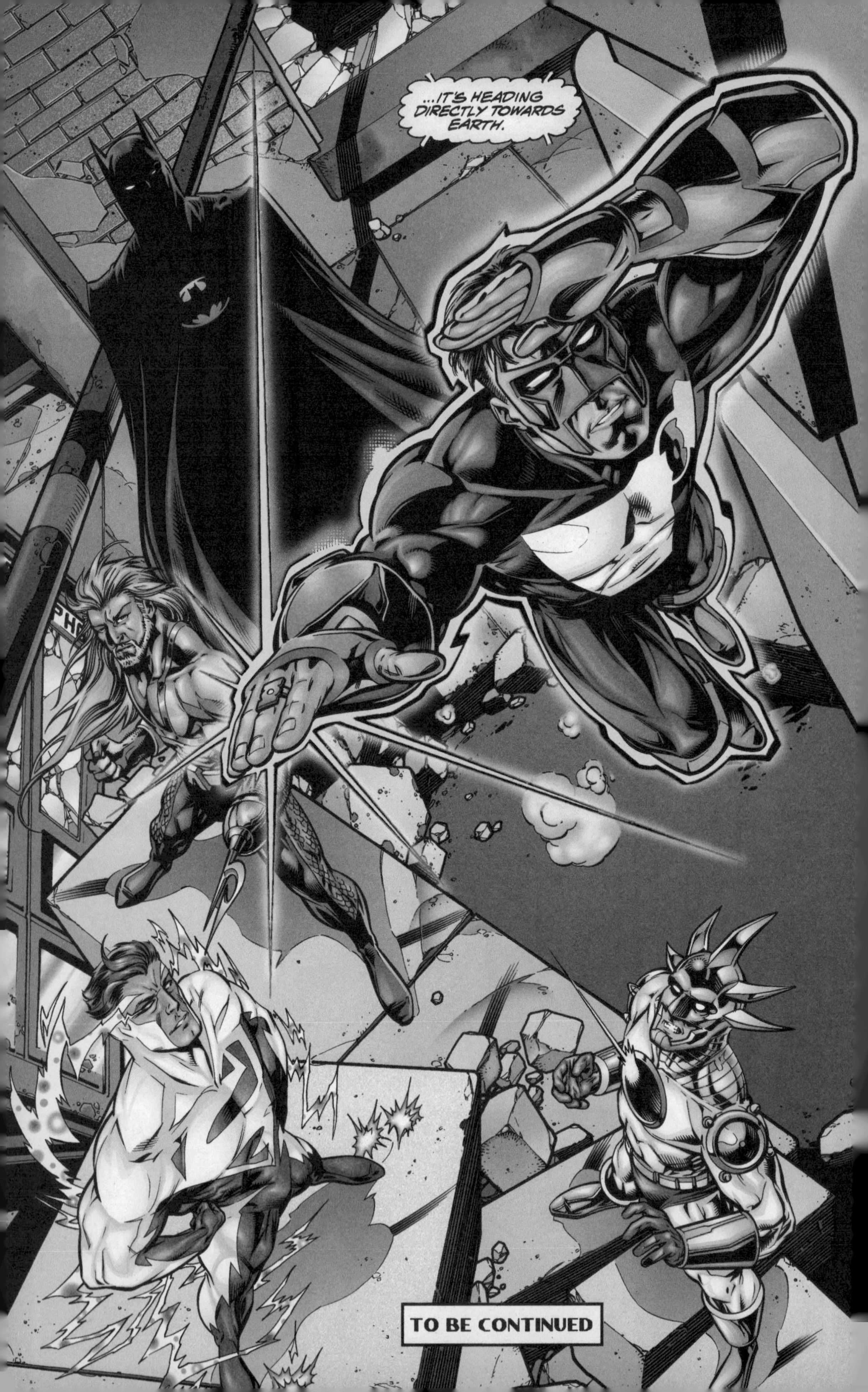
...IT'S HEADING DIRECTLY TOWARDS EARTH.
TO BE CONTINUED

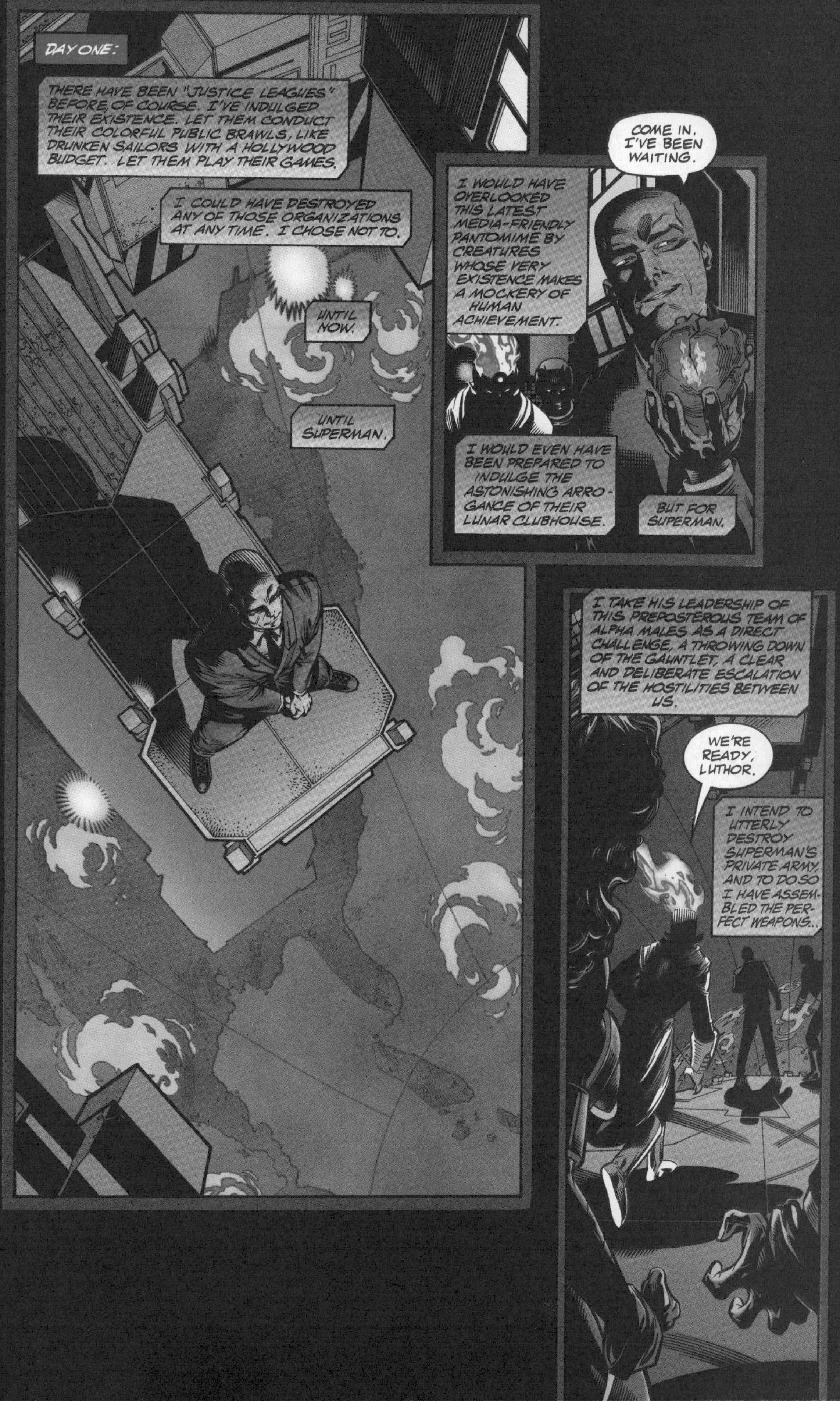
DAY ONE:
THERE HAVE BEEN "JUSTICE LEAGUES" BEFORE, OF COURSE. I'VE INDULGED THEIR EXISTENCE. LET THEM CONDUCT THEIR COLORFUL PUBLIC BRAWLS, LIKE DRUNKEN SAILORS WITH A HOLLYWOOD BUDGET. LET THEM PLAY THEIR GAMES.
I COULD HAVE DESTROYED ANY OF THOSE ORGANIZATIONS AT ANY TIME. I CHOSE NOT TO.
UNTIL NOW.
UNTIL SUPERMAN.
I WOULD HAVE OVERLOOKED THIS LATEST MEDIA-FRIENDLY PANTOMIME BY CREATURES WHOSE VERY EXISTENCE MAKES A MOCKERY OF HUMAN ACHIEVEMENT.
COME IN. I'VE BEEN WAITING.
I WOULD EVEN HAVE BEEN PREPARED TO INDULGE THE ASTONISHING ARRO-GANCE OF THEIR LUNAR CLUBHOUSE.
BUT FOR SUPERMAN.
I TAKE HIS LEADERSHIP OF THIS PREPOSTEROUS TEAM OF ALPHA MALES AS A DIRECT CHALLENGE, A THROWING DOWN OF THE GAUNTLET, A CLEAR AND DELIBERATE ESCALATION OF THE HOSTILITIES BETWEEN US.
WE'RE READY, LUTHOR.
I INTEND TO UTTERLY DESTROY SUPERMAN'S PRIVATE ARMY, AND TO DO SO I HAVE ASSEM-BLED THE PER-FECT WEAPONS...

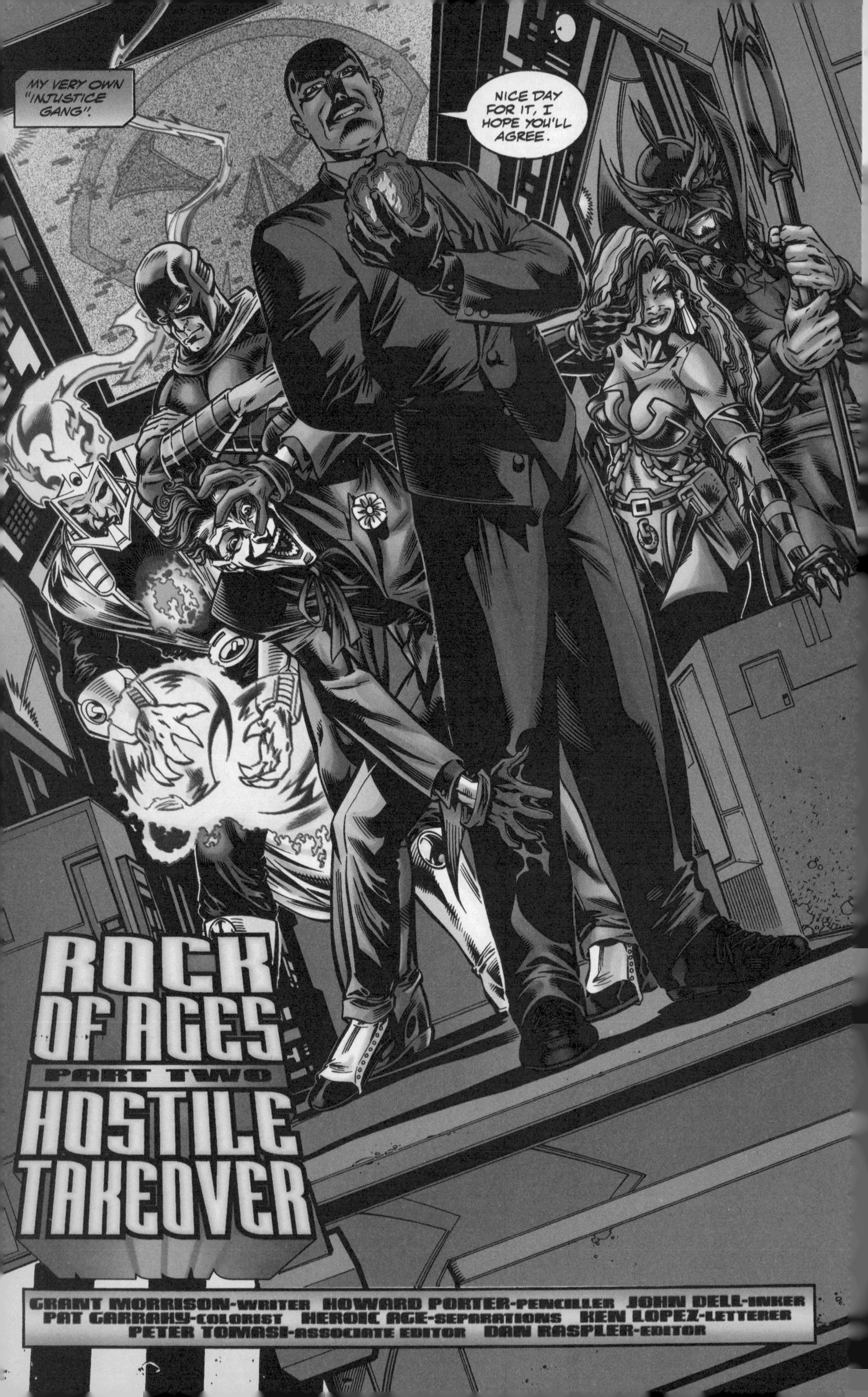

MY VERY OWN "INJUSTICE GANG".
NICE DAY FOR IT, I HOPE YOU'LL AGREE.
ROCK OF AGES
PART TWO
HOSTILE TAKEOVER
GRANT MORRISON-WRITER HOWARD PORTER-PENCILLER JOHN DELL-INKER
PAT GARRAHY-COLORIST HEROIC AGE-SEPARATIONS KEN LOPEZ-LETTERER
PETER TOMASI-ASSOCIATE EDITOR DAN RASPLER-EDITOR

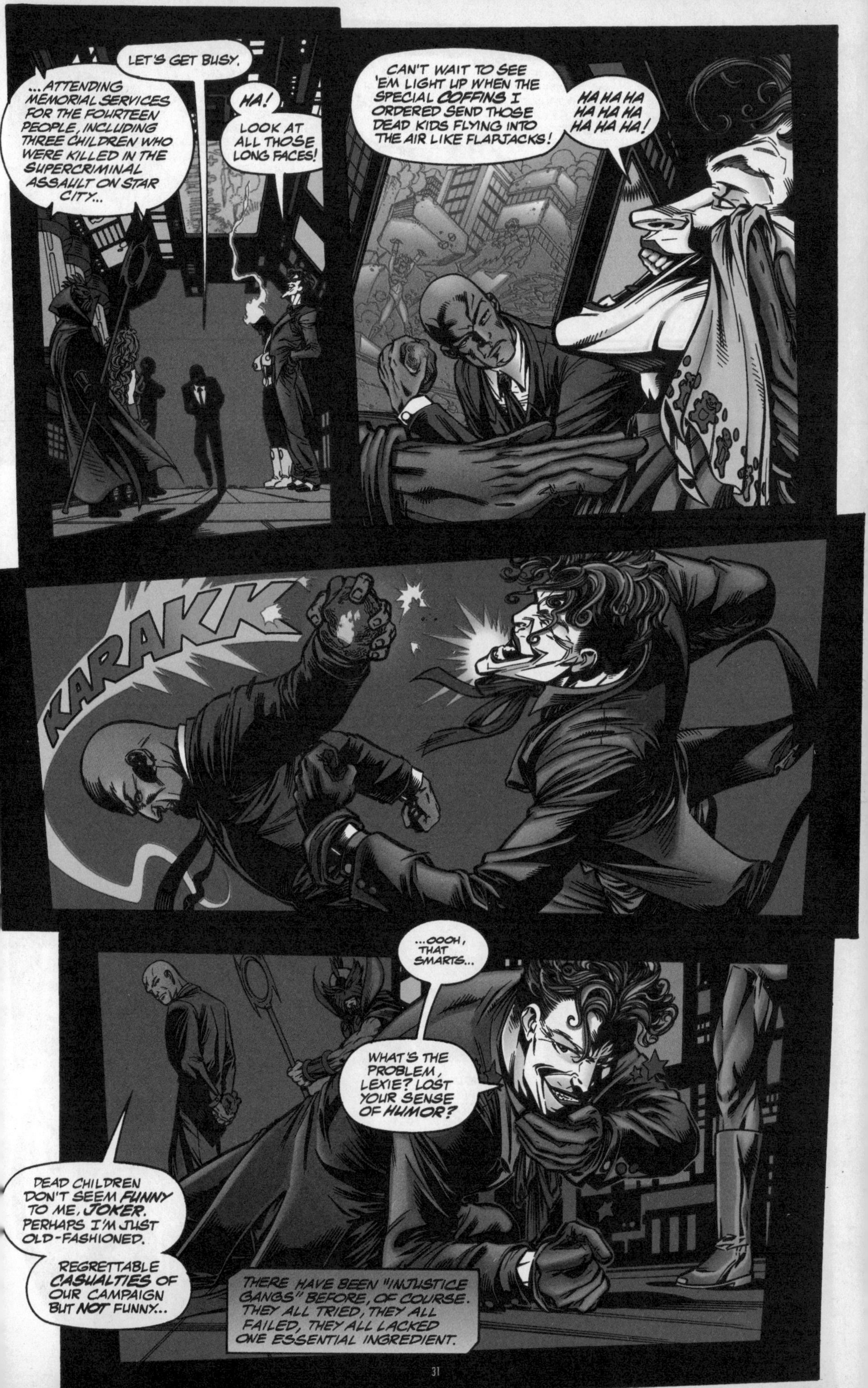
...ATTENDING MEMORIAL SERVICES FOR THE FOURTEEN PEOPLE, INCLUDING THREE CHILDREN WHO WERE KILLED IN THE SUPERCRIMINAL ASSAULT ON STAR CITY...
LET'S GET BUSY.
HA!
LOOK AT ALL THOSE LONG FACES!
CAN'T WAIT TO SEE 'EM LIGHT UP WHEN THE SPECIAL COFFINS I ORDERED SEND THOSE DEAD KIDS FLYING INTO THE AIR LIKE FLAPJACKS!
HA HA HA HA HA HA HA HA HA!
KARAKK
...OOOH, THAT SMARTS...
WHAT'S THE PROBLEM, LEXIE? LOST YOUR SENSE OF HUMOR?
DEAD CHILDREN DON'T SEEM FUNNY TO ME, JOKER. PERHAPS I'M JUST OLD-FASHIONED.
REGRETTABLE CASUALTIES OF OUR CAMPAIGN BUT NOT FUNNY...
THERE HAVE BEEN "INJUSTICE GANGS" BEFORE, OF COURSE. THEY ALL TRIED, THEY ALL FAILED, THEY ALL LACKED ONE ESSENTIAL INGREDIENT.

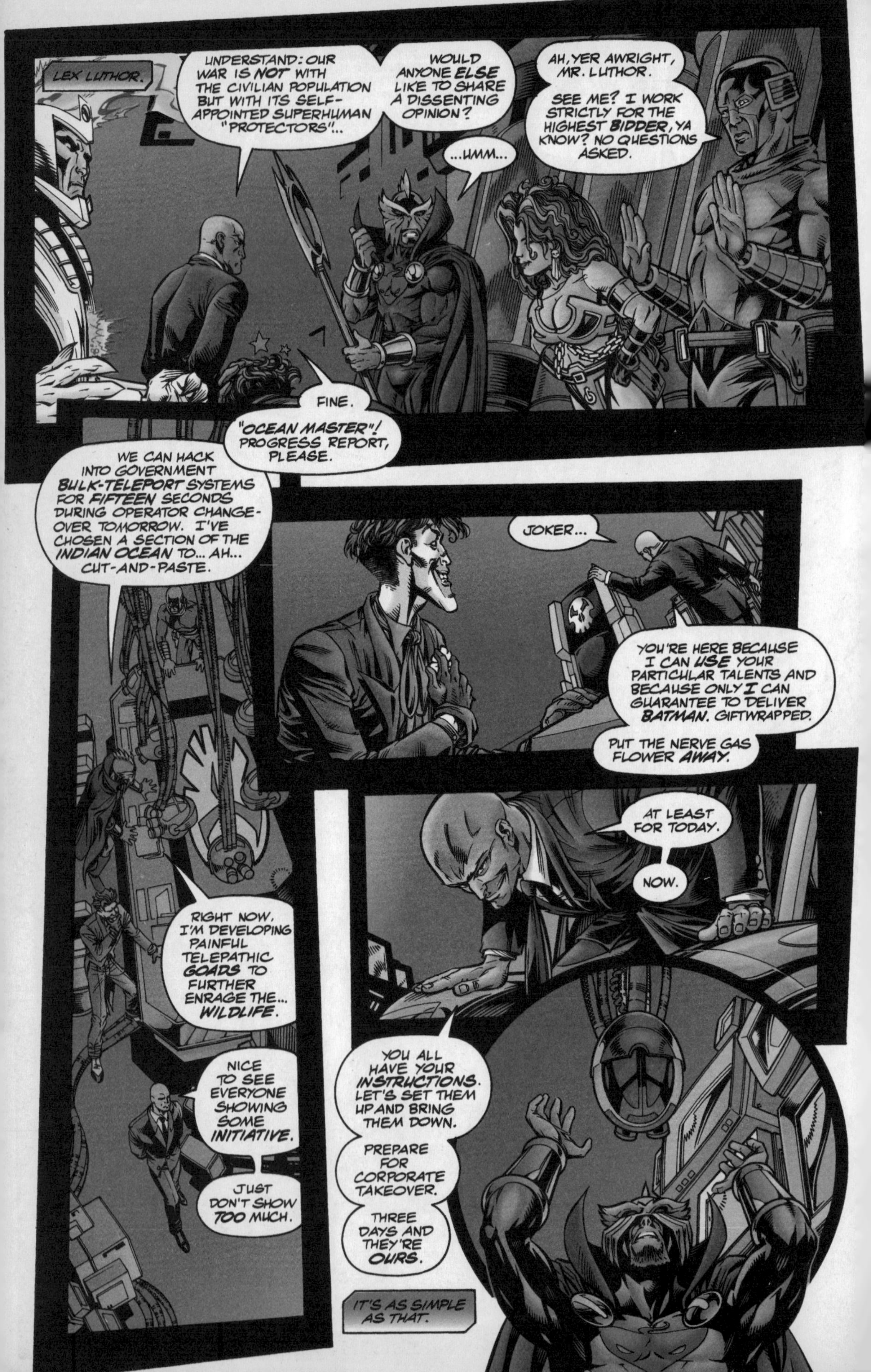
LEX LUTHOR.
UNDERSTAND: OUR WAR IS NOT WITH THE CIVILIAN POPULATION BUT WITH ITS SELF-APPOINTED SUPERHUMAN "PROTECTORS"...
WOULD ANYONE ELSE LIKE TO SHARE A DISSENTING OPINION?
...UMM...
AH, YER AWRIGHT, MR. LUTHOR.
SEE ME? I WORK STRICTLY FOR THE HIGHEST BIDDER, YA KNOW? NO QUESTIONS ASKED.
FINE.
"OCEAN MASTER"! PROGRESS REPORT, PLEASE.
WE CAN HACK INTO GOVERNMENT BULK-TELEPORT SYSTEMS FOR FIFTEEN SECONDS DURING OPERATOR CHANGE-OVER TOMORROW. I'VE CHOSEN A SECTION OF THE INDIAN OCEAN TO... AH... CUT-AND-PASTE.
JOKER...
YOU'RE HERE BECAUSE I CAN USE YOUR PARTICULAR TALENTS AND BECAUSE ONLY I CAN GUARANTEE TO DELIVER BATMAN. GIFTWRAPPED.
PUT THE NERVE GAS FLOWER AWAY.
AT LEAST FOR TODAY.
NOW.
RIGHT NOW, I'M DEVELOPING PAINFUL TELEPATHIC GOADS TO FURTHER ENRAGE THE... WILDLIFE.
NICE TO SEE EVERYONE SHOWING SOME INITIATIVE.
JUST DON'T SHOW TOO MUCH.
YOU ALL HAVE YOUR INSTRUCTIONS. LET'S SET THEM UP AND BRING THEM DOWN.
PREPARE FOR CORPORATE TAKEOVER.
THREE DAYS AND THEY'RE OURS.
IT'S AS SIMPLE AS THAT.

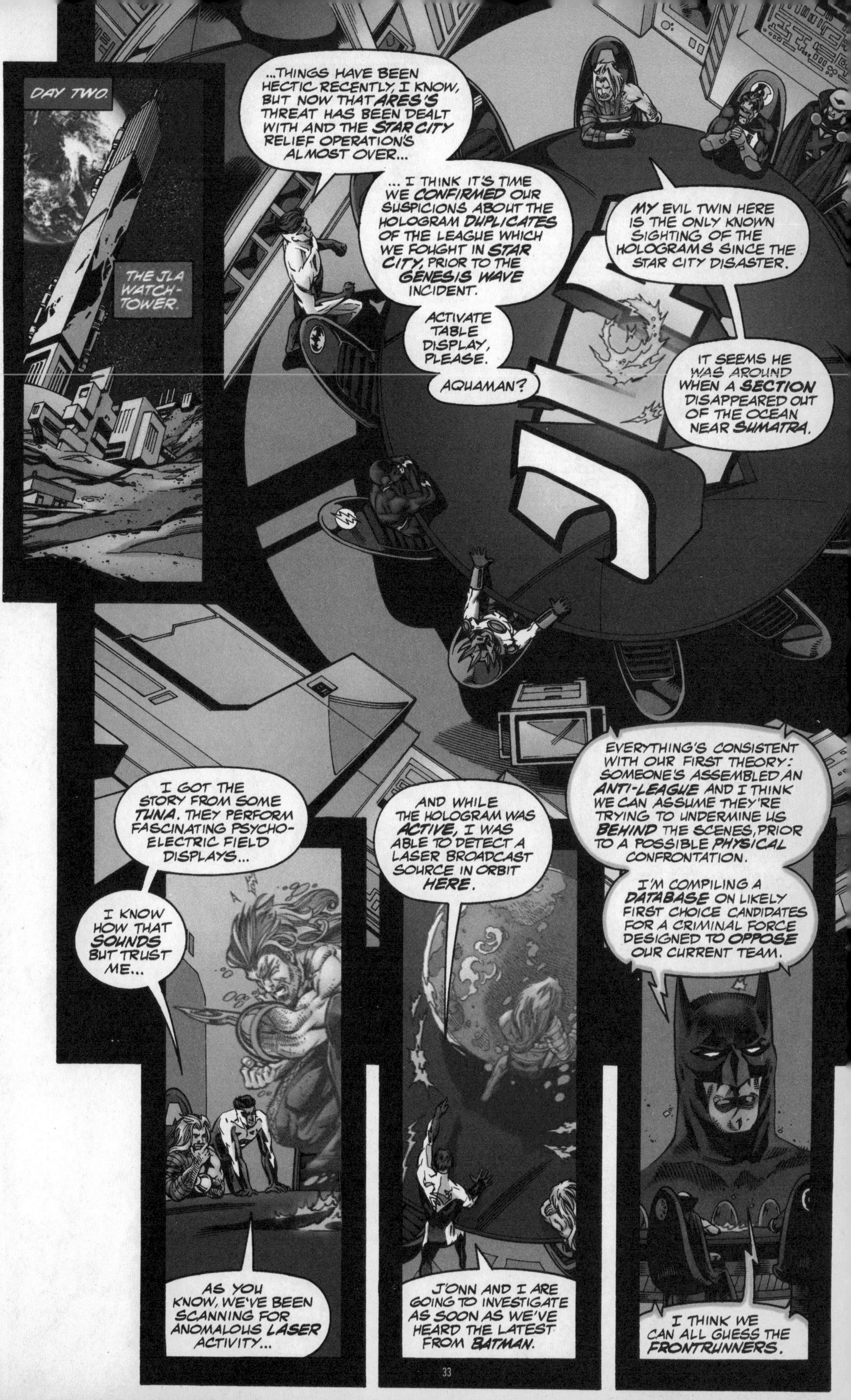
DAY TWO.
THE JLA WATCH-TOWER.
...THINGS HAVE BEEN HECTIC RECENTLY, I KNOW, BUT NOW THAT ARES'S THREAT HAS BEEN DEALT WITH AND THE STAR CITY RELIEF OPERATION'S ALMOST OVER...
... I THINK IT'S TIME WE CONFIRMED OUR SUSPICIONS ABOUT THE HOLOGRAM DUPLICATES OF THE LEAGUE WHICH WE FOUGHT IN STAR CITY, PRIOR TO THE GENESIS WAVE INCIDENT.
ACTIVATE TABLE DISPLAY, PLEASE.
AQUAMAN?
MY EVIL TWIN HERE IS THE ONLY KNOWN SIGHTING OF THE HOLOGRAMS SINCE THE STAR CITY DISASTER.
IT SEEMS HE WAS AROUND WHEN A SECTION DISAPPEARED OUT OF THE OCEAN NEAR SUMATRA.
I GOT THE STORY FROM SOME TUNA. THEY PERFORM FASCINATING PSYCHO-ELECTRIC FIELD DISPLAYS...
I KNOW HOW THAT SOUNDS BUT TRUST ME...
AS YOU KNOW, WE'VE BEEN SCANNING FOR ANOMALOUS LASER ACTIVITY...
AND WHILE THE HOLOGRAM WAS ACTIVE, I WAS ABLE TO DETECT A LASER BROADCAST SOURCE IN ORBIT HERE.
J'ONN AND I ARE GOING TO INVESTIGATE AS SOON AS WE'VE HEARD THE LATEST FROM BATMAN.
EVERYTHING'S CONSISTENT WITH OUR FIRST THEORY: SOMEONE'S ASSEMBLED AN ANTI-LEAGUE AND I THINK WE CAN ASSUME THEY'RE TRYING TO UNDERMINE US BEHIND THE SCENES, PRIOR TO A POSSIBLE PHYSICAL CONFRONTATION.
I'M COMPILING A DATABASE ON LIKELY FIRST CHOICE CANDIDATES FOR A CRIMINAL FORCE DESIGNED TO OPPOSE OUR CURRENT TEAM.
I THINK WE CAN ALL GUESS THE FRONTRUNNERS.

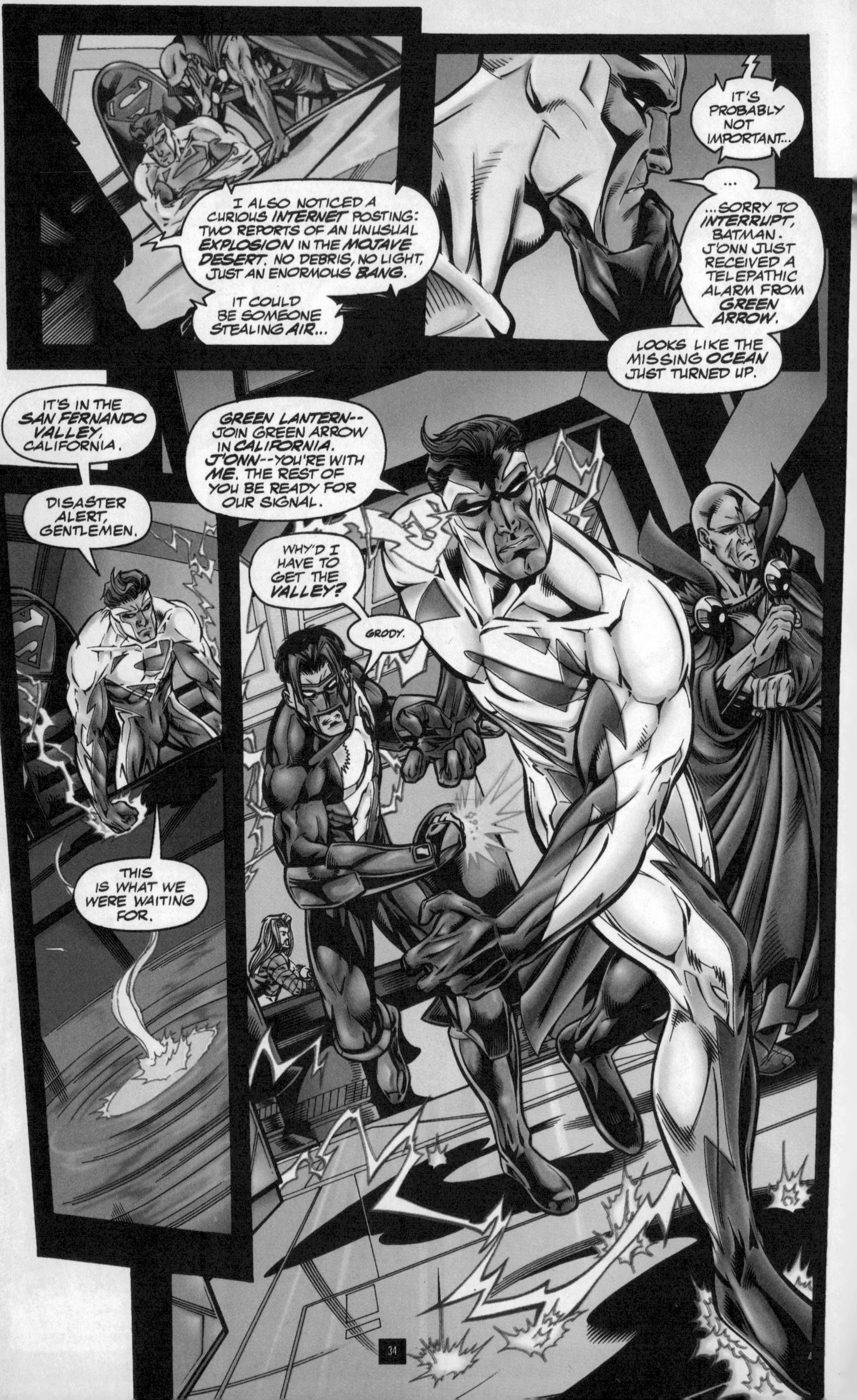
I ALSO NOTICED A CURIOUS INTERNET POSTING: TWO REPORTS OF AN UNUSUAL EXPLOSION IN THE MOJAVE DESERT. NO DEBRIS, NO LIGHT, JUST AN ENORMOUS BANG.
IT COULD BE SOMEONE STEALING AIR...
IT'S PROBABLY NOT IMPORTANT...
...
...SORRY TO INTERRUPT, BATMAN. J'ONN JUST RECEIVED A TELEPATHIC ALARM FROM GREEN ARROW.
LOOKS LIKE THE MISSING OCEAN JUST TURNED UP.
IT'S IN THE SAN FERNANDO VALLEY, CALIFORNIA.
DISASTER ALERT, GENTLEMEN.
THIS IS WHAT WE WERE WAITING FOR.
GREEN LANTERN-- JOIN GREEN ARROW IN CALIFORNIA. J'ONN--YOU'RE WITH ME. THE REST OF YOU BE READY FOR OUR SIGNAL.
WHY'D I HAVE TO GET THE VALLEY?
GRODY.

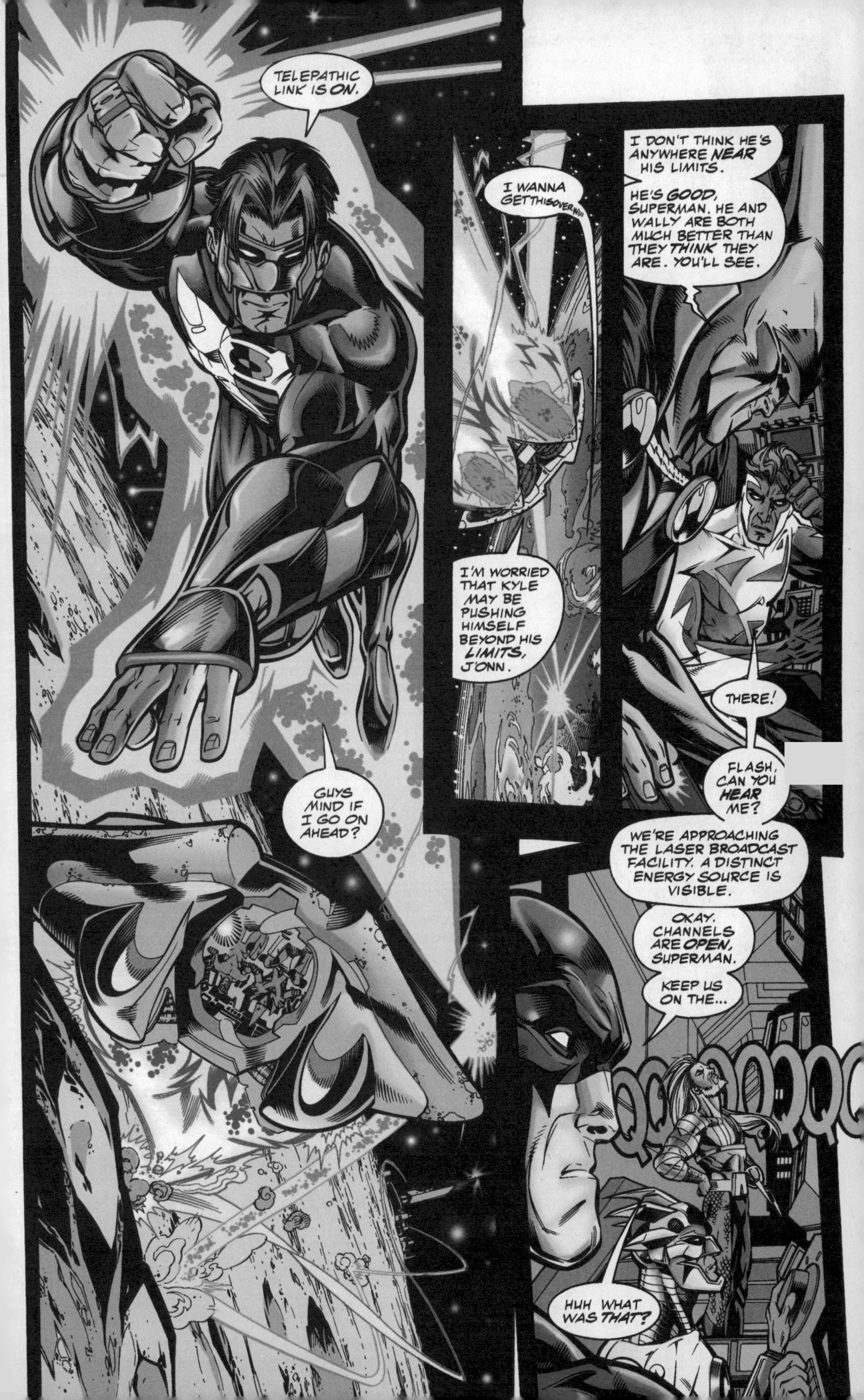
TELEPATHIC LINK IS ON.
I WANNA GET THIS OVER WITH
I'M WORRIED THAT KYLE MAY BE PUSHING HIMSELF BEYOND HIS LIMITS, J'ONN.
I DON'T THINK HE'S ANYWHERE NEAR HIS LIMITS.
HE'S GOOD, SUPERMAN. HE AND WALLY ARE BOTH MUCH BETTER THAN THEY THINK THEY ARE. YOU'LL SEE.
THERE!
GUYS MIND IF I GO ON AHEAD?
FLASH, CAN YOU HEAR ME?
WE'RE APPROACHING THE LASER BROADCAST FACILITY. A DISTINCT ENERGY SOURCE IS VISIBLE.
OKAY. CHANNELS ARE OPEN, SUPERMAN.
KEEP US ON THE...
QQQQQQQQ
HUH WHAT WAS THAT?

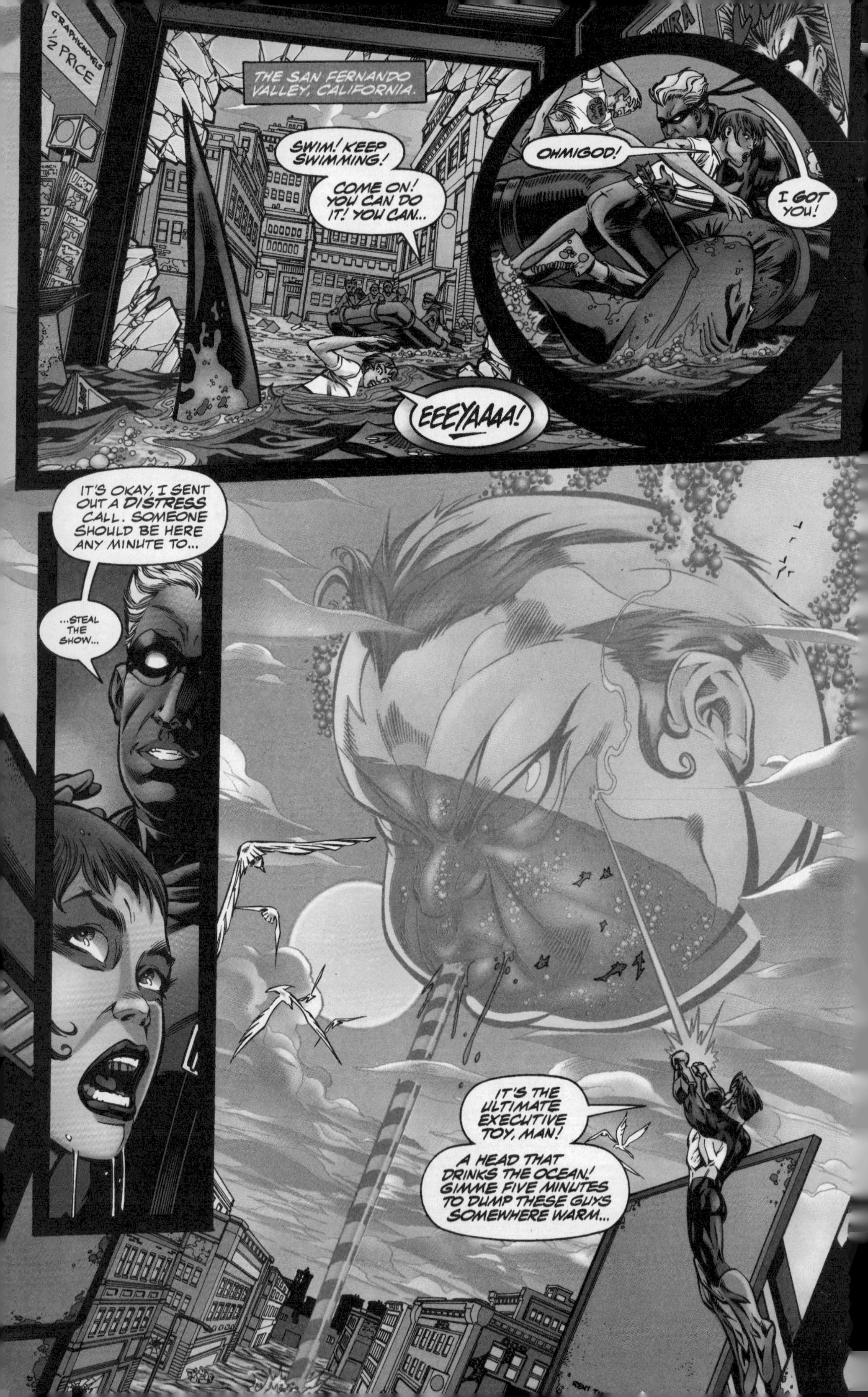
GRAPHIC NOVELS 1/2 PRICE
THE SAN FERNANDO VALLEY, CALIFORNIA.
SWIM! KEEP SWIMMING!
COME ON! YOU CAN DO IT! YOU CAN...
OHMIGOD!
I GOT YOU!
EEEYAAAA!
IT'S OKAY, I SENT OUT A DISTRESS CALL. SOMEONE SHOULD BE HERE ANY MINUTE TO...
...STEAL THE SHOW...
IT'S THE ULTIMATE EXECUTIVE TOY, MAN!
A HEAD THAT DRINKS THE OCEAN! GIMME FIVE MINUTES TO DUMP THESE GUYS SOMEWHERE WARM...

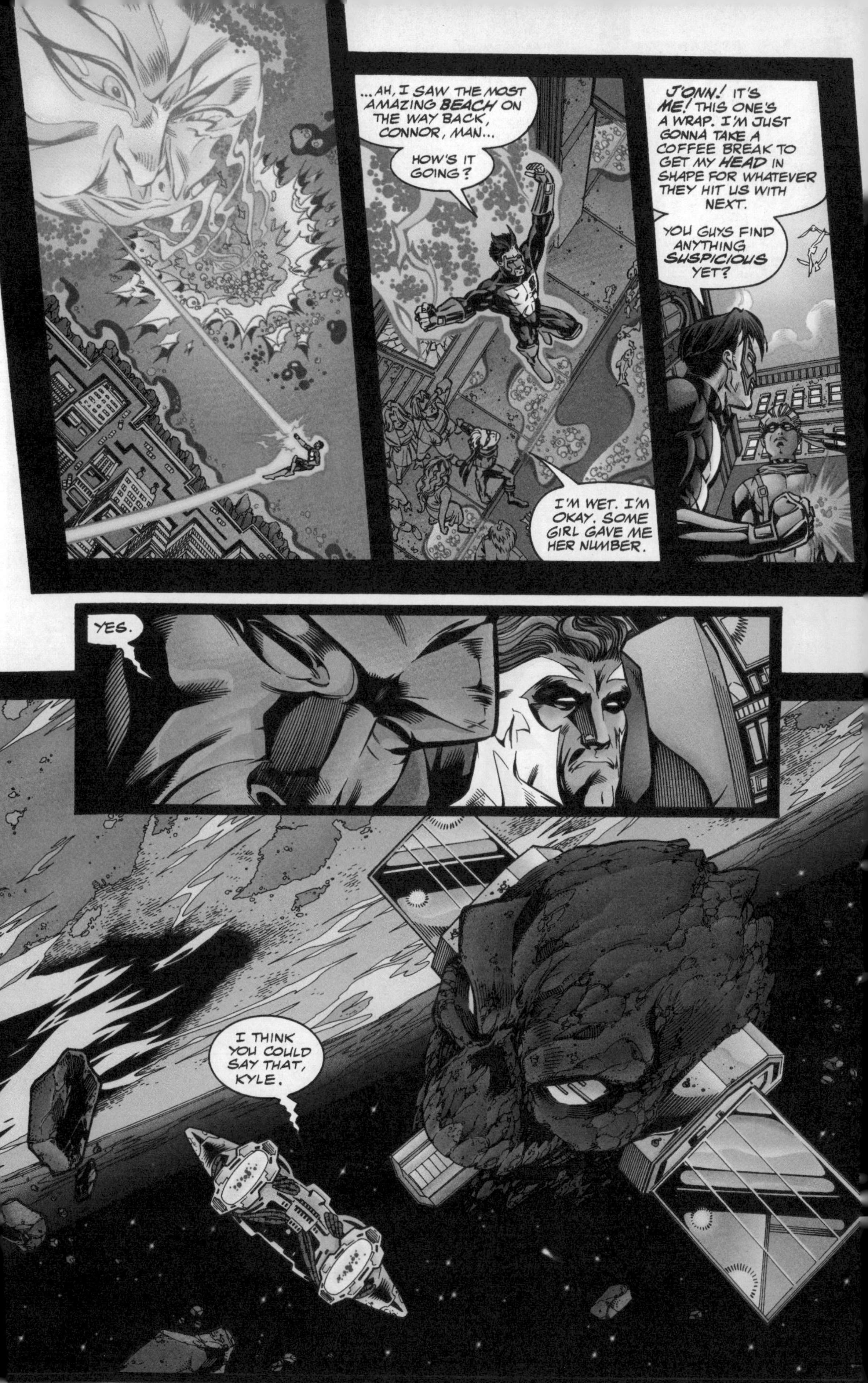
...AH, I SAW THE MOST AMAZING BEACH ON THE WAY BACK, CONNOR, MAN...
HOW'S IT GOING?
I'M WET. I'M OKAY. SOME GIRL GAVE ME HER NUMBER.
J'ONN! IT'S ME! THIS ONE'S A WRAP. I'M JUST GONNA TAKE A COFFEE BREAK TO GET MY HEAD IN SHAPE FOR WHATEVER THEY HIT US WITH NEXT.
YOU GUYS FIND ANYTHING SUSPICIOUS YET?
YES.
I THINK YOU COULD SAY THAT, KYLE.

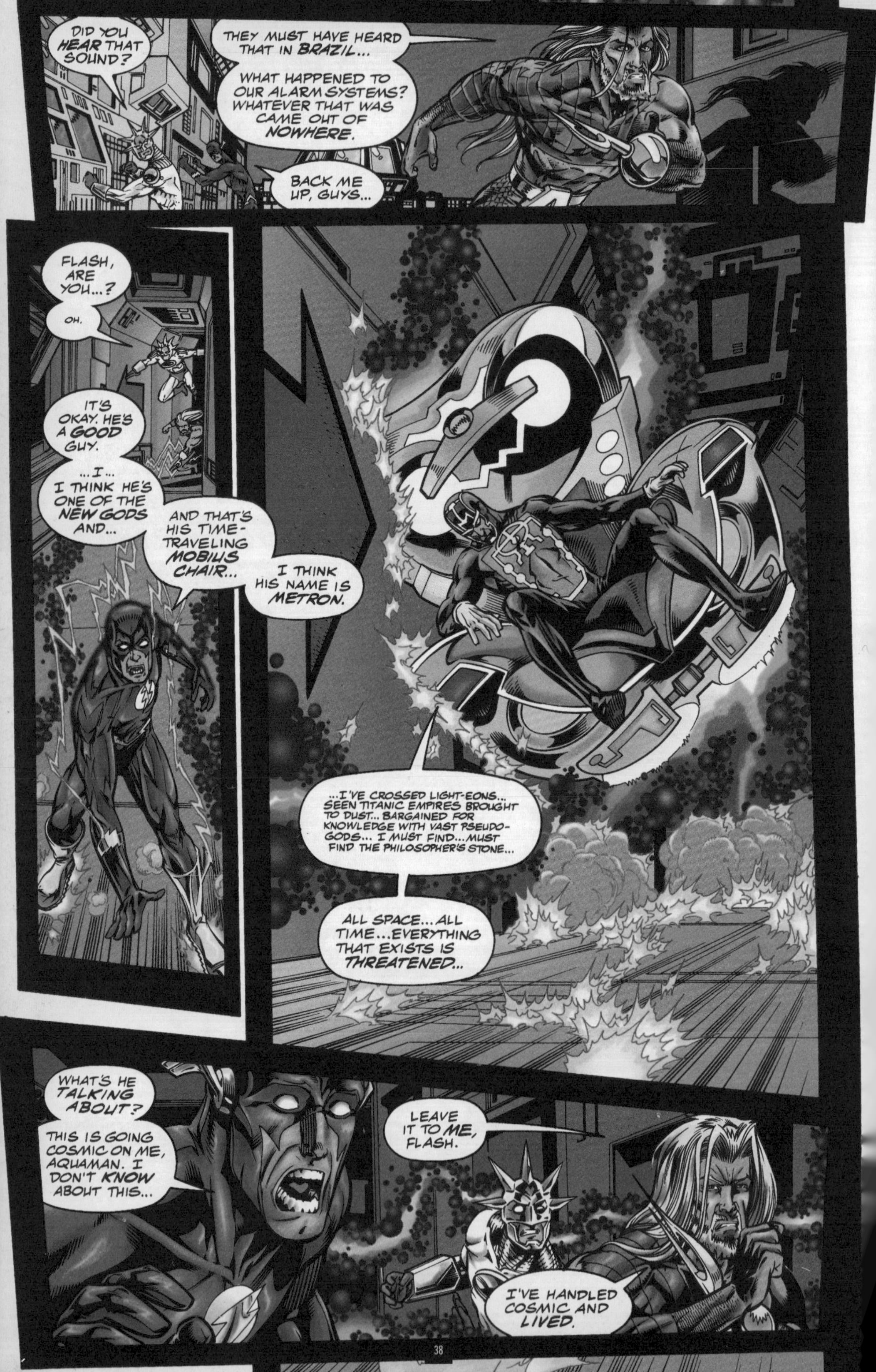
DID YOU HEAR THAT SOUND?
THEY MUST HAVE HEARD THAT IN BRAZIL...
WHAT HAPPENED TO OUR ALARM SYSTEMS? WHATEVER THAT WAS CAME OUT OF NOWHERE.
BACK ME UP, GUYS...
FLASH, ARE YOU...?
OH.
IT'S OKAY. HE'S A GOOD GUY.
...I... I THINK HE'S ONE OF THE NEW GODS AND...
AND THAT'S HIS TIME-TRAVELING MOBIUS CHAIR...
I THINK HIS NAME IS METRON.
...I'VE CROSSED LIGHT-EONS... SEEN TITANIC EMPIRES BROUGHT TO DUST... BARGAINED FOR KNOWLEDGE WITH VAST PSEUDO-GODS... I MUST FIND... MUST FIND THE PHILOSOPHER'S STONE...
ALL SPACE... ALL TIME... EVERYTHING THAT EXISTS IS THREATENED...
WHAT'S HE TALKING ABOUT?
THIS IS GOING COSMIC ON ME, AQUAMAN. I DON'T KNOW ABOUT THIS...
LEAVE IT TO ME, FLASH.
I'VE HANDLED COSMIC AND LIVED.

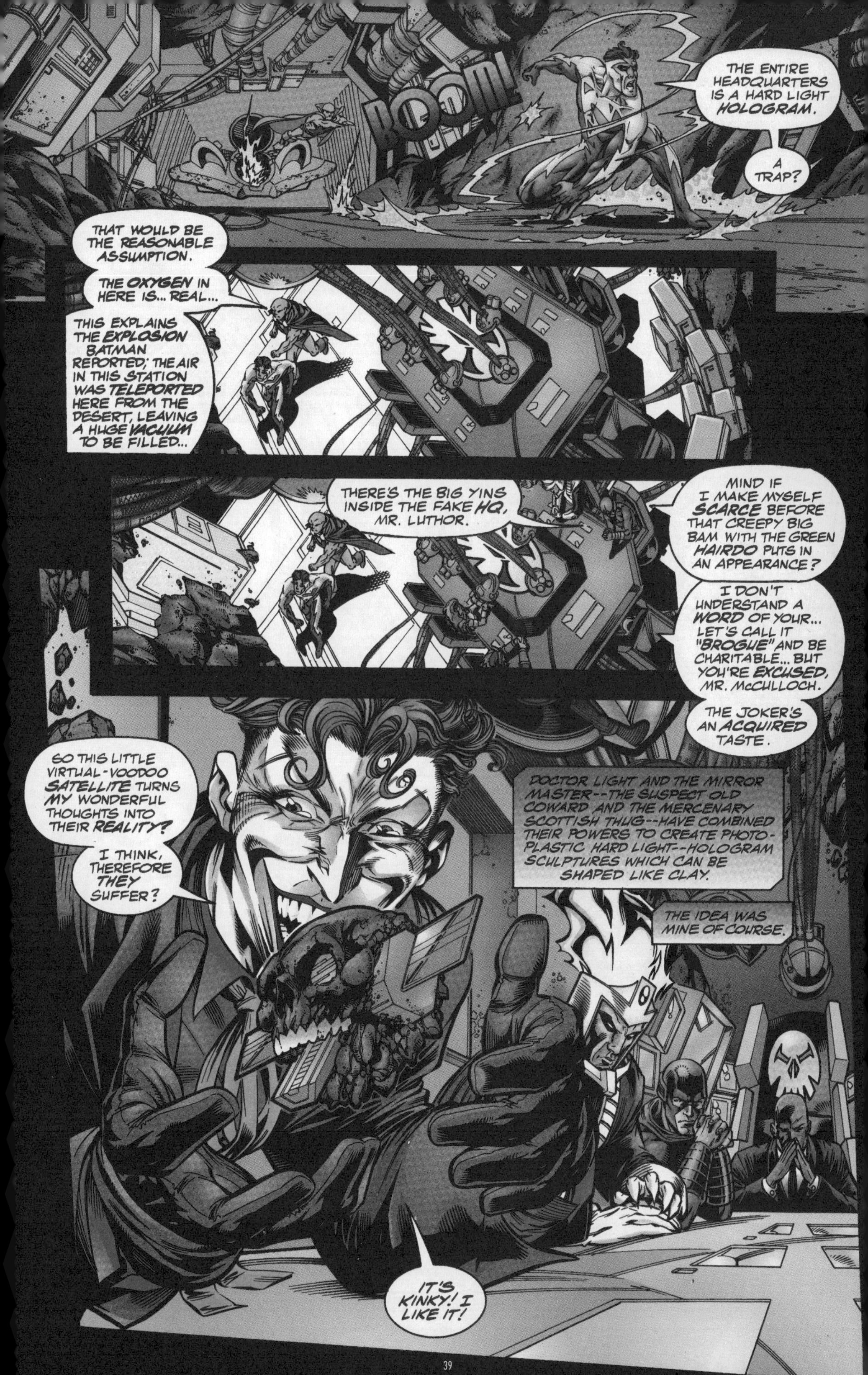
BOOM!
THE ENTIRE HEADQUARTERS IS A HARD LIGHT HOLOGRAM.
A TRAP?
THAT WOULD BE THE REASONABLE ASSUMPTION.
THE OXYGEN IN HERE IS... REAL...
THIS EXPLAINS THE EXPLOSION BATMAN REPORTED; THE AIR IN THIS STATION WAS TELEPORTED HERE FROM THE DESERT, LEAVING A HUGE VACUUM TO BE FILLED...
THERE'S THE BIG YINS INSIDE THE FAKE HQ, MR. LUTHOR.
MIND IF I MAKE MYSELF SCARCE BEFORE THAT CREEPY BIG BAM WITH THE GREEN HAIRDO PUTS IN AN APPEARANCE?
I DON'T UNDERSTAND A WORD OF YOUR... LET'S CALL IT "BROGUE" AND BE CHARITABLE... BUT YOU'RE EXCUSED, MR. McCULLOCH.
THE JOKER'S AN ACQUIRED TASTE.
SO THIS LITTLE VIRTUAL-VOODOO SATELLITE TURNS MY WONDERFUL THOUGHTS INTO THEIR REALITY?
I THINK, THEREFORE THEY SUFFER?
DOCTOR LIGHT AND THE MIRROR MASTER--THE SUSPECT OLD COWARD AND THE MERCENARY SCOTTISH THUG--HAVE COMBINED THEIR POWERS TO CREATE PHOTO-PLASTIC HARD LIGHT--HOLOGRAM SCULPTURES WHICH CAN BE SHAPED LIKE CLAY.
THE IDEA WAS MINE OF COURSE.
IT'S KINKY! I LIKE IT!

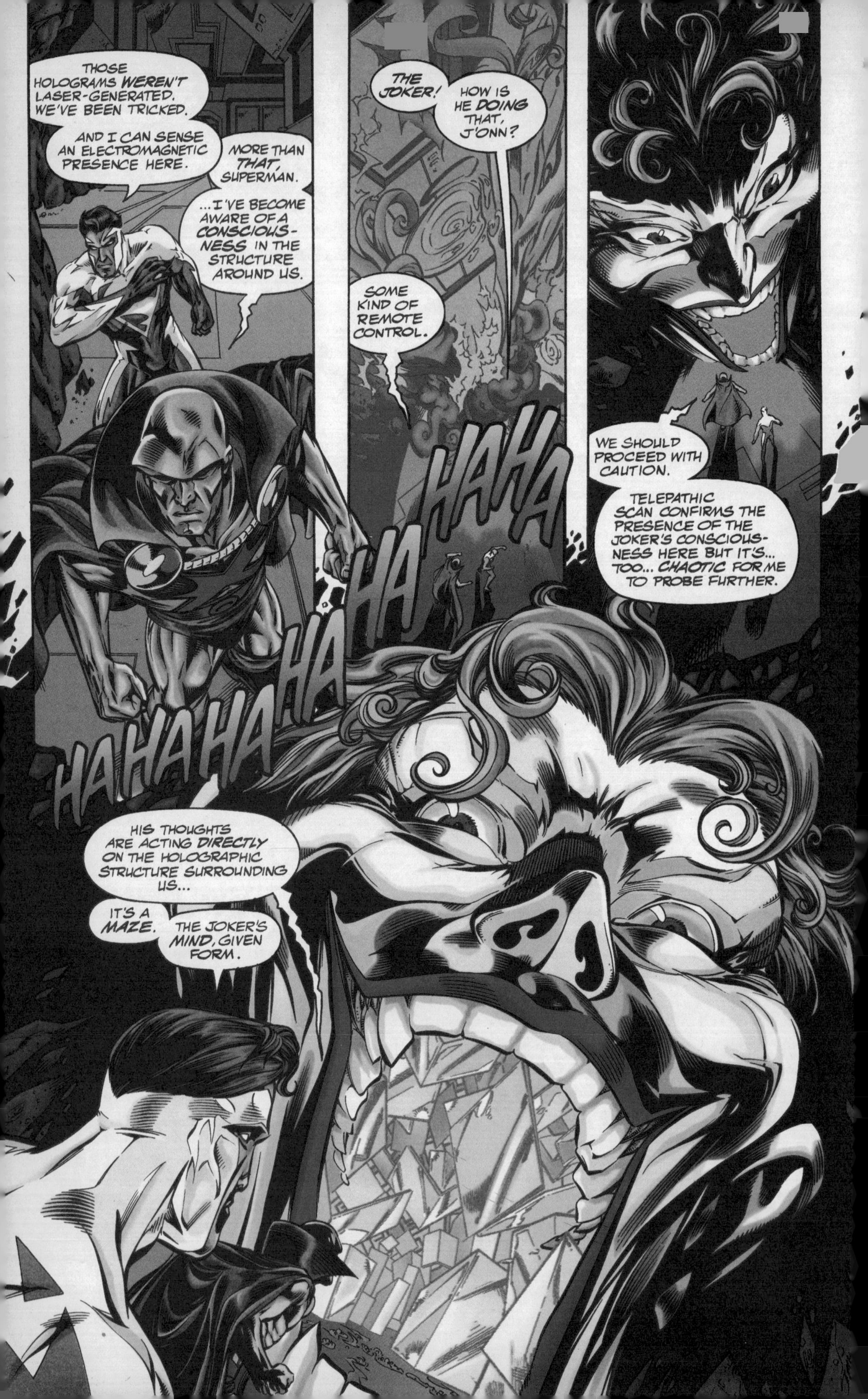
THOSE HOLOGRAMS WEREN'T LASER-GENERATED. WE'VE BEEN TRICKED.
AND I CAN SENSE AN ELECTROMAGNETIC PRESENCE HERE.
MORE THAN THAT, SUPERMAN.
...I'VE BECOME AWARE OF A CONSCIOUSNESS IN THE STRUCTURE AROUND US.
THE JOKER!
HOW IS HE DOING THAT, J'ONN?
SOME KIND OF REMOTE CONTROL.
WE SHOULD PROCEED WITH CAUTION.
TELEPATHIC SCAN CONFIRMS THE PRESENCE OF THE JOKER'S CONSCIOUSNESS HERE BUT IT'S... TOO... CHAOTIC FOR ME TO PROBE FURTHER.
HAHAHAHAHAHAHAHAHAHA
HIS THOUGHTS ARE ACTING DIRECTLY ON THE HOLOGRAPHIC STRUCTURE SURROUNDING US...
IT'S A MAZE.
THE JOKER'S MIND, GIVEN FORM.

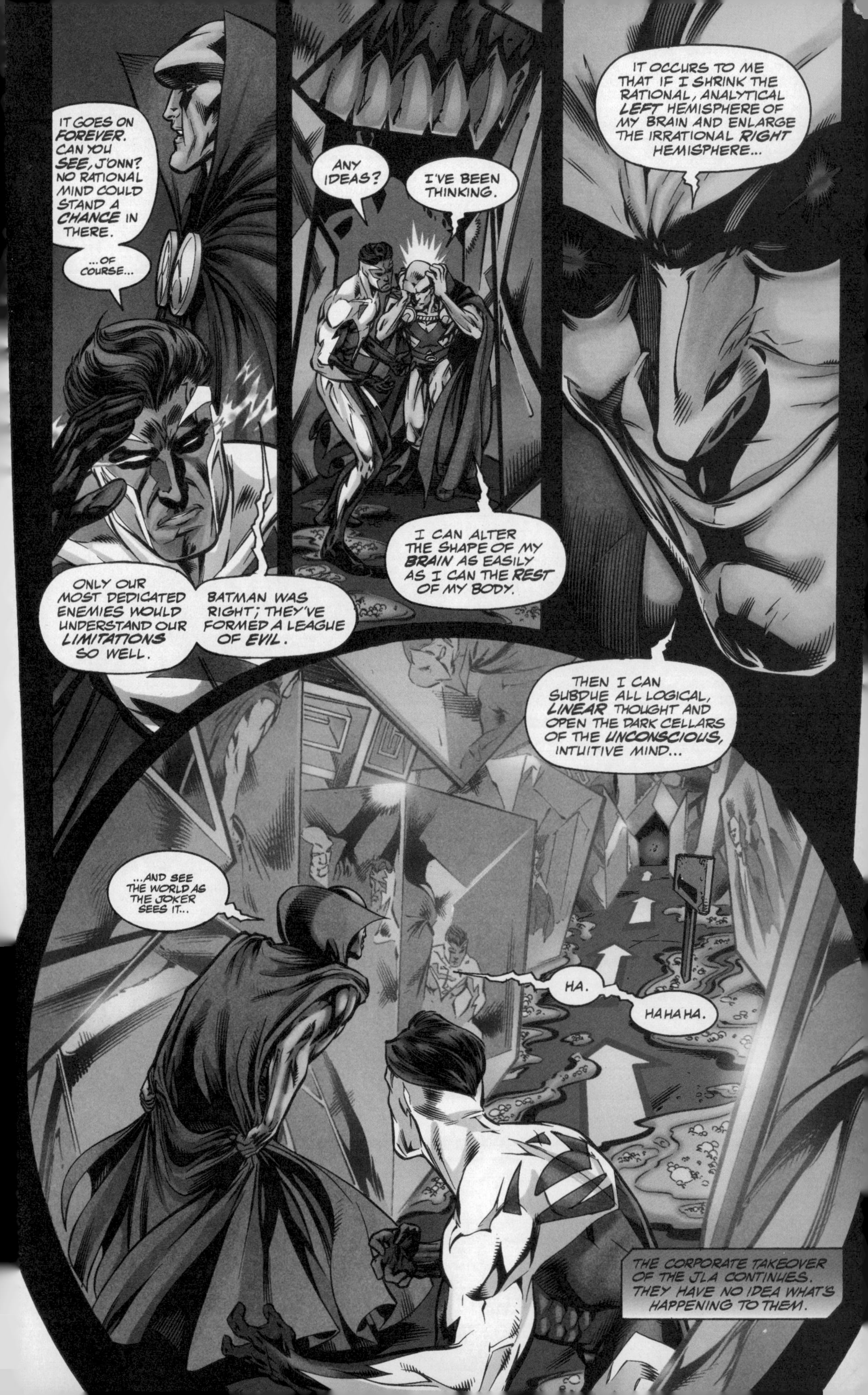
IT GOES ON FOREVER. CAN YOU SEE, J'ONN? NO RATIONAL MIND COULD STAND A CHANCE IN THERE.
...OF COURSE...
ONLY OUR MOST DEDICATED ENEMIES WOULD UNDERSTAND OUR LIMITATIONS SO WELL.
BATMAN WAS RIGHT; THEY'VE FORMED A LEAGUE OF EVIL.
ANY IDEAS?
I'VE BEEN THINKING.
I CAN ALTER THE SHAPE OF MY BRAIN AS EASILY AS I CAN THE REST OF MY BODY.
IT OCCURS TO ME THAT IF I SHRINK THE RATIONAL, ANALYTICAL LEFT HEMISPHERE OF MY BRAIN AND ENLARGE THE IRRATIONAL RIGHT HEMISPHERE...
THEN I CAN SUBDUE ALL LOGICAL, LINEAR THOUGHT AND OPEN THE DARK CELLARS OF THE UNCONSCIOUS, INTUITIVE MIND...
...AND SEE THE WORLD AS THE JOKER SEES IT...
HA.
HAHAHA.
THE CORPORATE TAKEOVER OF THE JLA CONTINUES. THEY HAVE NO IDEA WHAT'S HAPPENING TO THEM.

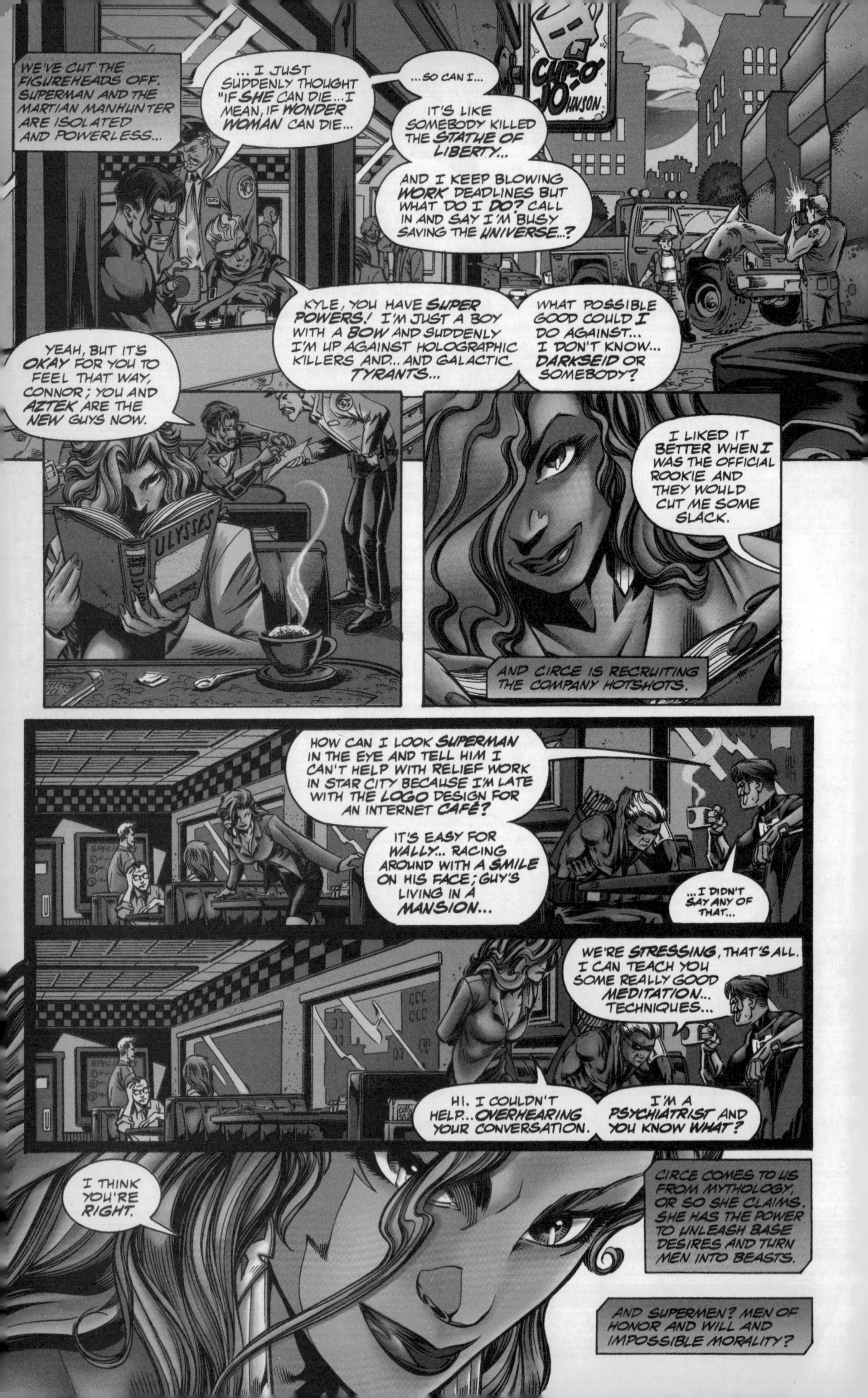
WE'VE CUT THE FIGUREHEADS OFF. SUPERMAN AND THE MARTIAN MANHUNTER ARE ISOLATED AND POWERLESS...
... I JUST SUDDENLY THOUGHT "IF SHE CAN DIE... I MEAN, IF WONDER WOMAN CAN DIE...
...SO CAN I...
IT'S LIKE SOMEBODY KILLED THE STATUE OF LIBERTY...
AND I KEEP BLOWING WORK DEADLINES BUT WHAT DO I DO? CALL IN AND SAY I'M BUSY SAVING THE UNIVERSE...?
CUP-O' JOHNSON
KYLE, YOU HAVE SUPER POWERS! I'M JUST A BOY WITH A BOW AND SUDDENLY I'M UP AGAINST HOLOGRAPHIC KILLERS AND... AND GALACTIC TYRANTS...
WHAT POSSIBLE GOOD COULD I DO AGAINST... I DON'T KNOW... DARKSEID OR SOMEBODY?
YEAH, BUT IT'S OKAY FOR YOU TO FEEL THAT WAY, CONNOR; YOU AND AZTEK ARE THE NEW GUYS NOW.
ULYSSES
JAMES JOYCE
I LIKED IT BETTER WHEN I WAS THE OFFICIAL ROOKIE AND THEY WOULD CUT ME SOME SLACK.
AND CIRCE IS RECRUITING THE COMPANY HOTSHOTS.
HOW CAN I LOOK SUPERMAN IN THE EYE AND TELL HIM I CAN'T HELP WITH RELIEF WORK IN STAR CITY BECAUSE I'M LATE WITH THE LOGO DESIGN FOR AN INTERNET CAFÉ?
IT'S EASY FOR WALLY... RACING AROUND WITH A SMILE ON HIS FACE; GUY'S LIVING IN A MANSION...
...I DIDN'T SAY ANY OF THAT...
WE'RE STRESSING, THAT'S ALL. I CAN TEACH YOU SOME REALLY GOOD MEDITATION... TECHNIQUES...
HI. I COULDN'T HELP... OVERHEARING YOUR CONVERSATION.
I'M A PSYCHIATRIST AND YOU KNOW WHAT?
I THINK YOU'RE RIGHT.
CIRCE COMES TO US FROM MYTHOLOGY, OR SO SHE CLAIMS. SHE HAS THE POWER TO UNLEASH BASE DESIRES AND TURN MEN INTO BEASTS.
AND SUPERMEN? MEN OF HONOR AND WILL AND IMPOSSIBLE MORALITY?

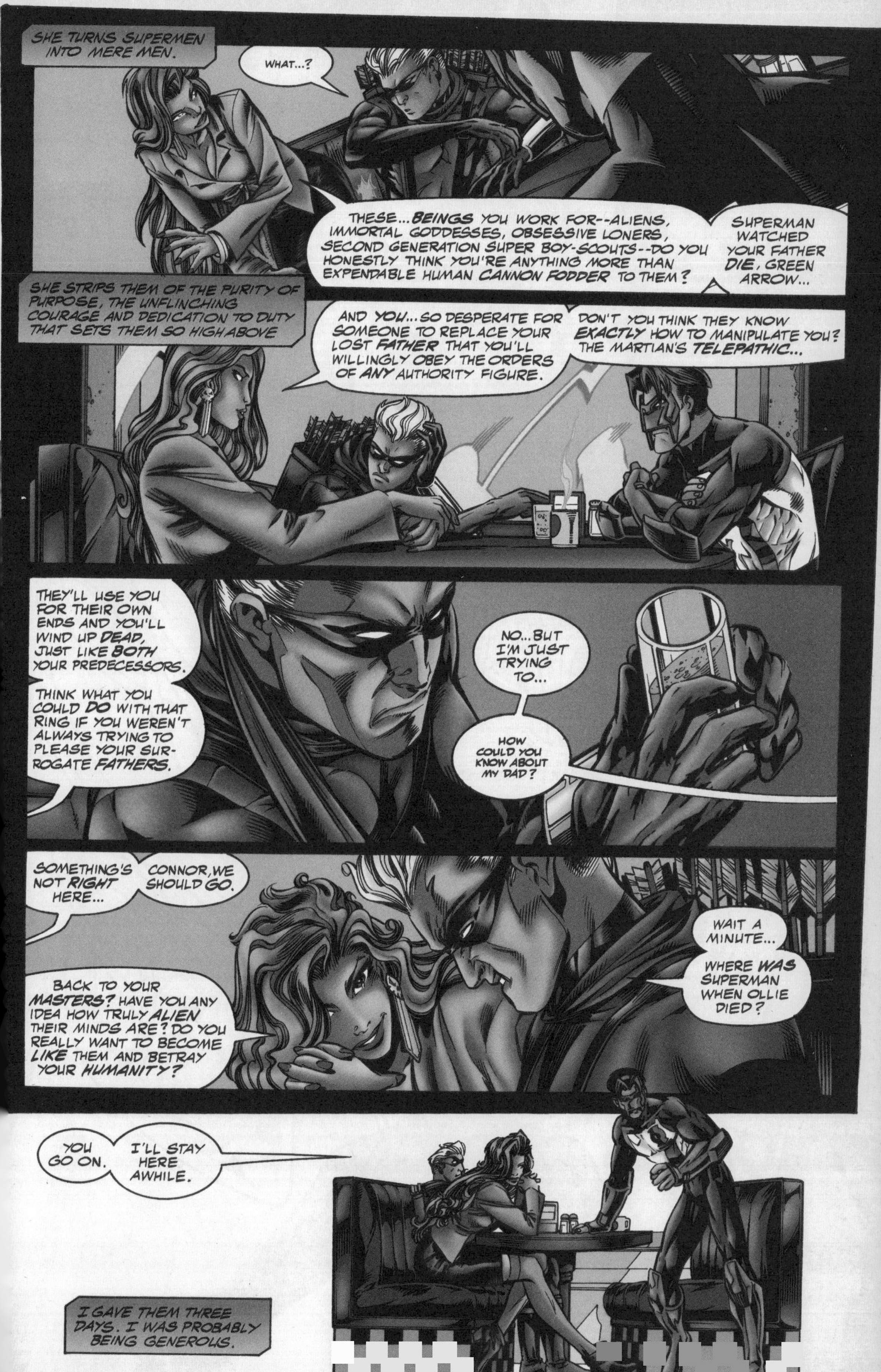

SHE TURNS SUPERMEN INTO MERE MEN.
WHAT...?
THESE...BEINGS YOU WORK FOR--ALIENS, IMMORTAL GODDESSES, OBSESSIVE LONERS, SECOND GENERATION SUPER BOY-SCOUTS--DO YOU HONESTLY THINK YOU'RE ANYTHING MORE THAN EXPENDABLE HUMAN CANNON FODDER TO THEM?
SUPERMAN WATCHED YOUR FATHER DIE, GREEN ARROW...
SHE STRIPS THEM OF THE PURITY OF PURPOSE, THE UNFLINCHING COURAGE AND DEDICATION TO DUTY THAT SETS THEM SO HIGH ABOVE
AND YOU...SO DESPERATE FOR SOMEONE TO REPLACE YOUR LOST FATHER THAT YOU'LL WILLINGLY OBEY THE ORDERS OF ANY AUTHORITY FIGURE.
DON'T YOU THINK THEY KNOW EXACTLY HOW TO MANIPULATE YOU? THE MARTIAN'S TELEPATHIC...
THEY'LL USE YOU FOR THEIR OWN ENDS AND YOU'LL WIND UP DEAD, JUST LIKE BOTH YOUR PREDECESSORS.
THINK WHAT YOU COULD DO WITH THAT RING IF YOU WEREN'T ALWAYS TRYING TO PLEASE YOUR SUR-ROGATE FATHERS.
NO...BUT I'M JUST TRYING TO...
HOW COULD YOU KNOW ABOUT MY DAD?
SOMETHING'S NOT RIGHT HERE...
CONNOR, WE SHOULD GO.
BACK TO YOUR MASTERS? HAVE YOU ANY IDEA HOW TRULY ALIEN THEIR MINDS ARE? DO YOU REALLY WANT TO BECOME LIKE THEM AND BETRAY YOUR HUMANITY?
WAIT A MINUTE...
WHERE WAS SUPERMAN WHEN OLLIE DIED?
YOU GO ON.
I'LL STAY HERE AWHILE.
I GAVE THEM THREE DAYS. I WAS PROBABLY BEING GENEROUS.

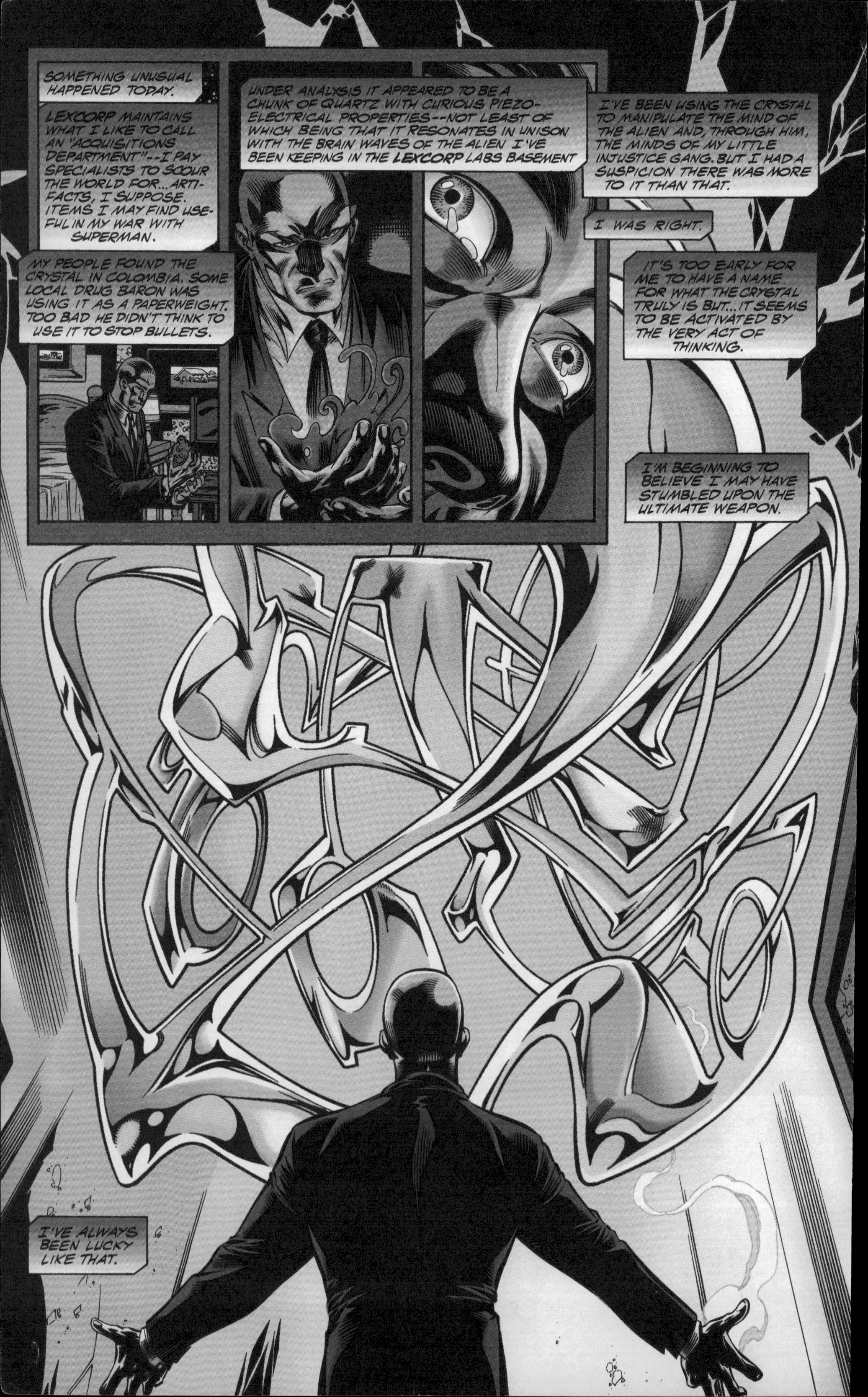
SOMETHING UNUSUAL HAPPENED TODAY.
LEXCORP MAINTAINS WHAT I LIKE TO CALL AN "ACQUISITIONS DEPARTMENT"--I PAY SPECIALISTS TO SCOUR THE WORLD FOR... ARTIFACTS, I SUPPOSE. ITEMS I MAY FIND USEFUL IN MY WAR WITH SUPERMAN.
MY PEOPLE FOUND THE CRYSTAL IN COLOMBIA. SOME LOCAL DRUG BARON WAS USING IT AS A PAPERWEIGHT. TOO BAD HE DIDN'T THINK TO USE IT TO STOP BULLETS.
UNDER ANALYSIS IT APPEARED TO BE A CHUNK OF QUARTZ WITH CURIOUS PIEZO-ELECTRICAL PROPERTIES--NOT LEAST OF WHICH BEING THAT IT RESONATES IN UNISON WITH THE BRAIN WAVES OF THE ALIEN I'VE BEEN KEEPING IN THE LEXCORP LABS BASEMENT
I'VE BEEN USING THE CRYSTAL TO MANIPULATE THE MIND OF THE ALIEN AND, THROUGH HIM, THE MINDS OF MY LITTLE INJUSTICE GANG. BUT I HAD A SUSPICION THERE WAS MORE TO IT THAN THAT.
I WAS RIGHT.
IT'S TOO EARLY FOR ME TO HAVE A NAME FOR WHAT THE CRYSTAL TRULY IS BUT... IT SEEMS TO BE ACTIVATED BY THE VERY ACT OF THINKING.
I'M BEGINNING TO BELIEVE I MAY HAVE STUMBLED UPON THE ULTIMATE WEAPON.
I'VE ALWAYS BEEN LUCKY LIKE THAT.

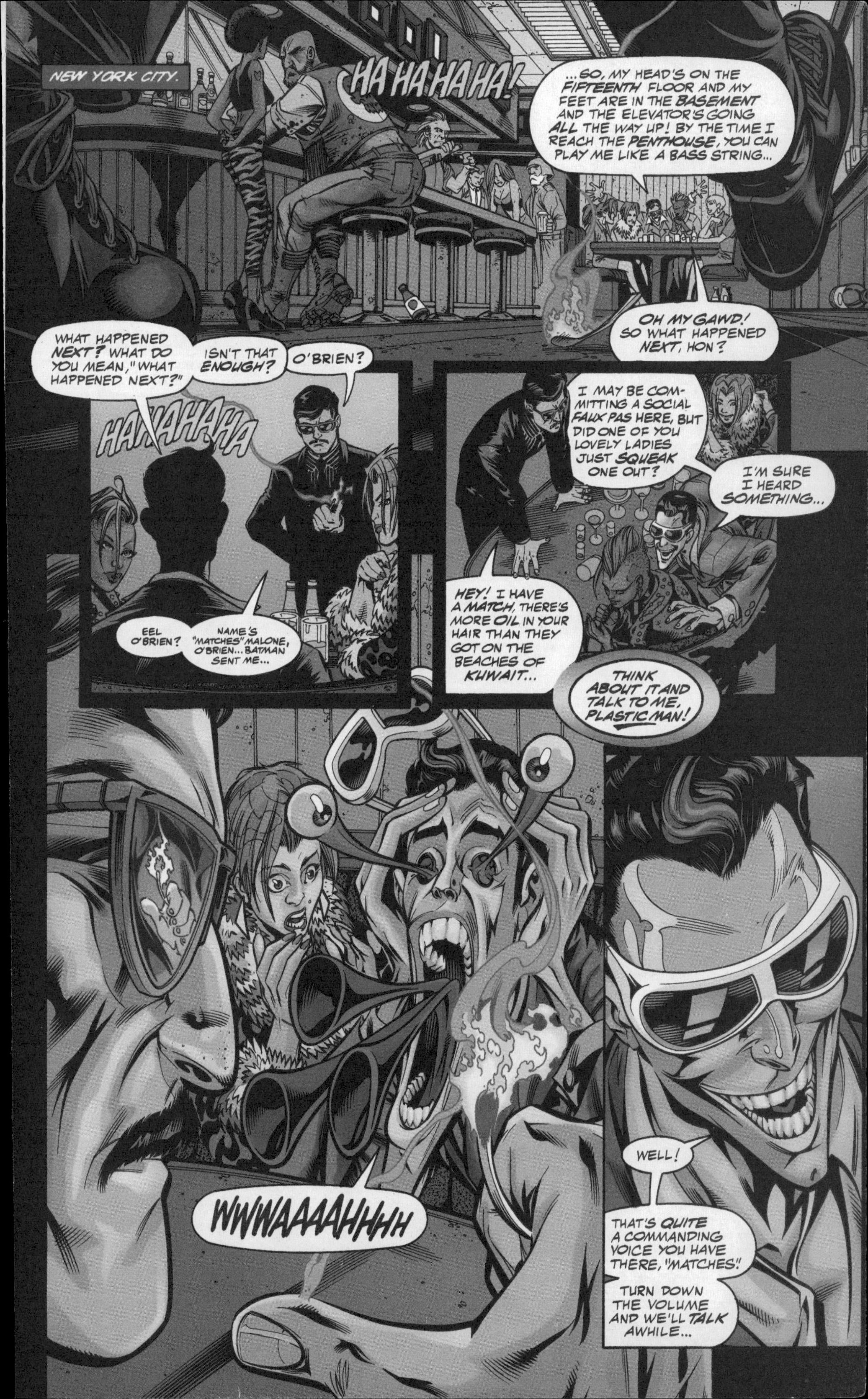
NEW YORK CITY.
HA HA HA HA HA!
...SO, MY HEAD'S ON THE FIFTEENTH FLOOR AND MY FEET ARE IN THE BASEMENT AND THE ELEVATOR'S GOING ALL THE WAY UP! BY THE TIME I REACH THE PENTHOUSE, YOU CAN PLAY ME LIKE A BASS STRING...
OH MY GAWD! SO WHAT HAPPENED NEXT, HON?
WHAT HAPPENED NEXT? WHAT DO YOU MEAN, "WHAT HAPPENED NEXT?"
ISN'T THAT ENOUGH?
O'BRIEN?
HAHAHAHA
EEL O'BRIEN?
NAME'S "MATCHES" MALONE, O'BRIEN... BATMAN SENT ME...
I MAY BE COMMITTING A SOCIAL FAUX PAS HERE, BUT DID ONE OF YOU LOVELY LADIES JUST SQUEAK ONE OUT?
I'M SURE I HEARD SOMETHING...
HEY! I HAVE A MATCH. THERE'S MORE OIL IN YOUR HAIR THAN THEY GOT ON THE BEACHES OF KUWAIT...
THINK ABOUT IT AND TALK TO ME, PLASTIC MAN!
WWWAAAAHHhh
WELL!
THAT'S QUITE A COMMANDING VOICE YOU HAVE THERE, "MATCHES."
TURN DOWN THE VOLUME AND WE'LL TALK AWHILE...

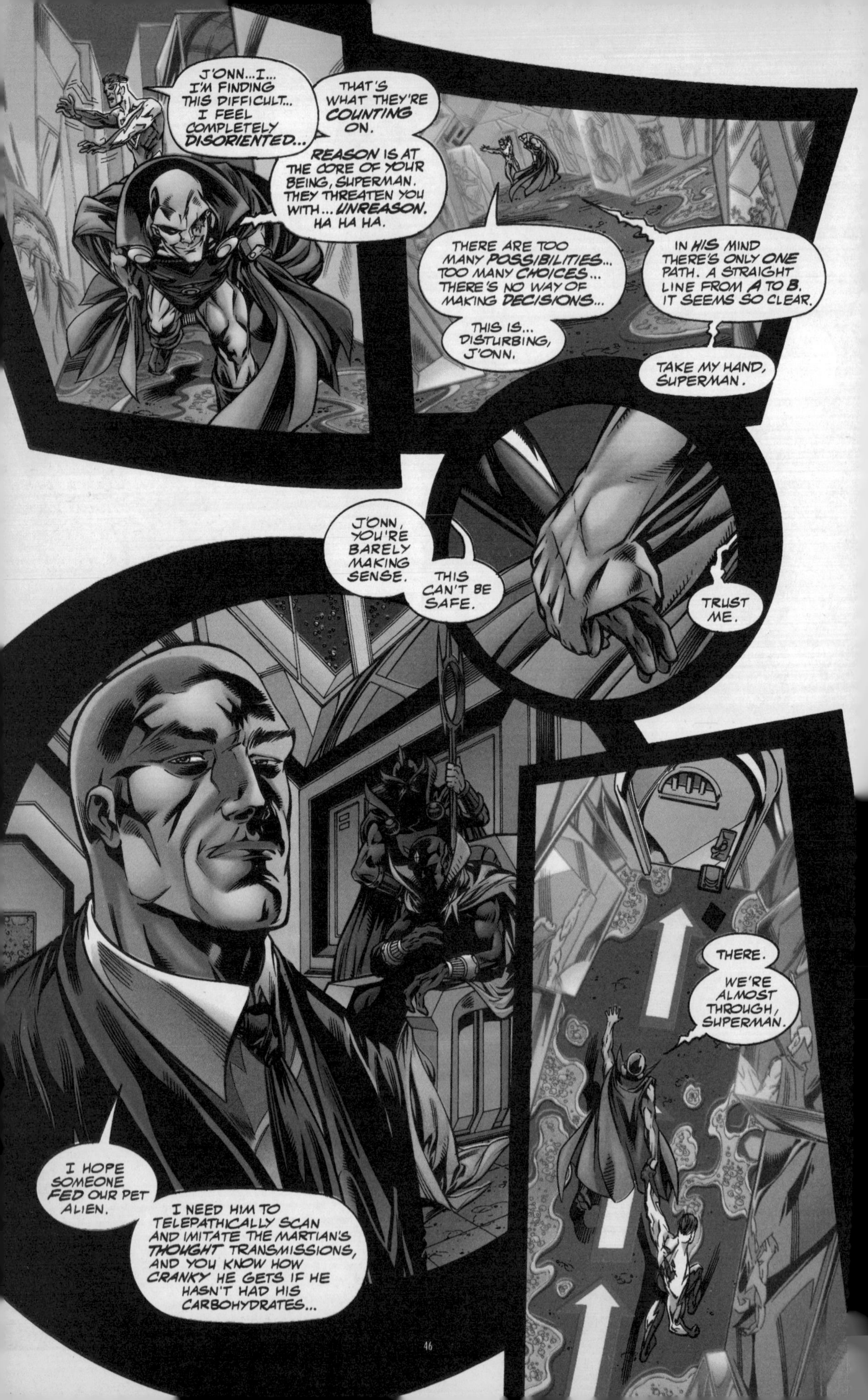
J'ONN...I... I'M FINDING THIS DIFFICULT... I FEEL COMPLETELY DISORIENTED...
THAT'S WHAT THEY'RE COUNTING ON.
REASON IS AT THE CORE OF YOUR BEING, SUPERMAN. THEY THREATEN YOU WITH... UNREASON. HA HA HA.
THERE ARE TOO MANY POSSIBILITIES... TOO MANY CHOICES... THERE'S NO WAY OF MAKING DECISIONS...
THIS IS... DISTURBING, J'ONN.
IN HIS MIND THERE'S ONLY ONE PATH. A STRAIGHT LINE FROM A TO B. IT SEEMS SO CLEAR.
TAKE MY HAND, SUPERMAN.
J'ONN, YOU'RE BARELY MAKING SENSE.
THIS CAN'T BE SAFE.
TRUST ME.
I HOPE SOMEONE FED OUR PET ALIEN.
I NEED HIM TO TELEPATHICALLY SCAN AND IMITATE THE MARTIAN'S THOUGHT TRANSMISSIONS, AND YOU KNOW HOW CRANKY HE GETS IF HE HASN'T HAD HIS CARBOHYDRATES...
THERE.
WE'RE ALMOST THROUGH, SUPERMAN.

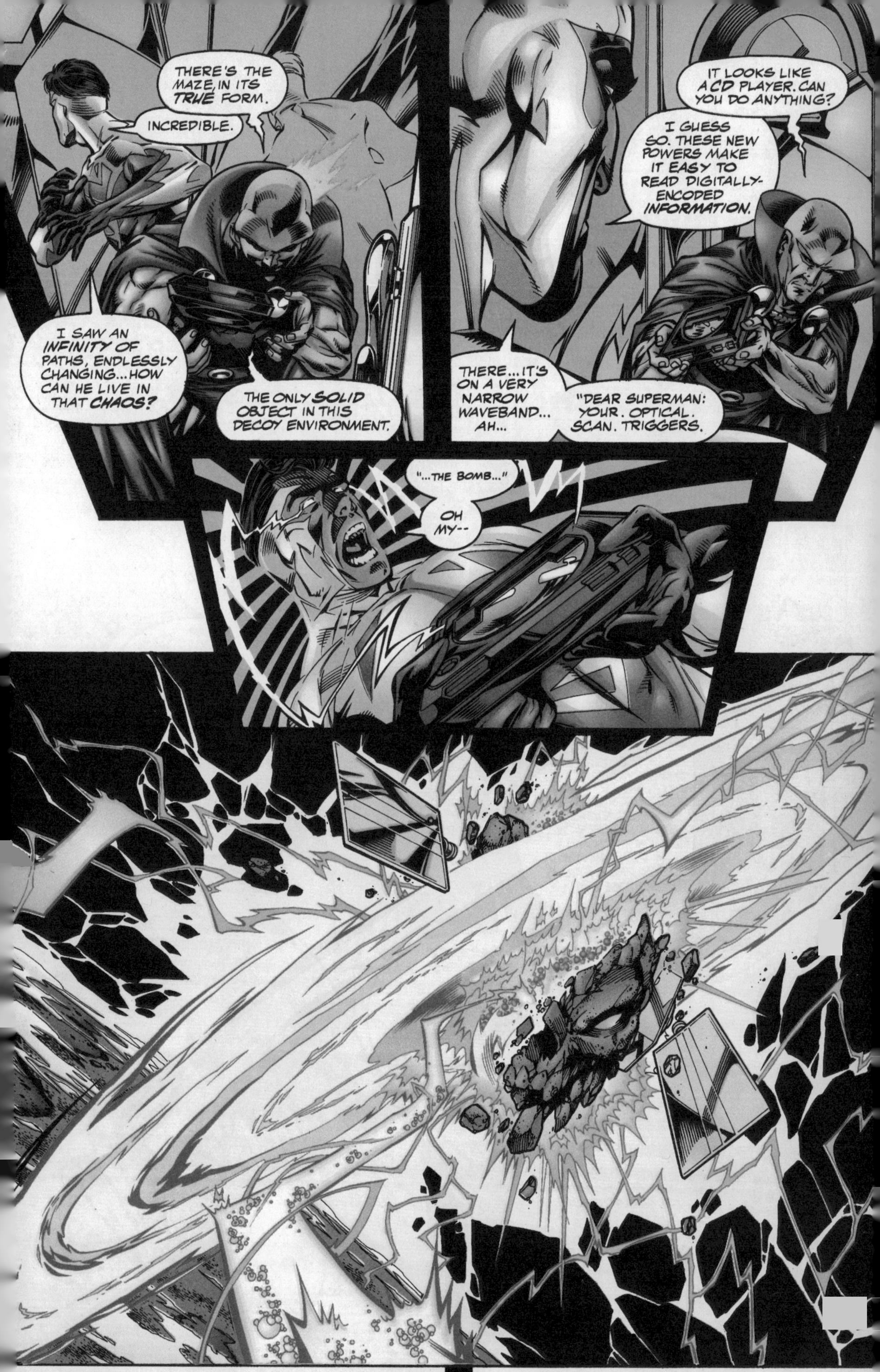
THERE'S THE MAZE, IN ITS TRUE FORM.
INCREDIBLE.
I SAW AN INFINITY OF PATHS, ENDLESSLY CHANGING...HOW CAN HE LIVE IN THAT CHAOS?
THE ONLY SOLID OBJECT IN THIS DECOY ENVIRONMENT.
IT LOOKS LIKE A CD PLAYER. CAN YOU DO ANYTHING?
I GUESS SO. THESE NEW POWERS MAKE IT EASY TO READ DIGITALLY-ENCODED INFORMATION.
THERE...IT'S ON A VERY NARROW WAVEBAND... AH...
"DEAR SUPERMAN: YOUR. OPTICAL. SCAN. TRIGGERS.
"...THE BOMB..."
OH MY--

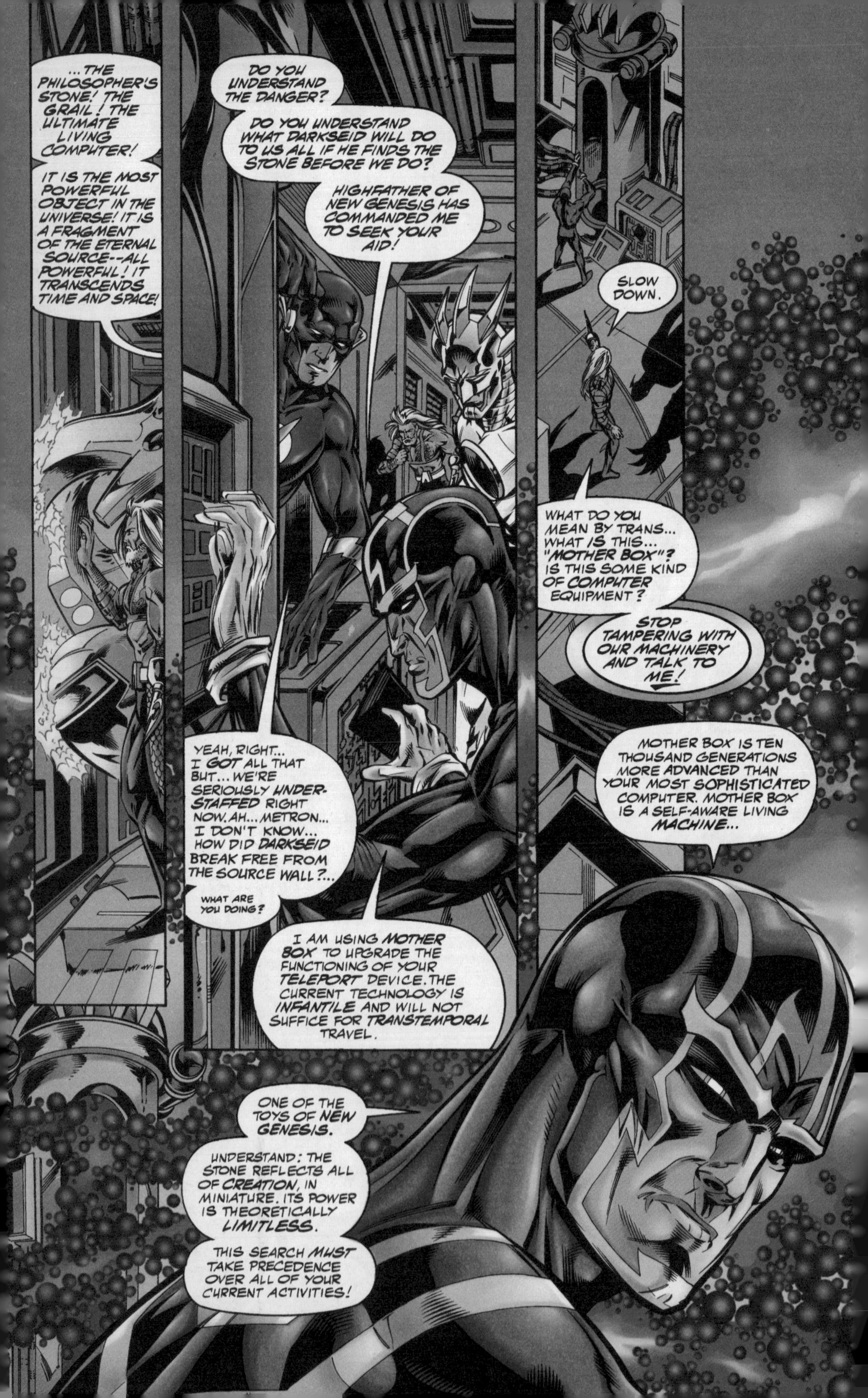
...THE PHILOSOPHER'S STONE! THE GRAIL! THE ULTIMATE LIVING COMPUTER!
IT IS THE MOST POWERFUL OBJECT IN THE UNIVERSE! IT IS A FRAGMENT OF THE ETERNAL SOURCE--ALL POWERFUL! IT TRANSCENDS TIME AND SPACE!
DO YOU UNDERSTAND THE DANGER?
DO YOU UNDERSTAND WHAT DARKSEID WILL DO TO US ALL IF HE FINDS THE STONE BEFORE WE DO?
HIGHFATHER OF NEW GENESIS HAS COMMANDED ME TO SEEK YOUR AID!
YEAH, RIGHT... I GOT ALL THAT BUT... WE'RE SERIOUSLY UNDER-STAFFED RIGHT NOW. AH... METRON... I DON'T KNOW... HOW DID DARKSEID BREAK FREE FROM THE SOURCE WALL?...
WHAT ARE YOU DOING?
I AM USING MOTHER BOX TO UPGRADE THE FUNCTIONING OF YOUR TELEPORT DEVICE. THE CURRENT TECHNOLOGY IS INFANTILE AND WILL NOT SUFFICE FOR TRANSTEMPORAL TRAVEL.
SLOW DOWN.
WHAT DO YOU MEAN BY TRANS... WHAT IS THIS... "MOTHER BOX"? IS THIS SOME KIND OF COMPUTER EQUIPMENT?
STOP TAMPERING WITH OUR MACHINERY AND TALK TO ME!
MOTHER BOX IS TEN THOUSAND GENERATIONS MORE ADVANCED THAN YOUR MOST SOPHISTICATED COMPUTER. MOTHER BOX IS A SELF-AWARE LIVING MACHINE...
ONE OF THE TOYS OF NEW GENESIS.
UNDERSTAND: THE STONE REFLECTS ALL OF CREATION, IN MINIATURE. ITS POWER IS THEORETICALLY LIMITLESS.
THIS SEARCH MUST TAKE PRECEDENCE OVER ALL OF YOUR CURRENT ACTIVITIES!

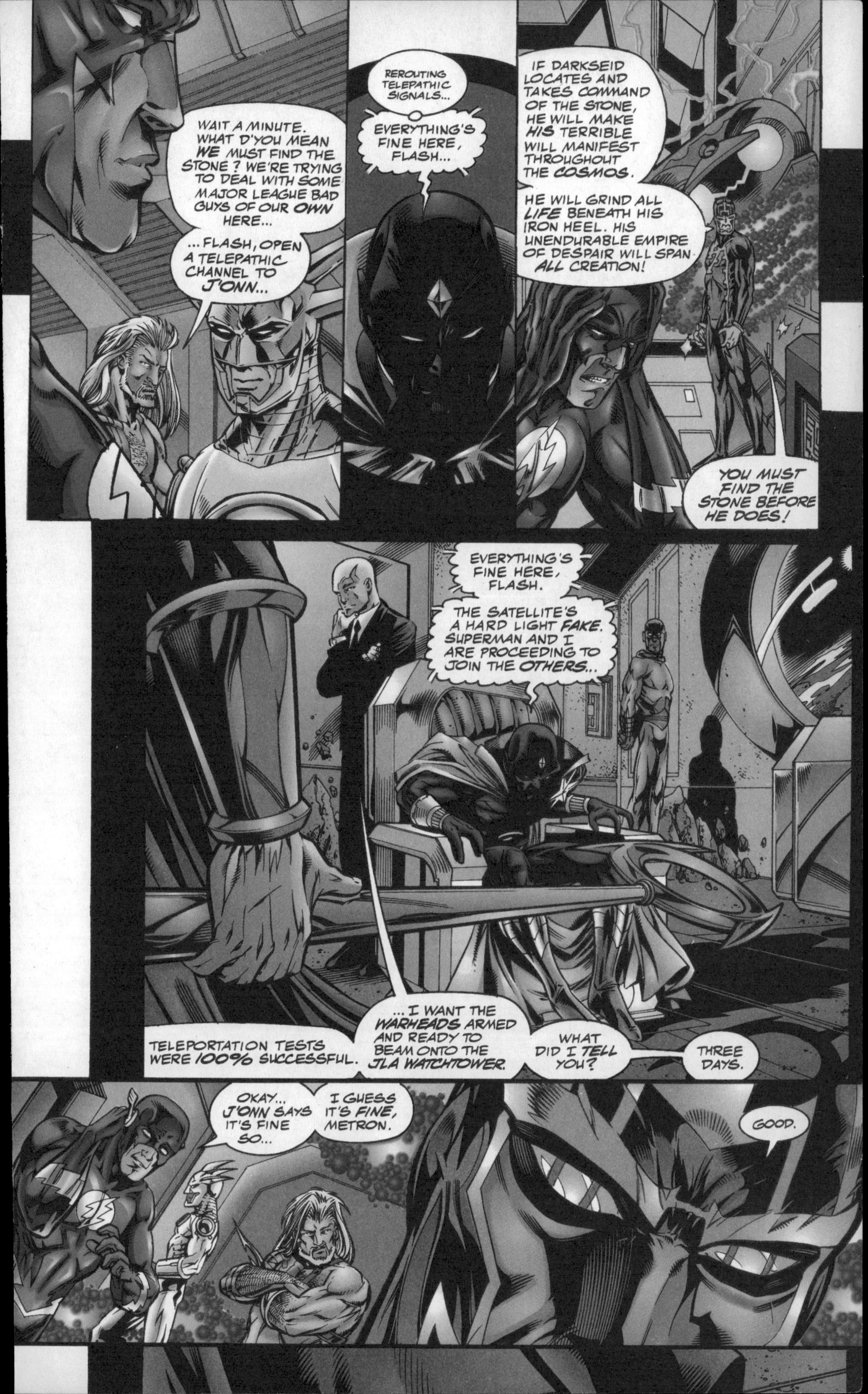
WAIT A MINUTE. WHAT D'YOU MEAN WE MUST FIND THE STONE? WE'RE TRYING TO DEAL WITH SOME MAJOR LEAGUE BAD GUYS OF OUR OWN HERE...
...FLASH, OPEN A TELEPATHIC CHANNEL TO J'ONN...
REROUTING TELEPATHIC SIGNALS...
EVERYTHING'S FINE HERE, FLASH...
IF DARKSEID LOCATES AND TAKES COMMAND OF THE STONE, HE WILL MAKE HIS TERRIBLE WILL MANIFEST THROUGHOUT THE COSMOS.
HE WILL GRIND ALL LIFE BENEATH HIS IRON HEEL. HIS UNENDURABLE EMPIRE OF DESPAIR WILL SPAN ALL CREATION!
YOU MUST FIND THE STONE BEFORE HE DOES!
EVERYTHING'S FINE HERE, FLASH.
THE SATELLITE'S A HARD LIGHT FAKE. SUPERMAN AND I ARE PROCEEDING TO JOIN THE OTHERS...
TELEPORTATION TESTS WERE 100% SUCCESSFUL.
...I WANT THE WARHEADS ARMED AND READY TO BEAM ONTO THE JLA WATCHTOWER.
WHAT DID I TELL YOU?
THREE DAYS.
OKAY... J'ONN SAYS IT'S FINE SO...
I GUESS IT'S FINE, METRON.
GOOD.

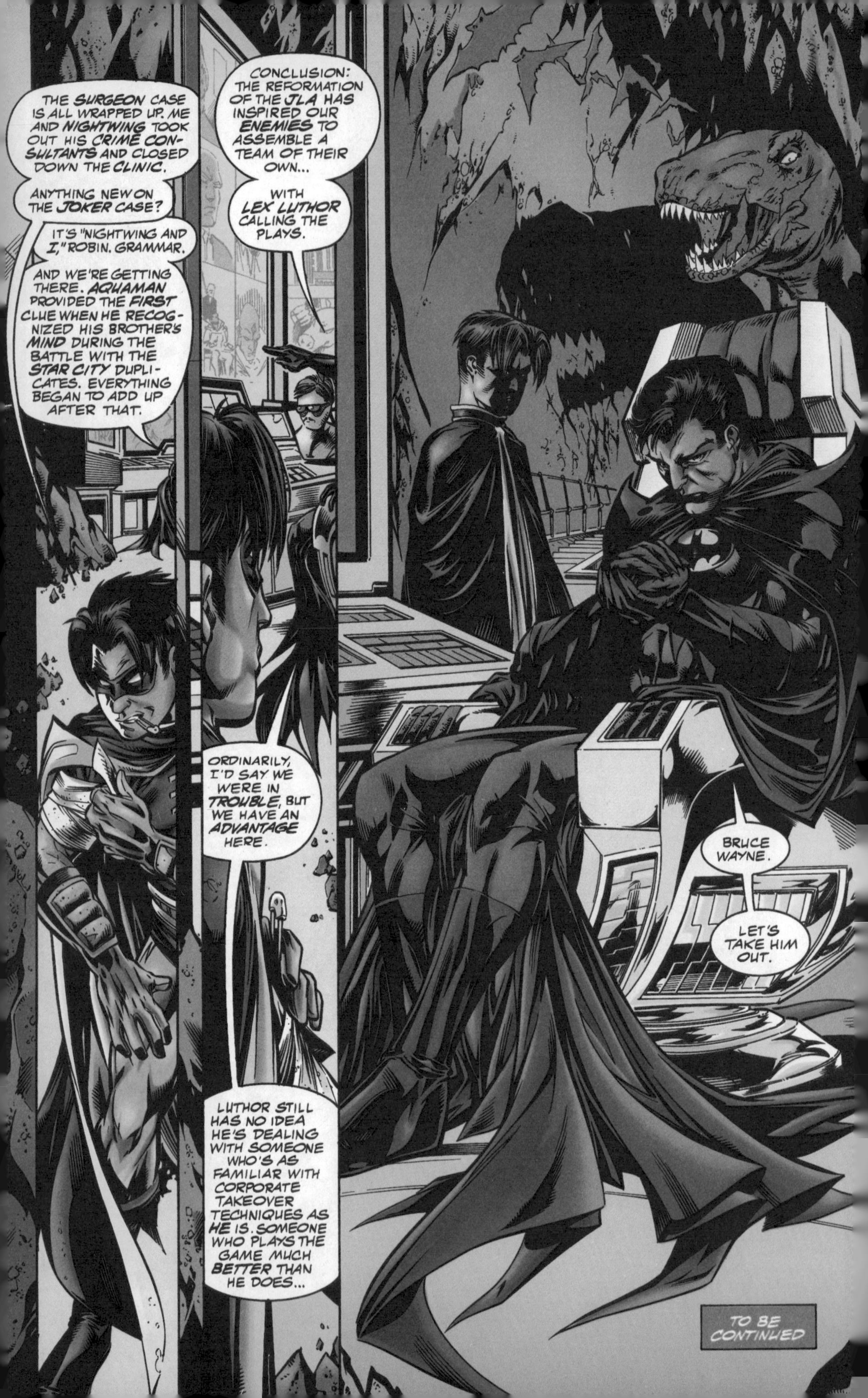
THE SURGEON CASE IS ALL WRAPPED UP. ME AND NIGHTWING TOOK OUT HIS CRIME CONSULTANTS AND CLOSED DOWN THE CLINIC.
ANYTHING NEW ON THE JOKER CASE?
IT'S "NIGHTWING AND I," ROBIN. GRAMMAR.
AND WE'RE GETTING THERE. AQUAMAN PROVIDED THE FIRST CLUE WHEN HE RECOGNIZED HIS BROTHER'S MIND DURING THE BATTLE WITH THE STAR CITY DUPLICATES. EVERYTHING BEGAN TO ADD UP AFTER THAT.
CONCLUSION: THE REFORMATION OF THE JLA HAS INSPIRED OUR ENEMIES TO ASSEMBLE A TEAM OF THEIR OWN...
WITH LEX LUTHOR CALLING THE PLAYS.
ORDINARILY, I'D SAY WE WERE IN TROUBLE, BUT WE HAVE AN ADVANTAGE HERE.
LUTHOR STILL HAS NO IDEA HE'S DEALING WITH SOMEONE WHO'S AS FAMILIAR WITH CORPORATE TAKEOVER TECHNIQUES AS HE IS. SOMEONE WHO PLAYS THE GAME MUCH BETTER THAN HE DOES...
BRUCE WAYNE.
LET'S TAKE HIM OUT.
TO BE CONTINUED

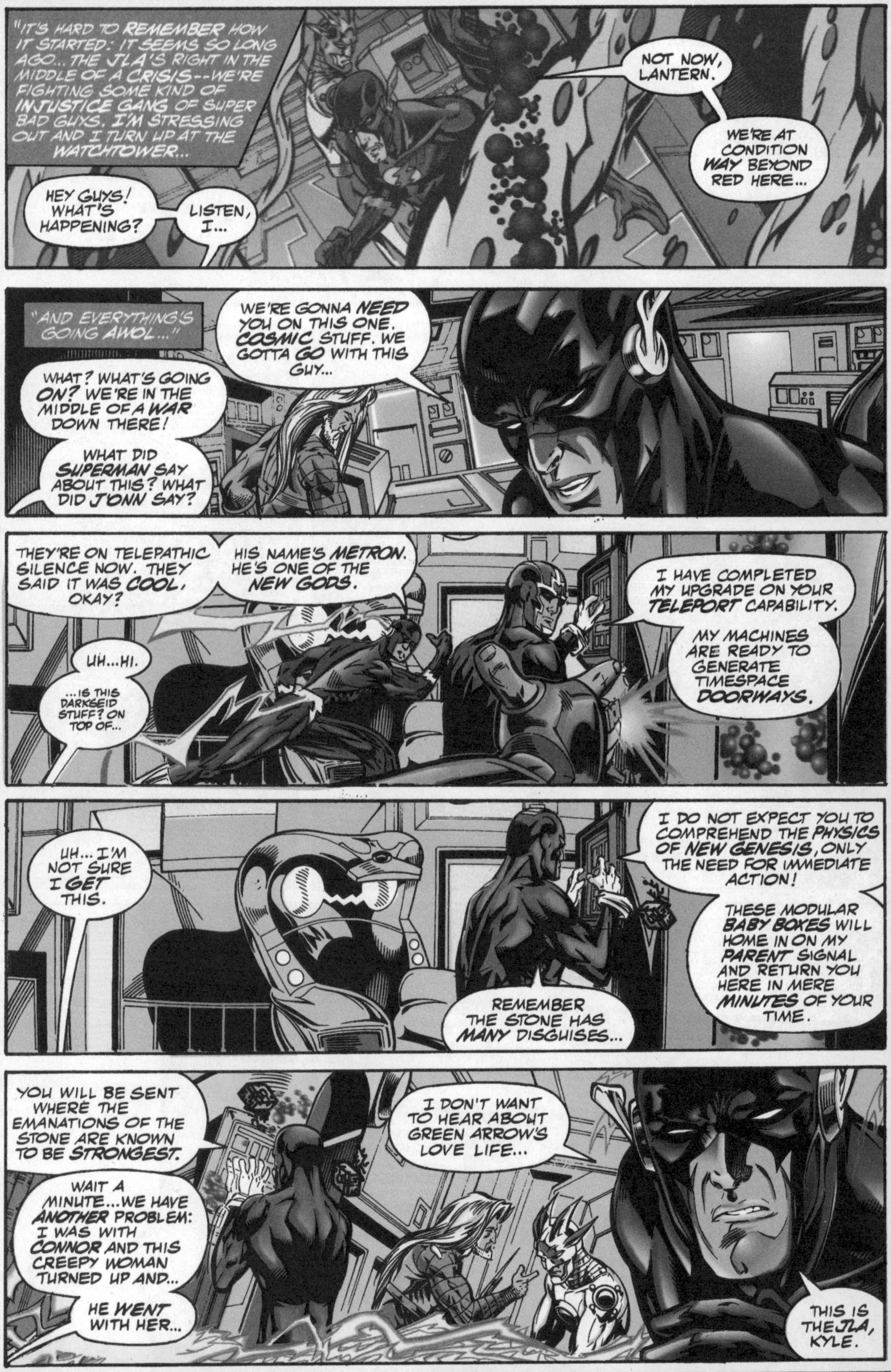
"IT'S HARD TO REMEMBER HOW IT STARTED: IT SEEMS SO LONG AGO... THE JLA'S RIGHT IN THE MIDDLE OF A CRISIS--WE'RE FIGHTING SOME KIND OF INJUSTICE GANG OF SUPER BAD GUYS. I'M STRESSING OUT AND I TURN UP AT THE WATCHTOWER...
HEY GUYS! WHAT'S HAPPENING?
LISTEN, I...
NOT NOW, LANTERN.
WE'RE AT CONDITION WAY BEYOND RED HERE...
"AND EVERYTHING'S GOING AWOL..."
WE'RE GONNA NEED YOU ON THIS ONE. COSMIC STUFF. WE GOTTA GO WITH THIS GUY...
WHAT? WHAT'S GOING ON? WE'RE IN THE MIDDLE OF A WAR DOWN THERE!
WHAT DID SUPERMAN SAY ABOUT THIS? WHAT DID J'ONN SAY?
THEY'RE ON TELEPATHIC SILENCE NOW. THEY SAID IT WAS COOL, OKAY?
HIS NAME'S METRON. HE'S ONE OF THE NEW GODS.
UH...HI.
...IS THIS DARKSEID STUFF? ON TOP OF...
I HAVE COMPLETED MY UPGRADE ON YOUR TELEPORT CAPABILITY.
MY MACHINES ARE READY TO GENERATE TIMESPACE DOORWAYS.
UH... I'M NOT SURE I GET THIS.
I DO NOT EXPECT YOU TO COMPREHEND THE PHYSICS OF NEW GENESIS, ONLY THE NEED FOR IMMEDIATE ACTION!
THESE MODULAR BABY BOXES WILL HOME IN ON MY PARENT SIGNAL AND RETURN YOU HERE IN MERE MINUTES OF YOUR TIME.
REMEMBER THE STONE HAS MANY DISGUISES...
YOU WILL BE SENT WHERE THE EMANATIONS OF THE STONE ARE KNOWN TO BE STRONGEST.
WAIT A MINUTE...WE HAVE ANOTHER PROBLEM: I WAS WITH CONNOR AND THIS CREEPY WOMAN TURNED UP AND...
HE WENT WITH HER...
I DON'T WANT TO HEAR ABOUT GREEN ARROW'S LOVE LIFE...
THIS IS THE JLA, KYLE.

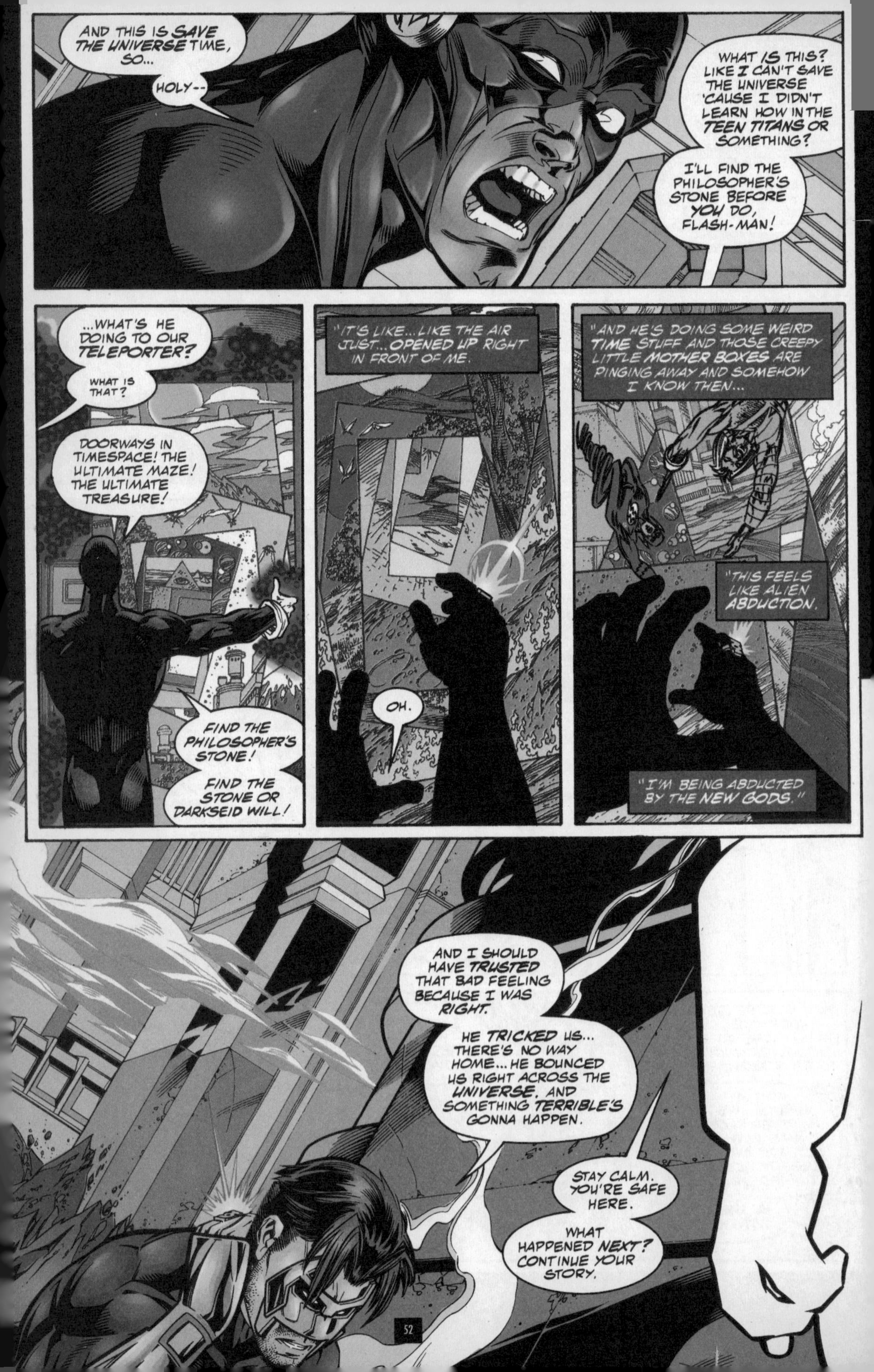
AND THIS IS SAVE THE UNIVERSE TIME, SO...
HOLY--
WHAT IS THIS? LIKE I CAN'T SAVE THE UNIVERSE 'CAUSE I DIDN'T LEARN HOW IN THE TEEN TITANS OR SOMETHING?
I'LL FIND THE PHILOSOPHER'S STONE BEFORE YOU DO, FLASH-MAN!
...WHAT'S HE DOING TO OUR TELEPORTER?
WHAT IS THAT?
DOORWAYS IN TIMESPACE! THE ULTIMATE MAZE! THE ULTIMATE TREASURE!
FIND THE PHILOSOPHER'S STONE!
FIND THE STONE OR DARKSEID WILL!
"IT'S LIKE... LIKE THE AIR JUST... OPENED UP RIGHT IN FRONT OF ME.
OH.
"AND HE'S DOING SOME WEIRD TIME STUFF AND THOSE CREEPY LITTLE MOTHER BOXES ARE PINGING AWAY AND SOMEHOW I KNOW THEN...
"THIS FEELS LIKE ALIEN ABDUCTION.
"I'M BEING ABDUCTED BY THE NEW GODS."
AND I SHOULD HAVE TRUSTED THAT BAD FEELING BECAUSE I WAS RIGHT.
HE TRICKED US... THERE'S NO WAY HOME... HE BOUNCED US RIGHT ACROSS THE UNIVERSE, AND SOMETHING TERRIBLE'S GONNA HAPPEN.
STAY CALM. YOU'RE SAFE HERE.
WHAT HAPPENED NEXT? CONTINUE YOUR STORY.

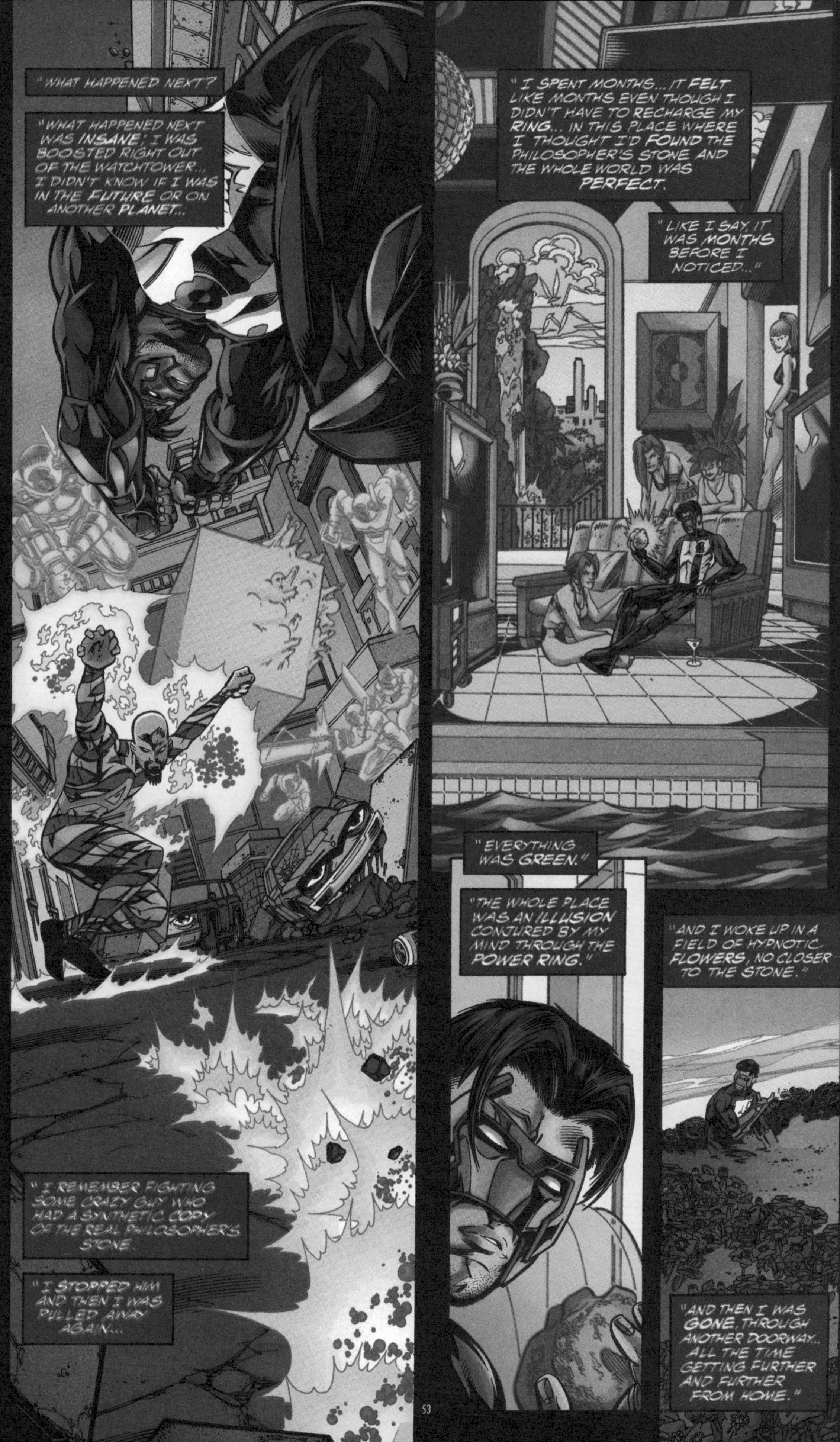
"WHAT HAPPENED NEXT?
"WHAT HAPPENED NEXT WAS INSANE; I WAS BOOSTED RIGHT OUT OF THE WATCHTOWER... I DIDN'T KNOW IF I WAS IN THE FUTURE OR ON ANOTHER PLANET...
"I REMEMBER FIGHTING SOME CRAZY GUY WHO HAD A SYNTHETIC COPY OF THE REAL PHILOSOPHERS STONE.
"I STOPPED HIM AND THEN I WAS PULLED AWAY AGAIN...
"I SPENT MONTHS... IT FELT LIKE MONTHS EVEN THOUGH I DIDN'T HAVE TO RECHARGE MY RING... IN THIS PLACE WHERE I THOUGHT I'D FOUND THE PHILOSOPHER'S STONE AND THE WHOLE WORLD WAS PERFECT.
"LIKE I SAY, IT WAS MONTHS BEFORE I NOTICED..."
"EVERYTHING WAS GREEN."
"THE WHOLE PLACE WAS AN ILLUSION CONJURED BY MY MIND THROUGH THE POWER RING."
"AND I WOKE UP IN A FIELD OF HYPNOTIC FLOWERS, NO CLOSER TO THE STONE."
"AND THEN I WAS GONE, THROUGH ANOTHER DOORWAY.. ALL THE TIME GETTING FURTHER AND FURTHER FROM HOME."

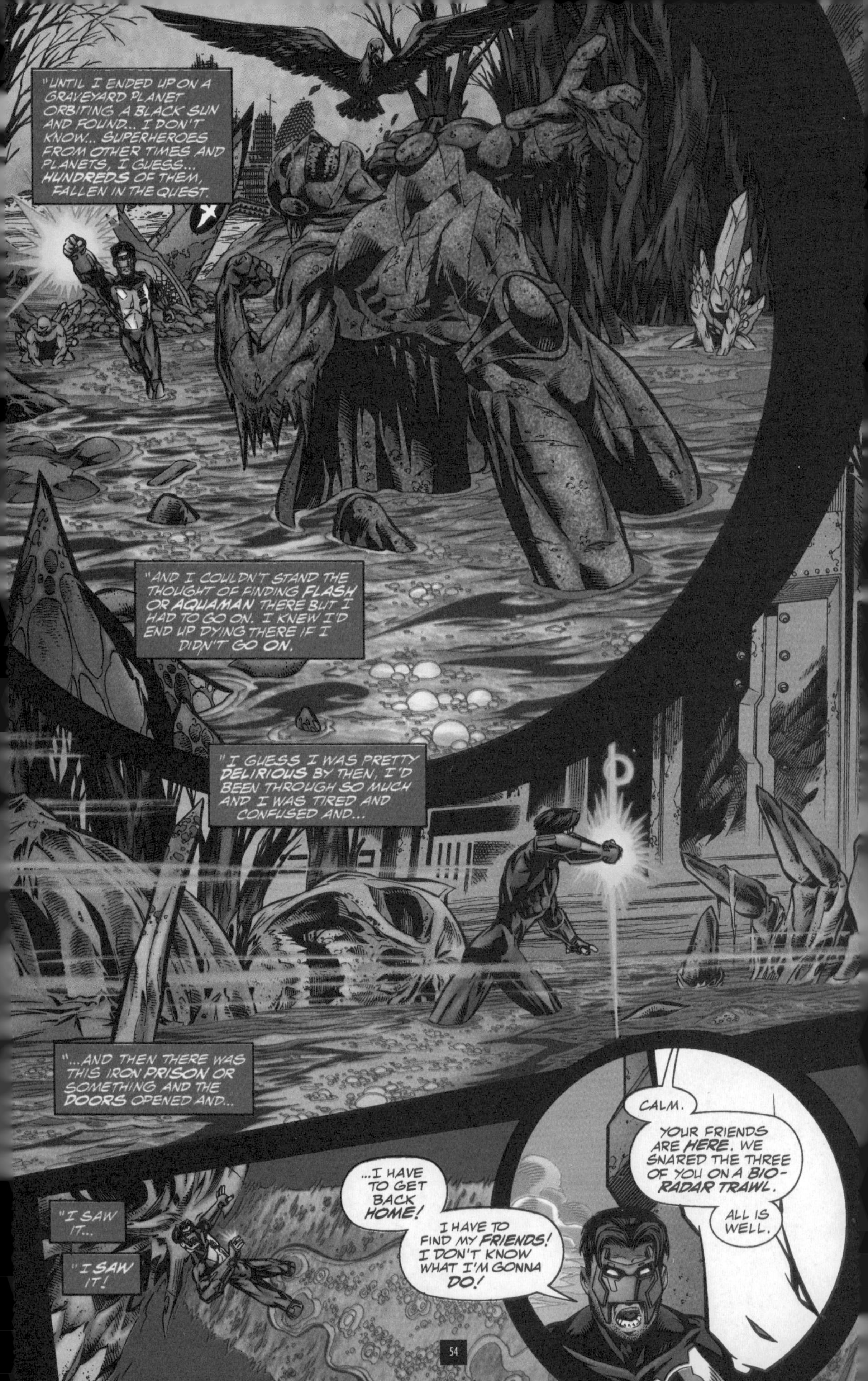
"UNTIL I ENDED UP ON A GRAVEYARD PLANET ORBITING A BLACK SUN AND FOUND... I DON'T KNOW... SUPERHEROES FROM OTHER TIMES AND PLANETS, I GUESS... HUNDREDS OF THEM, FALLEN IN THE QUEST.
"AND I COULDN'T STAND THE THOUGHT OF FINDING FLASH OR AQUAMAN THERE BUT I HAD TO GO ON. I KNEW I'D END UP DYING THERE IF I DIDN'T GO ON.
"I GUESS I WAS PRETTY DELIRIOUS BY THEN, I'D BEEN THROUGH SO MUCH AND I WAS TIRED AND CONFUSED AND...
"...AND THEN THERE WAS THIS IRON PRISON OR SOMETHING AND THE DOORS OPENED AND...
"I SAW IT...
"I SAW IT!
...I HAVE TO GET BACK HOME!
I HAVE TO FIND MY FRIENDS! I DON'T KNOW WHAT I'M GONNA DO!
CALM.
YOUR FRIENDS ARE HERE. WE SNARED THE THREE OF YOU ON A BIO-RADAR TRAWL.
ALL IS WELL.

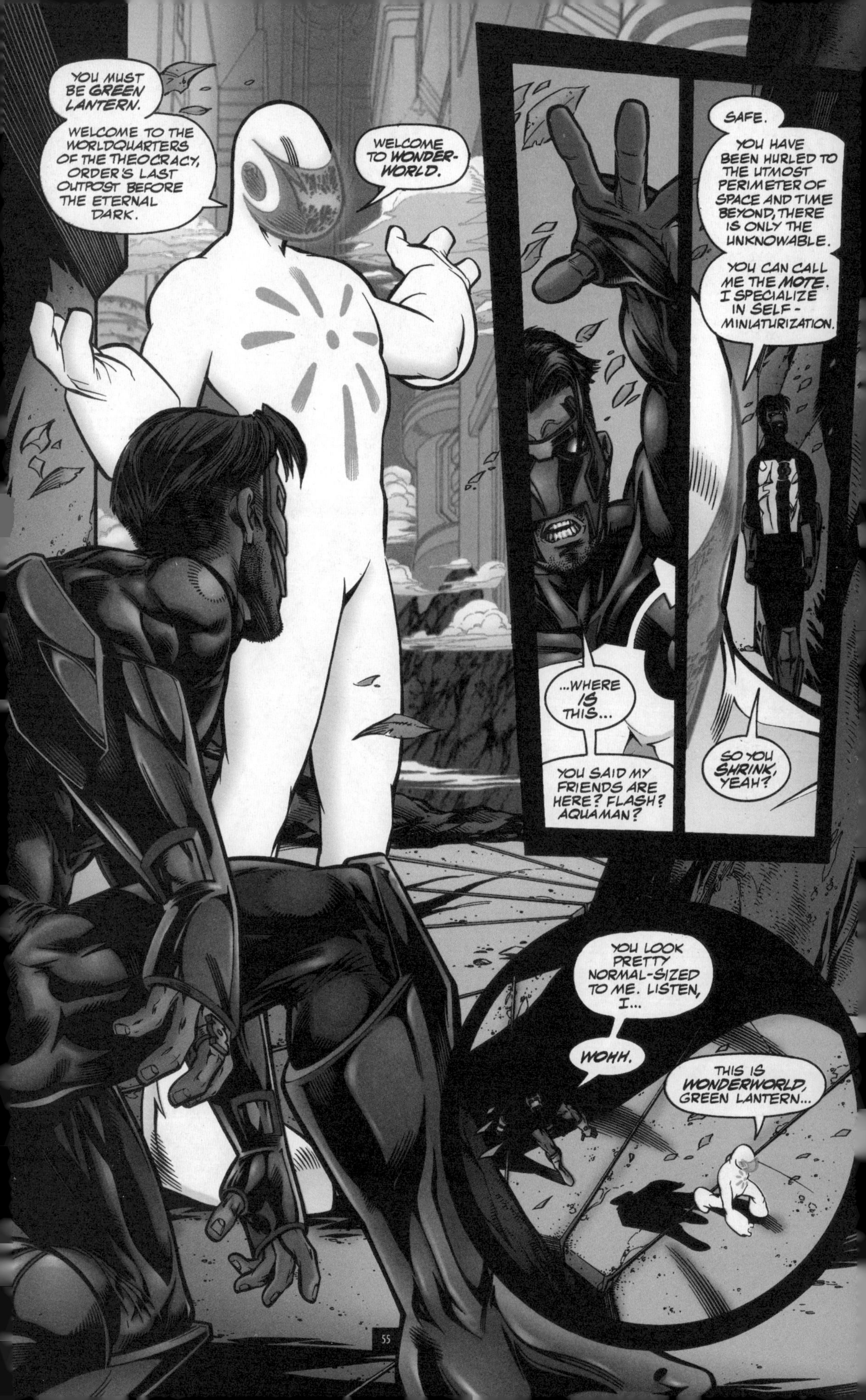

YOU MUST BE GREEN LANTERN.
WELCOME TO THE WORLDQUARTERS OF THE THEOCRACY, ORDER'S LAST OUTPOST BEFORE THE ETERNAL DARK.
WELCOME TO WONDER-WORLD.
SAFE.
YOU HAVE BEEN HURLED TO THE UTMOST PERIMETER OF SPACE AND TIME BEYOND, THERE IS ONLY THE UNKNOWABLE.
YOU CAN CALL ME THE MOTE. I SPECIALIZE IN SELF-MINIATURIZATION.
...WHERE IS THIS...
YOU SAID MY FRIENDS ARE HERE? FLASH? AQUAMAN?
SO YOU SHRINK, YEAH?
YOU LOOK PRETTY NORMAL-SIZED TO ME. LISTEN, I...
WOHH.
THIS IS WONDERWORLD, GREEN LANTERN...

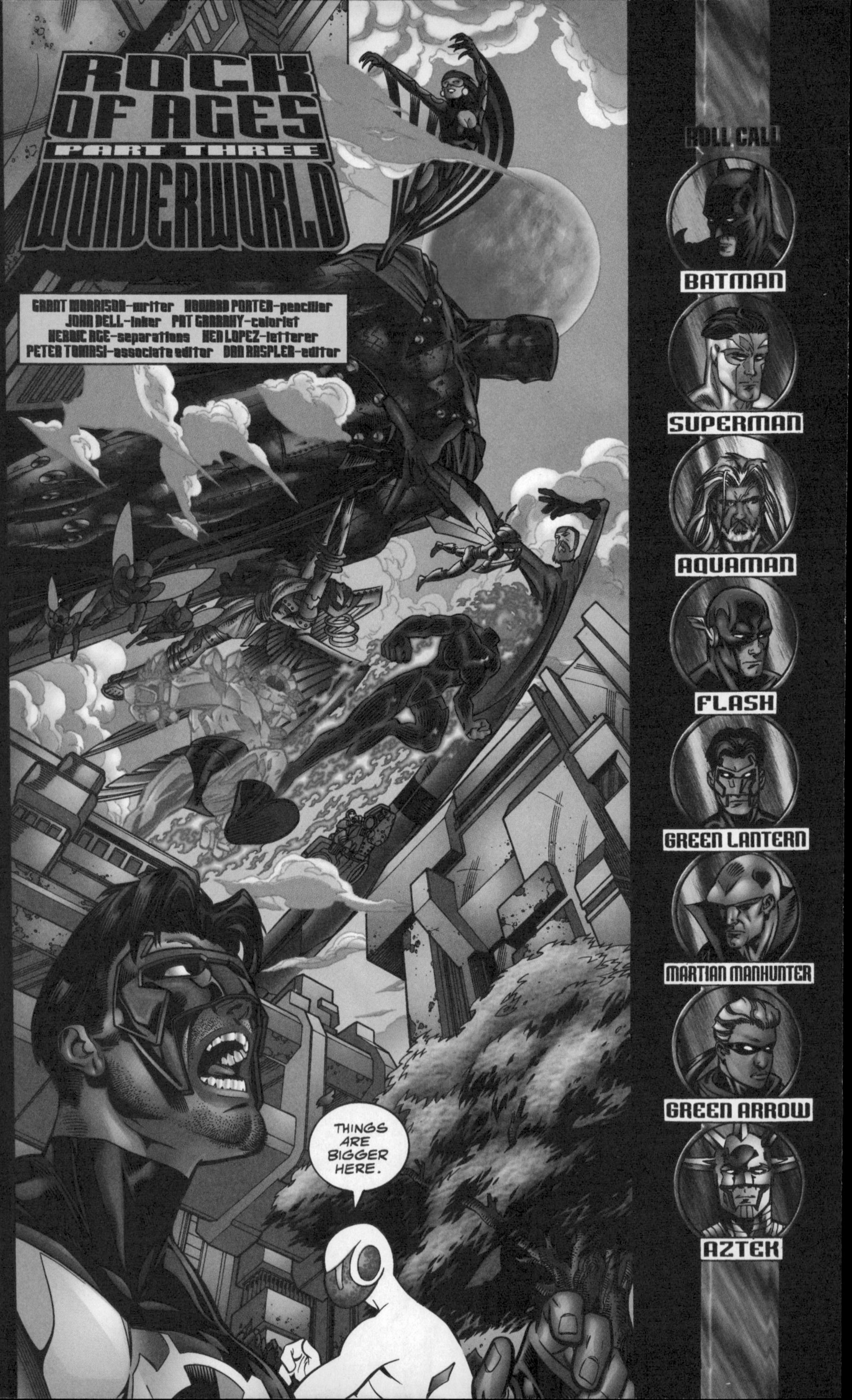
ROCK OF AGES
PART THREE
WONDERWORLD
GRANT MORRISON–writer HOWARD PORTER–penciller
JOHN DELL–inker PAT GARRAHY–colorist
HEROIC AGE–separations KEN LOPEZ–letterer
PETER TOMASI–associate editor DAN RASPLER–editor
ROLL CALL
BATMAN
SUPERMAN
AQUAMAN
FLASH
GREEN LANTERN
MARTIAN MANHUNTER
GREEN ARROW
AZTEK
THINGS ARE BIGGER HERE.

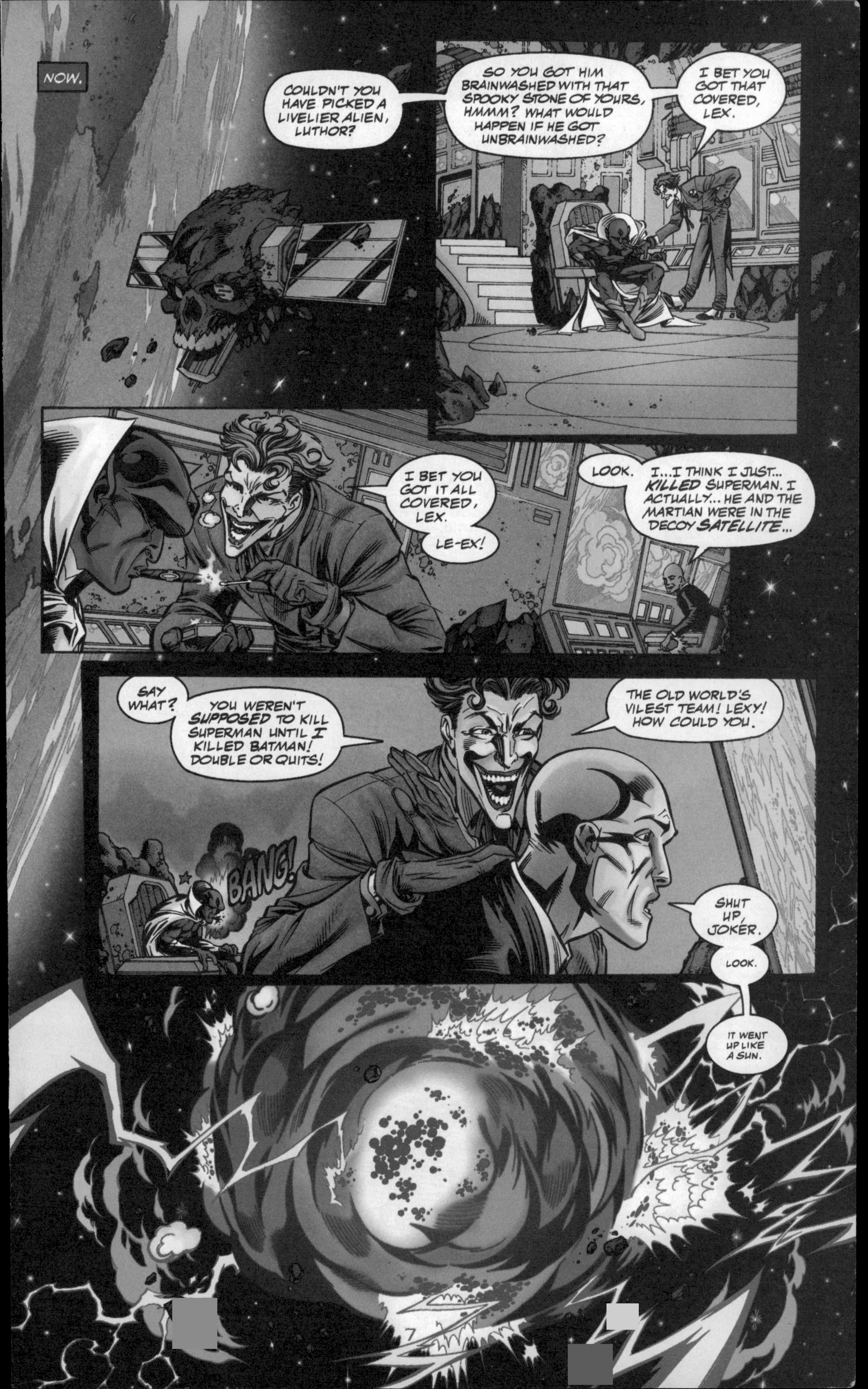
NOW.
COULDN'T YOU HAVE PICKED A LIVELIER ALIEN, LUTHOR?
SO YOU GOT HIM BRAINWASHED WITH THAT SPOOKY STONE OF YOURS, HMMM? WHAT WOULD HAPPEN IF HE GOT UNBRAINWASHED?
I BET YOU GOT THAT COVERED, LEX.
I BET YOU GOT IT ALL COVERED, LEX.
LE-EX!
LOOK.
I...I THINK I JUST... KILLED SUPERMAN. I ACTUALLY... HE AND THE MARTIAN WERE IN THE DECOY SATELLITE...
SAY WHAT?
YOU WEREN'T SUPPOSED TO KILL SUPERMAN UNTIL I KILLED BATMAN! DOUBLE OR QUITS!
THE OLD WORLD'S VILEST TEAM! LEXY! HOW COULD YOU.
BANG!
SHUT UP, JOKER.
LOOK.
IT WENT UP LIKE A SUN.

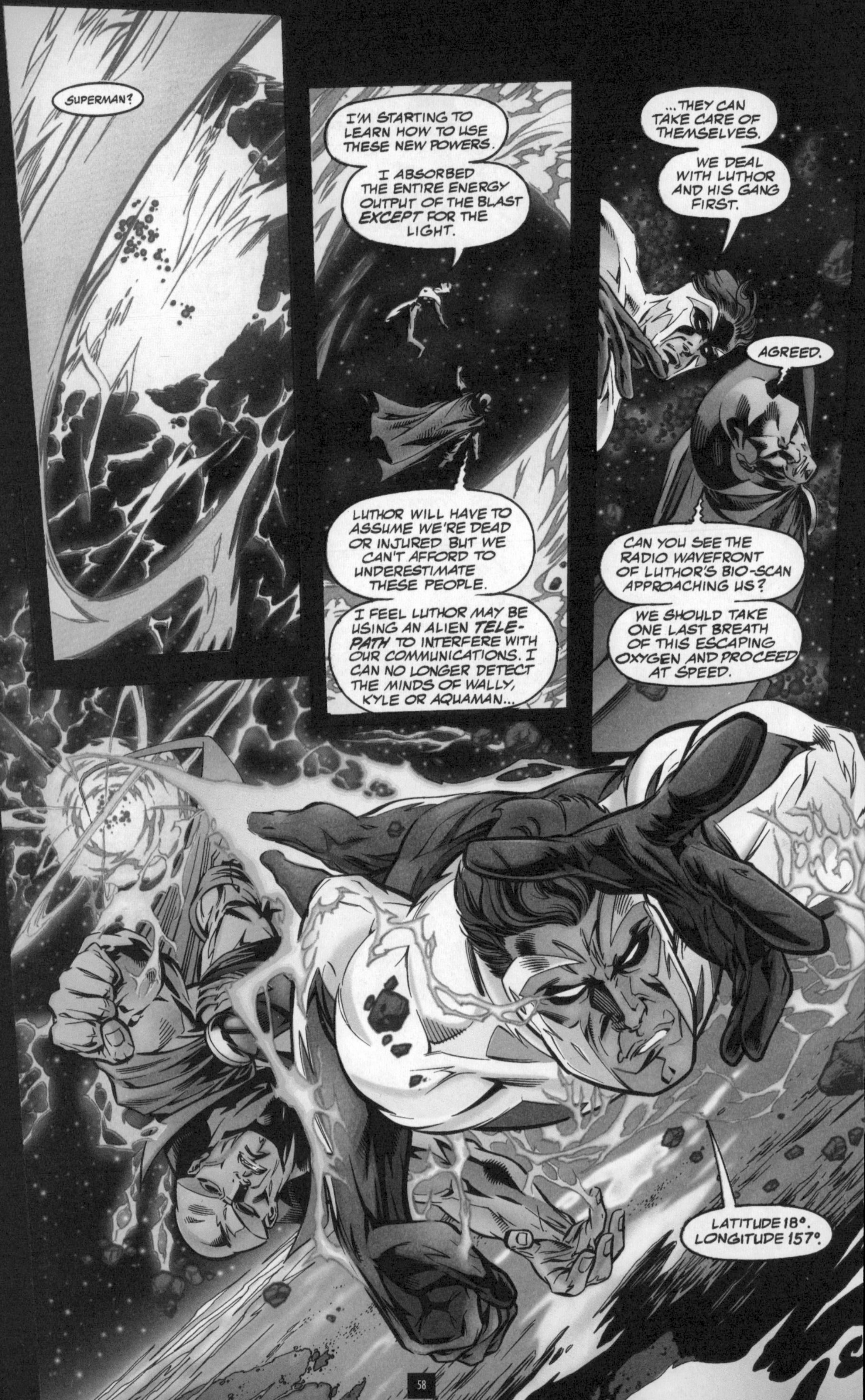
SUPERMAN?
I'M STARTING TO LEARN HOW TO USE THESE NEW POWERS.
I ABSORBED THE ENTIRE ENERGY OUTPUT OF THE BLAST EXCEPT FOR THE LIGHT.
LUTHOR WILL HAVE TO ASSUME WE'RE DEAD OR INJURED BUT WE CAN'T AFFORD TO UNDERESTIMATE THESE PEOPLE.
I FEEL LUTHOR MAY BE USING AN ALIEN TELE-PATH TO INTERFERE WITH OUR COMMUNICATIONS. I CAN NO LONGER DETECT THE MINDS OF WALLY, KYLE OR AQUAMAN...
...THEY CAN TAKE CARE OF THEMSELVES.
WE DEAL WITH LUTHOR AND HIS GANG FIRST.
AGREED.
CAN YOU SEE THE RADIO WAVEFRONT OF LUTHOR'S BIO-SCAN APPROACHING US?
WE SHOULD TAKE ONE LAST BREATH OF THIS ESCAPING OXYGEN AND PROCEED AT SPEED.
LATITUDE 18°. LONGITUDE 157°.

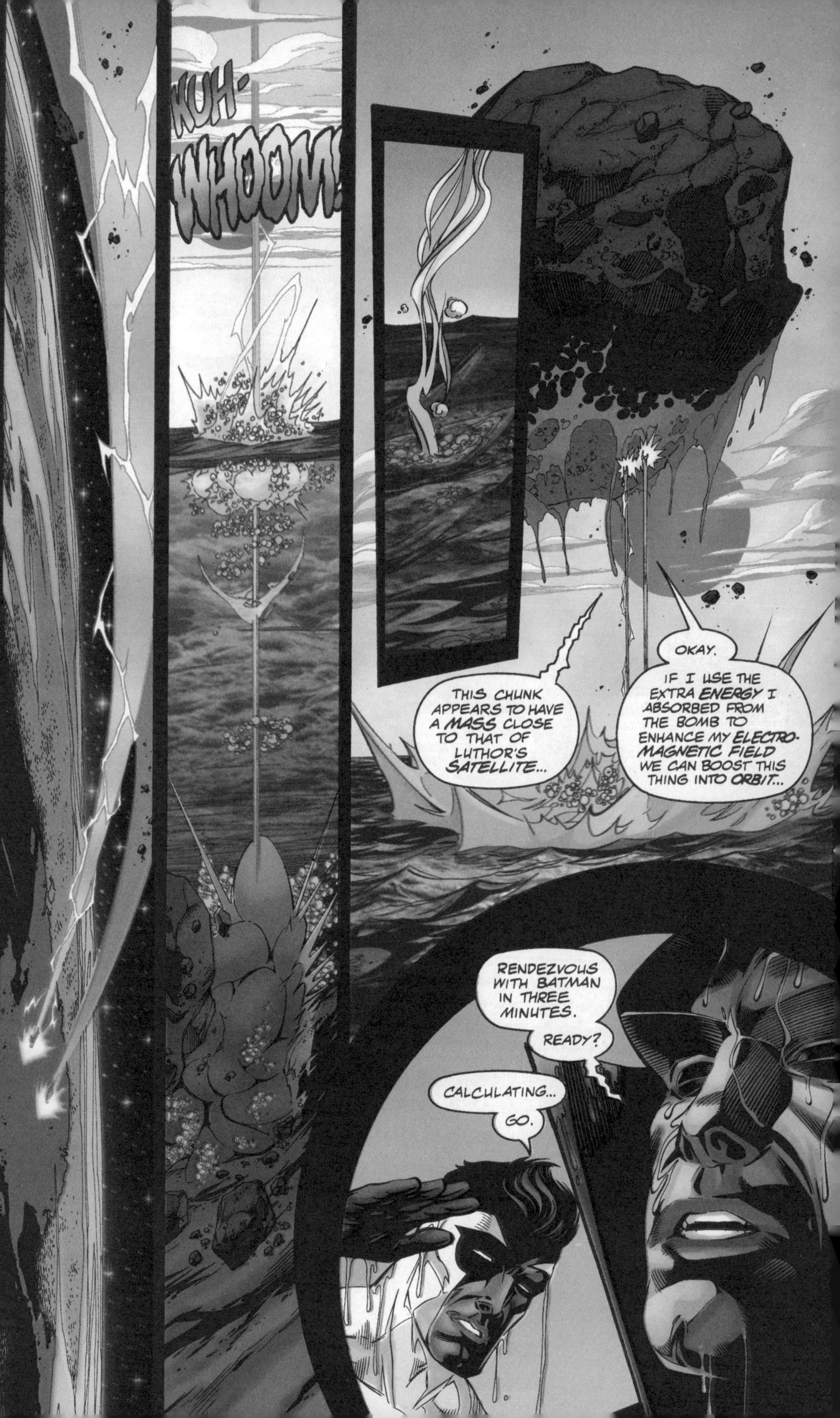
KUH-
WHOOM!
THIS CHUNK APPEARS TO HAVE A MASS CLOSE TO THAT OF LUTHOR'S SATELLITE...
OKAY.
IF I USE THE EXTRA ENERGY I ABSORBED FROM THE BOMB TO ENHANCE MY ELECTRO-MAGNETIC FIELD WE CAN BOOST THIS THING INTO ORBIT...
RENDEZVOUS WITH BATMAN IN THREE MINUTES.
READY?
CALCULATING...
GO.

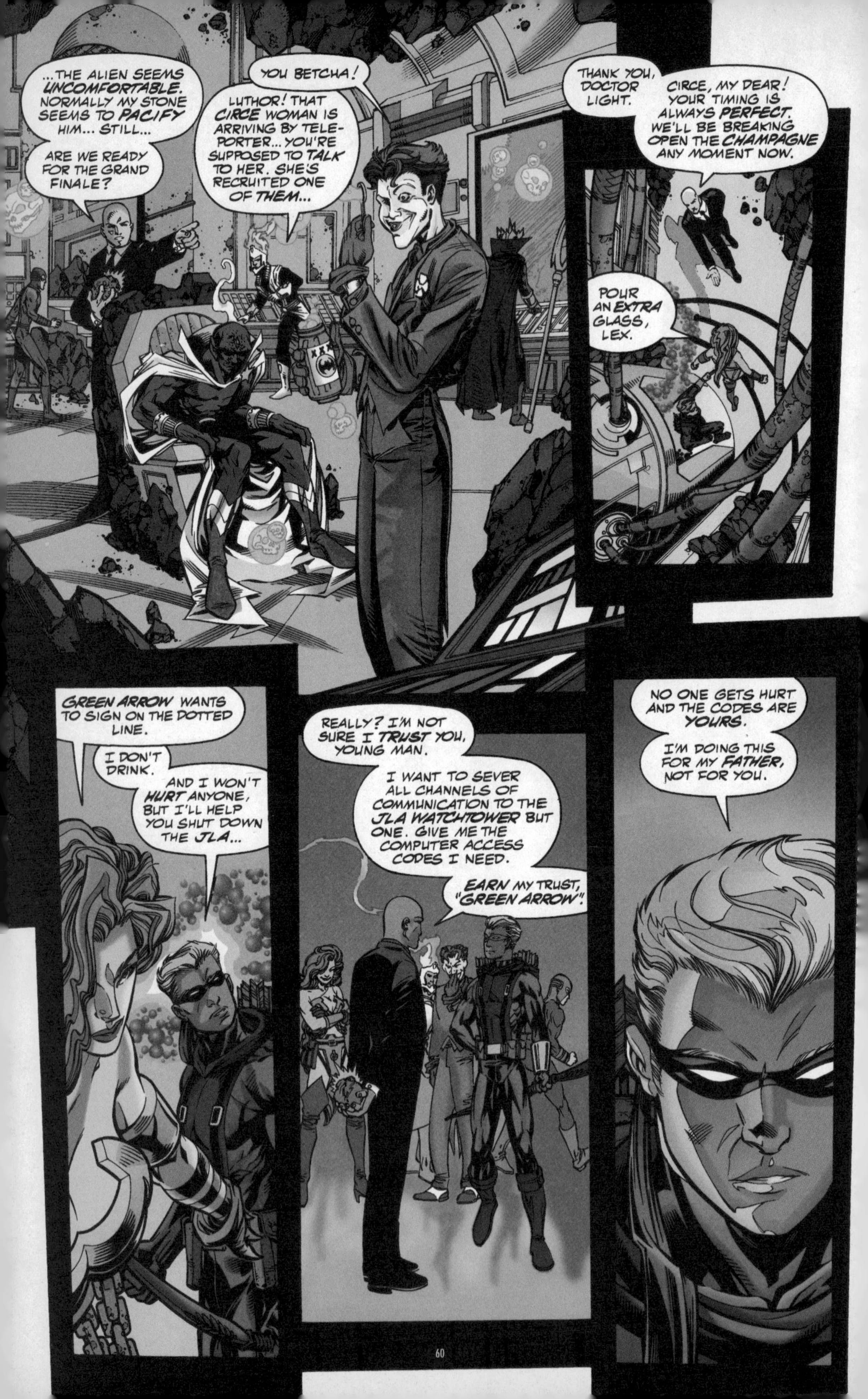
...THE ALIEN SEEMS UNCOMFORTABLE. NORMALLY MY STONE SEEMS TO PACIFY HIM... STILL...
ARE WE READY FOR THE GRAND FINALE?
YOU BETCHA!
LUTHOR! THAT CIRCE WOMAN IS ARRIVING BY TELE-PORTER... YOU'RE SUPPOSED TO TALK TO HER. SHE'S RECRUITED ONE OF THEM...
THANK YOU, DOCTOR LIGHT.
CIRCE, MY DEAR! YOUR TIMING IS ALWAYS PERFECT. WE'LL BE BREAKING OPEN THE CHAMPAGNE ANY MOMENT NOW.
POUR AN EXTRA GLASS, LEX.
GREEN ARROW WANTS TO SIGN ON THE DOTTED LINE.
I DON'T DRINK.
AND I WON'T HURT ANYONE, BUT I'LL HELP YOU SHUT DOWN THE JLA...
REALLY? I'M NOT SURE I TRUST YOU, YOUNG MAN.
I WANT TO SEVER ALL CHANNELS OF COMMUNICATION TO THE JLA WATCHTOWER BUT ONE. GIVE ME THE COMPUTER ACCESS CODES I NEED.
EARN MY TRUST, "GREEN ARROW".
NO ONE GETS HURT AND THE CODES ARE YOURS.
I'M DOING THIS FOR MY FATHER, NOT FOR YOU.

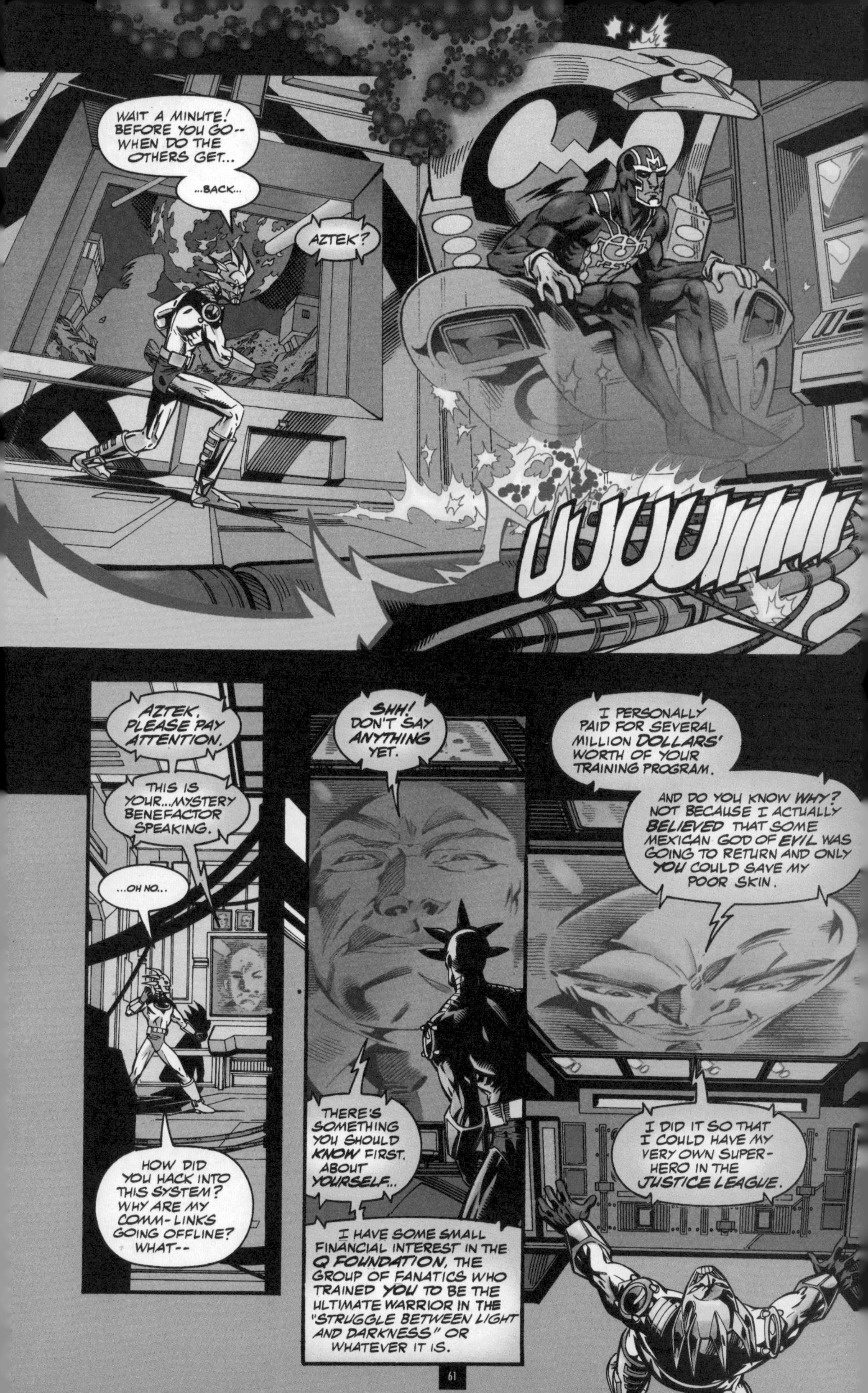
WAIT A MINUTE! BEFORE YOU GO-- WHEN DO THE OTHERS GET...
...BACK...
AZTEK?
UUUUMMM!!!
AZTEK, PLEASE PAY ATTENTION.
THIS IS YOUR...MYSTERY BENEFACTOR SPEAKING.
...OH NO...
HOW DID YOU HACK INTO THIS SYSTEM? WHY ARE MY COMM-LINKS GOING OFFLINE? WHAT--
SHH! DON'T SAY ANYTHING YET.
THERE'S SOMETHING YOU SHOULD KNOW FIRST. ABOUT YOURSELF...
I HAVE SOME SMALL FINANCIAL INTEREST IN THE Q FOUNDATION, THE GROUP OF FANATICS WHO TRAINED YOU TO BE THE ULTIMATE WARRIOR IN THE "STRUGGLE BETWEEN LIGHT AND DARKNESS" OR WHATEVER IT IS.
I PERSONALLY PAID FOR SEVERAL MILLION DOLLARS' WORTH OF YOUR TRAINING PROGRAM.
AND DO YOU KNOW WHY? NOT BECAUSE I ACTUALLY BELIEVED THAT SOME MEXICAN GOD OF EVIL WAS GOING TO RETURN AND ONLY YOU COULD SAVE MY POOR SKIN.
I DID IT SO THAT I COULD HAVE MY VERY OWN SUPER-HERO IN THE JUSTICE LEAGUE.

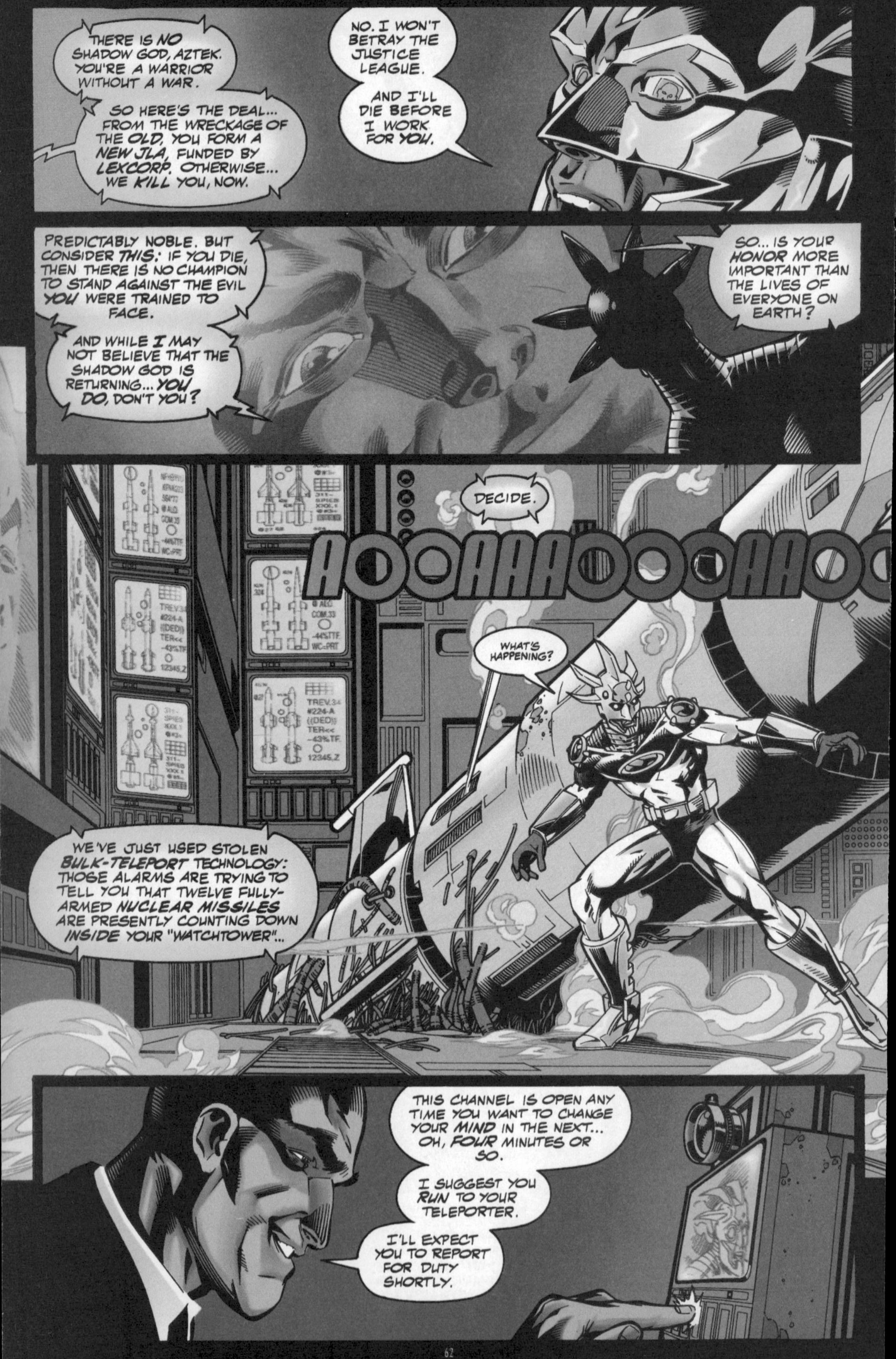
THERE IS NO SHADOW GOD, AZTEK. YOU'RE A WARRIOR WITHOUT A WAR.
SO HERE'S THE DEAL... FROM THE WRECKAGE OF THE OLD, YOU FORM A NEW JLA, FUNDED BY LEXCORP. OTHERWISE... WE KILL YOU, NOW.
NO. I WON'T BETRAY THE JUSTICE LEAGUE.
AND I'LL DIE BEFORE I WORK FOR YOU.
PREDICTABLY NOBLE. BUT CONSIDER THIS: IF YOU DIE, THEN THERE IS NO CHAMPION TO STAND AGAINST THE EVIL YOU WERE TRAINED TO FACE.
AND WHILE I MAY NOT BELIEVE THAT THE SHADOW GOD IS RETURNING... YOU DO, DON'T YOU?
SO... IS YOUR HONOR MORE IMPORTANT THAN THE LIVES OF EVERYONE ON EARTH?
DECIDE.
AOOAAAOOOOAAOO
WHAT'S HAPPENING?
WE'VE JUST USED STOLEN BULK-TELEPORT TECHNOLOGY: THOSE ALARMS ARE TRYING TO TELL YOU THAT TWELVE FULLY-ARMED NUCLEAR MISSILES ARE PRESENTLY COUNTING DOWN INSIDE YOUR "WATCHTOWER"...
THIS CHANNEL IS OPEN ANY TIME YOU WANT TO CHANGE YOUR MIND IN THE NEXT... OH, FOUR MINUTES OR SO.
I SUGGEST YOU RUN TO YOUR TELEPORTER.
I'LL EXPECT YOU TO REPORT FOR DUTY SHORTLY.

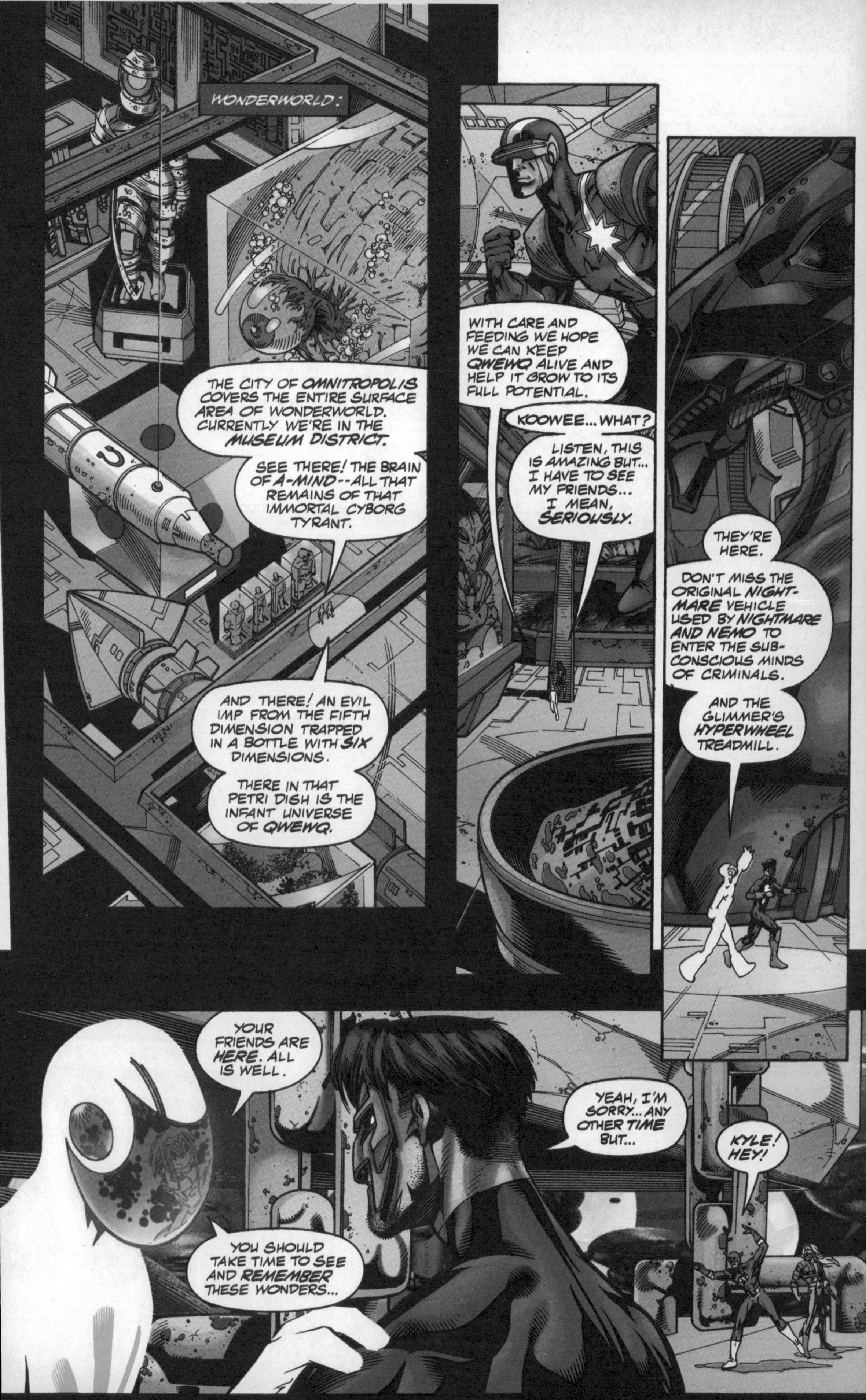
WONDERWORLD:
THE CITY OF OMNITROPOLIS COVERS THE ENTIRE SURFACE AREA OF WONDERWORLD. CURRENTLY WE'RE IN THE MUSEUM DISTRICT.
SEE THERE! THE BRAIN OF A-MIND--ALL THAT REMAINS OF THAT IMMORTAL CYBORG TYRANT.
AND THERE! AN EVIL IMP FROM THE FIFTH DIMENSION TRAPPED IN A BOTTLE WITH SIX DIMENSIONS.
THERE IN THAT PETRI DISH IS THE INFANT UNIVERSE OF QWEWQ.
WITH CARE AND FEEDING WE HOPE WE CAN KEEP QWEWQ ALIVE AND HELP IT GROW TO ITS FULL POTENTIAL.
KOOWEE... WHAT?
LISTEN, THIS IS AMAZING BUT... I HAVE TO SEE MY FRIENDS... I MEAN, SERIOUSLY.
THEY'RE HERE.
DON'T MISS THE ORIGINAL NIGHT-MARE VEHICLE USED BY NIGHTMARE AND NEMO TO ENTER THE SUB-CONSCIOUS MINDS OF CRIMINALS.
AND THE GLIMMER'S HYPERWHEEL TREADMILL.
YOUR FRIENDS ARE HERE. ALL IS WELL.
YOU SHOULD TAKE TIME TO SEE AND REMEMBER THESE WONDERS...
YEAH, I'M SORRY... ANY OTHER TIME BUT...
KYLE! HEY!

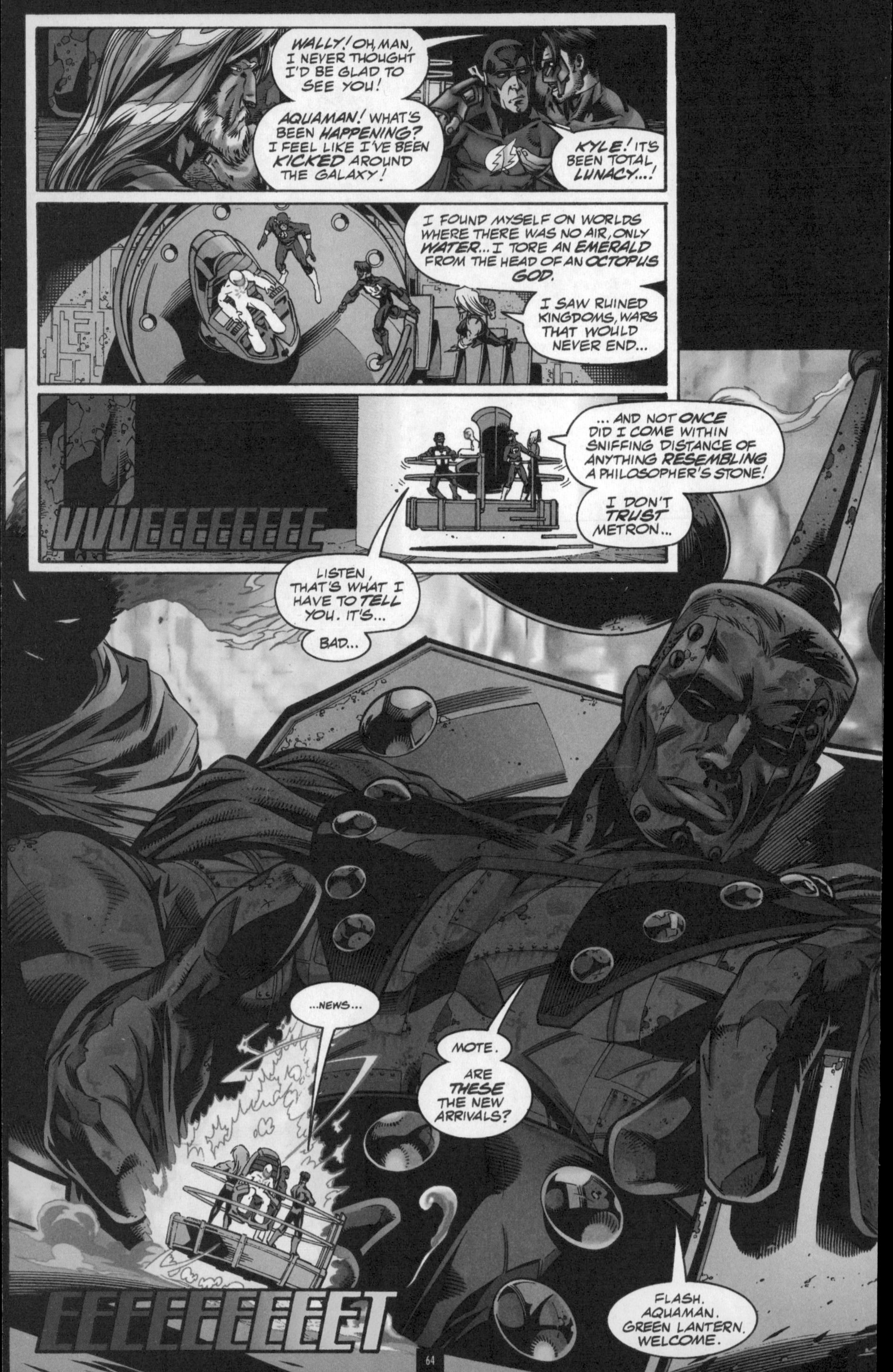
WALLY! OH, MAN, I NEVER THOUGHT I'D BE GLAD TO SEE YOU!
AQUAMAN! WHAT'S BEEN HAPPENING? I FEEL LIKE I'VE BEEN KICKED AROUND THE GALAXY!
KYLE! IT'S BEEN TOTAL LUNACY...!
I FOUND MYSELF ON WORLDS WHERE THERE WAS NO AIR, ONLY WATER... I TORE AN EMERALD FROM THE HEAD OF AN OCTOPUS GOD.
I SAW RUINED KINGDOMS, WARS THAT WOULD NEVER END...
VVVEEEEEEEEE
... AND NOT ONCE DID I COME WITHIN SNIFFING DISTANCE OF ANYTHING RESEMBLING A PHILOSOPHER'S STONE!
I DON'T TRUST METRON...
LISTEN, THAT'S WHAT I HAVE TO TELL YOU. IT'S...
BAD...
...NEWS...
MOTE.
ARE THESE THE NEW ARRIVALS?
EEEEEEEEET
FLASH. AQUAMAN. GREEN LANTERN. WELCOME.

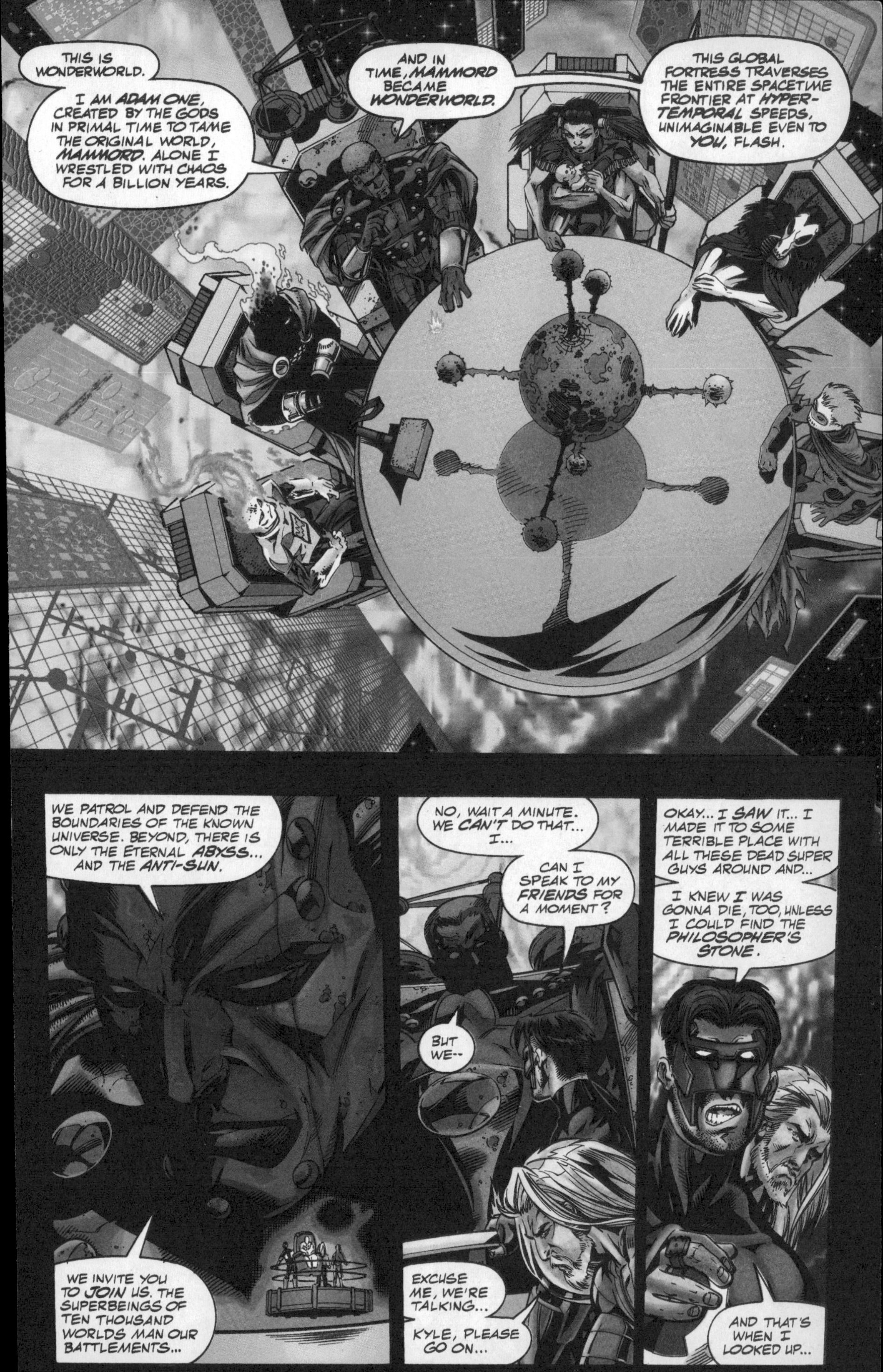
THIS IS WONDERWORLD.
I AM ADAM ONE, CREATED BY THE GODS IN PRIMAL TIME TO TAME THE ORIGINAL WORLD, MAMMORD. ALONE I WRESTLED WITH CHAOS FOR A BILLION YEARS.
AND IN TIME, MAMMORD BECAME WONDERWORLD.
THIS GLOBAL FORTRESS TRAVERSES THE ENTIRE SPACETIME FRONTIER AT HYPER-TEMPORAL SPEEDS, UNIMAGINABLE EVEN TO YOU, FLASH.
WE PATROL AND DEFEND THE BOUNDARIES OF THE KNOWN UNIVERSE. BEYOND, THERE IS ONLY THE ETERNAL ABYSS... AND THE ANTI-SUN.
WE INVITE YOU TO JOIN US. THE SUPERBEINGS OF TEN THOUSAND WORLDS MAN OUR BATTLEMENTS...
NO, WAIT A MINUTE. WE CAN'T DO THAT... I...
CAN I SPEAK TO MY FRIENDS FOR A MOMENT?
BUT WE--
EXCUSE ME, WE'RE TALKING...
KYLE, PLEASE GO ON...
OKAY... I SAW IT... I MADE IT TO SOME TERRIBLE PLACE WITH ALL THESE DEAD SUPER GUYS AROUND AND...
I KNEW I WAS GONNA DIE, TOO, UNLESS I COULD FIND THE PHILOSOPHER'S STONE.
AND THAT'S WHEN I LOOKED UP...

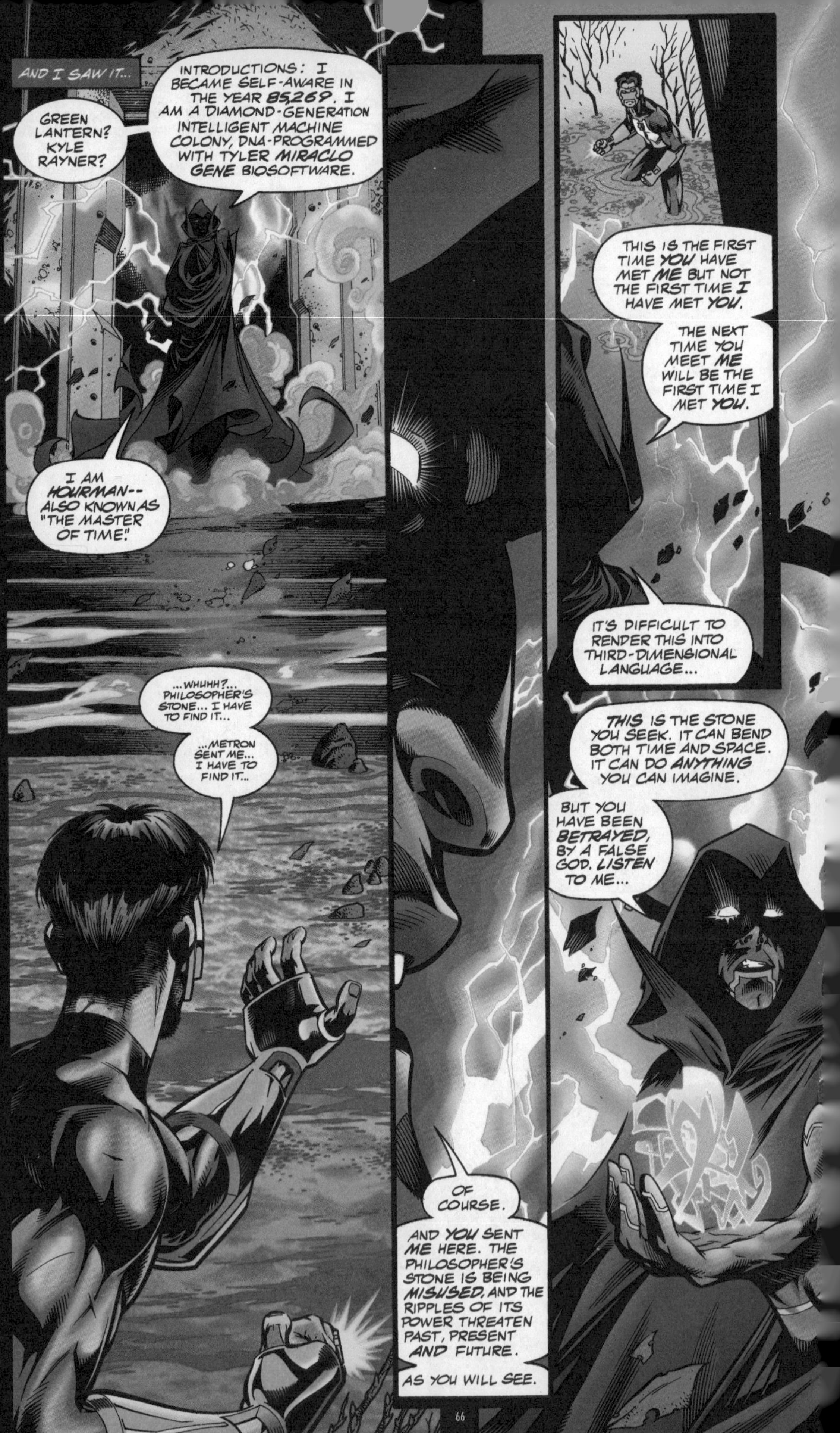
AND I SAW IT...
GREEN LANTERN? KYLE RAYNER?
INTRODUCTIONS: I BECAME SELF-AWARE IN THE YEAR 85,269. I AM A DIAMOND-GENERATION INTELLIGENT MACHINE COLONY, DNA-PROGRAMMED WITH TYLER MIRACLO GENE BIOSOFTWARE.
I AM HOURMAN-- ALSO KNOWN AS "THE MASTER OF TIME."
...WHUHH?... PHILOSOPHER'S STONE... I HAVE TO FIND IT...
...METRON SENT ME... I HAVE TO FIND IT...
THIS IS THE FIRST TIME YOU HAVE MET ME BUT NOT THE FIRST TIME I HAVE MET YOU.
THE NEXT TIME YOU MEET ME WILL BE THE FIRST TIME I MET YOU.
IT'S DIFFICULT TO RENDER THIS INTO THIRD-DIMENSIONAL LANGUAGE...
THIS IS THE STONE YOU SEEK. IT CAN BEND BOTH TIME AND SPACE. IT CAN DO ANYTHING YOU CAN IMAGINE.
BUT YOU HAVE BEEN BETRAYED, BY A FALSE GOD. LISTEN TO ME...
OF COURSE.
AND YOU SENT ME HERE. THE PHILOSOPHER'S STONE IS BEING MISUSED, AND THE RIPPLES OF ITS POWER THREATEN PAST, PRESENT AND FUTURE.
AS YOU WILL SEE.

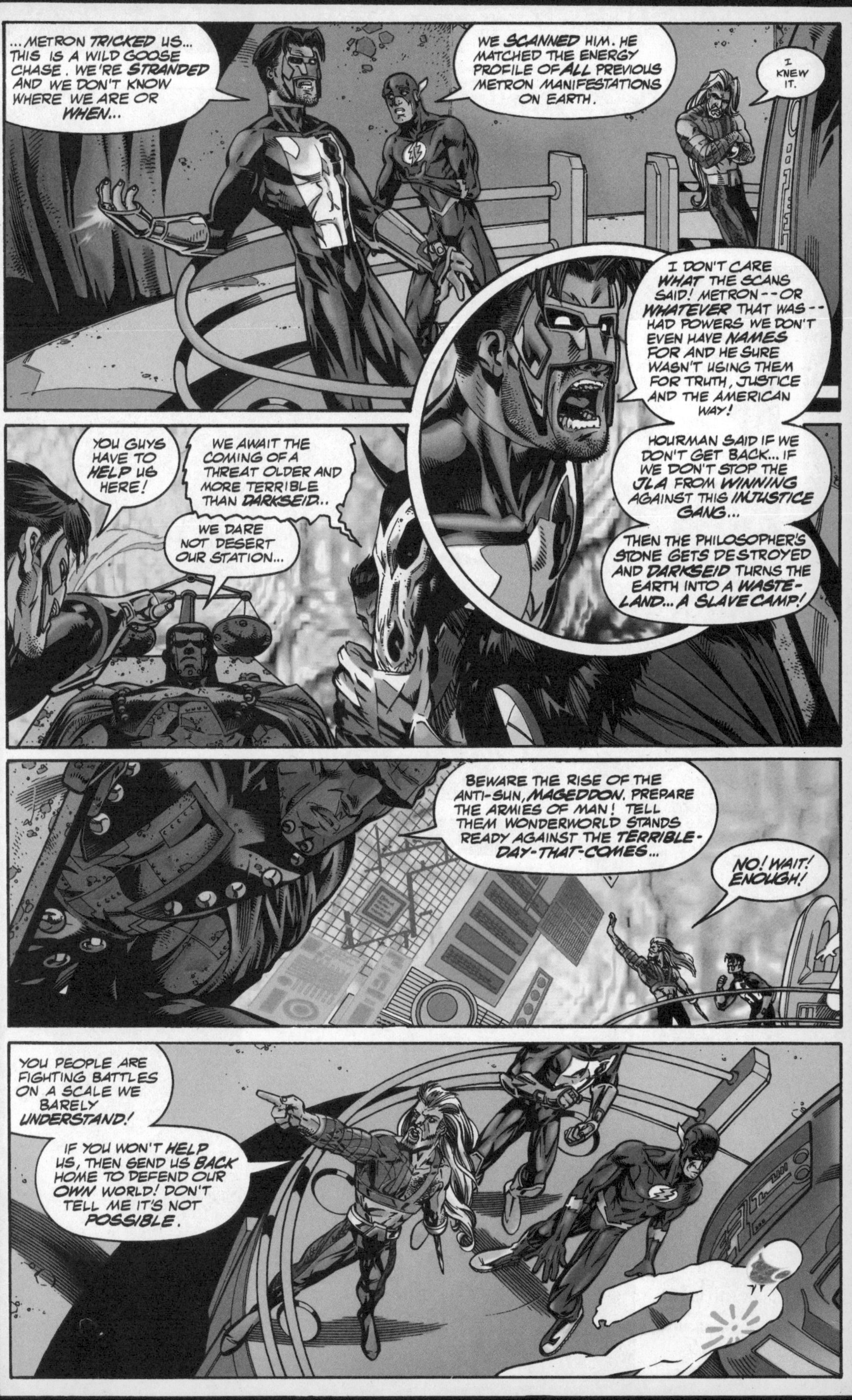
...METRON TRICKED US... THIS IS A WILD GOOSE CHASE. WE'RE STRANDED AND WE DON'T KNOW WHERE WE ARE OR WHEN...
WE SCANNED HIM. HE MATCHED THE ENERGY PROFILE OF ALL PREVIOUS METRON MANIFESTATIONS ON EARTH.
I KNEW IT.
I DON'T CARE WHAT THE SCANS SAID! METRON--OR WHATEVER THAT WAS--HAD POWERS WE DON'T EVEN HAVE NAMES FOR AND HE SURE WASN'T USING THEM FOR TRUTH, JUSTICE AND THE AMERICAN WAY!
HOURMAN SAID IF WE DON'T GET BACK... IF WE DON'T STOP THE JLA FROM WINNING AGAINST THIS INJUSTICE GANG...
THEN THE PHILOSOPHER'S STONE GETS DESTROYED AND DARKSEID TURNS THE EARTH INTO A WASTE-LAND... A SLAVE CAMP!
YOU GUYS HAVE TO HELP US HERE!
WE AWAIT THE COMING OF A THREAT OLDER AND MORE TERRIBLE THAN DARKSEID...
WE DARE NOT DESERT OUR STATION...
BEWARE THE RISE OF THE ANTI-SUN, MAGEDDON. PREPARE THE ARMIES OF MAN! TELL THEM WONDERWORLD STANDS READY AGAINST THE TERRIBLE-DAY-THAT-COMES...
NO! WAIT! ENOUGH!
YOU PEOPLE ARE FIGHTING BATTLES ON A SCALE WE BARELY UNDERSTAND!
IF YOU WON'T HELP US, THEN SEND US BACK HOME TO DEFEND OUR OWN WORLD! DON'T TELL ME IT'S NOT POSSIBLE.

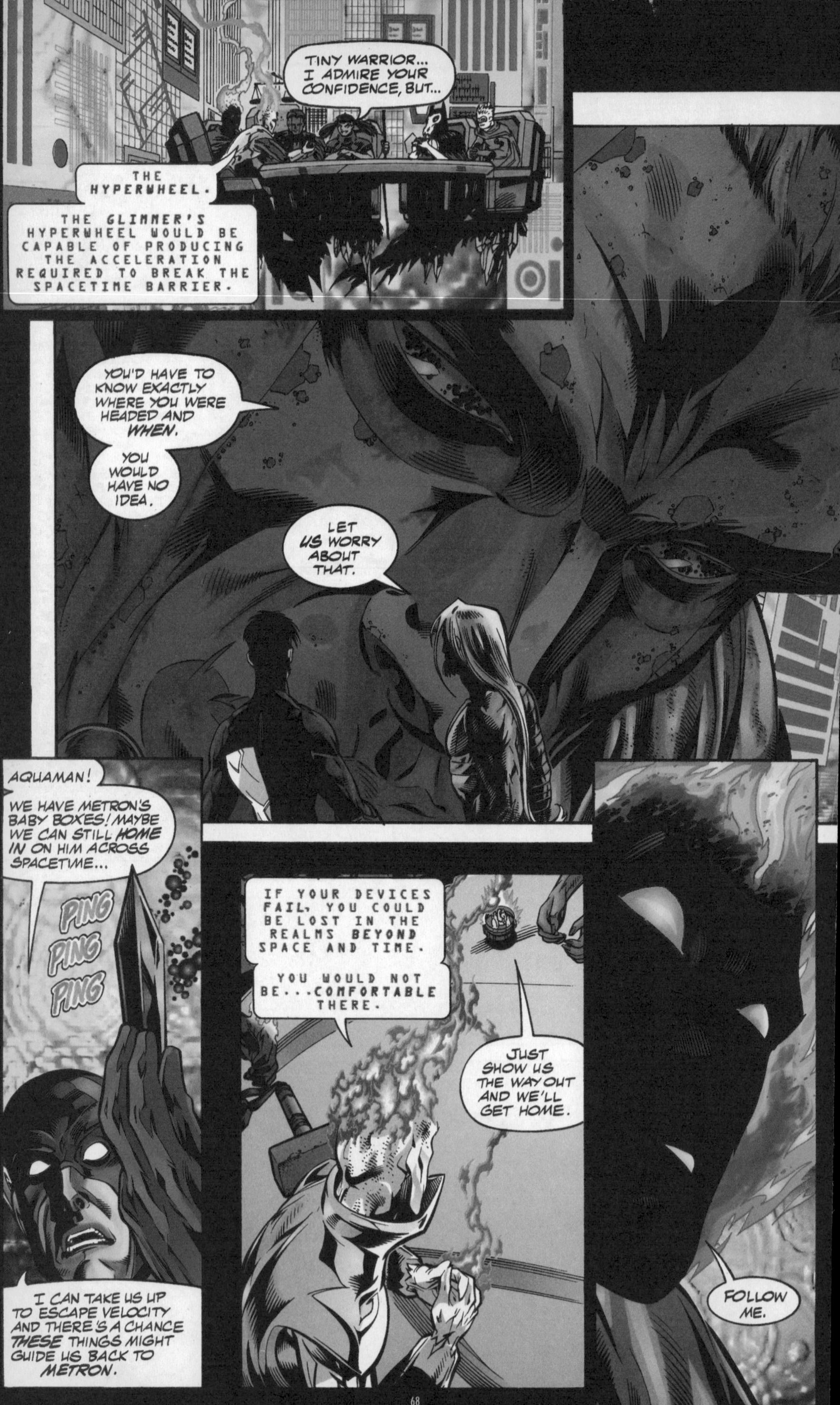

TINY WARRIOR... I ADMIRE YOUR CONFIDENCE, BUT...
THE HYPERWHEEL.
THE GLIMMER'S HYPERWHEEL WOULD BE CAPABLE OF PRODUCING THE ACCELERATION REQUIRED TO BREAK THE SPACETIME BARRIER.
YOU'D HAVE TO KNOW EXACTLY WHERE YOU WERE HEADED AND WHEN.
YOU WOULD HAVE NO IDEA.
LET US WORRY ABOUT THAT.
AQUAMAN!
WE HAVE METRON'S BABY BOXES! MAYBE WE CAN STILL HOME IN ON HIM ACROSS SPACETIME...
PING PING PING
I CAN TAKE US UP TO ESCAPE VELOCITY AND THERE'S A CHANCE THESE THINGS MIGHT GUIDE US BACK TO METRON.
IF YOUR DEVICES FAIL, YOU COULD BE LOST IN THE REALMS BEYOND SPACE AND TIME.
YOU WOULD NOT BE...COMFORTABLE THERE.
JUST SHOW US THE WAY OUT AND WE'LL GET HOME.
FOLLOW ME.

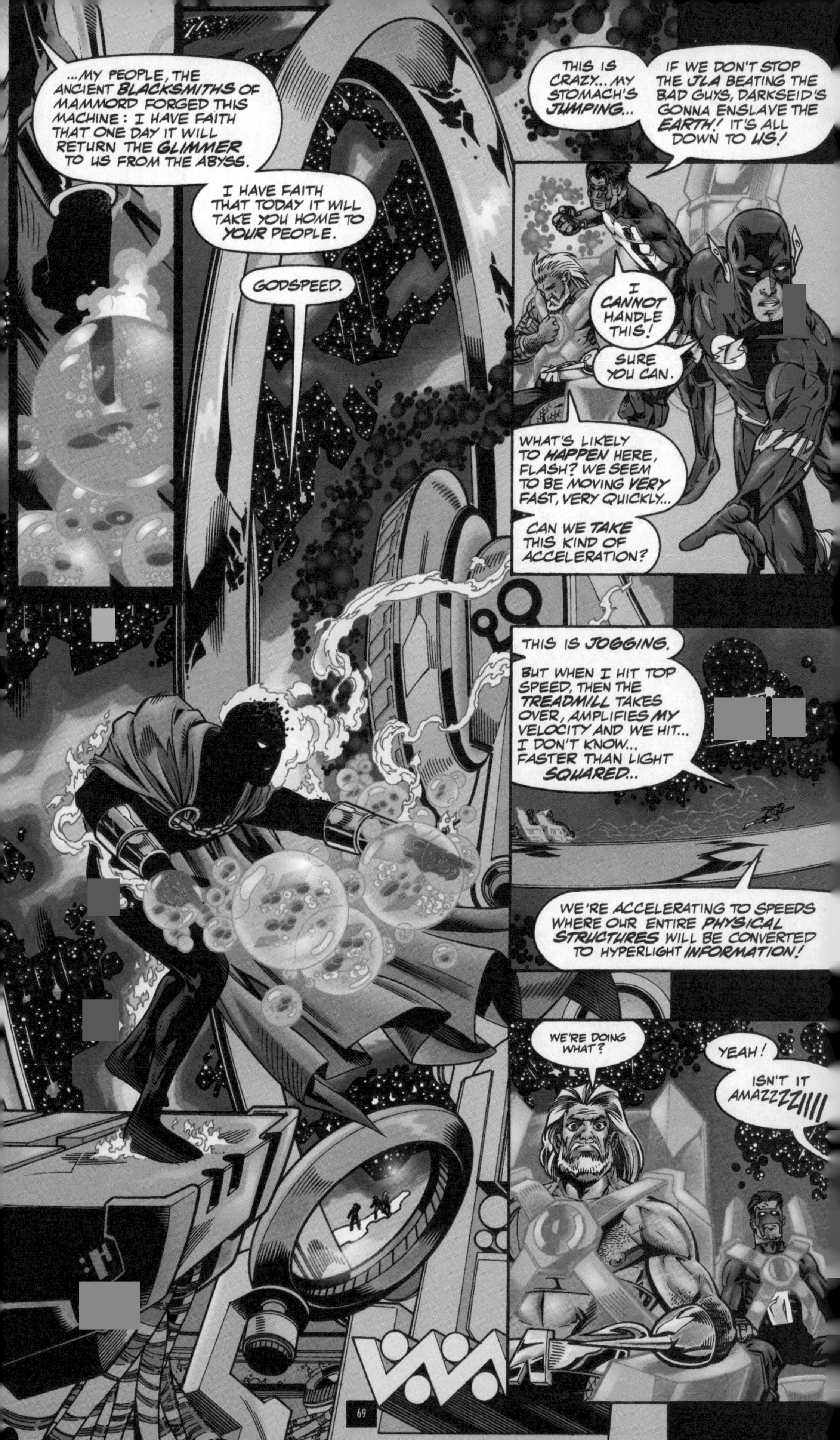
...MY PEOPLE, THE ANCIENT BLACKSMITHS OF MAMMORD FORGED THIS MACHINE : I HAVE FAITH THAT ONE DAY IT WILL RETURN THE GLIMMER TO US FROM THE ABYSS.
I HAVE FAITH THAT TODAY IT WILL TAKE YOU HOME TO YOUR PEOPLE.
GODSPEED.
THIS IS CRAZY... MY STOMACH'S JUMPING...
IF WE DON'T STOP THE JLA BEATING THE BAD GUYS, DARKSEID'S GONNA ENSLAVE THE EARTH! IT'S ALL DOWN TO US!
I CANNOT HANDLE THIS!
SURE YOU CAN.
WHAT'S LIKELY TO HAPPEN HERE, FLASH? WE SEEM TO BE MOVING VERY FAST, VERY QUICKLY...
CAN WE TAKE THIS KIND OF ACCELERATION?
THIS IS JOGGING.
BUT WHEN I HIT TOP SPEED, THEN THE TREADMILL TAKES OVER, AMPLIFIES MY VELOCITY AND WE HIT... I DON'T KNOW... FASTER THAN LIGHT SQUARED...
WE'RE ACCELERATING TO SPEEDS WHERE OUR ENTIRE PHYSICAL STRUCTURES WILL BE CONVERTED TO HYPERLIGHT INFORMATION!
WE'RE DOING WHAT?
YEAH!
ISN'T IT AMAZZZZIIII

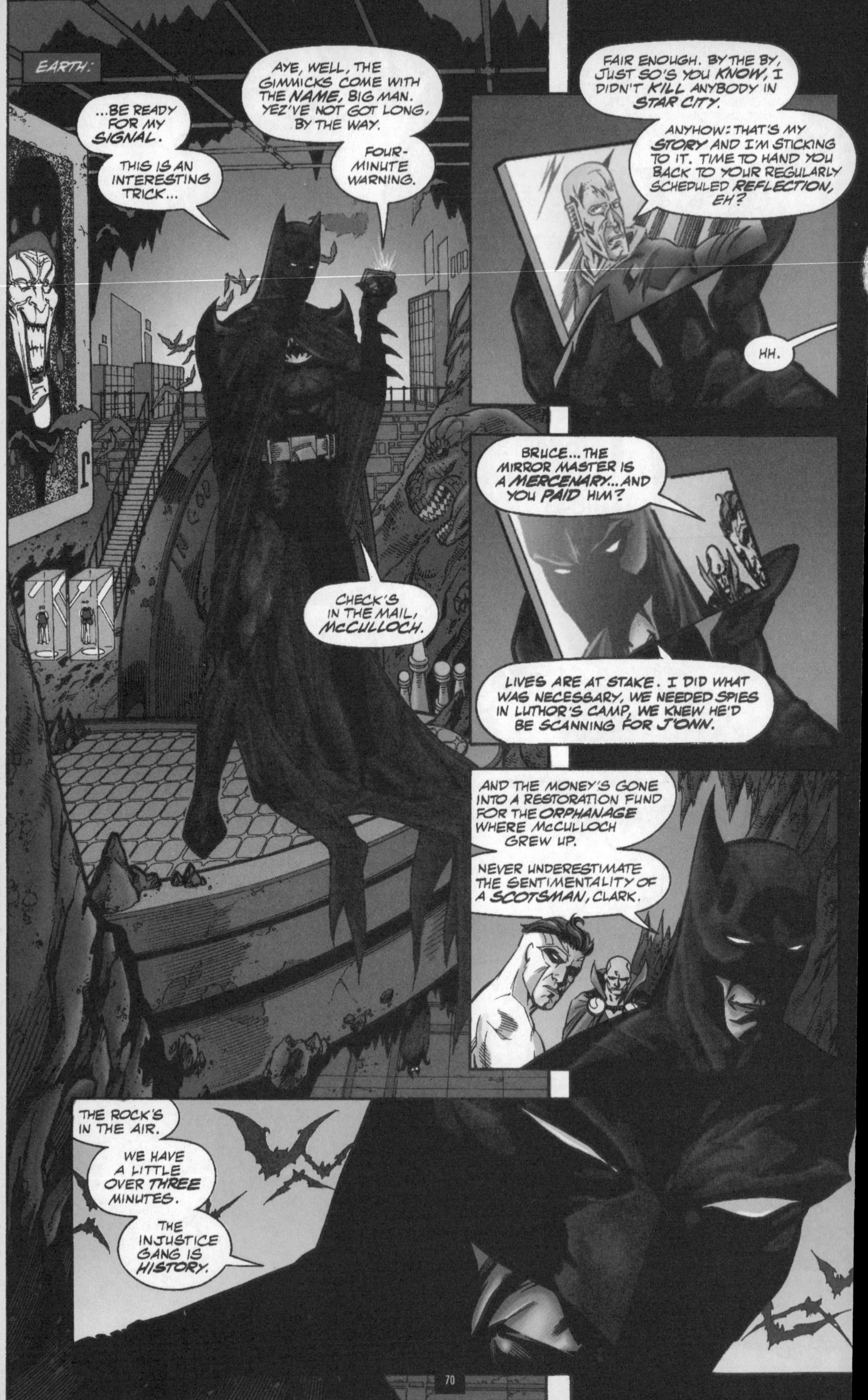
EARTH:
...BE READY FOR MY SIGNAL.
THIS IS AN INTERESTING TRICK...
AYE, WELL, THE GIMMICKS COME WITH THE NAME, BIG MAN. YEZ'VE NOT GOT LONG, BY THE WAY.
FOUR-MINUTE WARNING.
CHECK'S IN THE MAIL, McCULLOCH.
FAIR ENOUGH. BY THE BY, JUST SO'S YOU KNOW, I DIDN'T KILL ANYBODY IN STAR CITY.
ANYHOW: THAT'S MY STORY AND I'M STICKING TO IT. TIME TO HAND YOU BACK TO YOUR REGULARLY SCHEDULED REFLECTION, EH?
HH.
BRUCE... THE MIRROR MASTER IS A MERCENARY... AND YOU PAID HIM?
LIVES ARE AT STAKE. I DID WHAT WAS NECESSARY. WE NEEDED SPIES IN LUTHOR'S CAMP. WE KNEW HE'D BE SCANNING FOR J'ONN.
AND THE MONEY'S GONE INTO A RESTORATION FUND FOR THE ORPHANAGE WHERE McCULLOCH GREW UP.
NEVER UNDERESTIMATE THE SENTIMENTALITY OF A SCOTSMAN, CLARK.
THE ROCK'S IN THE AIR.
WE HAVE A LITTLE OVER THREE MINUTES.
THE INJUSTICE GANG IS HISTORY.

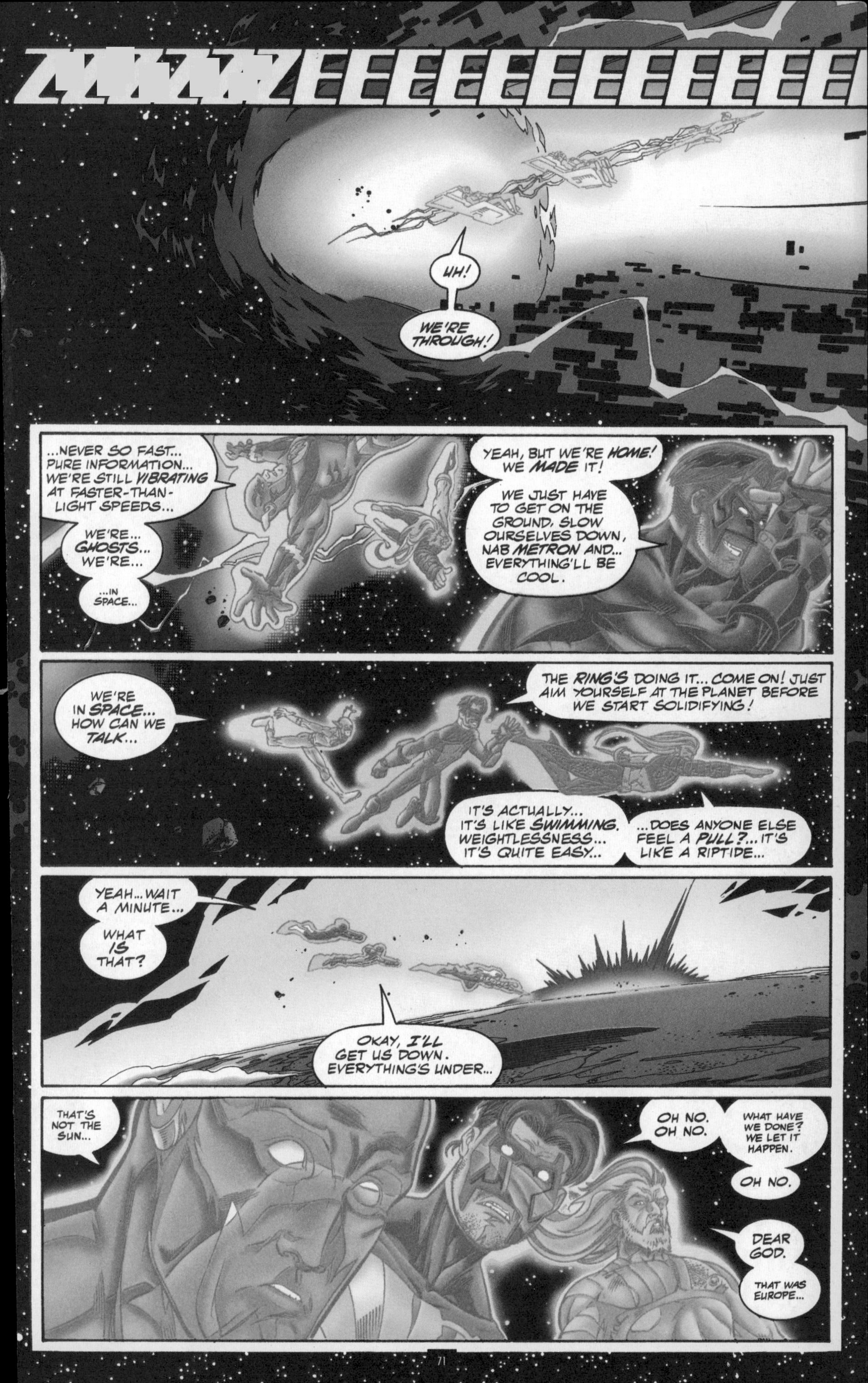
ZZZZZZEEEEEEEEEEEEE
UH!
WE'RE THROUGH!
...NEVER SO FAST... PURE INFORMATION... WE'RE STILL VIBRATING AT FASTER-THAN-LIGHT SPEEDS...
WE'RE... GHOSTS... WE'RE...
...IN SPACE...
YEAH, BUT WE'RE HOME! WE MADE IT!
WE JUST HAVE TO GET ON THE GROUND, SLOW OURSELVES DOWN, NAB METRON AND... EVERYTHING'LL BE COOL.
WE'RE IN SPACE... HOW CAN WE TALK...
THE RING'S DOING IT... COME ON! JUST AIM YOURSELF AT THE PLANET BEFORE WE START SOLIDIFYING!
IT'S ACTUALLY... IT'S LIKE SWIMMING. WEIGHTLESSNESS... IT'S QUITE EASY...
...DOES ANYONE ELSE FEEL A PULL?... IT'S LIKE A RIPTIDE...
YEAH... WAIT A MINUTE...
WHAT IS THAT?
OKAY, I'LL GET US DOWN. EVERYTHING'S UNDER...
THAT'S NOT THE SUN...
OH NO. OH NO.
WHAT HAVE WE DONE? WE LET IT HAPPEN.
OH NO.
DEAR GOD.
THAT WAS EUROPE...

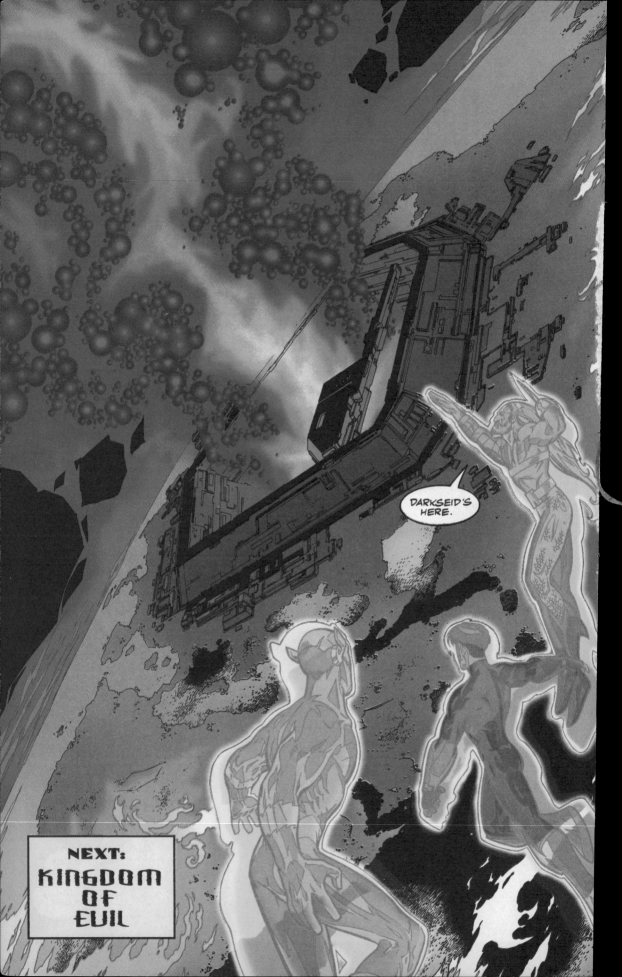

DARKSEID'S HERE.

NEXT:
KINGDOM
OF
EVIL

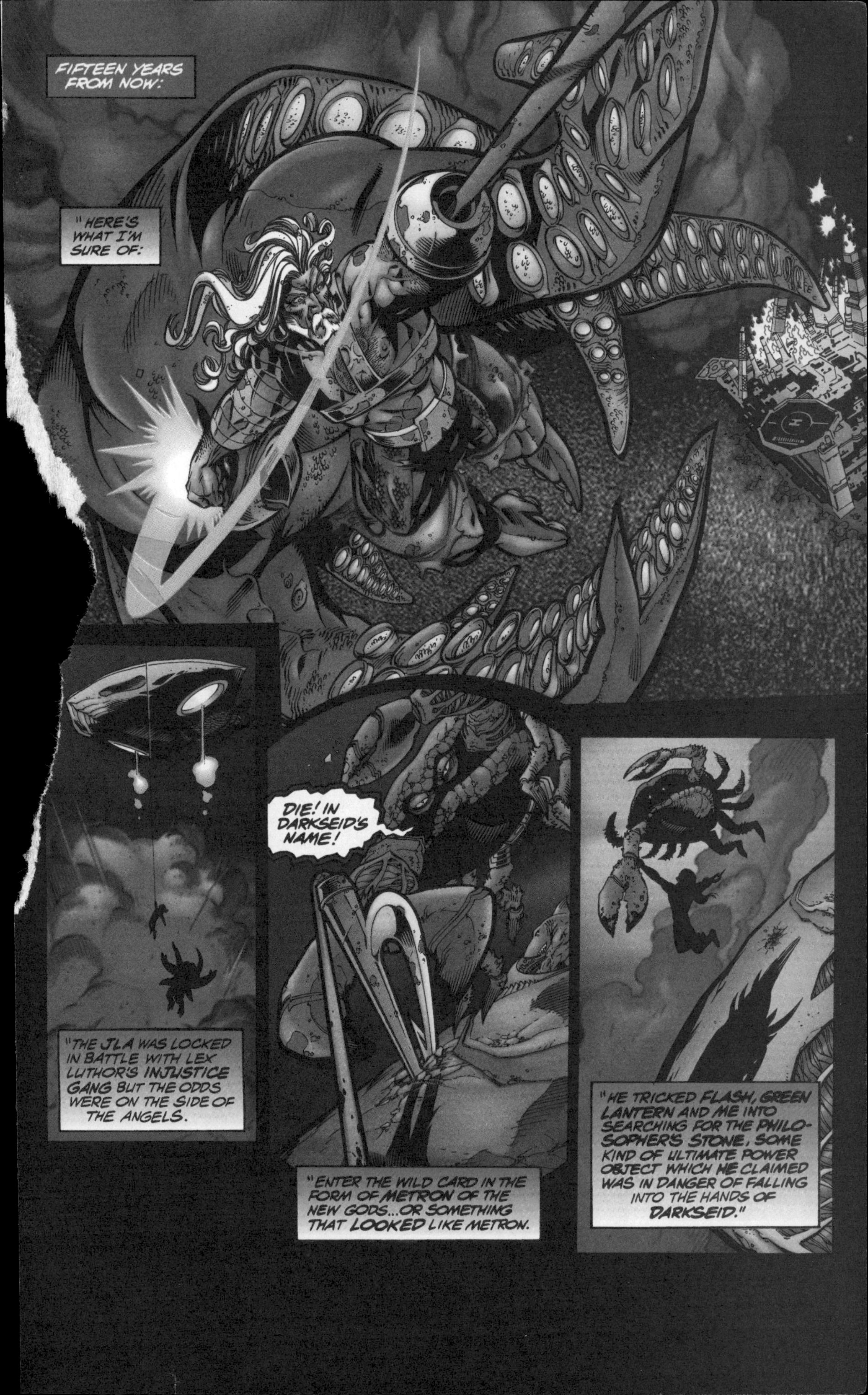
FIFTEEN YEARS FROM NOW:
"HERE'S WHAT I'M SURE OF:
"THE JLA WAS LOCKED IN BATTLE WITH LEX LUTHOR'S INJUSTICE GANG BUT THE ODDS WERE ON THE SIDE OF THE ANGELS.
DIE! IN DARKSEID'S NAME!
"ENTER THE WILD CARD IN THE FORM OF METRON OF THE NEW GODS...OR SOMETHING THAT LOOKED LIKE METRON.
"HE TRICKED FLASH, GREEN LANTERN AND ME INTO SEARCHING FOR THE PHILOSOPHER'S STONE, SOME KIND OF ULTIMATE POWER OBJECT WHICH HE CLAIMED WAS IN DANGER OF FALLING INTO THE HANDS OF DARKSEID."

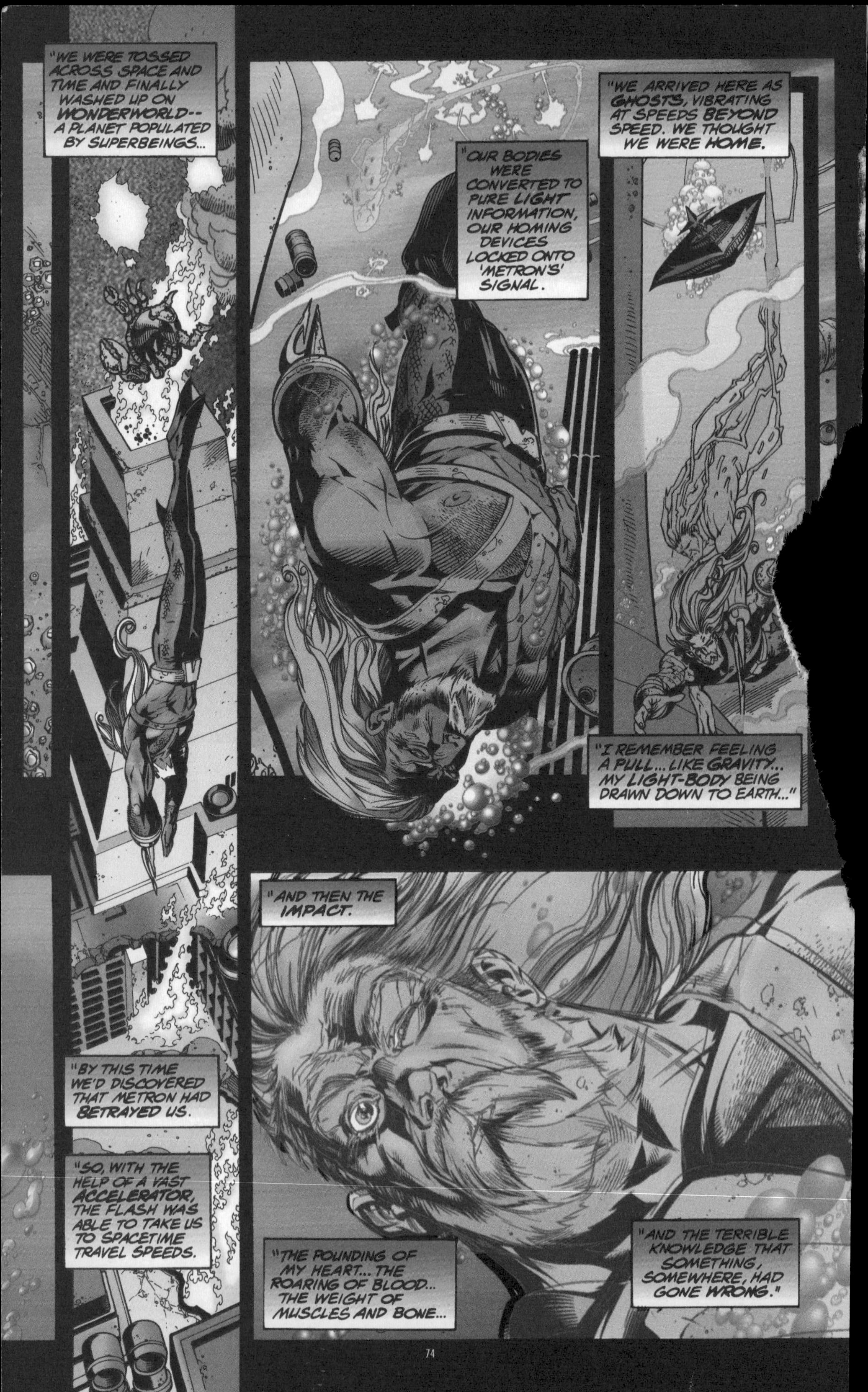

"WE WERE TOSSED ACROSS SPACE AND TIME AND FINALLY WASHED UP ON WONDERWORLD-- A PLANET POPULATED BY SUPERBEINGS...
"OUR BODIES WERE CONVERTED TO PURE LIGHT INFORMATION, OUR HOMING DEVICES LOCKED ONTO 'METRON'S' SIGNAL.
"WE ARRIVED HERE AS GHOSTS, VIBRATING AT SPEEDS BEYOND SPEED. WE THOUGHT WE WERE HOME.
"I REMEMBER FEELING A PULL... LIKE GRAVITY... MY LIGHT-BODY BEING DRAWN DOWN TO EARTH..."
"BY THIS TIME WE'D DISCOVERED THAT METRON HAD BETRAYED US.
"SO, WITH THE HELP OF A VAST ACCELERATOR, THE FLASH WAS ABLE TO TAKE US TO SPACETIME TRAVEL SPEEDS.
"AND THEN THE IMPACT.
"THE POUNDING OF MY HEART... THE ROARING OF BLOOD... THE WEIGHT OF MUSCLES AND BONE...
"AND THE TERRIBLE KNOWLEDGE THAT SOMETHING, SOMEWHERE, HAD GONE WRONG."

"IT CAME OUT OF NOWHERE.

"THAT WAS HOW I GOT HERE. IT WAS THE SAME FOR THE OTHERS.

"IT...TAKES A LITTLE GETTING USED TO.

"WE SEEM TO HAVE TAKEN POSSESSION OF THE BODIES OF OUR FUTURE SELVES.

"BUT I WAS LUCKY; MY OLDER SELF HAD MANAGED TO TRANSMIT A TELEPATHIC COMMAND JUST BEFORE I ARRIVED.

SOME COLOSSAL, MUTATED THING.

"I SWAM WEST.

DEEP VI

75

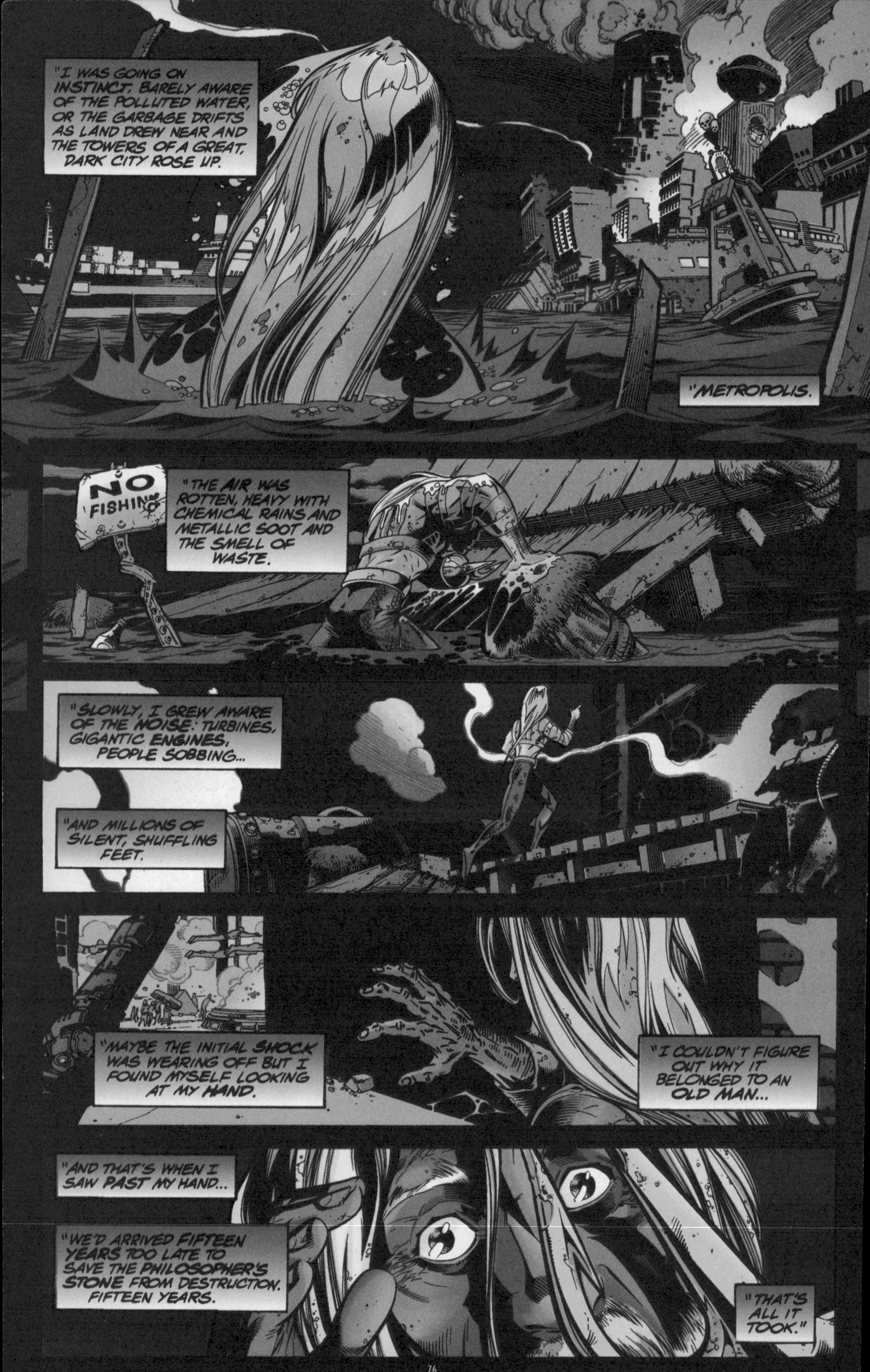
"I WAS GOING ON INSTINCT, BARELY AWARE OF THE POLLUTED WATER, OR THE GARBAGE DRIFTS AS LAND DREW NEAR AND THE TOWERS OF A GREAT, DARK CITY ROSE UP.
"METROPOLIS.
NO FISHING
"THE AIR WAS ROTTEN, HEAVY WITH CHEMICAL RAINS AND METALLIC SOOT AND THE SMELL OF WASTE.
"SLOWLY, I GREW AWARE OF THE NOISE: TURBINES, GIGANTIC ENGINES, PEOPLE SOBBING...
"AND MILLIONS OF SILENT, SHUFFLING FEET.
"MAYBE THE INITIAL SHOCK WAS WEARING OFF BUT I FOUND MYSELF LOOKING AT MY HAND.
"I COULDN'T FIGURE OUT WHY IT BELONGED TO AN OLD MAN...
"AND THAT'S WHEN I SAW PAST MY HAND...
"WE'D ARRIVED FIFTEEN YEARS TOO LATE TO SAVE THE PHILOSOPHER'S STONE FROM DESTRUCTION. FIFTEEN YEARS.
"THAT'S ALL IT TOOK."

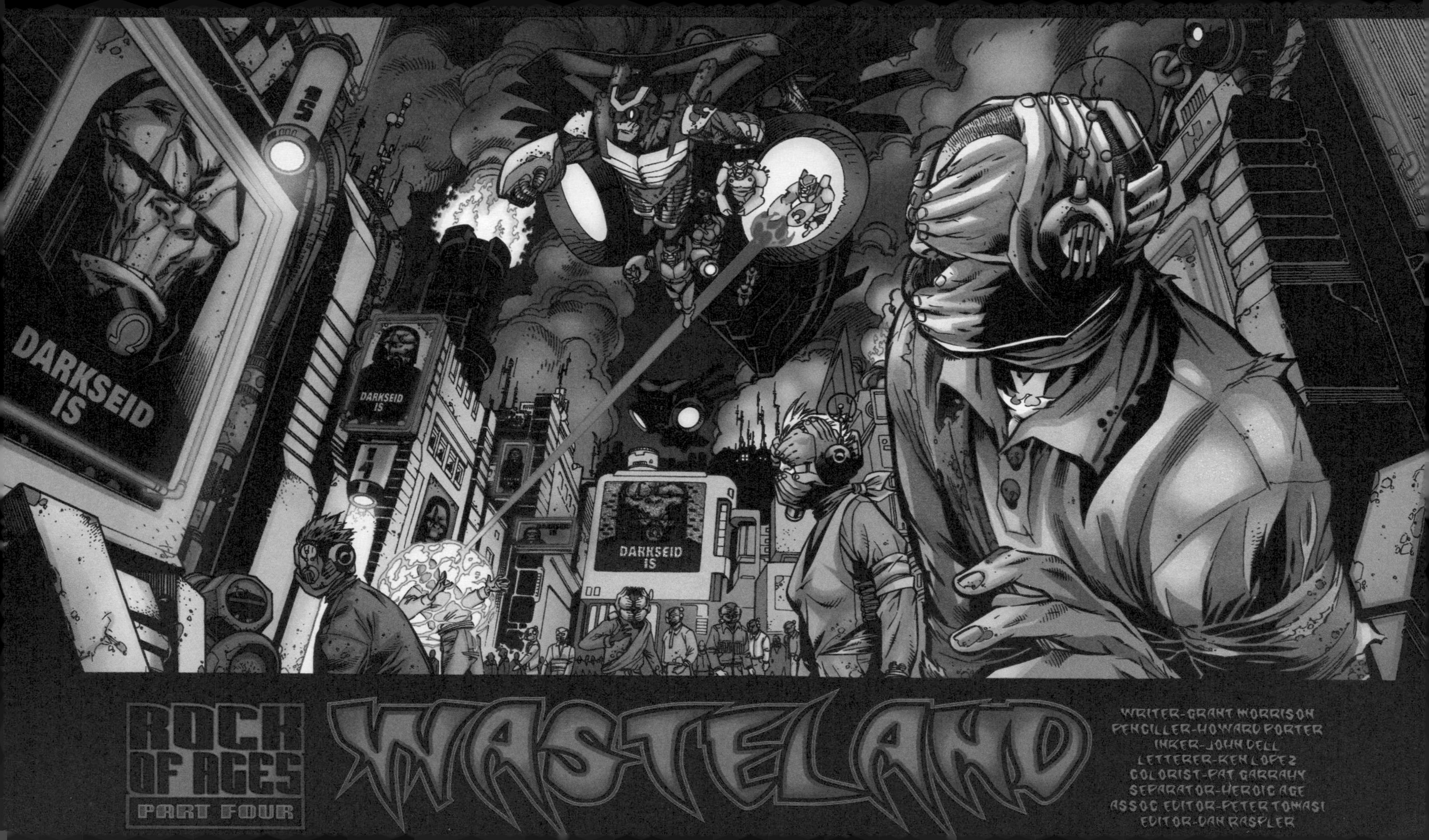
DARKSEID IS
DARKSEID IS
DARKSEID IS
ROCK OF AGES
PART FOUR
WASTELAND
WRITER-GRANT MORRISON
PENCILLER-HOWARD PORTER
INKER-JOHN DELL
LETTERER-KEN LOPEZ
COLORIST-PAT GARRAHY
SEPARATOR-HEROIC AGE
ASSOC EDITOR-PETER TOMASI
EDITOR-DAN RASPLER

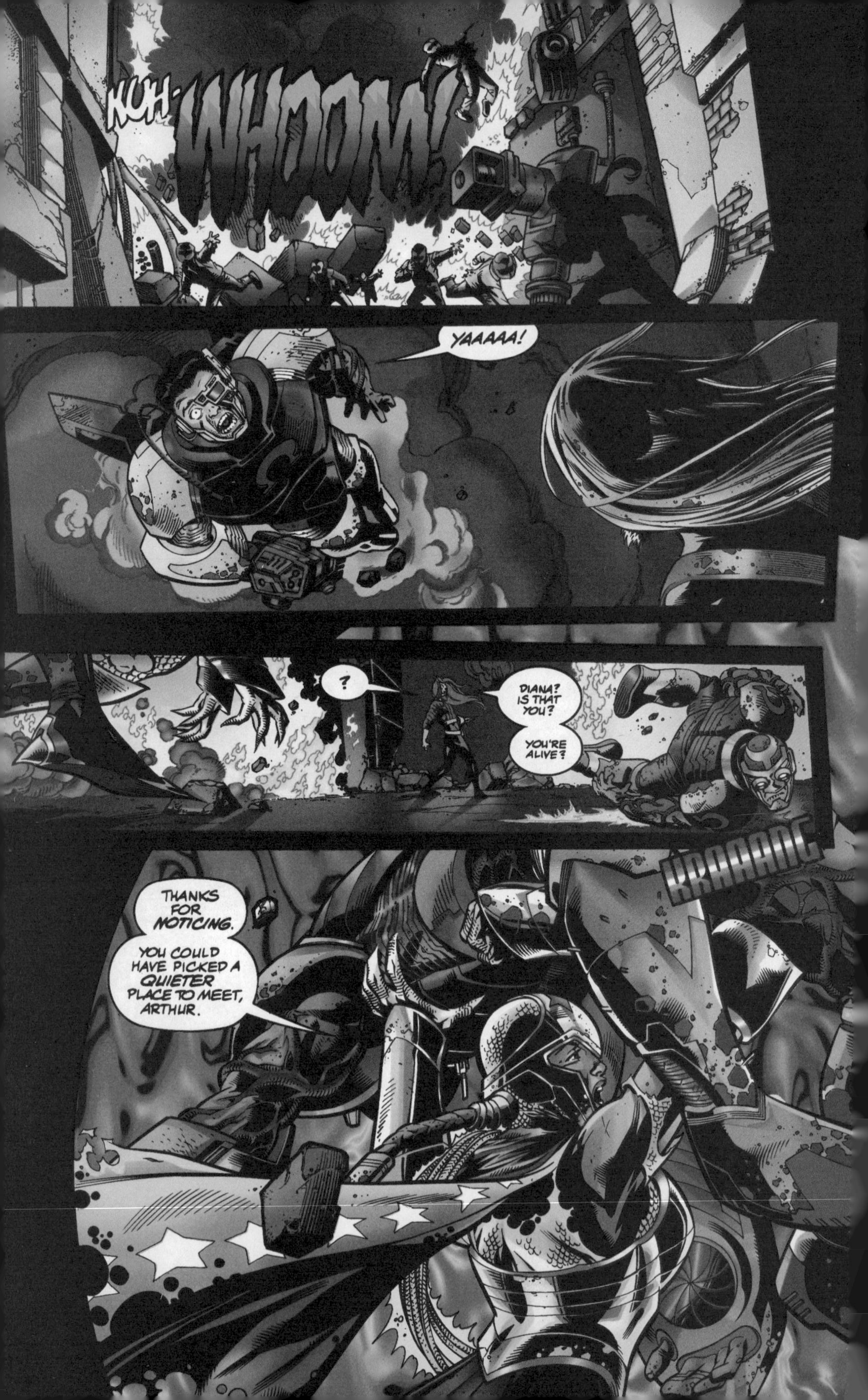
KUH-WHOOM!
YAAAAA!
?
DIANA? IS THAT YOU?
YOU'RE ALIVE?
KRAAANG
THANKS FOR NOTICING.
YOU COULD HAVE PICKED A QUIETER PLACE TO MEET, ARTHUR.

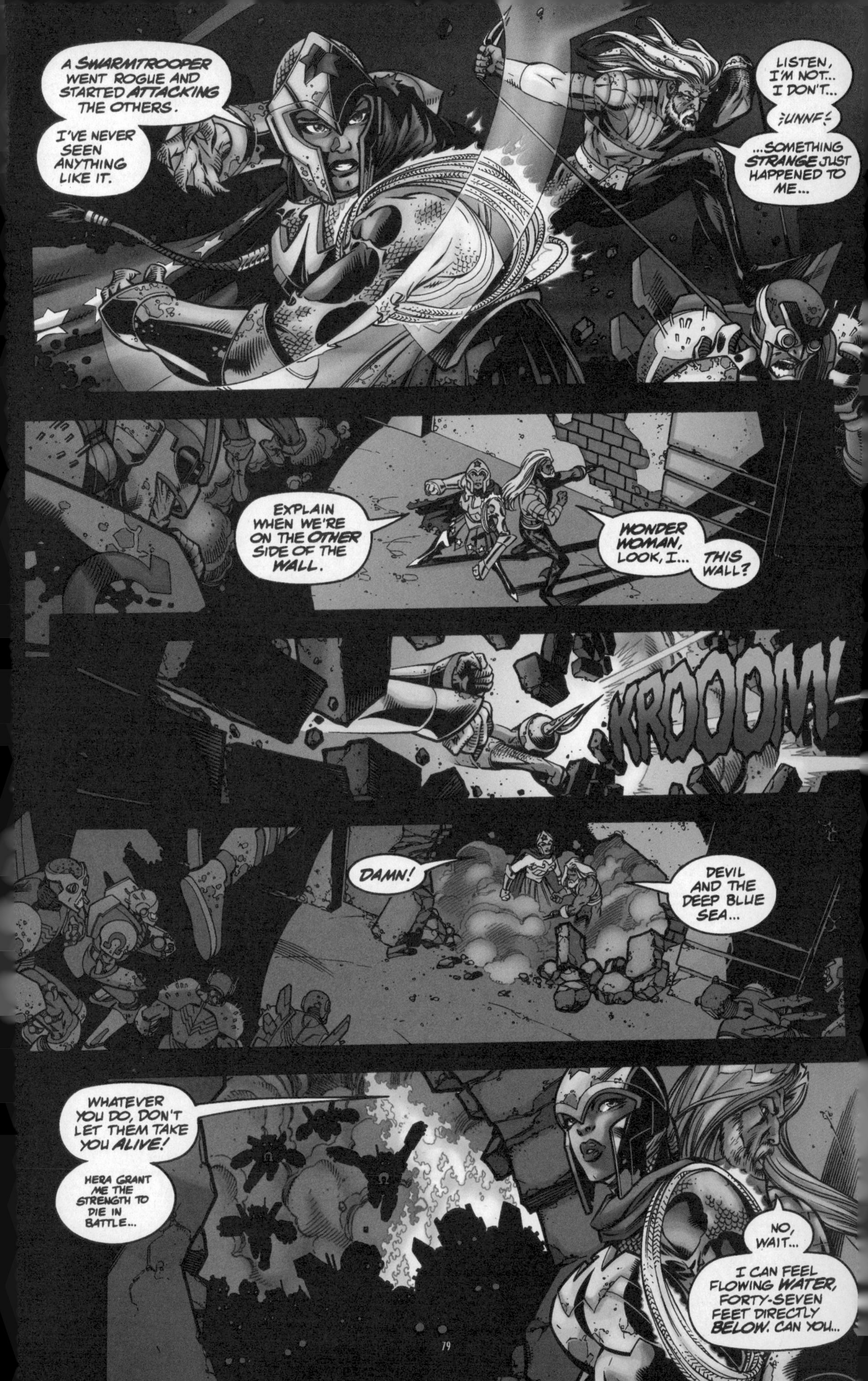
A SWARMTROOPER WENT ROGUE AND STARTED ATTACKING THE OTHERS.
I'VE NEVER SEEN ANYTHING LIKE IT.
LISTEN, I'M NOT... I DON'T...
UNNF
...SOMETHING STRANGE JUST HAPPENED TO ME...
EXPLAIN WHEN WE'RE ON THE OTHER SIDE OF THE WALL.
WONDER WOMAN, LOOK, I...
THIS WALL?
KROOOM!
DAMN!
DEVIL AND THE DEEP BLUE SEA...
WHATEVER YOU DO, DON'T LET THEM TAKE YOU ALIVE!
HERA GRANT ME THE STRENGTH TO DIE IN BATTLE...
NO, WAIT...
I CAN FEEL FLOWING WATER, FORTY-SEVEN FEET DIRECTLY BELOW. CAN YOU...

THOOOM!

ZZz

"THEN SILENCE."

SHH!

SWARMTROOPER.

DIANA...WE NEED TO *TALK*...

ACTUALLY, WE NEED TO *FIGHT,* ARTHUR...

NO!

"HER HEEL STRUCK THE FLOOR ONCE AND I FELT THE *BOTTOM* DROPPING OUT OF THE WORLD. OVERHEAD, THERMO-BOLTS FLASHED AND ROARED.

"WE HIT THE *SEWAGE* IN A RAIN OF DEBRIS, HER ARMBANDS RINGING AS SHE DEFLECTED FALLING STONES.

NO FIGHTING! IT'S *ME.*   IT'S KYLE.

HELP.

"THAT'S HOW WE FOUND *GREEN LANTERN.*"

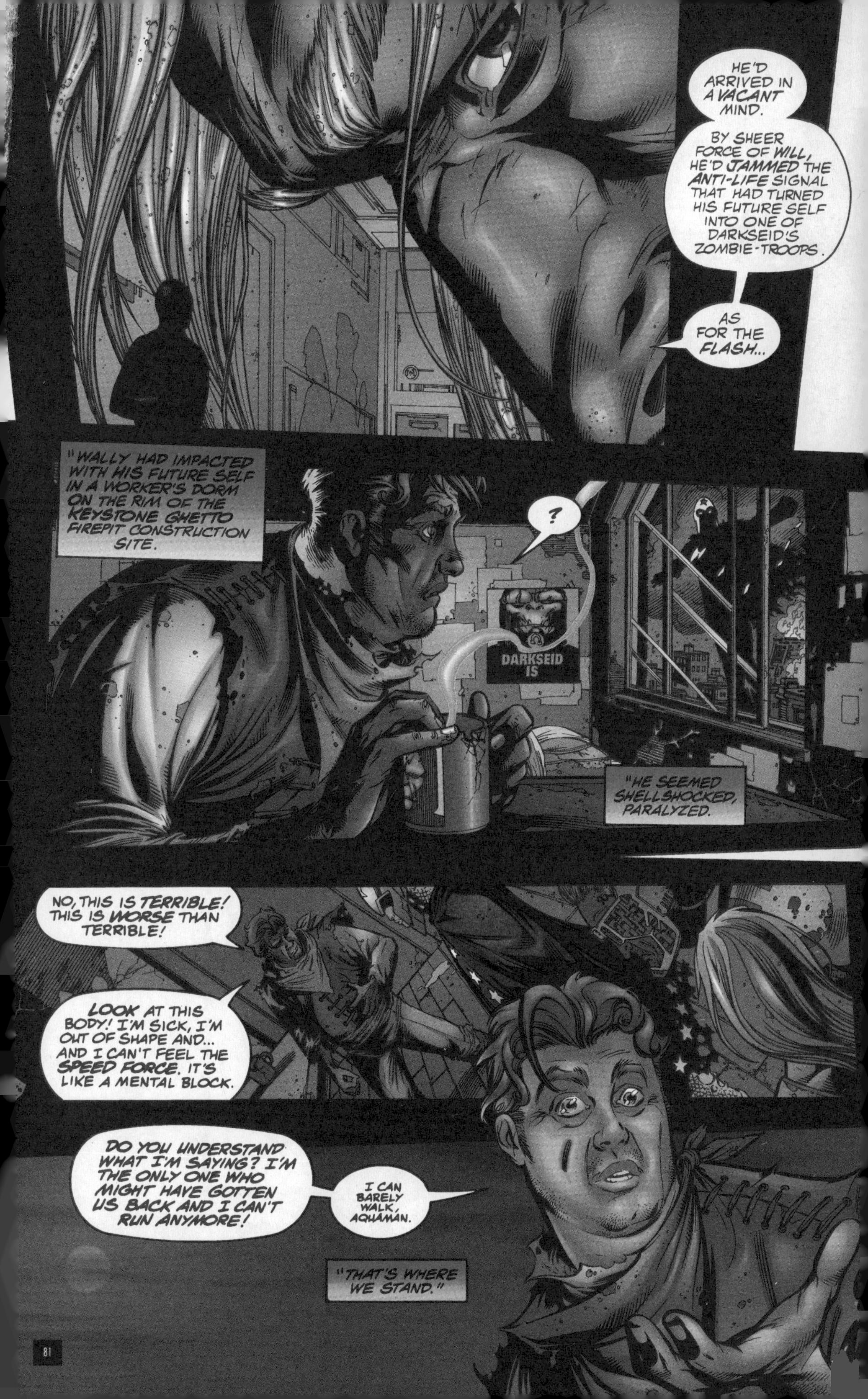
HE'D ARRIVED IN A VACANT MIND.
BY SHEER FORCE OF WILL, HE'D JAMMED THE ANTI-LIFE SIGNAL THAT HAD TURNED HIS FUTURE SELF INTO ONE OF DARKSEID'S ZOMBIE-TROOPS.
AS FOR THE FLASH...
"WALLY HAD IMPACTED WITH HIS FUTURE SELF IN A WORKER'S DORM ON THE RIM OF THE KEYSTONE GHETTO FIREPIT CONSTRUCTION SITE.
?
DARKSEID IS
"HE SEEMED SHELLSHOCKED, PARALYZED.
NO, THIS IS TERRIBLE! THIS IS WORSE THAN TERRIBLE!
LOOK AT THIS BODY! I'M SICK, I'M OUT OF SHAPE AND... AND I CAN'T FEEL THE SPEED FORCE. IT'S LIKE A MENTAL BLOCK.
DO YOU UNDERSTAND WHAT I'M SAYING? I'M THE ONLY ONE WHO MIGHT HAVE GOTTEN US BACK AND I CAN'T RUN ANYMORE!
I CAN BARELY WALK, AQUAMAN.
"THAT'S WHERE WE STAND."

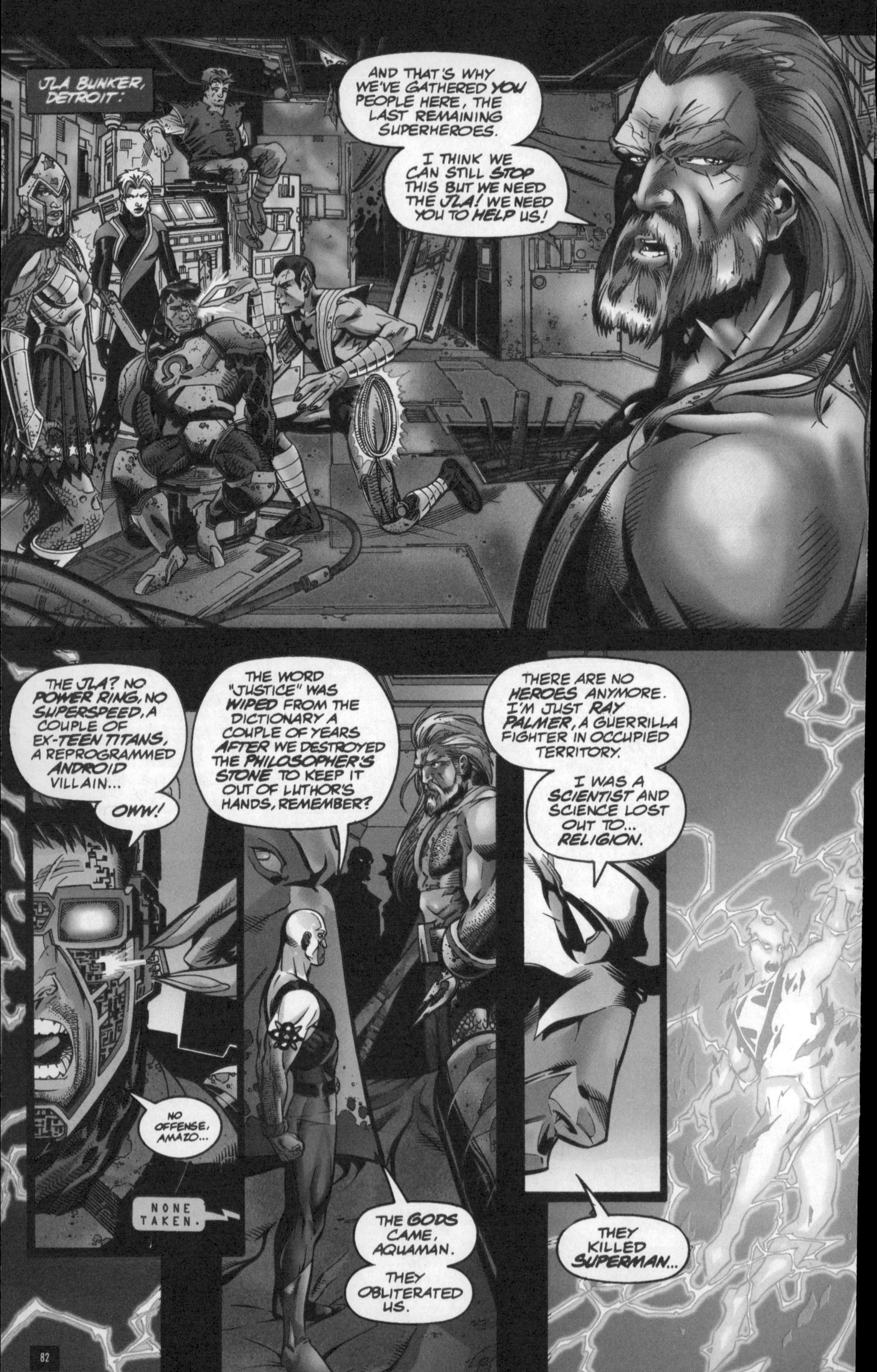
JLA BUNKER, DETROIT:
AND THAT'S WHY WE'VE GATHERED YOU PEOPLE HERE, THE LAST REMAINING SUPERHEROES.
I THINK WE CAN STILL STOP THIS BUT WE NEED THE JLA! WE NEED YOU TO HELP US!
THE JLA? NO POWER RING, NO SUPERSPEED, A COUPLE OF EX-TEEN TITANS, A REPROGRAMMED ANDROID VILLAIN...
OWW!
NO OFFENSE, AMAZO...
NONE TAKEN.
THE WORD "JUSTICE" WAS WIPED FROM THE DICTIONARY A COUPLE OF YEARS AFTER WE DESTROYED THE PHILOSOPHER'S STONE TO KEEP IT OUT OF LUTHOR'S HANDS, REMEMBER?
THE GODS CAME, AQUAMAN.
THEY OBLITERATED US.
THERE ARE NO HEROES ANYMORE. I'M JUST RAY PALMER, A GUERRILLA FIGHTER IN OCCUPIED TERRITORY.
I WAS A SCIENTIST AND SCIENCE LOST OUT TO... RELIGION.
THEY KILLED SUPERMAN...

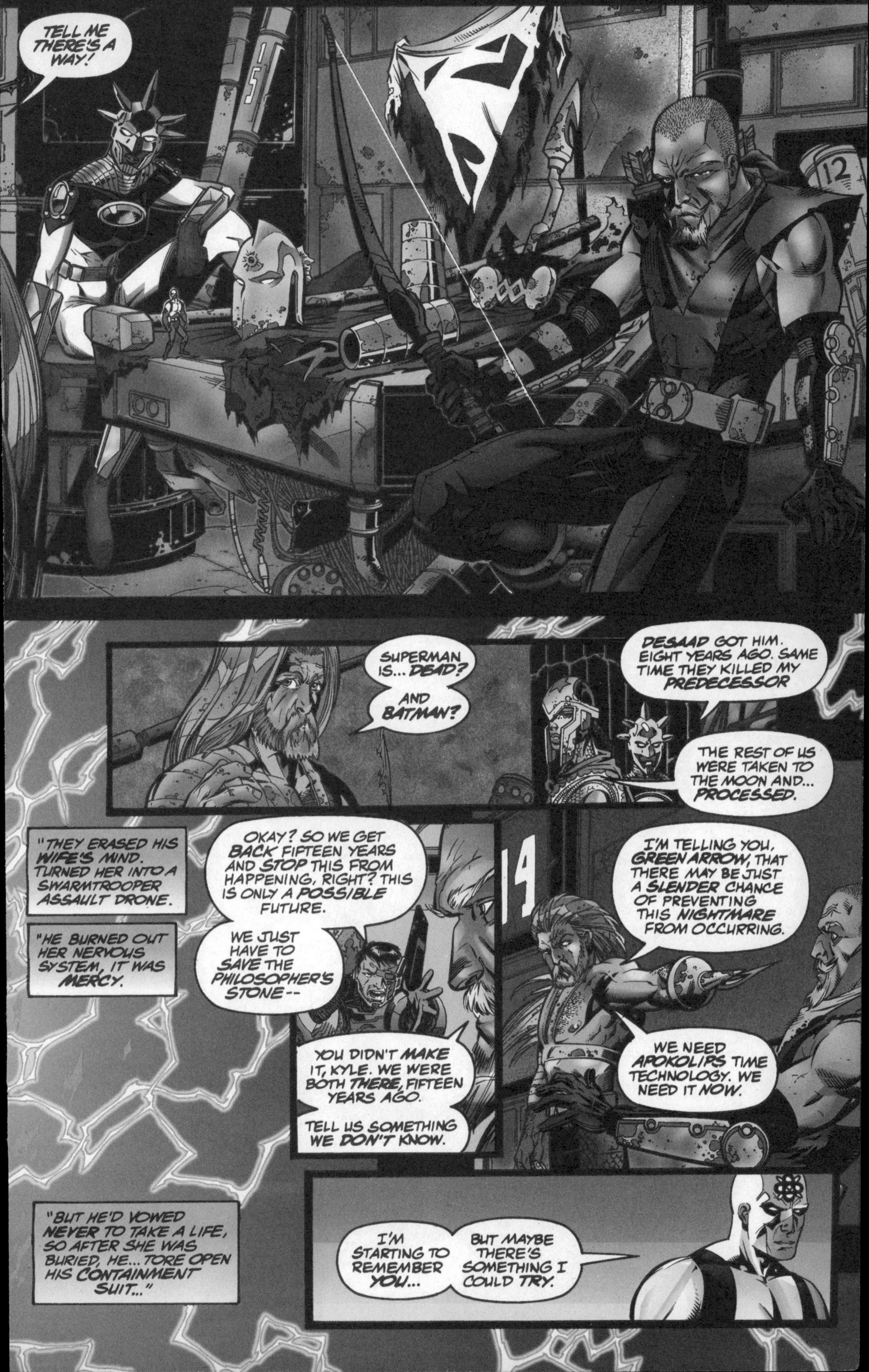
TELL ME THERE'S A WAY!
SUPERMAN IS... DEAD?
AND BATMAN?
DESAAD GOT HIM. EIGHT YEARS AGO. SAME TIME THEY KILLED MY PREDECESSOR
THE REST OF US WERE TAKEN TO THE MOON AND... PROCESSED.
"THEY ERASED HIS WIFE'S MIND. TURNED HER INTO A SWARMTROOPER ASSAULT DRONE.
"HE BURNED OUT HER NERVOUS SYSTEM, IT WAS MERCY.
OKAY? SO WE GET BACK FIFTEEN YEARS AND STOP THIS FROM HAPPENING, RIGHT? THIS IS ONLY A POSSIBLE FUTURE.
WE JUST HAVE TO SAVE THE PHILOSOPHER'S STONE--
YOU DIDN'T MAKE IT, KYLE. WE WERE BOTH THERE, FIFTEEN YEARS AGO.
TELL US SOMETHING WE DON'T KNOW.
I'M TELLING YOU, GREEN ARROW, THAT THERE MAY BE JUST A SLENDER CHANCE OF PREVENTING THIS NIGHTMARE FROM OCCURRING.
WE NEED APOKOLIPS TIME TECHNOLOGY. WE NEED IT NOW.
"BUT HE'D VOWED NEVER TO TAKE A LIFE, SO AFTER SHE WAS BURIED, HE... TORE OPEN HIS CONTAINMENT SUIT..."
I'M STARTING TO REMEMBER YOU...
BUT MAYBE THERE'S SOMETHING I COULD TRY.

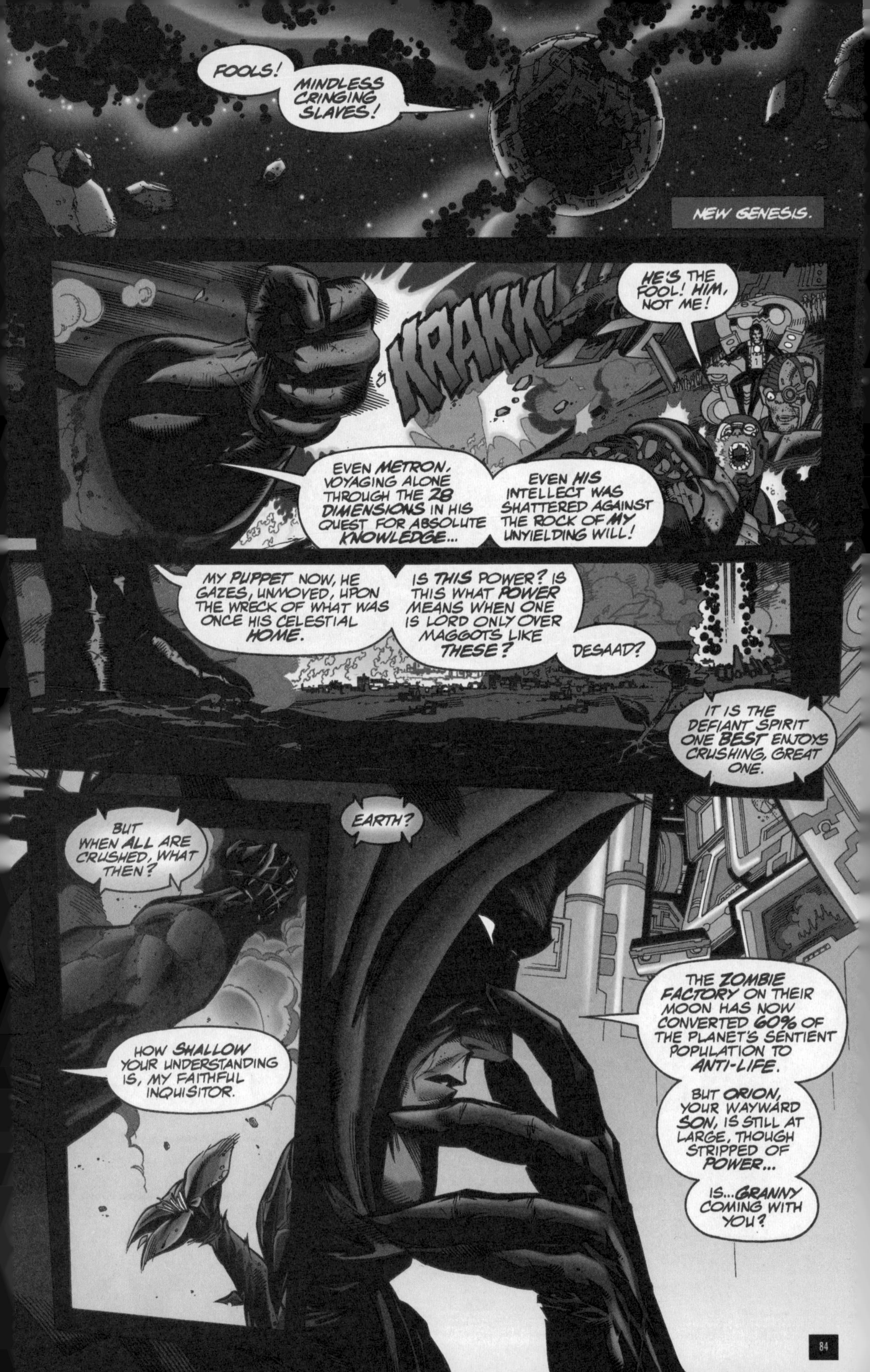
FOOLS!
MINDLESS CRINGING SLAVES!
NEW GENESIS.
KRAKK!
HE'S THE FOOL! HIM, NOT ME!
EVEN METRON, VOYAGING ALONE THROUGH THE 28 DIMENSIONS IN HIS QUEST FOR ABSOLUTE KNOWLEDGE...
EVEN HIS INTELLECT WAS SHATTERED AGAINST THE ROCK OF MY UNYIELDING WILL!
MY PUPPET NOW, HE GAZES, UNMOVED, UPON THE WRECK OF WHAT WAS ONCE HIS CELESTIAL HOME.
IS THIS POWER? IS THIS WHAT POWER MEANS WHEN ONE IS LORD ONLY OVER MAGGOTS LIKE THESE?
DESAAD?
IT IS THE DEFIANT SPIRIT ONE BEST ENJOYS CRUSHING, GREAT ONE.
BUT WHEN ALL ARE CRUSHED, WHAT THEN?
EARTH?
HOW SHALLOW YOUR UNDERSTANDING IS, MY FAITHFUL INQUISITOR.
THE ZOMBIE FACTORY ON THEIR MOON HAS NOW CONVERTED 60% OF THE PLANET'S SENTIENT POPULATION TO ANTI-LIFE.
BUT ORION, YOUR WAYWARD SON, IS STILL AT LARGE, THOUGH STRIPPED OF POWER...
IS...GRANNY COMING WITH YOU?

OF COURSE.
"BUT PERHAPS HE RELIES TOO MUCH ON HER MEANINGLESS 'PROPHECIES'..." THAT'S WHAT SOME SAY... UNDER TORTURE, GREAT ONE.
"PERHAPS HE HEARS ONLY WHAT APPEALS TO HIS VANITY," THEY SAY...
ORION-DOG OF WAR-GOD NO MORE-ALL IS RUIN
I REMEMBER WATCHING OUR DEAR GRANNY GOODNESS INVADING THE CORE SOFTDRIVE OF NEW GENESIS, TRANSFORMING THEIR ALL-GIVING MOTHER BOX INTO THIS...OUR PITILESS GRANDMOTHER BOX.
AWE-INSPIRING.
VANITY?
NEW GENESIS IS A STINKING COSMIC SEWER! I HAVE FOULED PARADISE BEYOND REPAIR AND BROKEN IN THE MIRE THE SHINING CITIES OF THE GODS! I HAVE WON!.
IS THIS VANITY?
THEN I WILL REMAKE THE ENTIRE UNIVERSE IN THE IMAGE OF MY SOUL, DESAAD.
AND WHEN AT LAST I TURN TO LOOK UPON THE ETERNAL DESOLATION I HAVE WROUGHT...
I WILL SEE DARKSEID, AS IN A MIRROR...
AND KNOW WHAT FEAR IS.
HAHAHAHAHAH

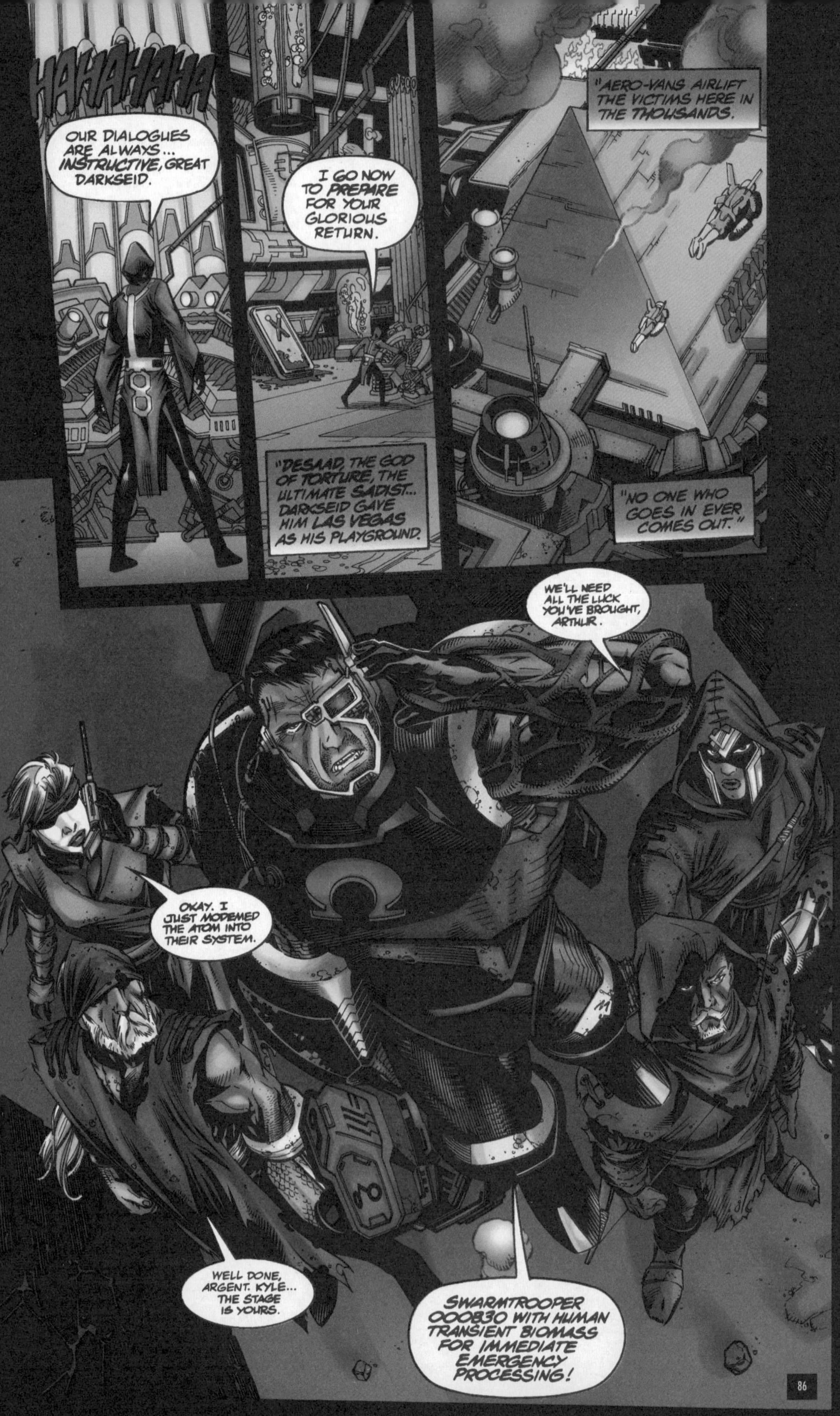
HAHAHAHA
OUR DIALOGUES ARE ALWAYS... INSTRUCTIVE, GREAT DARKSEID.
I GO NOW TO PREPARE FOR YOUR GLORIOUS RETURN.
"DESAAD, THE GOD OF TORTURE, THE ULTIMATE SADIST... DARKSEID GAVE HIM LAS VEGAS AS HIS PLAYGROUND.
"AERO-VANS AIRLIFT THE VICTIMS HERE IN THE THOUSANDS.
"NO ONE WHO GOES IN EVER COMES OUT."
WE'LL NEED ALL THE LUCK YOU'VE BROUGHT, ARTHUR.
OKAY. I JUST MODEMED THE ATOM INTO THEIR SYSTEM.
WELL DONE, ARGENT. KYLE... THE STAGE IS YOURS.
SWARMTROOPER 000B30 WITH HUMAN TRANSIENT BIOMASS FOR IMMEDIATE EMERGENCY PROCESSING!

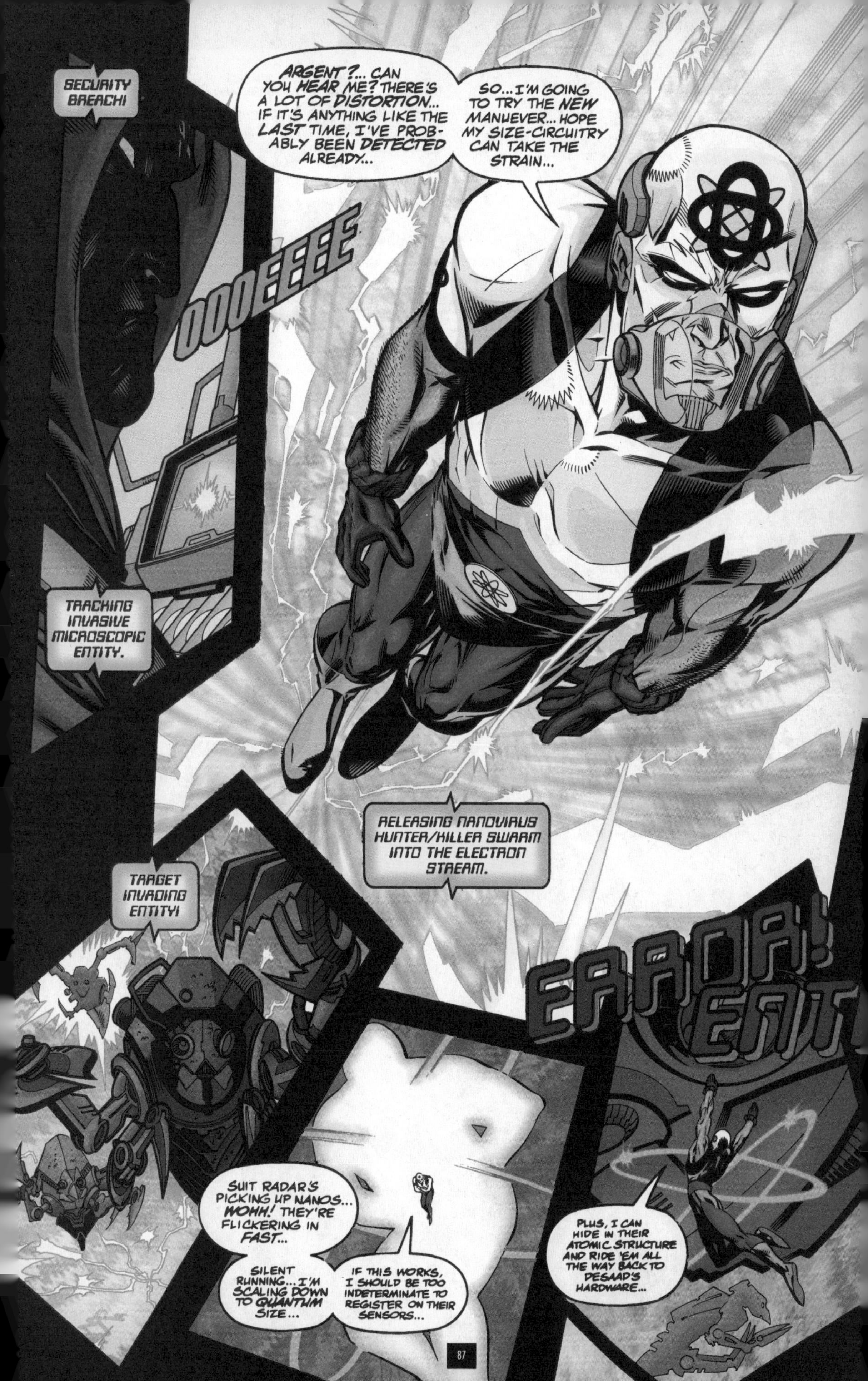
SECURITY BREACH!
ARGENT?... CAN YOU HEAR ME? THERE'S A LOT OF DISTORTION... IF IT'S ANYTHING LIKE THE LAST TIME, I'VE PROBABLY BEEN DETECTED ALREADY...
SO... I'M GOING TO TRY THE NEW MANUEVER... HOPE MY SIZE-CIRCUITRY CAN TAKE THE STRAIN...
OOOEEEE
TRACKING INVASIVE MICROSCOPIC ENTITY.
RELEASING NANOVIRUS HUNTER/KILLER SWARM INTO THE ELECTRON STREAM.
TARGET INVADING ENTITY!
ERROR! ENTI
SUIT RADAR'S PICKING UP NANOS... WOHH! THEY'RE FLICKERING IN FAST...
SILENT RUNNING... I'M SCALING DOWN TO QUANTUM SIZE...
IF THIS WORKS, I SHOULD BE TOO INDETERMINATE TO REGISTER ON THEIR SENSORS...
PLUS, I CAN HIDE IN THEIR ATOMIC STRUCTURE AND RIDE 'EM ALL THE WAY BACK TO DESAAD'S HARDWARE...

HE'S IN.
WHY'S NOTHING HAPPENING?
SHOULDN'T THEY BE OPENING THE GATES OR FRYING US WITH RAYGUNS BY NOW?
SOMETHING SMELLS.
PLAN B.
MAN, I WISH I HAD MY RING!
ZZZZZZZZZOM!
SHRRRAAA KOOM!
I SEE.
SUDDENLY IT'S A SUICIDE MISSION.
WE'RE THE JUSTICE LEAGUE, DIANA; WE DON'T DO SUICIDE MISSIONS.
FAN OUT.

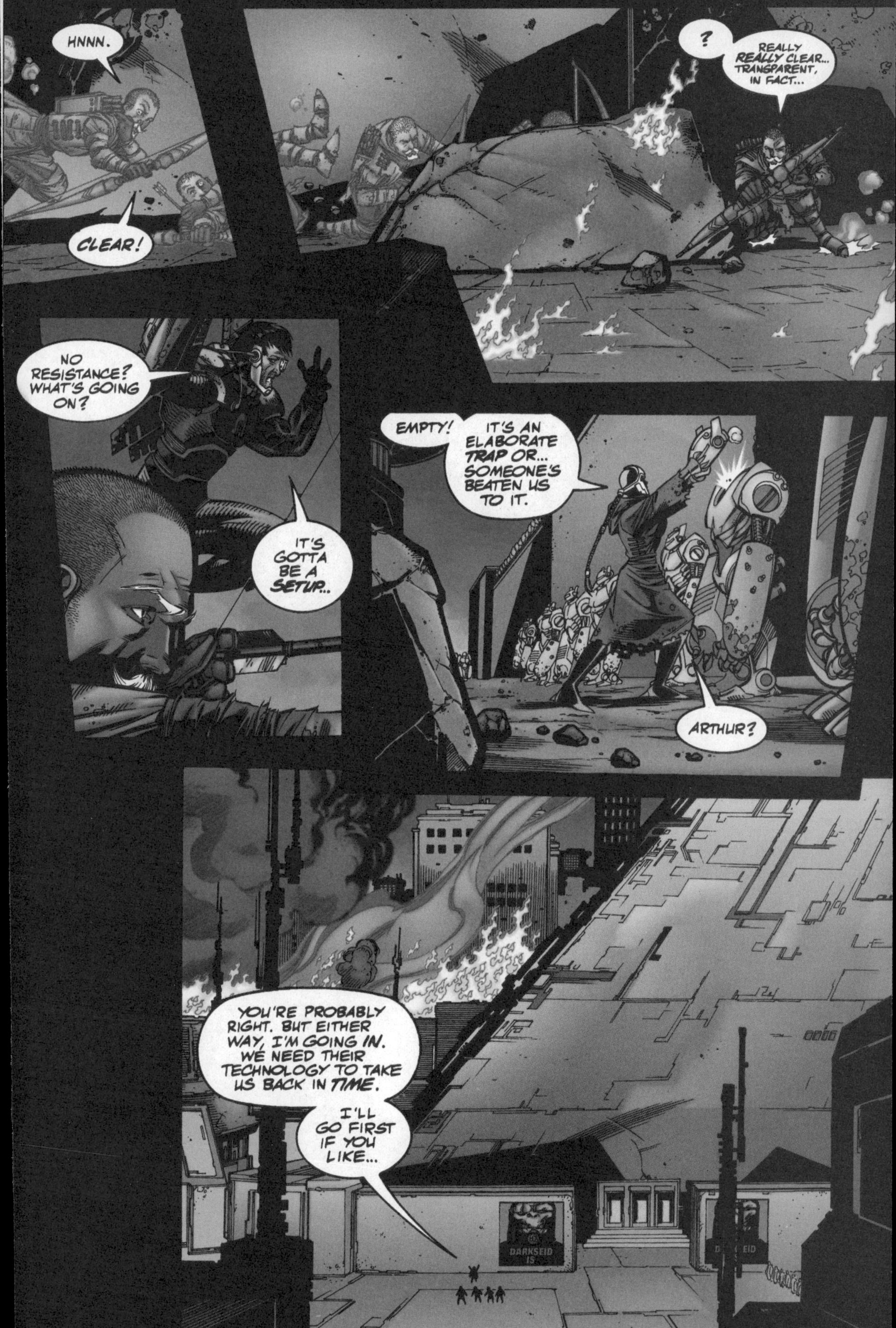
HNNN.
CLEAR!
?
REALLY REALLY CLEAR... TRANSPARENT, IN FACT...
NO RESISTANCE? WHAT'S GOING ON?
IT'S GOTTA BE A SETUP...
EMPTY!
IT'S AN ELABORATE TRAP OR... SOMEONE'S BEATEN US TO IT.
ARTHUR?
YOU'RE PROBABLY RIGHT. BUT EITHER WAY, I'M GOING IN. WE NEED THEIR TECHNOLOGY TO TAKE US BACK IN TIME.
I'LL GO FIRST IF YOU LIKE...
DARKSEID IS

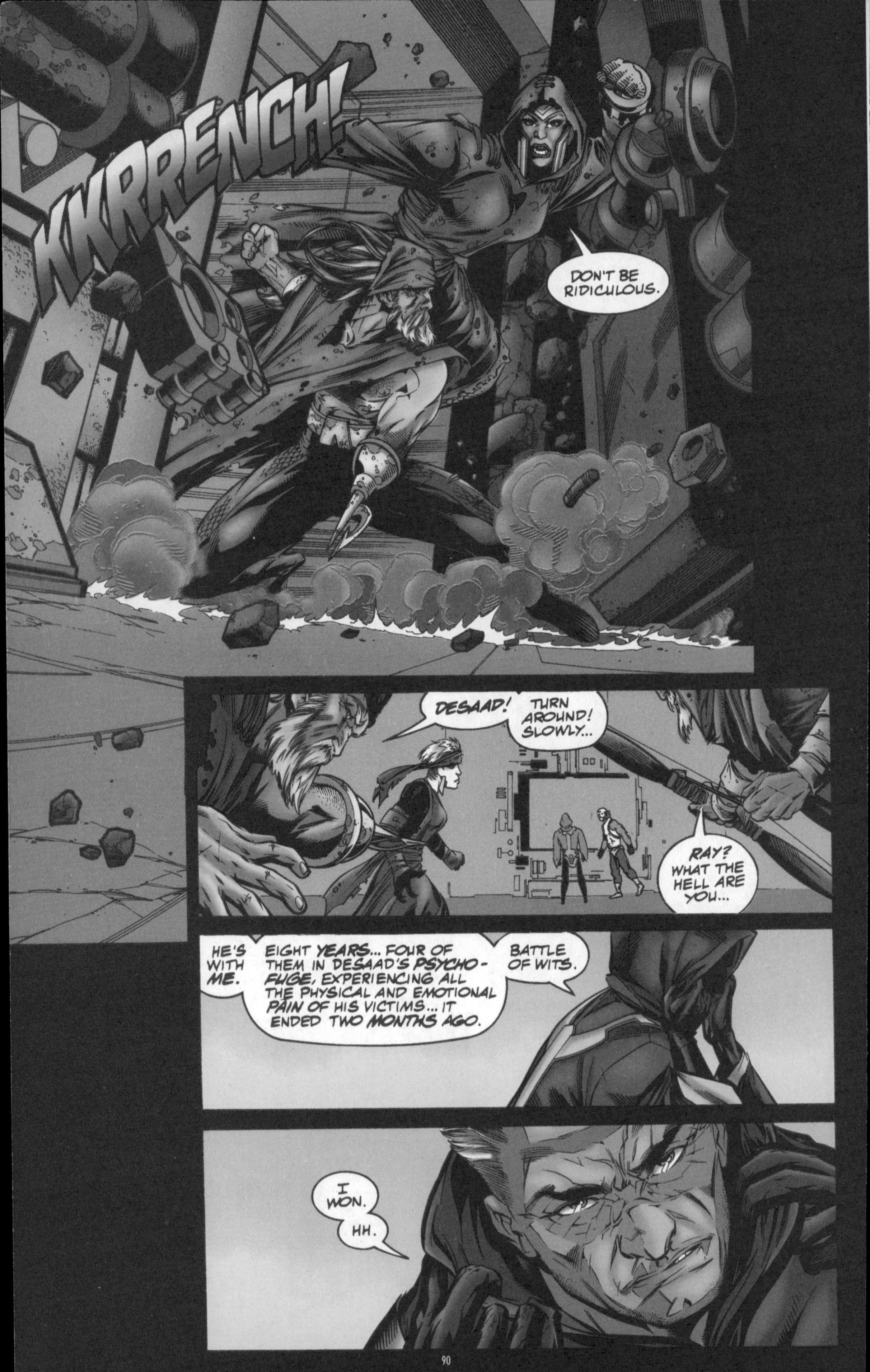
KKRRENCH!
DON'T BE RIDICULOUS.
DESAAD!
TURN AROUND! SLOWLY...
RAY? WHAT THE HELL ARE YOU...
HE'S WITH ME.
EIGHT YEARS... FOUR OF THEM IN DESAAD'S PSYCHO-FUGE, EXPERIENCING ALL THE PHYSICAL AND EMOTIONAL PAIN OF HIS VICTIMS... IT ENDED TWO MONTHS AGO.
BATTLE OF WITS.
I WON.
HH.

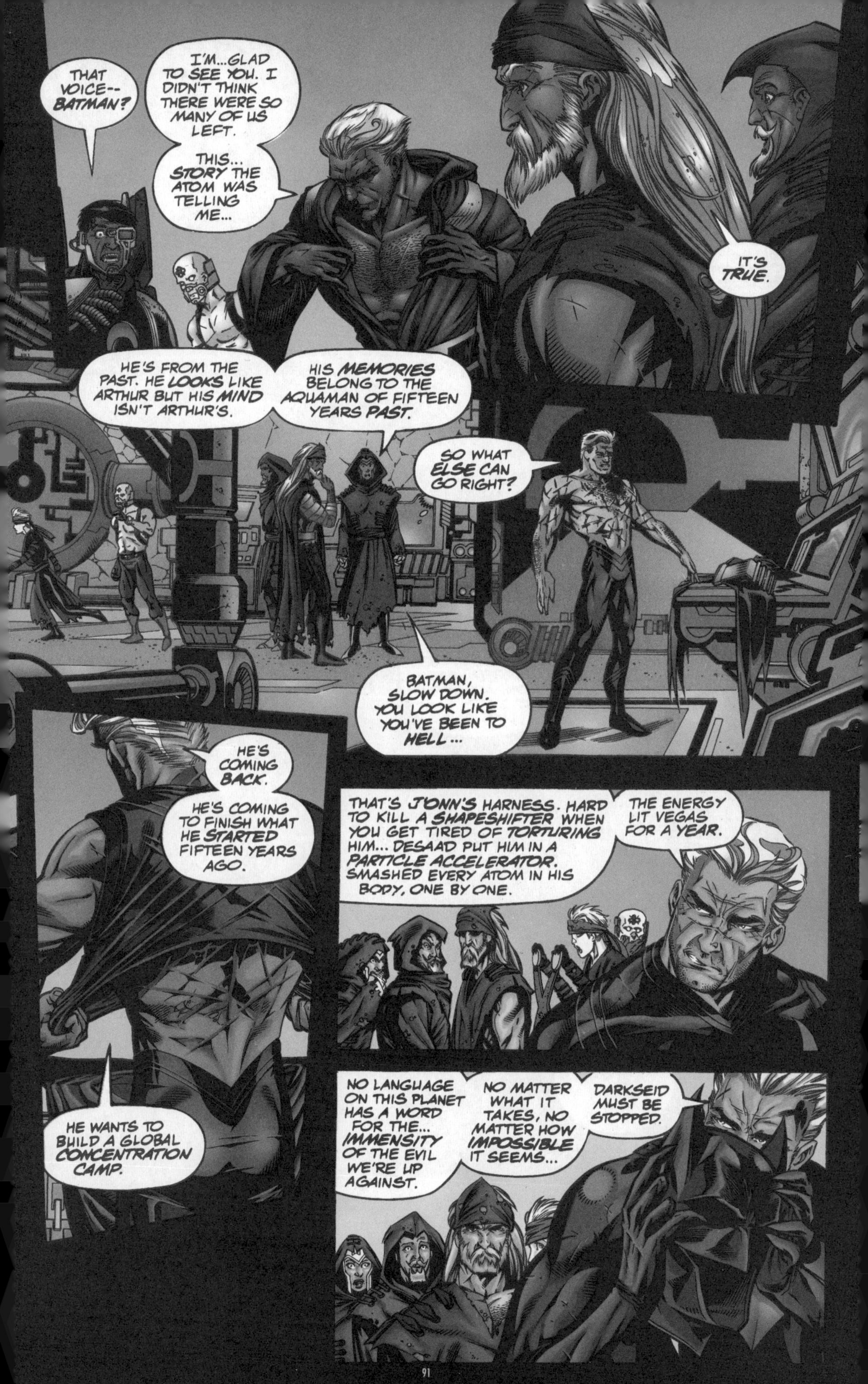
THAT VOICE-- BATMAN?
I'M...GLAD TO SEE YOU. I DIDN'T THINK THERE WERE SO MANY OF US LEFT.
THIS... STORY THE ATOM WAS TELLING ME...
IT'S TRUE.
HE'S FROM THE PAST. HE LOOKS LIKE ARTHUR BUT HIS MIND ISN'T ARTHUR'S.
HIS MEMORIES BELONG TO THE AQUAMAN OF FIFTEEN YEARS PAST.
SO WHAT ELSE CAN GO RIGHT?
BATMAN, SLOW DOWN. YOU LOOK LIKE YOU'VE BEEN TO HELL...
HE'S COMING BACK.
HE'S COMING TO FINISH WHAT HE STARTED FIFTEEN YEARS AGO.
HE WANTS TO BUILD A GLOBAL CONCENTRATION CAMP.
THAT'S J'ONN'S HARNESS. HARD TO KILL A SHAPESHIFTER WHEN YOU GET TIRED OF TORTURING HIM... DESAAD PUT HIM IN A PARTICLE ACCELERATOR. SMASHED EVERY ATOM IN HIS BODY, ONE BY ONE.
THE ENERGY LIT VEGAS FOR A YEAR.
NO LANGUAGE ON THIS PLANET HAS A WORD FOR THE... IMMENSITY OF THE EVIL WE'RE UP AGAINST.
NO MATTER WHAT IT TAKES, NO MATTER HOW IMPOSSIBLE IT SEEMS...
DARKSEID MUST BE STOPPED.

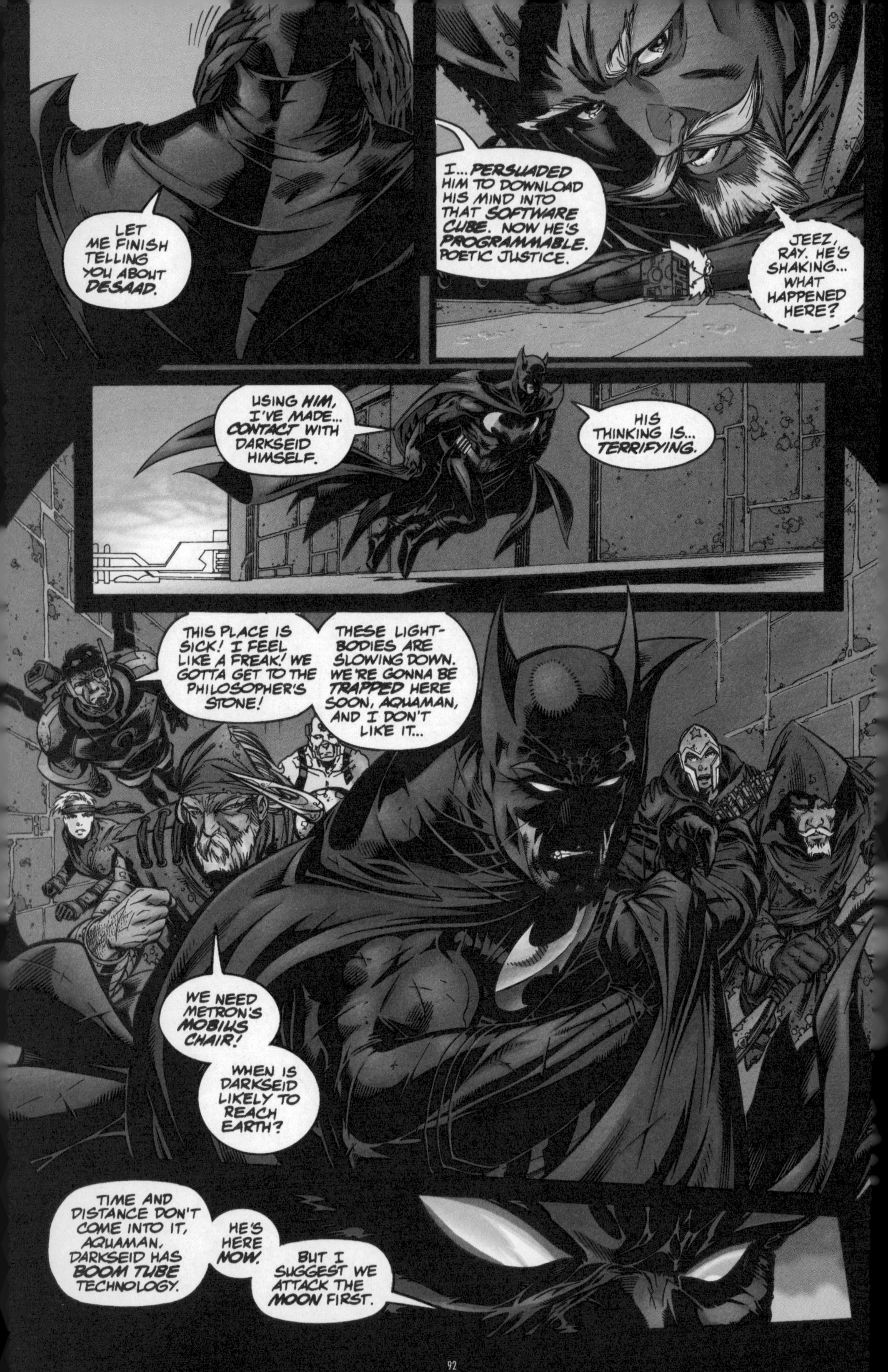

LET ME FINISH TELLING YOU ABOUT DESAAD.
I... PERSUADED HIM TO DOWNLOAD HIS MIND INTO THAT SOFTWARE CUBE. NOW HE'S PROGRAMMABLE. POETIC JUSTICE.
JEEZ, RAY. HE'S SHAKING... WHAT HAPPENED HERE?
USING HIM, I'VE MADE... CONTACT WITH DARKSEID HIMSELF.
HIS THINKING IS... TERRIFYING.
THIS PLACE IS SICK! I FEEL LIKE A FREAK! WE GOTTA GET TO THE PHILOSOPHER'S STONE!
THESE LIGHT-BODIES ARE SLOWING DOWN. WE'RE GONNA BE TRAPPED HERE SOON, AQUAMAN, AND I DON'T LIKE IT...
WE NEED METRON'S MOBIUS CHAIR!
WHEN IS DARKSEID LIKELY TO REACH EARTH?
TIME AND DISTANCE DON'T COME INTO IT, AQUAMAN. DARKSEID HAS BOOM TUBE TECHNOLOGY.
HE'S HERE NOW.
BUT I SUGGEST WE ATTACK THE MOON FIRST.

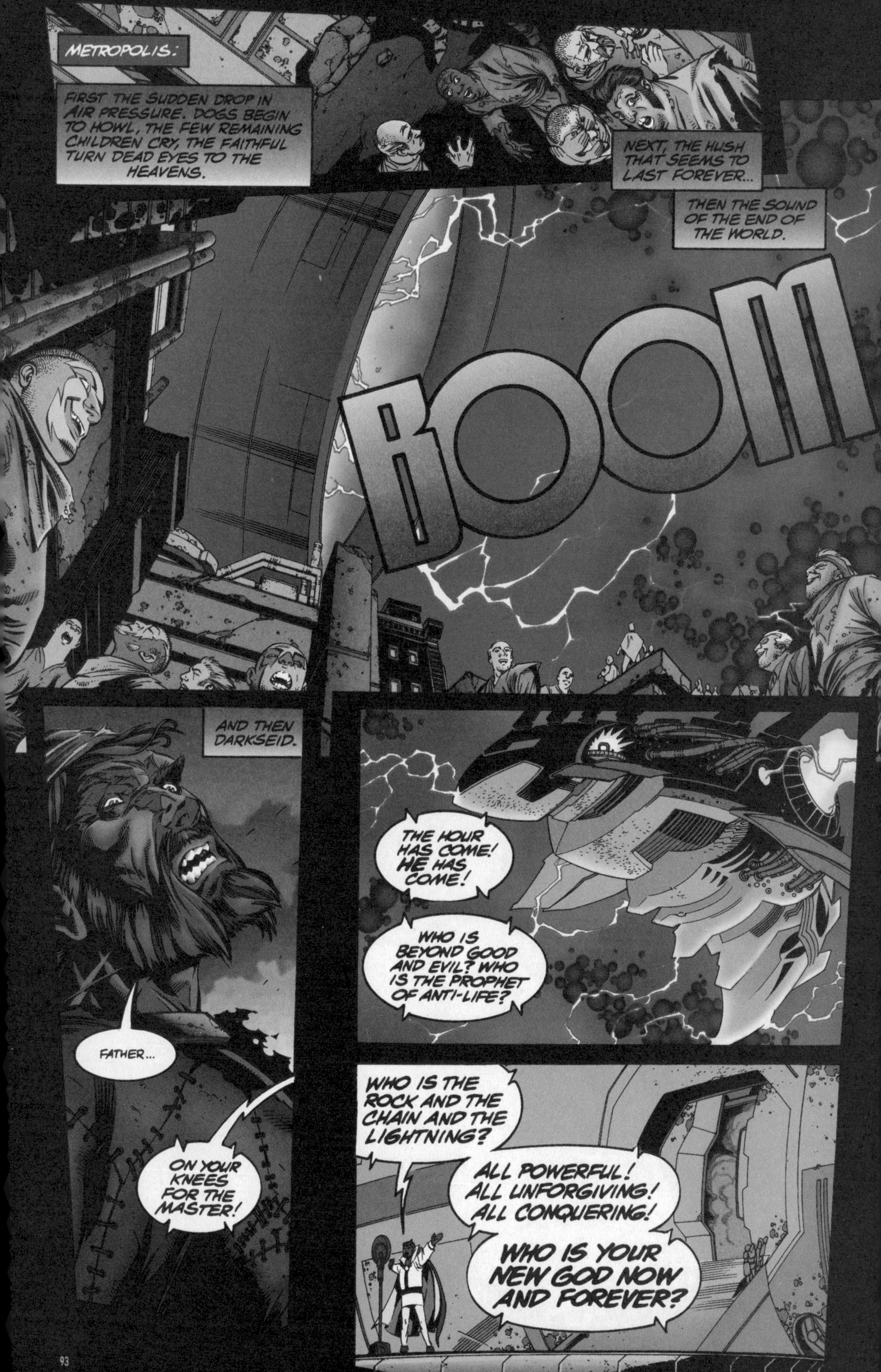
METROPOLIS:
FIRST THE SUDDEN DROP IN AIR PRESSURE. DOGS BEGIN TO HOWL, THE FEW REMAINING CHILDREN CRY, THE FAITHFUL TURN DEAD EYES TO THE HEAVENS.
NEXT, THE HUSH THAT SEEMS TO LAST FOREVER...
THEN THE SOUND OF THE END OF THE WORLD.
BOOM
AND THEN DARKSEID.
FATHER...
ON YOUR KNEES FOR THE MASTER!
THE HOUR HAS COME! HE HAS COME!
WHO IS BEYOND GOOD AND EVIL? WHO IS THE PROPHET OF ANTI-LIFE?
WHO IS THE ROCK AND THE CHAIN AND THE LIGHTNING?
ALL POWERFUL! ALL UNFORGIVING! ALL CONQUERING!
WHO IS YOUR NEW GOD NOW AND FOREVER?

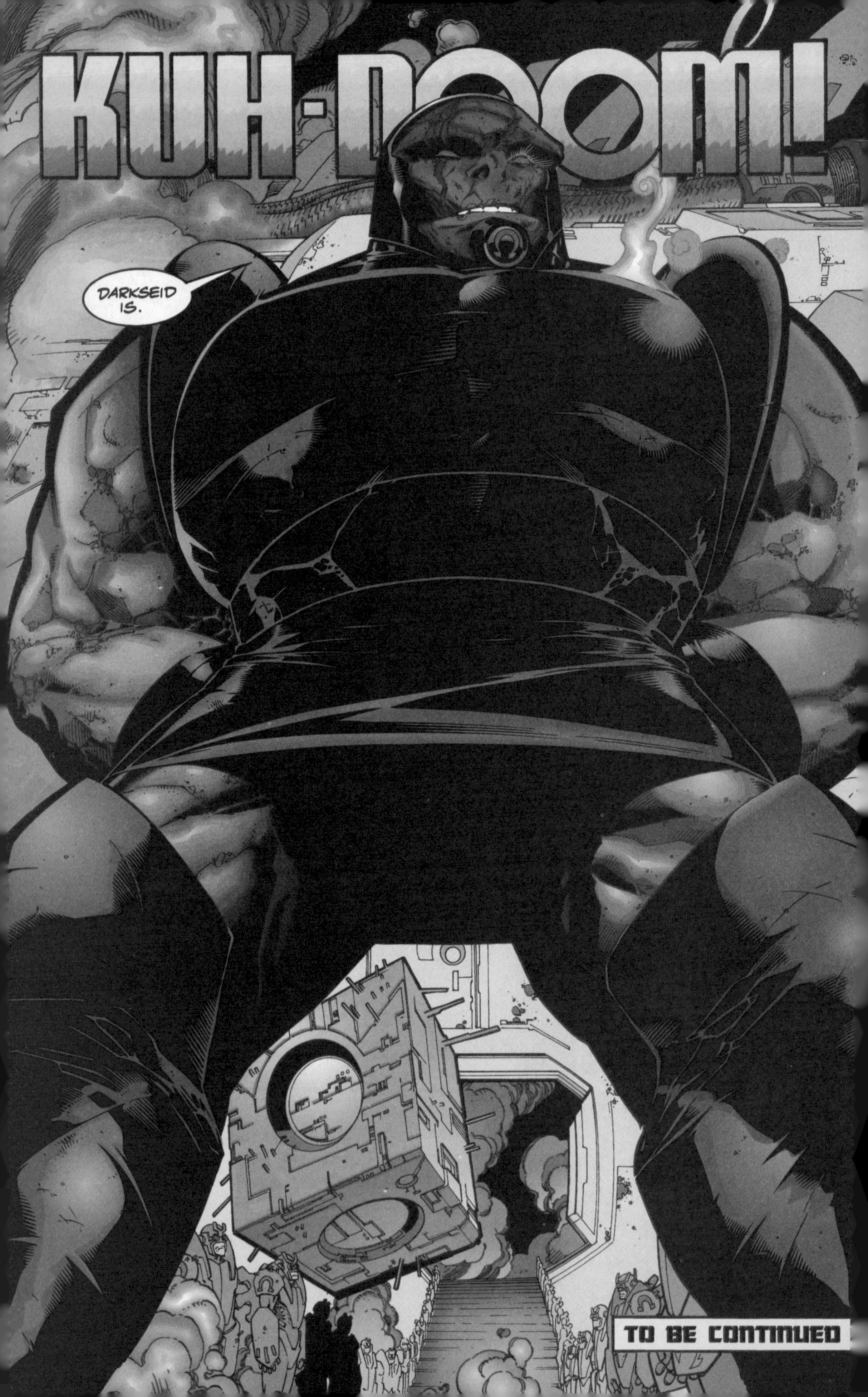
KUH-DOOM!
DARKSEID IS.
TO BE CONTINUED

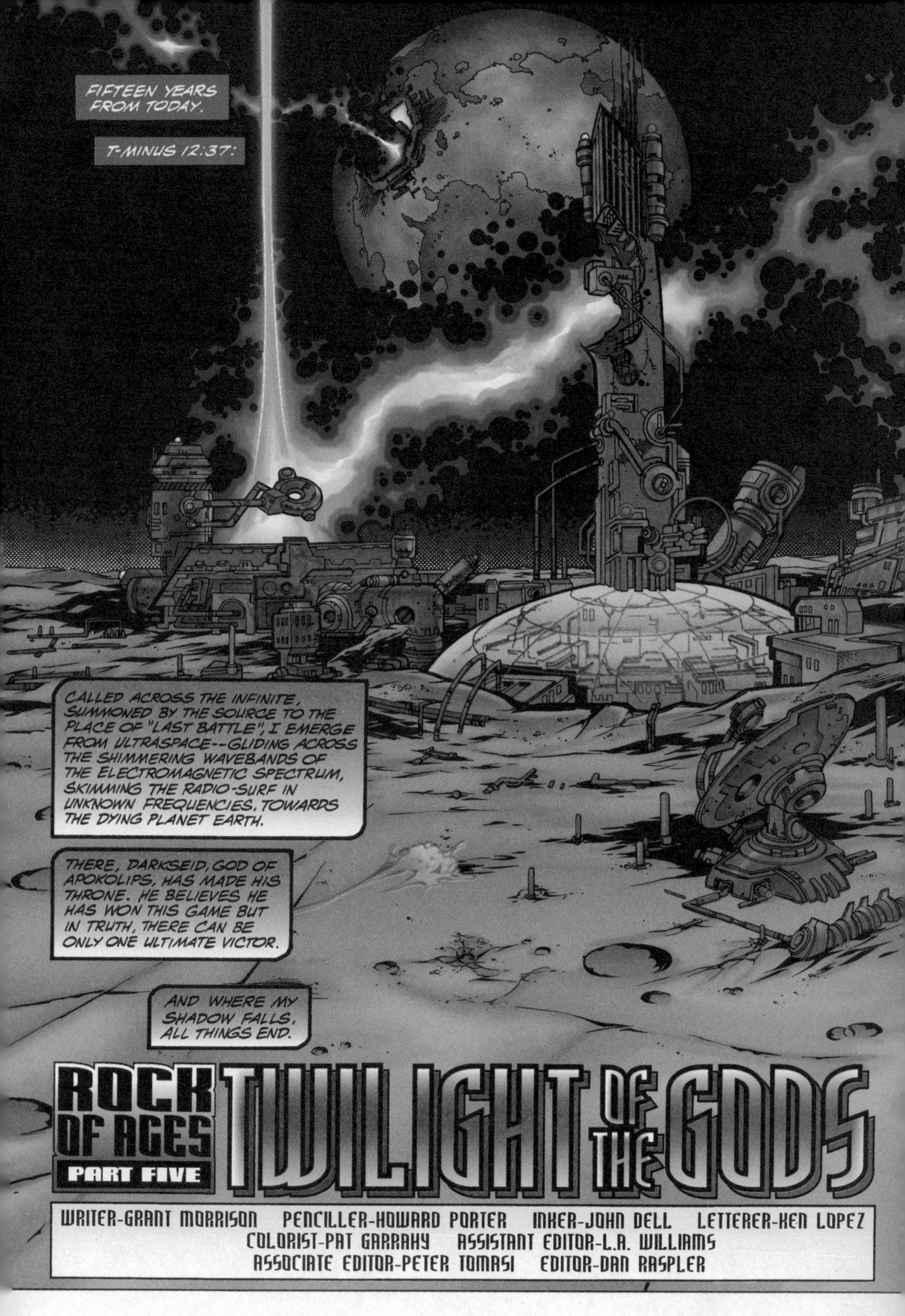
FIFTEEN YEARS FROM TODAY.
T-MINUS 12:37:
CALLED ACROSS THE INFINITE, SUMMONED BY THE SOURCE TO THE PLACE OF "LAST BATTLE", I EMERGE FROM ULTRASPACE--GLIDING ACROSS THE SHIMMERING WAVEBANDS OF THE ELECTROMAGNETIC SPECTRUM, SKIMMING THE RADIO-SURF IN UNKNOWN FREQUENCIES, TOWARDS THE DYING PLANET EARTH.
THERE, DARKSEID, GOD OF APOKOLIPS, HAS MADE HIS THRONE. HE BELIEVES HE HAS WON THIS GAME BUT IN TRUTH, THERE CAN BE ONLY ONE ULTIMATE VICTOR.
AND WHERE MY SHADOW FALLS, ALL THINGS END.
ROCK OF AGES
PART FIVE
TWILIGHT OF THE GODS
WRITER-GRANT MORRISON PENCILLER-HOWARD PORTER INKER-JOHN DELL LETTERER-KEN LOPEZ
COLORIST-PAT GARRAHY ASSISTANT EDITOR-L.A. WILLIAMS
ASSOCIATE EDITOR-PETER TOMASI EDITOR-DAN RASPLER

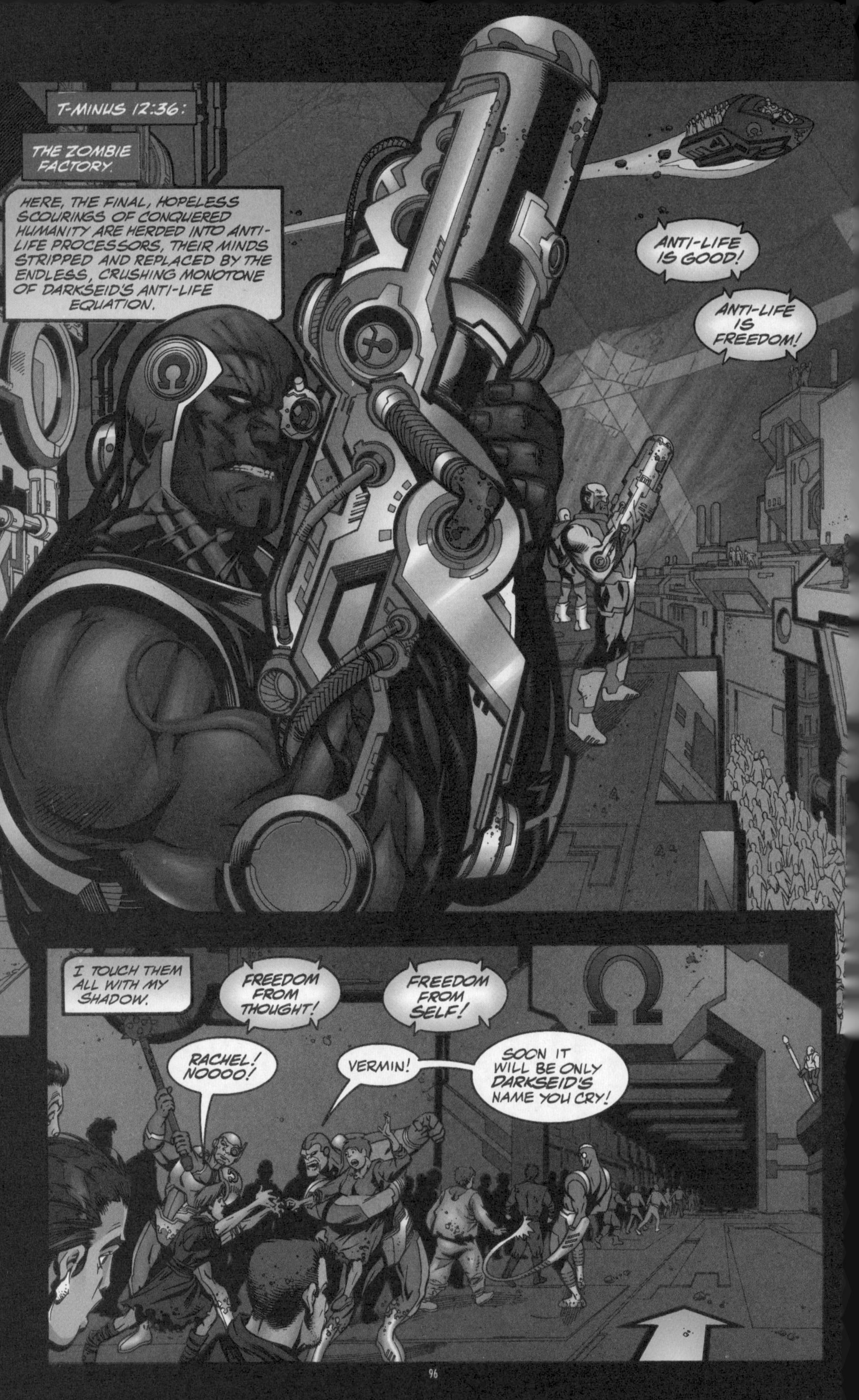
T-MINUS 12:36:
THE ZOMBIE FACTORY.
HERE, THE FINAL, HOPELESS SCOURINGS OF CONQUERED HUMANITY ARE HERDED INTO ANTI-LIFE PROCESSORS, THEIR MINDS STRIPPED AND REPLACED BY THE ENDLESS, CRUSHING MONOTONE OF DARKSEID'S ANTI-LIFE EQUATION.
ANTI-LIFE IS GOOD!
ANTI-LIFE IS FREEDOM!
I TOUCH THEM ALL WITH MY SHADOW.
FREEDOM FROM THOUGHT!
FREEDOM FROM SELF!
RACHEL! NOOOO!
VERMIN!
SOON IT WILL BE ONLY DARKSEID'S NAME YOU CRY!

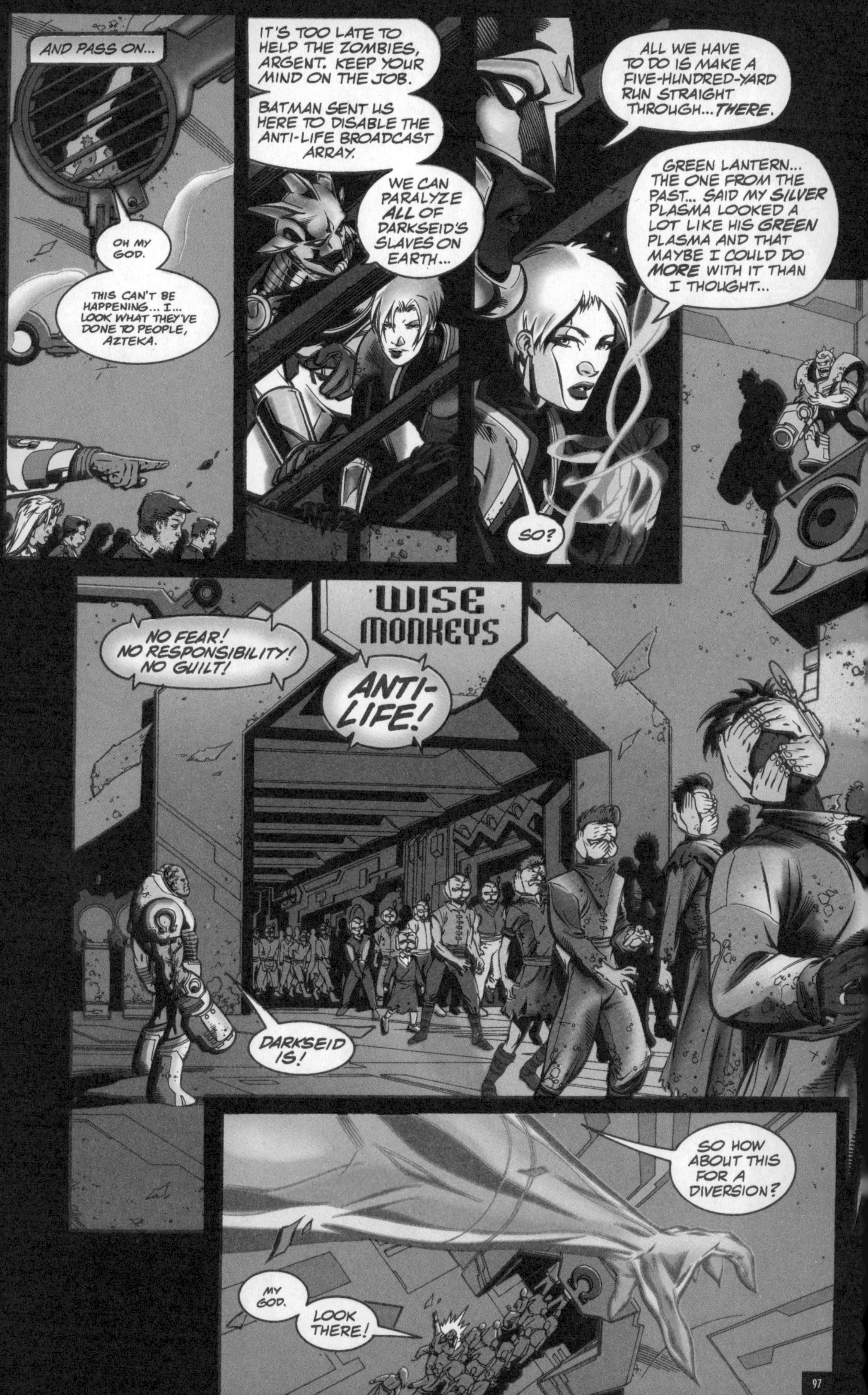
AND PASS ON...
OH MY GOD.
THIS CAN'T BE HAPPENING... I... LOOK WHAT THEY'VE DONE TO PEOPLE, AZTEKA.
IT'S TOO LATE TO HELP THE ZOMBIES, ARGENT. KEEP YOUR MIND ON THE JOB.
BATMAN SENT US HERE TO DISABLE THE ANTI-LIFE BROADCAST ARRAY.
WE CAN PARALYZE ALL OF DARKSEID'S SLAVES ON EARTH...
ALL WE HAVE TO DO IS MAKE A FIVE-HUNDRED-YARD RUN STRAIGHT THROUGH... THERE.
SO?
GREEN LANTERN... THE ONE FROM THE PAST... SAID MY SILVER PLASMA LOOKED A LOT LIKE HIS GREEN PLASMA AND THAT MAYBE I COULD DO MORE WITH IT THAN I THOUGHT...
WISE MONKEYS
NO FEAR! NO RESPONSIBILITY! NO GUILT!
ANTI-LIFE!
DARKSEID IS!
SO HOW ABOUT THIS FOR A DIVERSION?
MY GOD.
LOOK THERE!

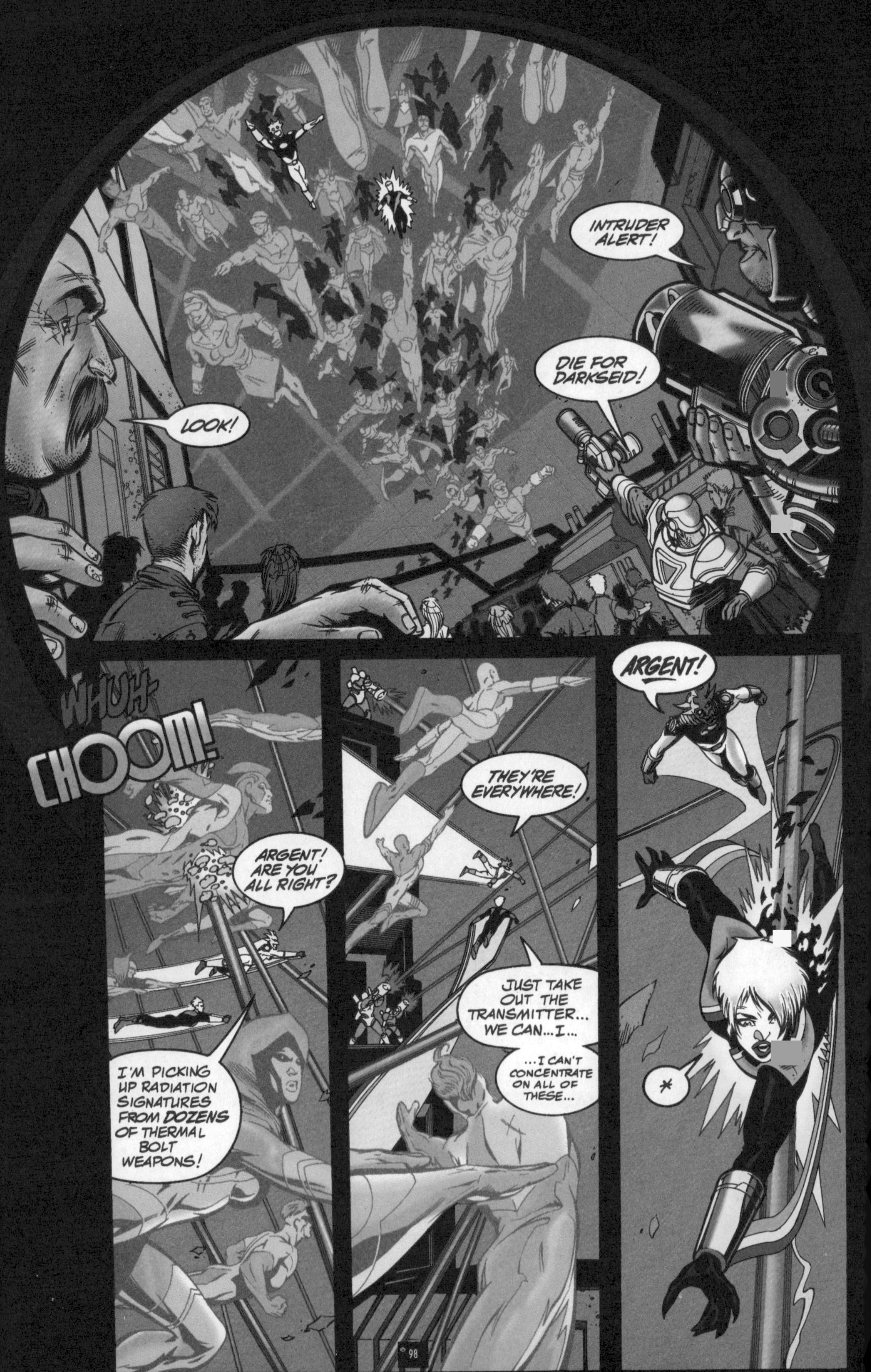
INTRUDER ALERT!
DIE FOR DARKSEID!
LOOK!
WHUH-CHOOM!
ARGENT! ARE YOU ALL RIGHT?
I'M PICKING UP RADIATION SIGNATURES FROM DOZENS OF THERMAL BOLT WEAPONS!
THEY'RE EVERYWHERE!
JUST TAKE OUT THE TRANSMITTER... WE CAN...I...
...I CAN'T CONCENTRATE ON ALL OF THESE...
ARGENT!
*

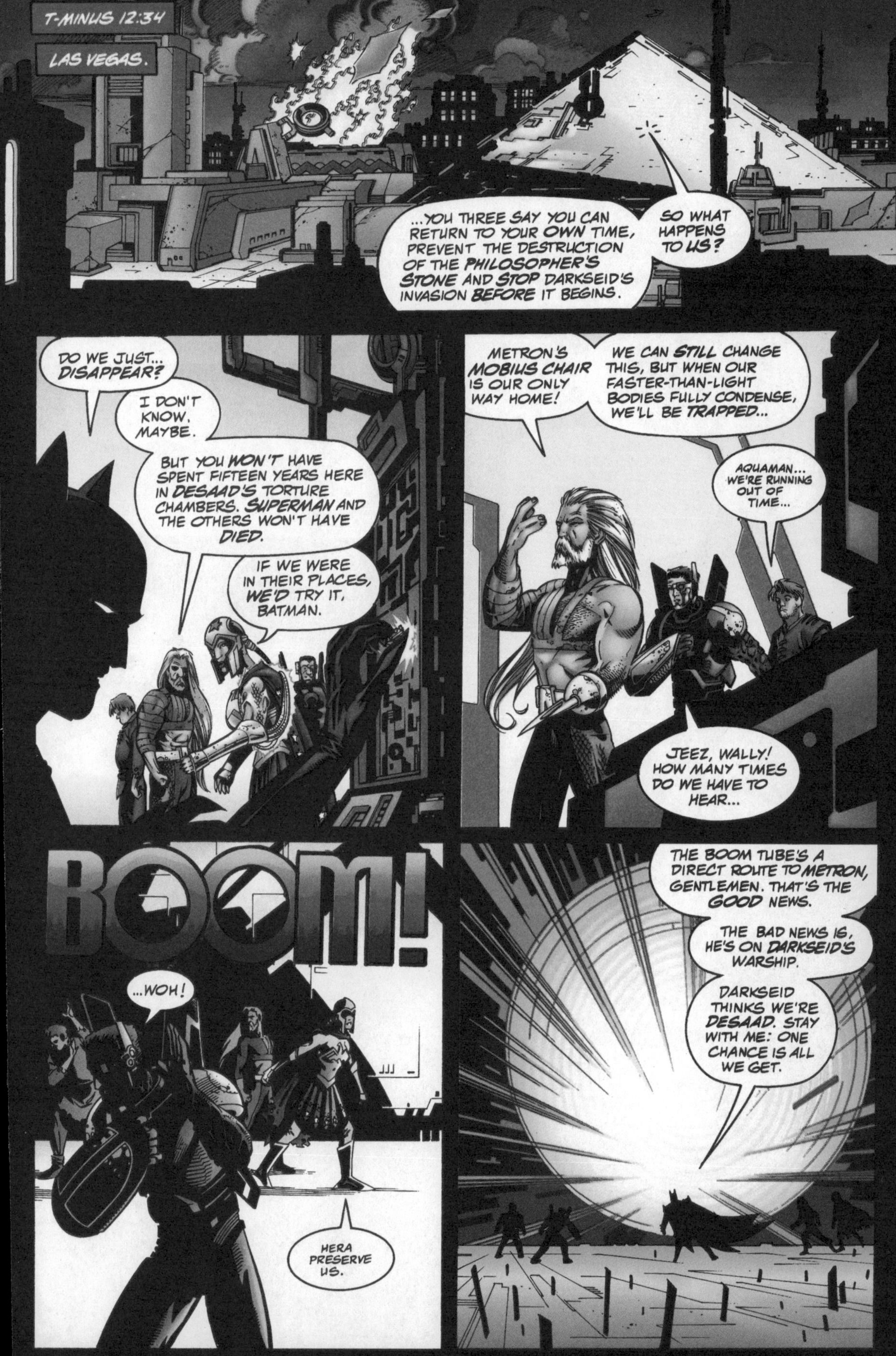
T-MINUS 12:34
LAS VEGAS.
...YOU THREE SAY YOU CAN RETURN TO YOUR OWN TIME, PREVENT THE DESTRUCTION OF THE PHILOSOPHER'S STONE AND STOP DARKSEID'S INVASION BEFORE IT BEGINS.
SO WHAT HAPPENS TO US?
DO WE JUST... DISAPPEAR?
I DON'T KNOW. MAYBE.
BUT YOU WON'T HAVE SPENT FIFTEEN YEARS HERE IN DESAAD'S TORTURE CHAMBERS. SUPERMAN AND THE OTHERS WON'T HAVE DIED.
IF WE WERE IN THEIR PLACES, WE'D TRY IT, BATMAN.
METRON'S MOBIUS CHAIR IS OUR ONLY WAY HOME!
WE CAN STILL CHANGE THIS, BUT WHEN OUR FASTER-THAN-LIGHT BODIES FULLY CONDENSE, WE'LL BE TRAPPED...
AQUAMAN... WE'RE RUNNING OUT OF TIME...
JEEZ, WALLY! HOW MANY TIMES DO WE HAVE TO HEAR...
BOOM!
...WOH!
HERA PRESERVE US.
THE BOOM TUBE'S A DIRECT ROUTE TO METRON, GENTLEMEN. THAT'S THE GOOD NEWS.
THE BAD NEWS IS, HE'S ON DARKSEID'S WARSHIP.
DARKSEID THINKS WE'RE DESAAD. STAY WITH ME: ONE CHANCE IS ALL WE GET.

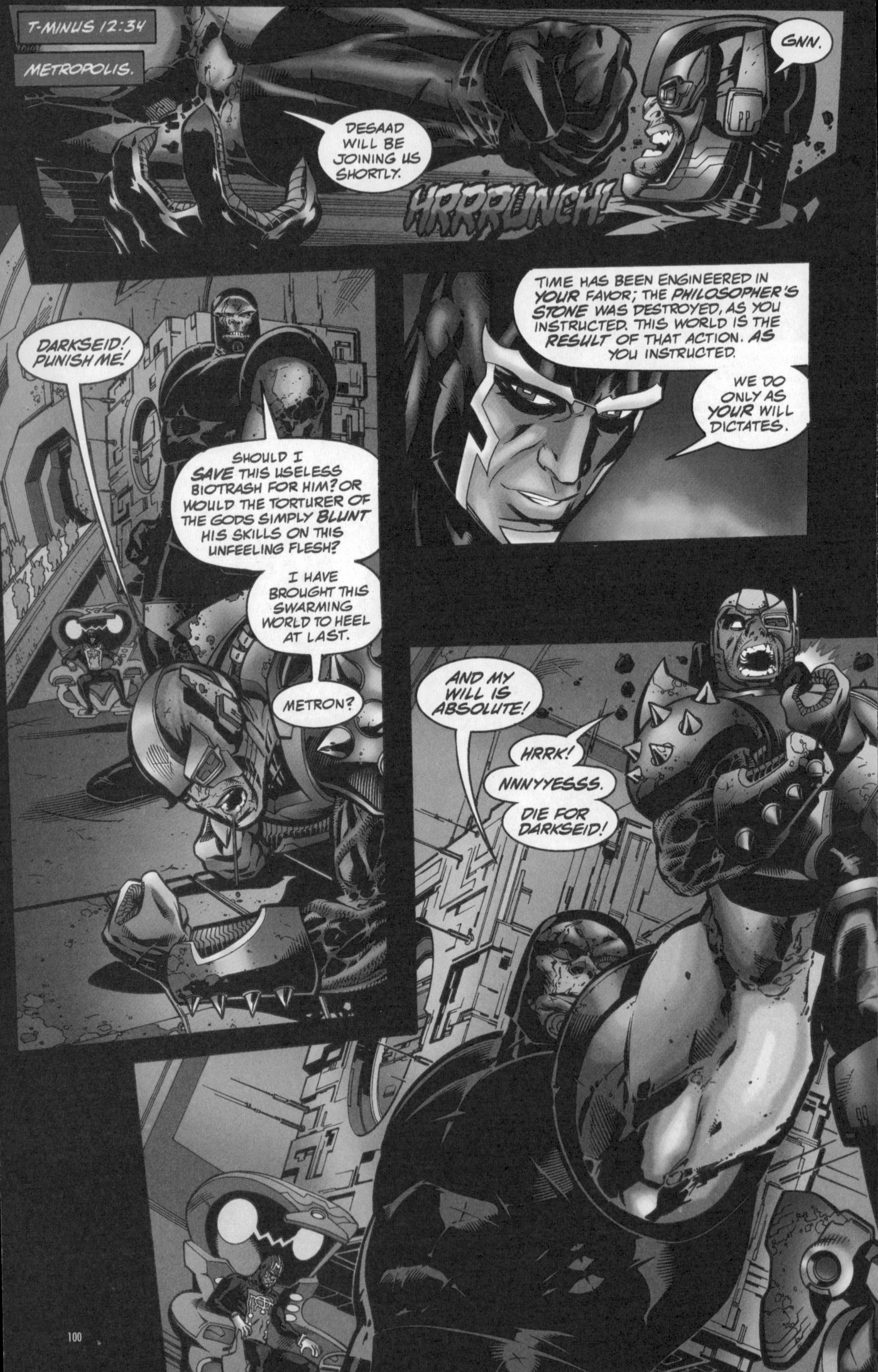
T-MINUS 12:34
METROPOLIS.
DESAAD WILL BE JOINING US SHORTLY.
GNN.
HRRRUNCH!
TIME HAS BEEN ENGINEERED IN YOUR FAVOR; THE PHILOSOPHER'S STONE WAS DESTROYED, AS YOU INSTRUCTED. THIS WORLD IS THE RESULT OF THAT ACTION. AS YOU INSTRUCTED.
WE DO ONLY AS YOUR WILL DICTATES.
DARKSEID! PUNISH ME!
SHOULD I SAVE THIS USELESS BIOTRASH FOR HIM? OR WOULD THE TORTURER OF THE GODS SIMPLY BLUNT HIS SKILLS ON THIS UNFEELING FLESH?
I HAVE BROUGHT THIS SWARMING WORLD TO HEEL AT LAST.
METRON?
AND MY WILL IS ABSOLUTE!
HRRK!
NNNYYESSS.
DIE FOR DARKSEID!

SEE WHAT I HAVE MADE!
IMAGINE WHAT IS YET TO COME!
LET ME DIE FOR DARKSEID!
I TAKE AWAY THEIR CONFUSION AND GIVE THEM OBEDIENCE.
I TAKE AWAY THEIR FEAR OF THEMSELVES AND GIVE THEM FEAR OF DARKSEID.
UNRULY CHILDREN- MUST BE TAKEN IN HAND BY THEIR GRANNY-
COME TO GRANDMOTHER BOX-
HAND ME YOUR CHILDREN-TO RULE WITH MY ROD-
I HAVE LIBERATED THEM FROM THE CHAOS OF INDECISION!
I HAVE GIVEN THEM ONE STRAIGHT PATH! ONE CLEAR PURPOSE!
ONE GOAL: TO DIE FOR DARKSEID!
BBBBBBOOOMM

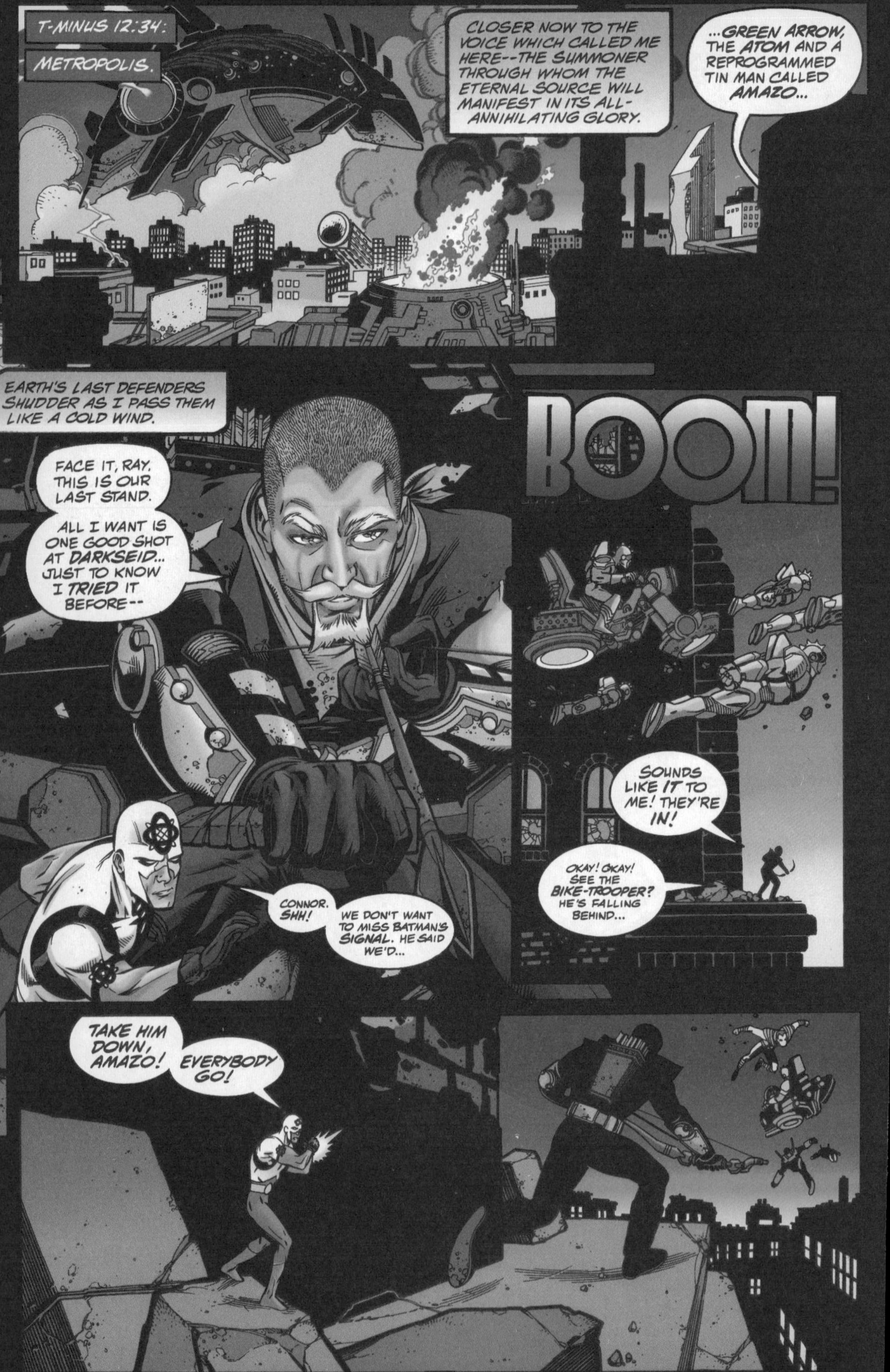
T-MINUS 12:34:
METROPOLIS.
CLOSER NOW TO THE VOICE WHICH CALLED ME HERE--THE SUMMONER THROUGH WHOM THE ETERNAL SOURCE WILL MANIFEST IN ITS ALL-ANNIHILATING GLORY.
...GREEN ARROW, THE ATOM AND A REPROGRAMMED TIN MAN CALLED AMAZO...
EARTH'S LAST DEFENDERS SHUDDER AS I PASS THEM LIKE A COLD WIND.
FACE IT, RAY. THIS IS OUR LAST STAND.
ALL I WANT IS ONE GOOD SHOT AT DARKSEID... JUST TO KNOW I TRIED IT BEFORE--
CONNOR. SHH!
WE DON'T WANT TO MISS BATMAN'S SIGNAL. HE SAID WE'D...
BOOM!
SOUNDS LIKE IT TO ME! THEY'RE IN!
OKAY! OKAY! SEE THE BIKE-TROOPER? HE'S FALLING BEHIND...
TAKE HIM DOWN, AMAZO!
EVERYBODY GO!

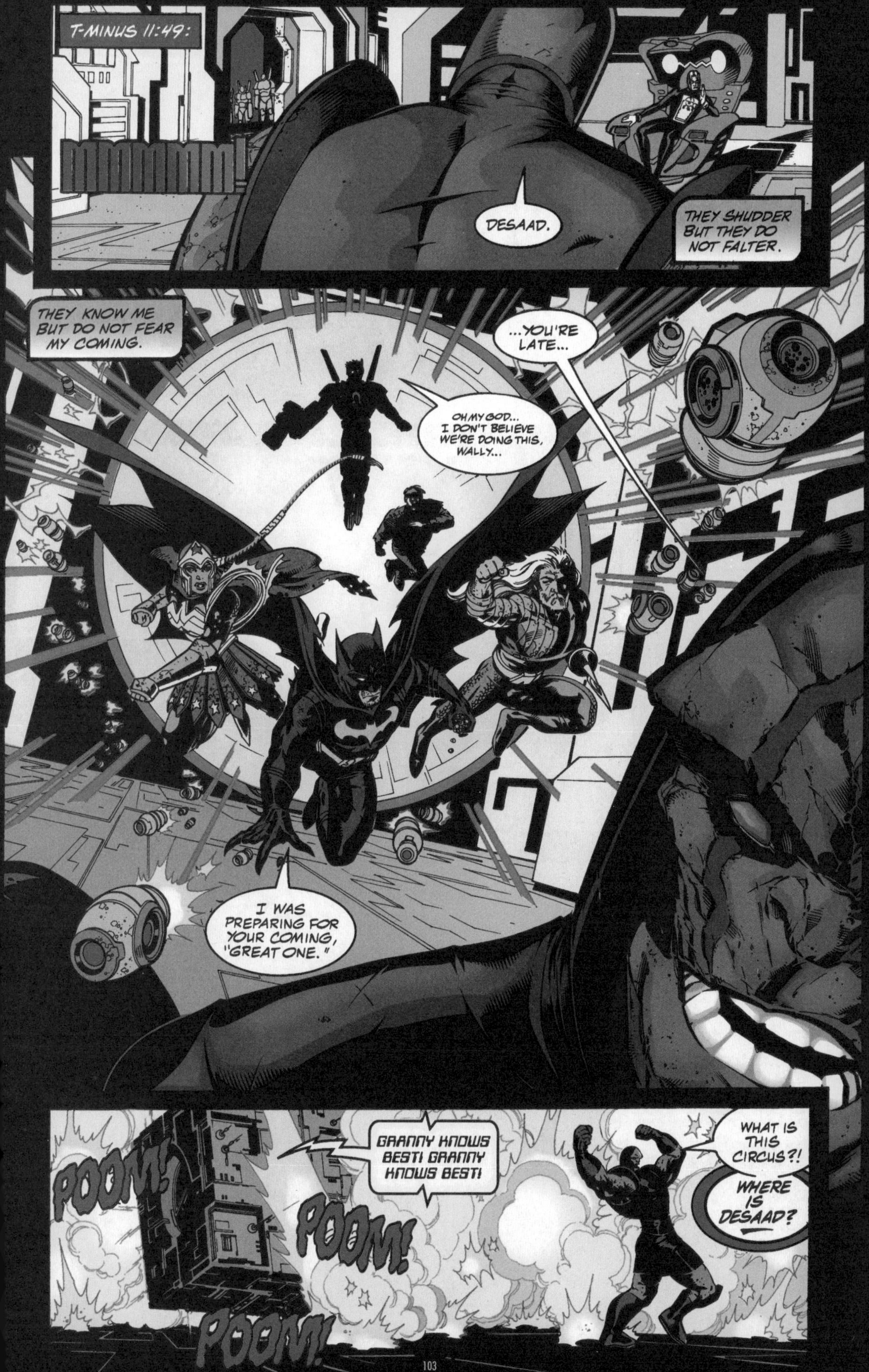
T-MINUS 11:49:
MMMMMM!
DESAAD.
THEY SHUDDER BUT THEY DO NOT FALTER.
THEY KNOW ME BUT DO NOT FEAR MY COMING.
...YOU'RE LATE...
OH MY GOD... I DON'T BELIEVE WE'RE DOING THIS, WALLY...
I WAS PREPARING FOR YOUR COMING, "GREAT ONE."
POOM!
GRANNY KNOWS BEST! GRANNY KNOWS BEST!
POOM!
WHAT IS THIS CIRCUS?!
WHERE IS DESAAD?
POOM!

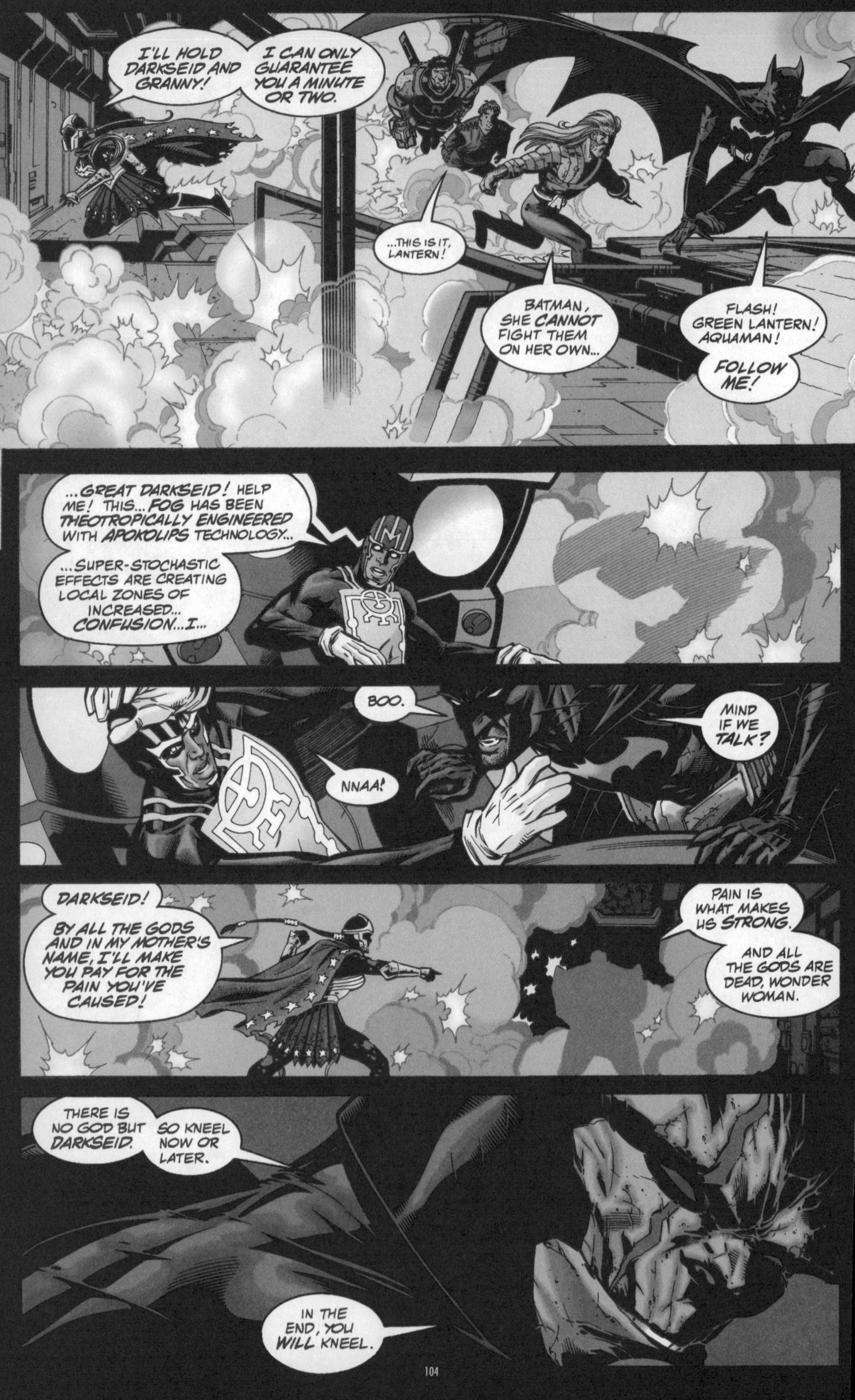
I'LL HOLD DARKSEID AND GRANNY!
I CAN ONLY GUARANTEE YOU A MINUTE OR TWO.
...THIS IS IT, LANTERN!
BATMAN, SHE CANNOT FIGHT THEM ON HER OWN...
FLASH! GREEN LANTERN! AQUAMAN!
FOLLOW ME!
...GREAT DARKSEID! HELP ME! THIS... FOG HAS BEEN THEOTROPICALLY ENGINEERED WITH APOKOLIPS TECHNOLOGY...
...SUPER-STOCHASTIC EFFECTS ARE CREATING LOCAL ZONES OF INCREASED... CONFUSION...I...
BOO.
MIND IF WE TALK?
NNAA!
DARKSEID!
BY ALL THE GODS AND IN MY MOTHER'S NAME, I'LL MAKE YOU PAY FOR THE PAIN YOU'VE CAUSED!
PAIN IS WHAT MAKES US STRONG.
AND ALL THE GODS ARE DEAD, WONDER WOMAN.
THERE IS NO GOD BUT DARKSEID.
SO KNEEL NOW OR LATER.
IN THE END, YOU WILL KNEEL.

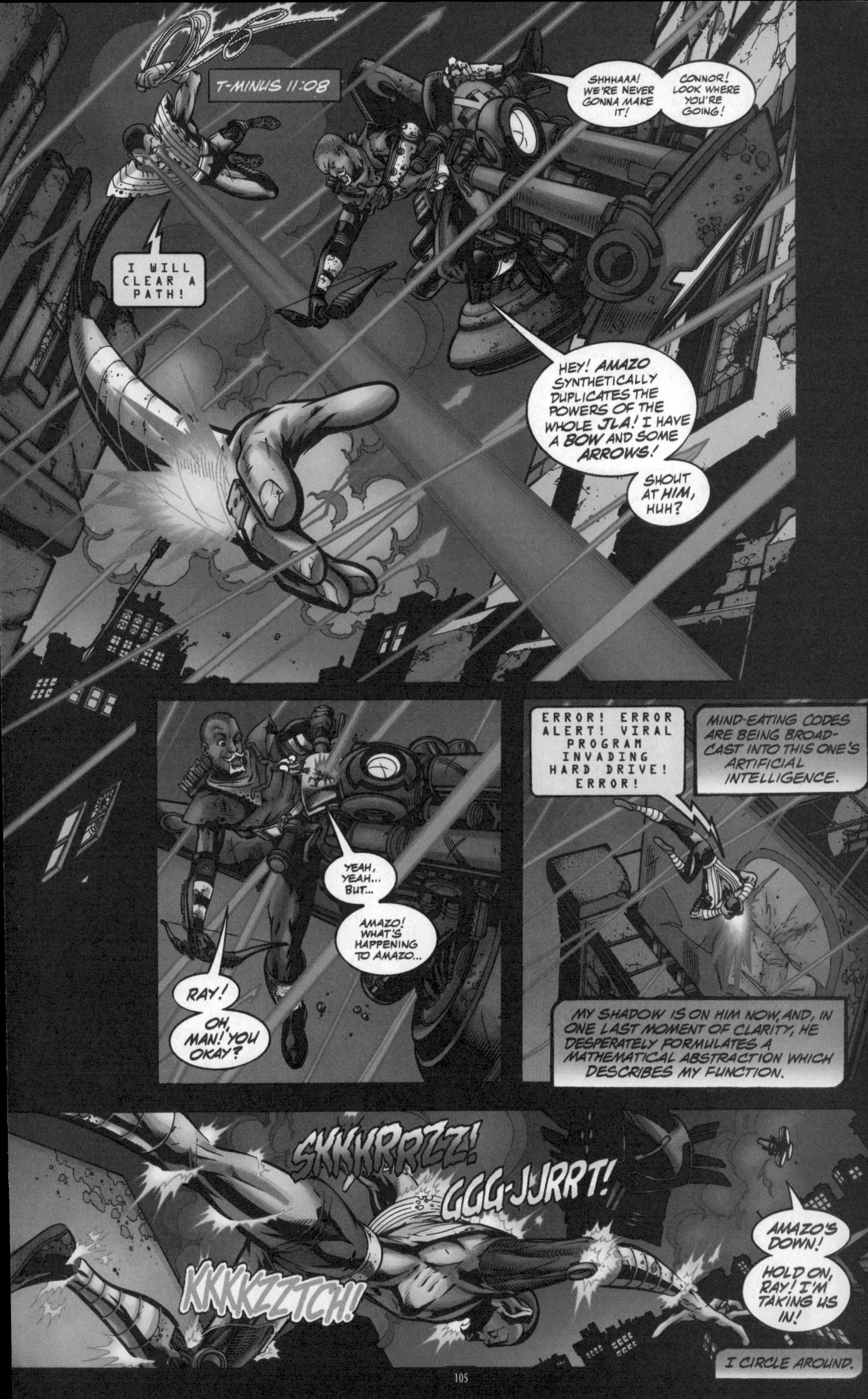
T-MINUS 11:08
SHHHAAA! WE'RE NEVER GONNA MAKE IT!
CONNOR! LOOK WHERE YOU'RE GOING!
I WILL CLEAR A PATH!
HEY! AMAZO SYNTHETICALLY DUPLICATES THE POWERS OF THE WHOLE JLA! I HAVE A BOW AND SOME ARROWS!
SHOUT AT HIM, HUH?
YEAH, YEAH... BUT...
AMAZO! WHAT'S HAPPENING TO AMAZO...
RAY!
OH, MAN! YOU OKAY?
ERROR! ERROR ALERT! VIRAL PROGRAM INVADING HARD DRIVE! ERROR!
MIND-EATING CODES ARE BEING BROAD-CAST INTO THIS ONE'S ARTIFICIAL INTELLIGENCE.
MY SHADOW IS ON HIM NOW, AND, IN ONE LAST MOMENT OF CLARITY, HE DESPERATELY FORMULATES A MATHEMATICAL ABSTRACTION WHICH DESCRIBES MY FUNCTION.
SKKKRRZZZ!
GGG-JJRRT!
KKKKZZZTCH!
AMAZO'S DOWN!
HOLD ON, RAY! I'M TAKING US IN!
I CIRCLE AROUND.

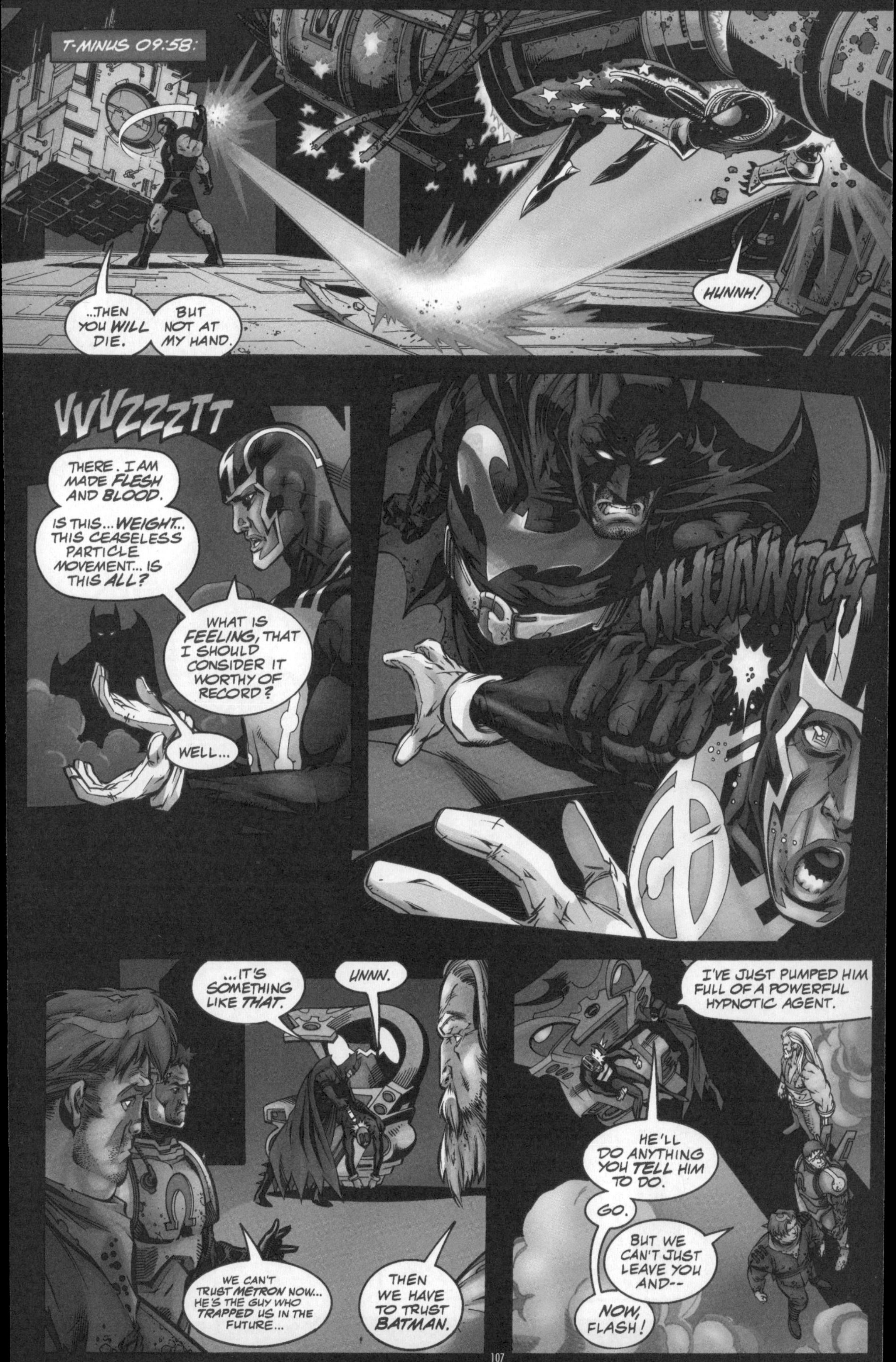
T-MINUS 09:58:
...THEN YOU WILL DIE.
BUT NOT AT MY HAND.
HUNNH!
VVVZZZTT
THERE. I AM MADE FLESH AND BLOOD.
IS THIS... WEIGHT... THIS CEASELESS PARTICLE MOVEMENT... IS THIS ALL?
WHAT IS FEELING, THAT I SHOULD CONSIDER IT WORTHY OF RECORD?
WELL...
WHUNNTCH
...IT'S SOMETHING LIKE THAT.
UNNN.
WE CAN'T TRUST METRON NOW... HE'S THE GUY WHO TRAPPED US IN THE FUTURE...
THEN WE HAVE TO TRUST BATMAN.
I'VE JUST PUMPED HIM FULL OF A POWERFUL HYPNOTIC AGENT.
HE'LL DO ANYTHING YOU TELL HIM TO DO.
GO.
BUT WE CAN'T JUST LEAVE YOU AND--
NOW, FLASH!

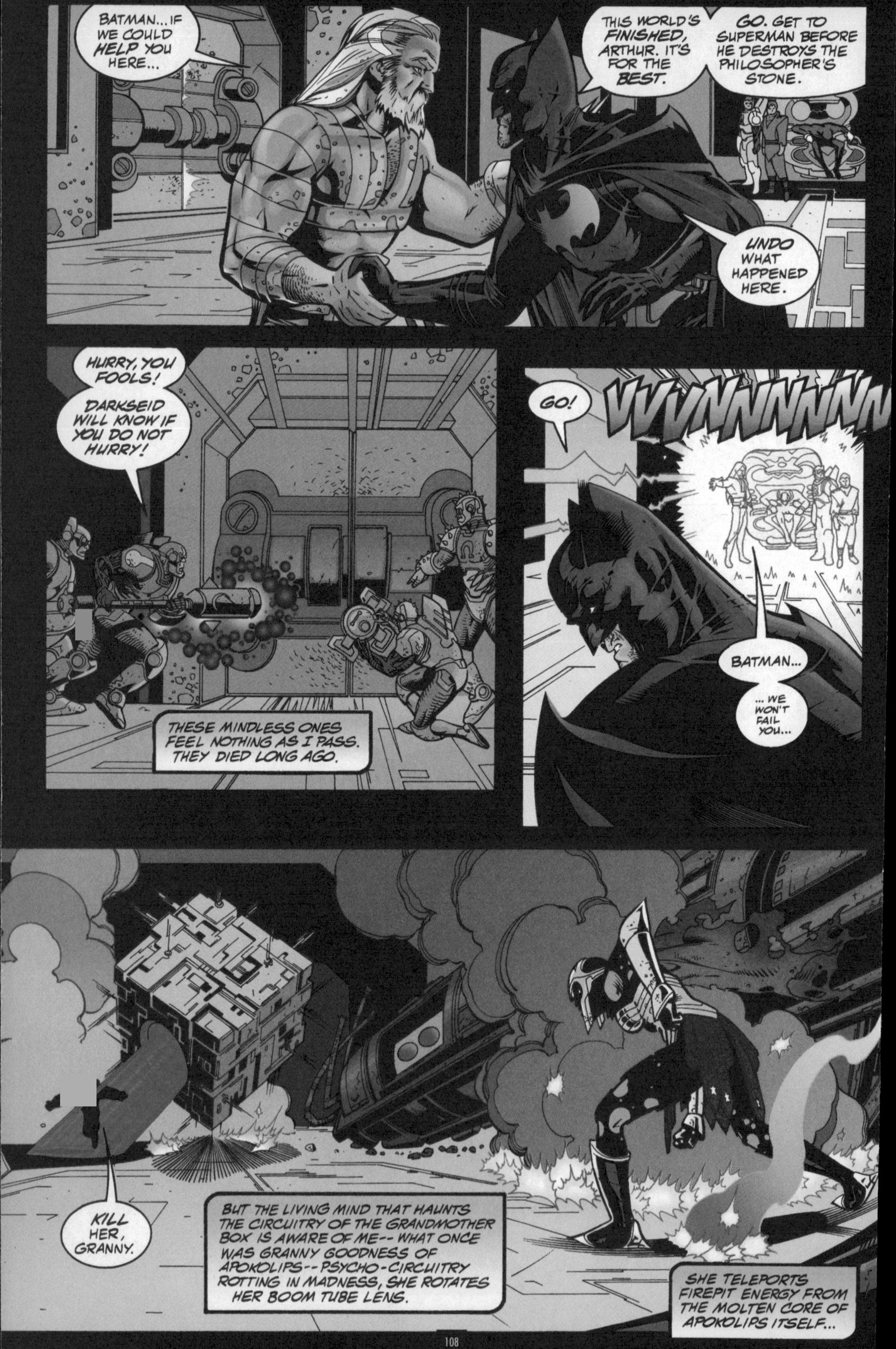
BATMAN... IF WE COULD HELP YOU HERE...
THIS WORLD'S FINISHED, ARTHUR. IT'S FOR THE BEST.
GO. GET TO SUPERMAN BEFORE HE DESTROYS THE PHILOSOPHER'S STONE.
UNDO WHAT HAPPENED HERE.
HURRY, YOU FOOLS!
DARKSEID WILL KNOW IF YOU DO NOT HURRY!
THESE MINDLESS ONES FEEL NOTHING AS I PASS. THEY DIED LONG AGO.
GO!
VVVNNNNNNN
BATMAN...
... WE WON'T FAIL YOU...
KILL HER, GRANNY.
BUT THE LIVING MIND THAT HAUNTS THE CIRCUITRY OF THE GRANDMOTHER BOX IS AWARE OF ME-- WHAT ONCE WAS GRANNY GOODNESS OF APOKOLIPS-- PSYCHO-CIRCUITRY ROTTING IN MADNESS, SHE ROTATES HER BOOM TUBE LENS.
SHE TELEPORTS FIREPIT ENERGY FROM THE MOLTEN CORE OF APOKOLIPS ITSELF...

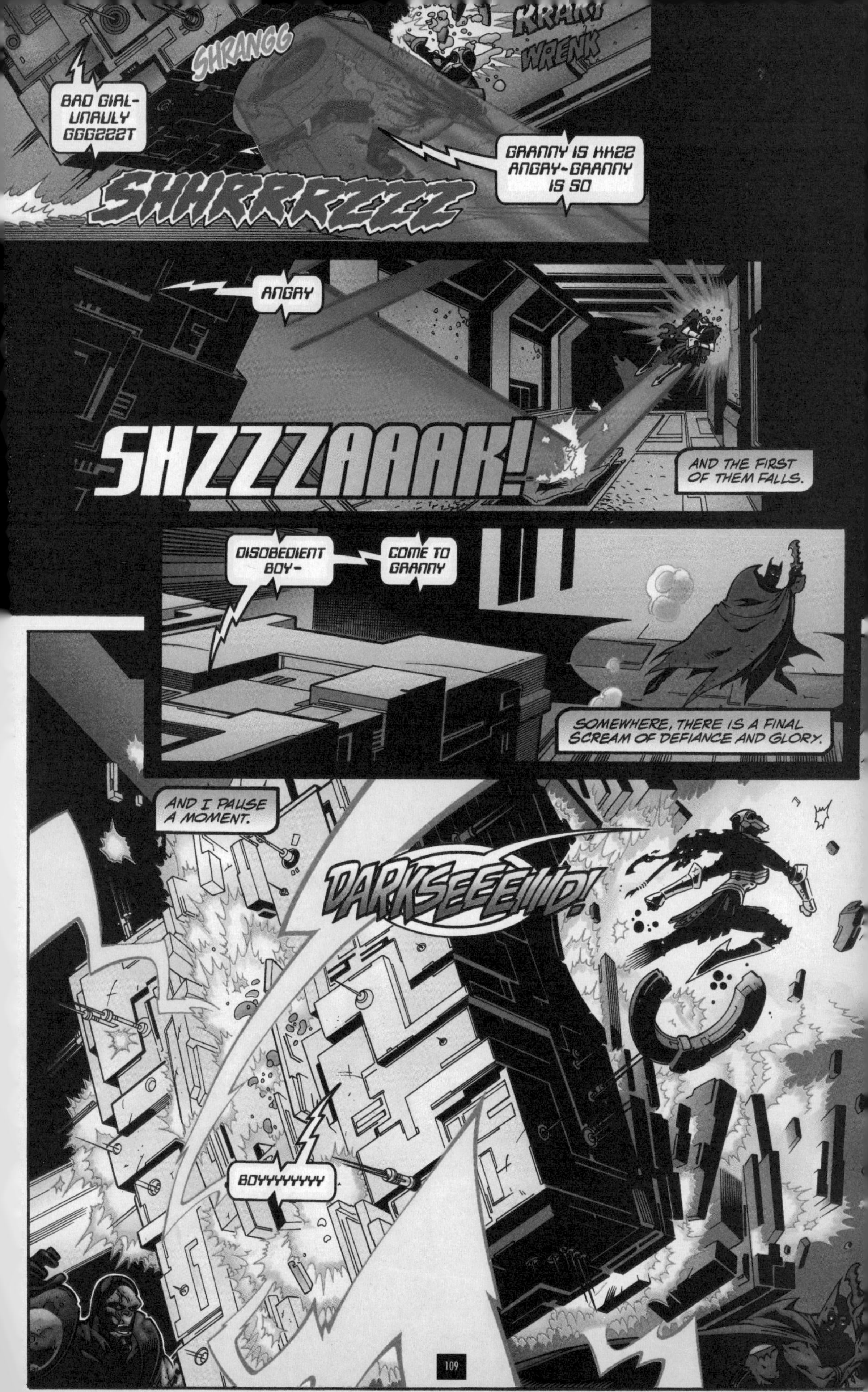
KRAK!
WRENK
SHRANGG
BAD GIRL-
UNRULY
GGGZZZT
GRANNY IS KKZZ
ANGRY-GRANNY
IS SO
SHHRRRZZZZ
ANGRY
SHZZZAAAK!
AND THE FIRST
OF THEM FALLS.
DISOBEDIENT
BOY-
COME TO
GRANNY
SOMEWHERE, THERE IS A FINAL
SCREAM OF DEFIANCE AND GLORY.
AND I PAUSE
A MOMENT.
DARKSEEEIIID!
BOYYYYYYYY

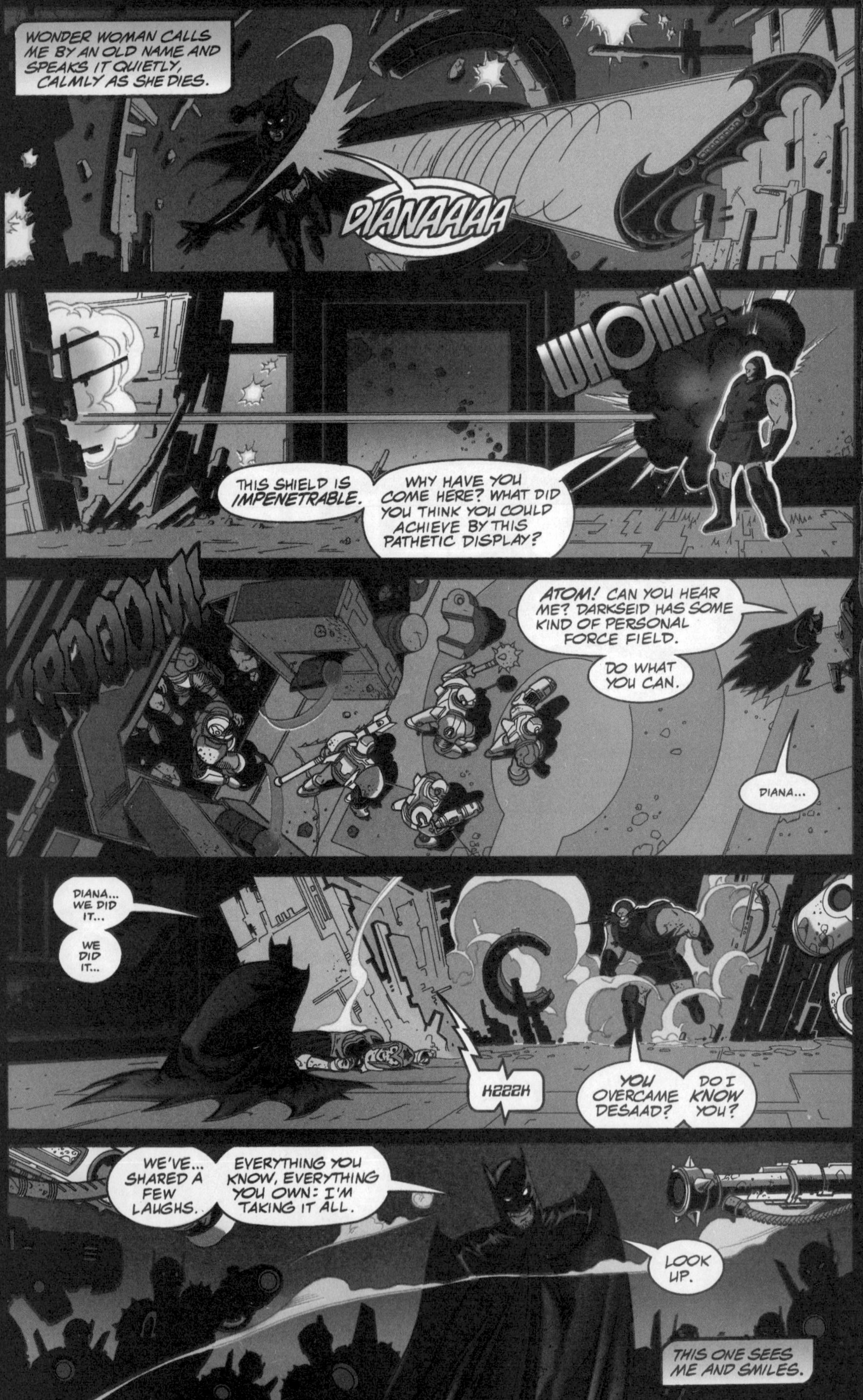
WONDER WOMAN CALLS ME BY AN OLD NAME AND SPEAKS IT QUIETLY, CALMLY AS SHE DIES.
DIANAAAA
WHOMP!
THIS SHIELD IS IMPENETRABLE.
WHY HAVE YOU COME HERE? WHAT DID YOU THINK YOU COULD ACHIEVE BY THIS PATHETIC DISPLAY?
ATOM! CAN YOU HEAR ME? DARKSEID HAS SOME KIND OF PERSONAL FORCE FIELD.
DO WHAT YOU CAN.
DIANA...
DIANA... WE DID IT...
WE DID IT...
KZZZH
YOU OVERCAME DESAAD?
DO I KNOW YOU?
WE'VE... SHARED A FEW LAUGHS.
EVERYTHING YOU KNOW, EVERYTHING YOU OWN: I'M TAKING IT ALL.
LOOK UP.
THIS ONE SEES ME AND SMILES.

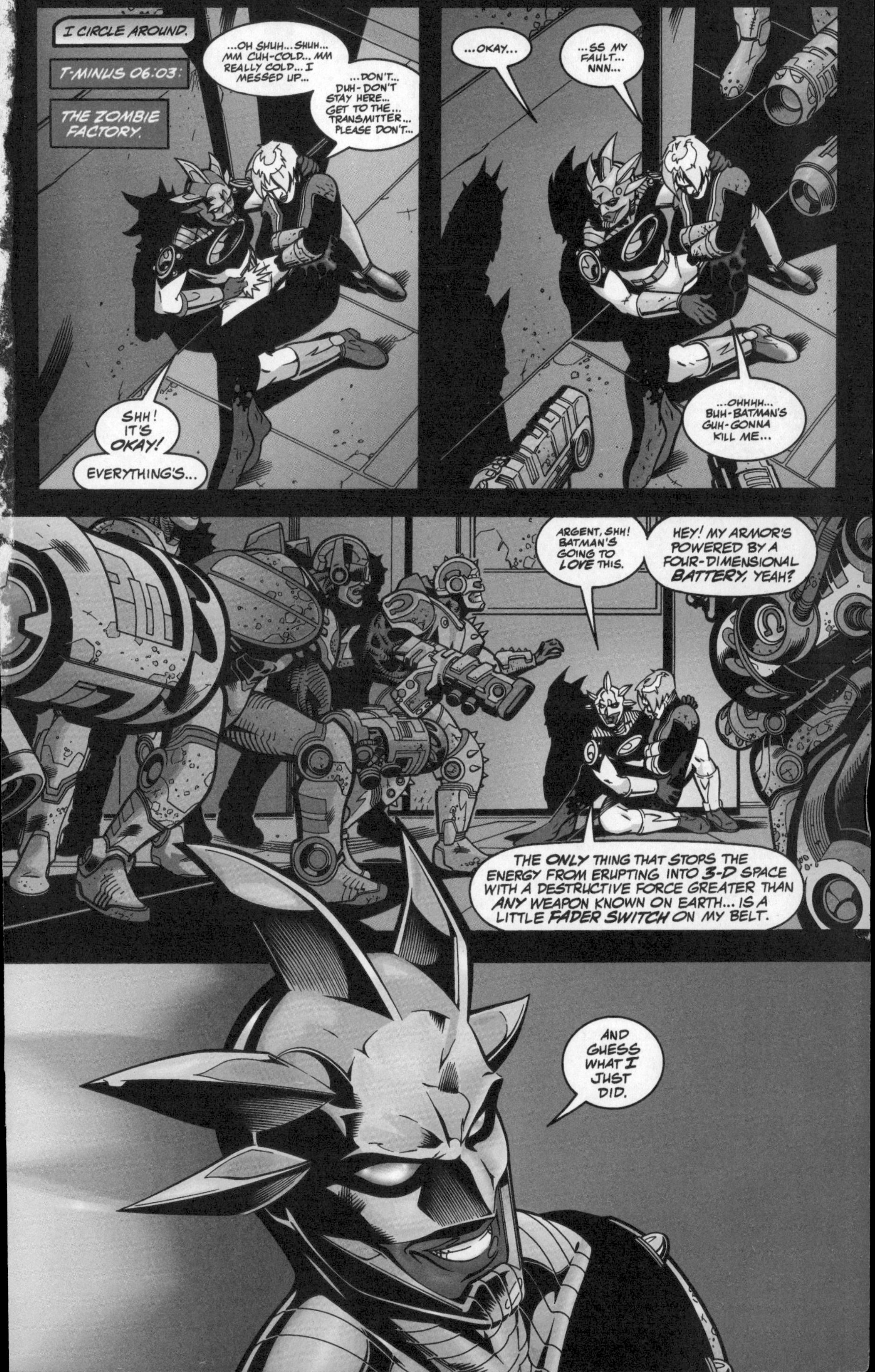

I CIRCLE AROUND.
T-MINUS 06:03:
THE ZOMBIE FACTORY.
...OH SHUH... SHUH... MM CUH-COLD... MM REALLY COLD... I MESSED UP...
...DON'T... DUH-DON'T STAY HERE... GET TO THE... TRANSMITTER... PLEASE DON'T...
SHH! IT'S OKAY!
EVERYTHING'S...
...OKAY...
...SS MY FAULT... NNN...
...OHHHH... BUH-BATMAN'S GUH-GONNA KILL ME...
ARGENT, SHH! BATMAN'S GOING TO LOVE THIS.
HEY! MY ARMOR'S POWERED BY A FOUR-DIMENSIONAL BATTERY, YEAH?
THE ONLY THING THAT STOPS THE ENERGY FROM ERUPTING INTO 3-D SPACE WITH A DESTRUCTIVE FORCE GREATER THAN ANY WEAPON KNOWN ON EARTH... IS A LITTLE FADER SWITCH ON MY BELT.
AND GUESS WHAT I JUST DID.

I CIRCLE AROUND.

STAY OUT

NO. MY ZOMBIE FACTORY.

KUH

KKKK

LOOK!

AND COME AT LAST TO THE SUMMONER.

EVEN SHORN OF HIS DIVINITY, I RECOGNIZE HIM.

THE MOON'S FEATURES BLUR. MY WORK IS OVER SWIFTLY, BEFORE THE DUST SETTLES.

LOOK AT THE MOON!

WE ARE OLD COMPANIONS.

AND ORION HAS BEEN BUSY AT HIS ART TOO.

THE END IS HERE.

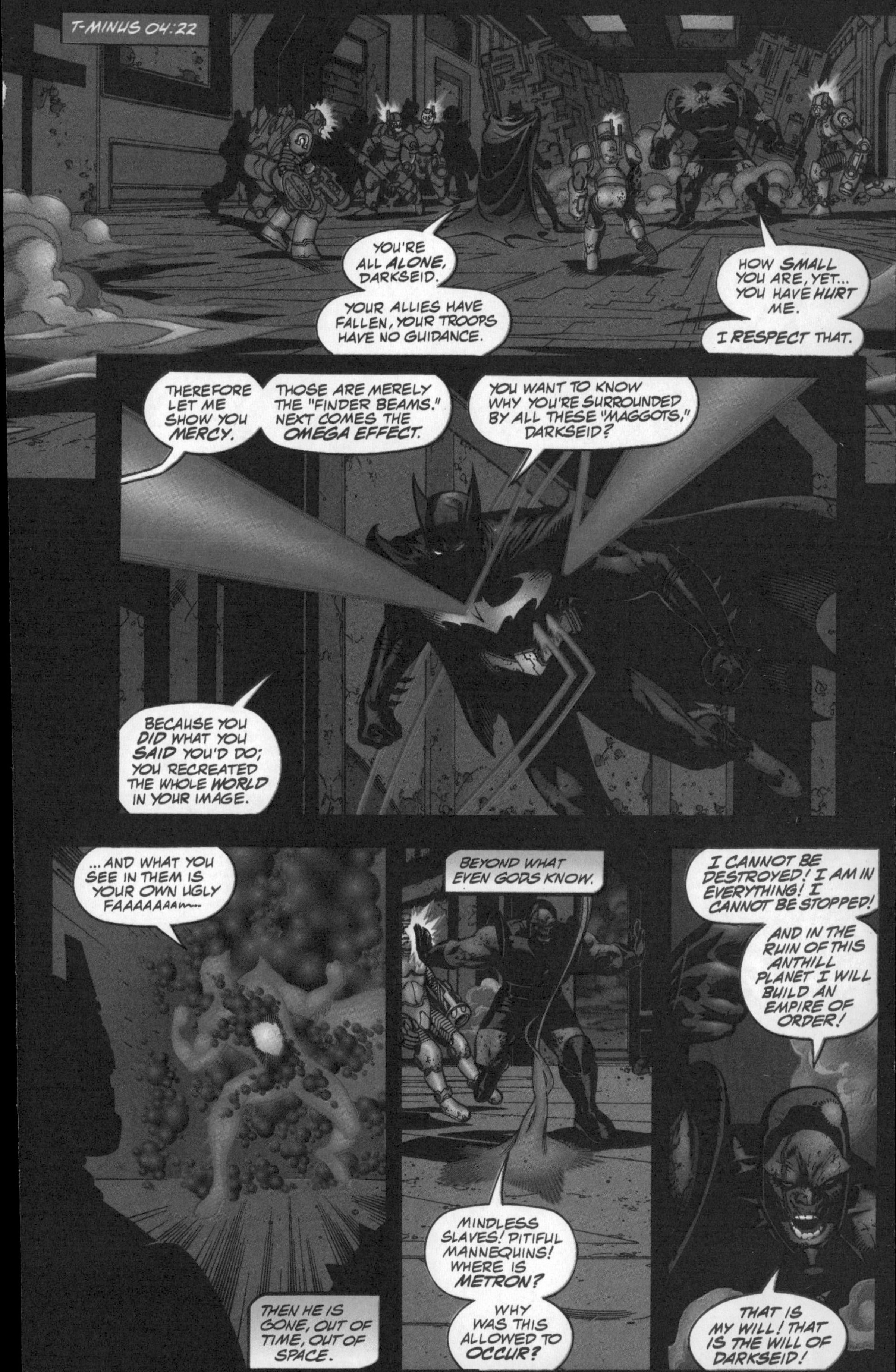
T-MINUS 04:22
YOU'RE ALL ALONE, DARKSEID.
YOUR ALLIES HAVE FALLEN, YOUR TROOPS HAVE NO GUIDANCE.
HOW SMALL YOU ARE, YET... YOU HAVE HURT ME.
I RESPECT THAT.
THEREFORE LET ME SHOW YOU MERCY.
THOSE ARE MERELY THE "FINDER BEAMS." NEXT COMES THE OMEGA EFFECT.
YOU WANT TO KNOW WHY YOU'RE SURROUNDED BY ALL THESE "MAGGOTS," DARKSEID?
BECAUSE YOU DID WHAT YOU SAID YOU'D DO; YOU RECREATED THE WHOLE WORLD IN YOUR IMAGE.
...AND WHAT YOU SEE IN THEM IS YOUR OWN UGLY FAAAAAAAm...
THEN HE IS GONE, OUT OF TIME, OUT OF SPACE.
BEYOND WHAT EVEN GODS KNOW.
MINDLESS SLAVES! PITIFUL MANNEQUINS! WHERE IS METRON?
WHY WAS THIS ALLOWED TO OCCUR?
I CANNOT BE DESTROYED! I AM IN EVERYTHING! I CANNOT BE STOPPED!
AND IN THE RUIN OF THIS ANTHILL PLANET I WILL BUILD AN EMPIRE OF ORDER!
THAT IS MY WILL! THAT IS THE WILL OF DARKSEID!

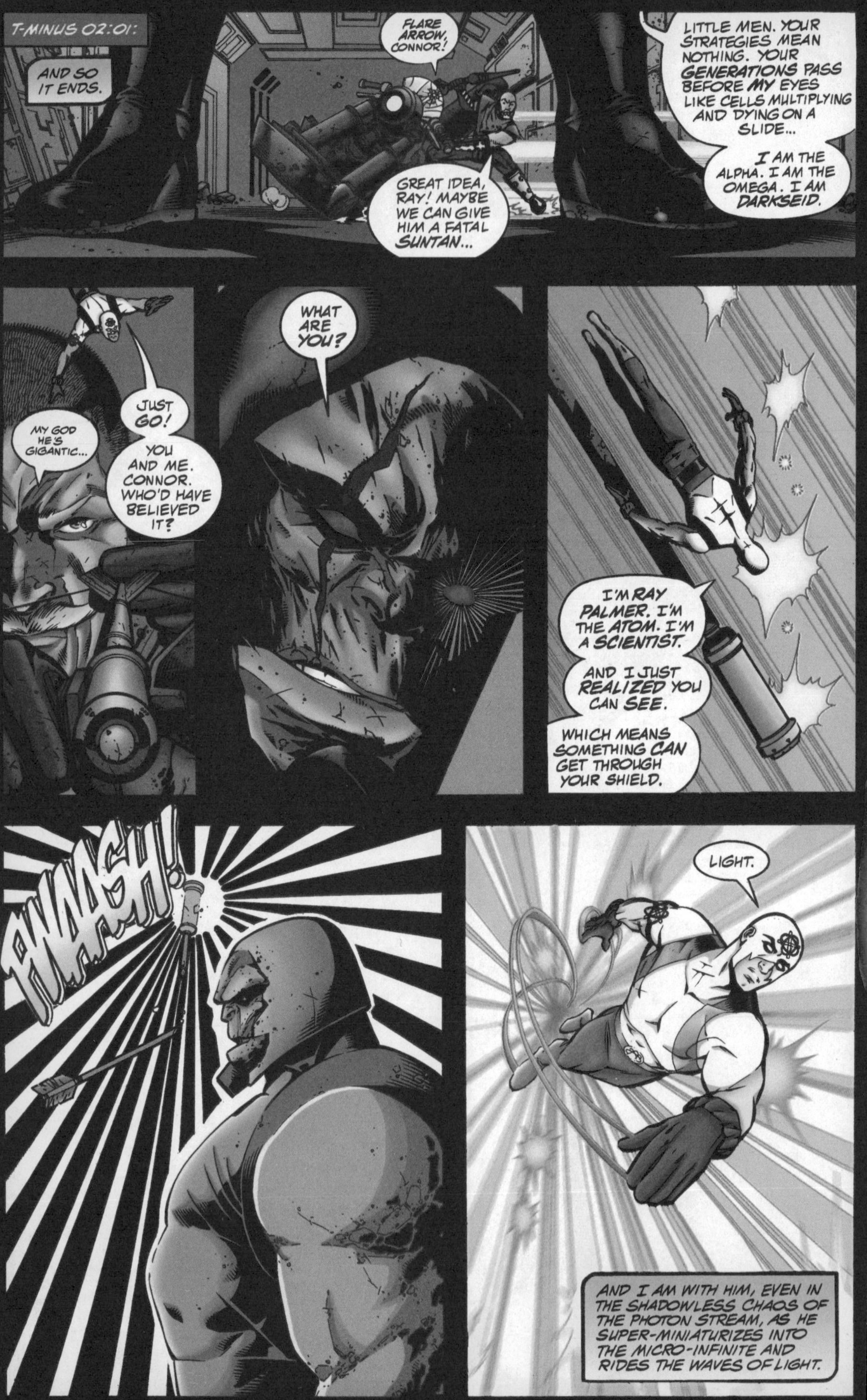
T-MINUS 02:01:
AND SO IT ENDS.
FLARE ARROW, CONNOR!
GREAT IDEA, RAY! MAYBE WE CAN GIVE HIM A FATAL SUNTAN...
LITTLE MEN. YOUR STRATEGIES MEAN NOTHING. YOUR GENERATIONS PASS BEFORE MY EYES LIKE CELLS MULTIPLYING AND DYING ON A SLIDE...
I AM THE ALPHA. I AM THE OMEGA. I AM DARKSEID.
MY GOD HE'S GIGANTIC...
JUST GO!
YOU AND ME. CONNOR. WHO'D HAVE BELIEVED IT?
WHAT ARE YOU?
I'M RAY PALMER. I'M THE ATOM. I'M A SCIENTIST.
AND I JUST REALIZED YOU CAN SEE.
WHICH MEANS SOMETHING CAN GET THROUGH YOUR SHIELD.
PHAASH!
LIGHT.
AND I AM WITH HIM, EVEN IN THE SHADOWLESS CHAOS OF THE PHOTON STREAM, AS HE SUPER-MINIATURIZES INTO THE MICRO-INFINITE AND RIDES THE WAVES OF LIGHT.

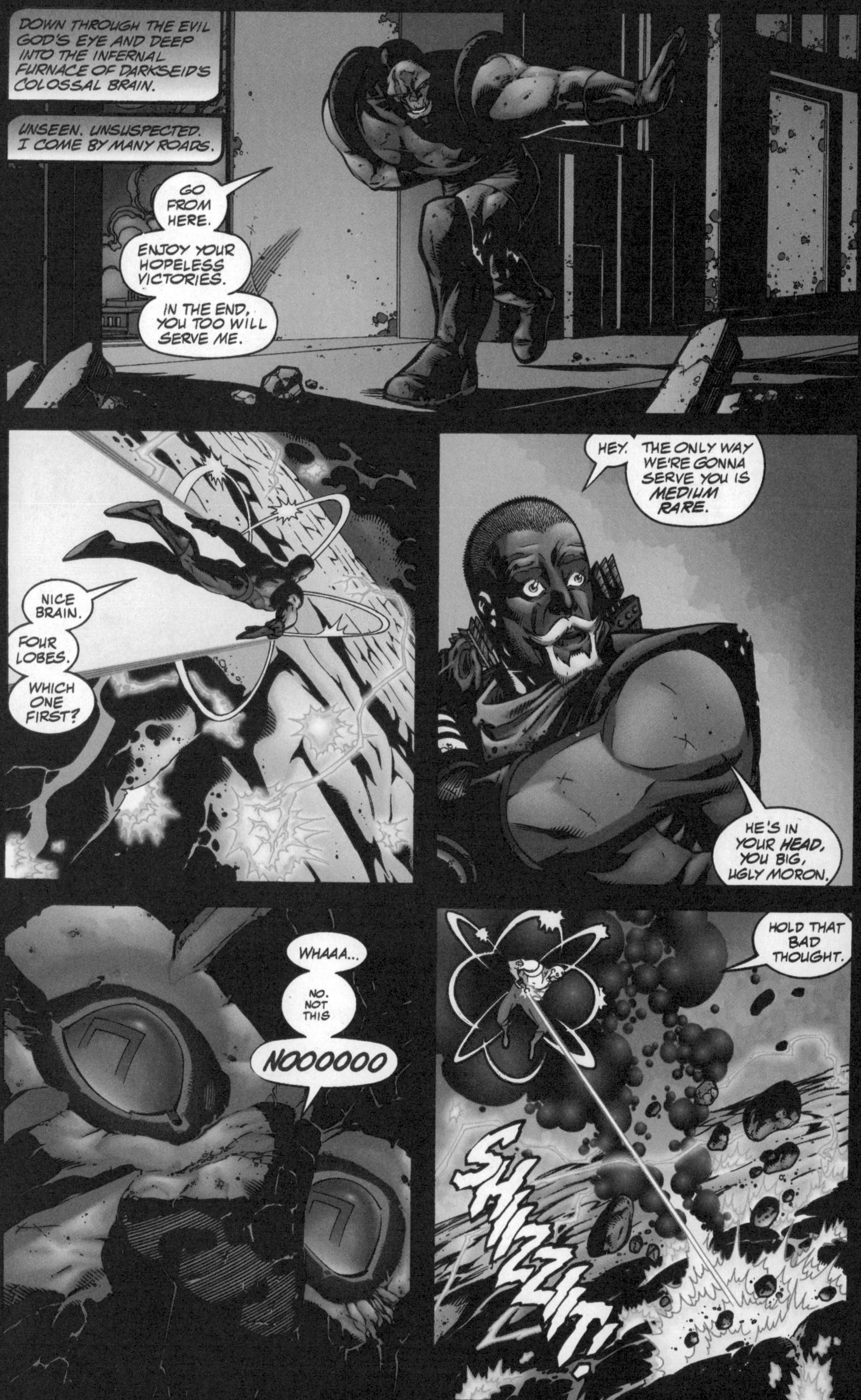
DOWN THROUGH THE EVIL GOD'S EYE AND DEEP INTO THE INFERNAL FURNACE OF DARKSEID'S COLOSSAL BRAIN.
UNSEEN. UNSUSPECTED. I COME BY MANY ROADS.
GO FROM HERE.
ENJOY YOUR HOPELESS VICTORIES.
IN THE END, YOU TOO WILL SERVE ME.
NICE BRAIN.
FOUR LOBES.
WHICH ONE FIRST?
HEY.
THE ONLY WAY WE'RE GONNA SERVE YOU IS MEDIUM RARE.
HE'S IN YOUR HEAD, YOU BIG, UGLY MORON.
WHAAA...
NO. NOT THIS
NOOOOOO
HOLD THAT BAD THOUGHT.
SHHZZIIT!

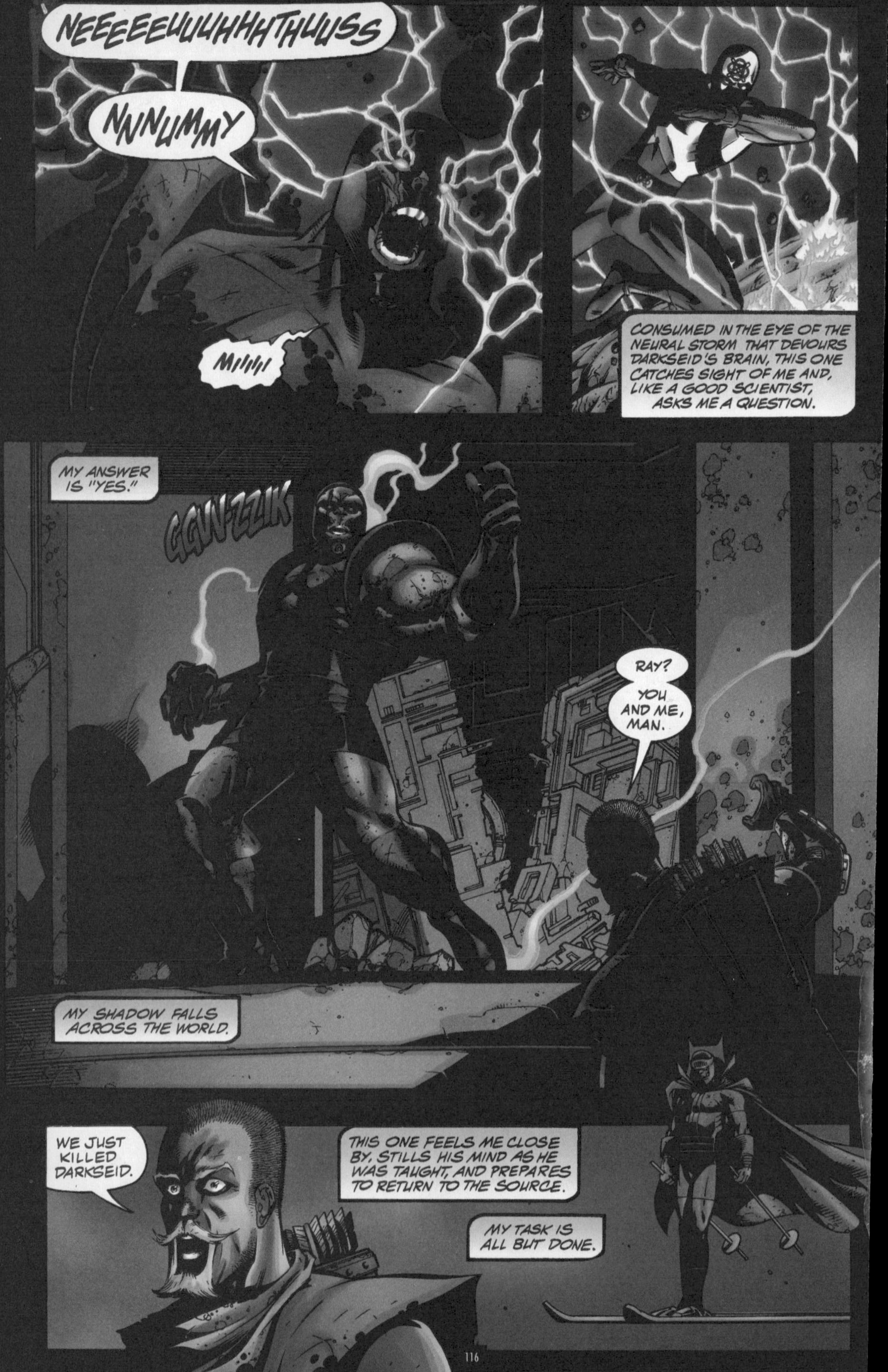
NEEEEEUUUHHHTHUUSS
NNNUMMY
MIIII
CONSUMED IN THE EYE OF THE NEURAL STORM THAT DEVOURS DARKSEID'S BRAIN, THIS ONE CATCHES SIGHT OF ME AND, LIKE A GOOD SCIENTIST, ASKS ME A QUESTION.
MY ANSWER IS "YES."
GGWZZIK
RAY?
YOU AND ME, MAN.
MY SHADOW FALLS ACROSS THE WORLD.
WE JUST KILLED DARKSEID.
THIS ONE FEELS ME CLOSE BY, STILLS HIS MIND AS HE WAS TAUGHT, AND PREPARES TO RETURN TO THE SOURCE.
MY TASK IS ALL BUT DONE.

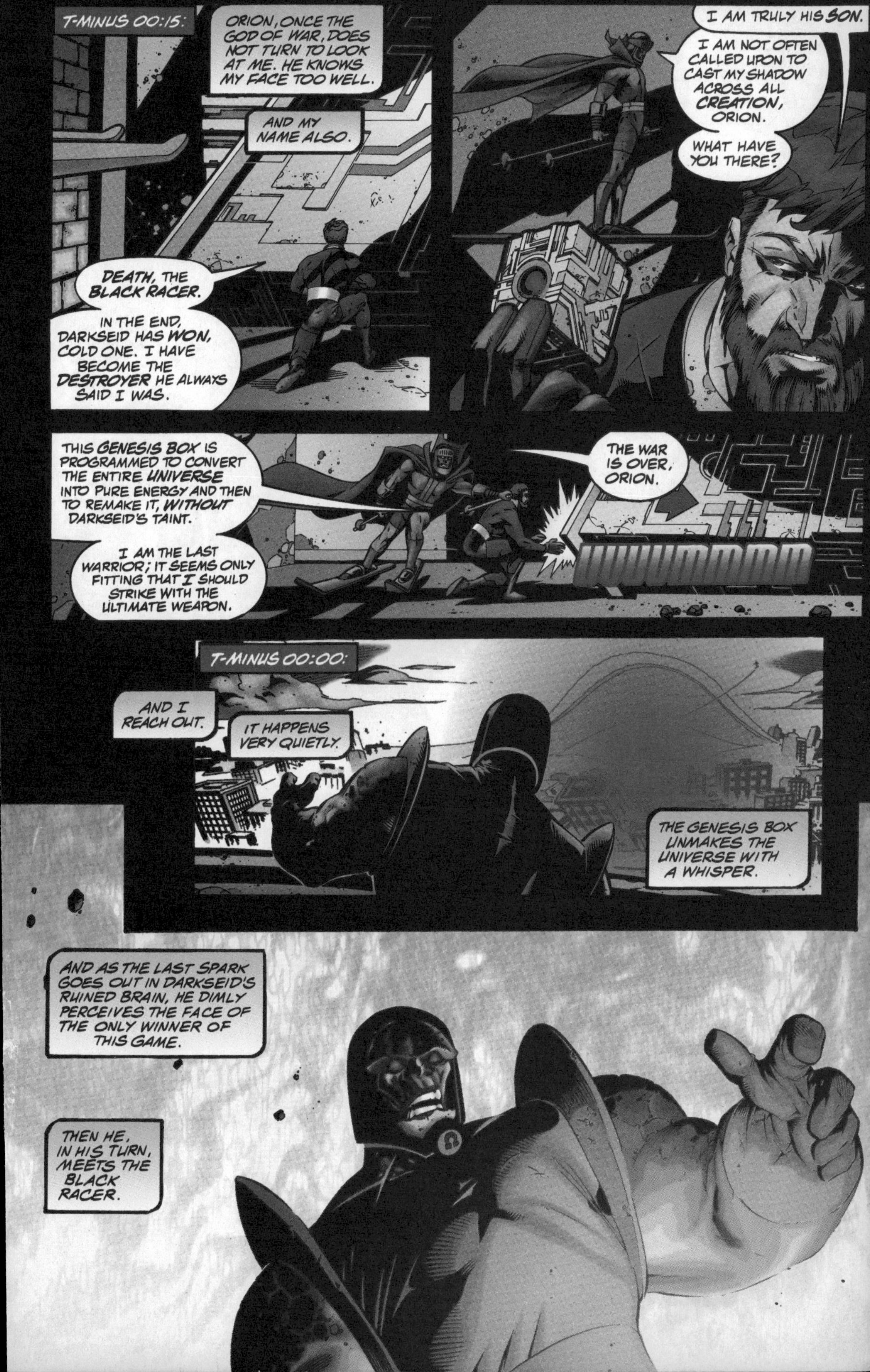

T-MINUS 00:15:
ORION, ONCE THE GOD OF WAR, DOES NOT TURN TO LOOK AT ME. HE KNOWS MY FACE TOO WELL.
AND MY NAME ALSO.
DEATH, THE BLACK RACER.
IN THE END, DARKSEID HAS WON, COLD ONE. I HAVE BECOME THE DESTROYER HE ALWAYS SAID I WAS.
I AM TRULY HIS SON.
I AM NOT OFTEN CALLED UPON TO CAST MY SHADOW ACROSS ALL CREATION, ORION.
WHAT HAVE YOU THERE?
THIS GENESIS BOX IS PROGRAMMED TO CONVERT THE ENTIRE UNIVERSE INTO PURE ENERGY AND THEN TO REMAKE IT, WITHOUT DARKSEID'S TAINT.
I AM THE LAST WARRIOR; IT SEEMS ONLY FITTING THAT I SHOULD STRIKE WITH THE ULTIMATE WEAPON.
THE WAR IS OVER, ORION.
WWWWMMMM
T-MINUS 00:00:
AND I REACH OUT.
IT HAPPENS VERY QUIETLY.
THE GENESIS BOX UNMAKES THE UNIVERSE WITH A WHISPER.
AND AS THE LAST SPARK GOES OUT IN DARKSEID'S RUINED BRAIN, HE DIMLY PERCEIVES THE FACE OF THE ONLY WINNER OF THIS GAME.
THEN HE, IN HIS TURN, MEETS THE BLACK RACER.

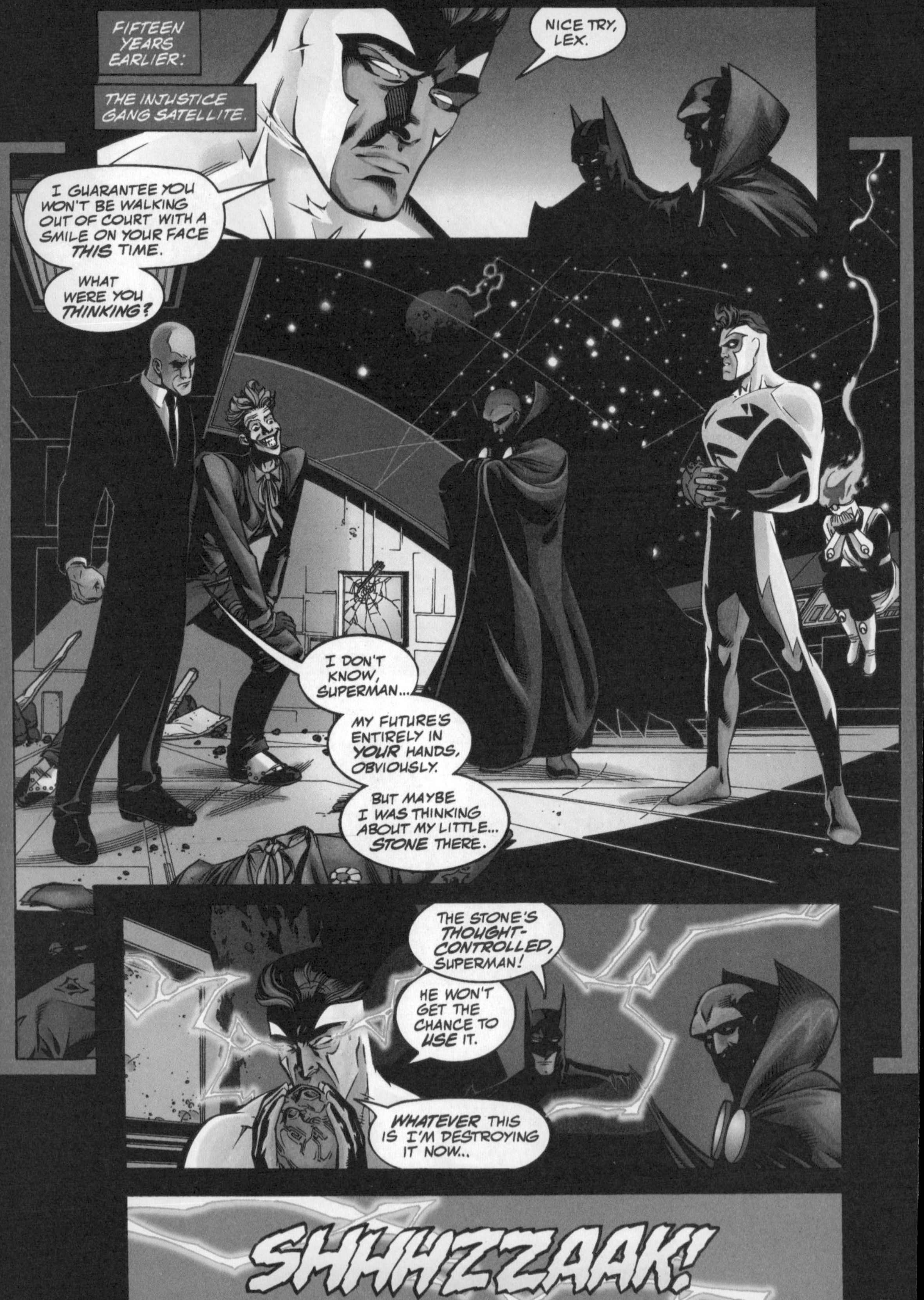
FIFTEEN YEARS EARLIER:
THE INJUSTICE GANG SATELLITE.
NICE TRY, LEX.
I GUARANTEE YOU WON'T BE WALKING OUT OF COURT WITH A SMILE ON YOUR FACE THIS TIME.
WHAT WERE YOU THINKING?
I DON'T KNOW, SUPERMAN...
MY FUTURE'S ENTIRELY IN YOUR HANDS, OBVIOUSLY.
BUT MAYBE I WAS THINKING ABOUT MY LITTLE... STONE THERE.
THE STONE'S THOUGHT-CONTROLLED, SUPERMAN!
HE WON'T GET THE CHANCE TO USE IT.
WHATEVER THIS IS I'M DESTROYING IT NOW...
SHHHZZAAK!

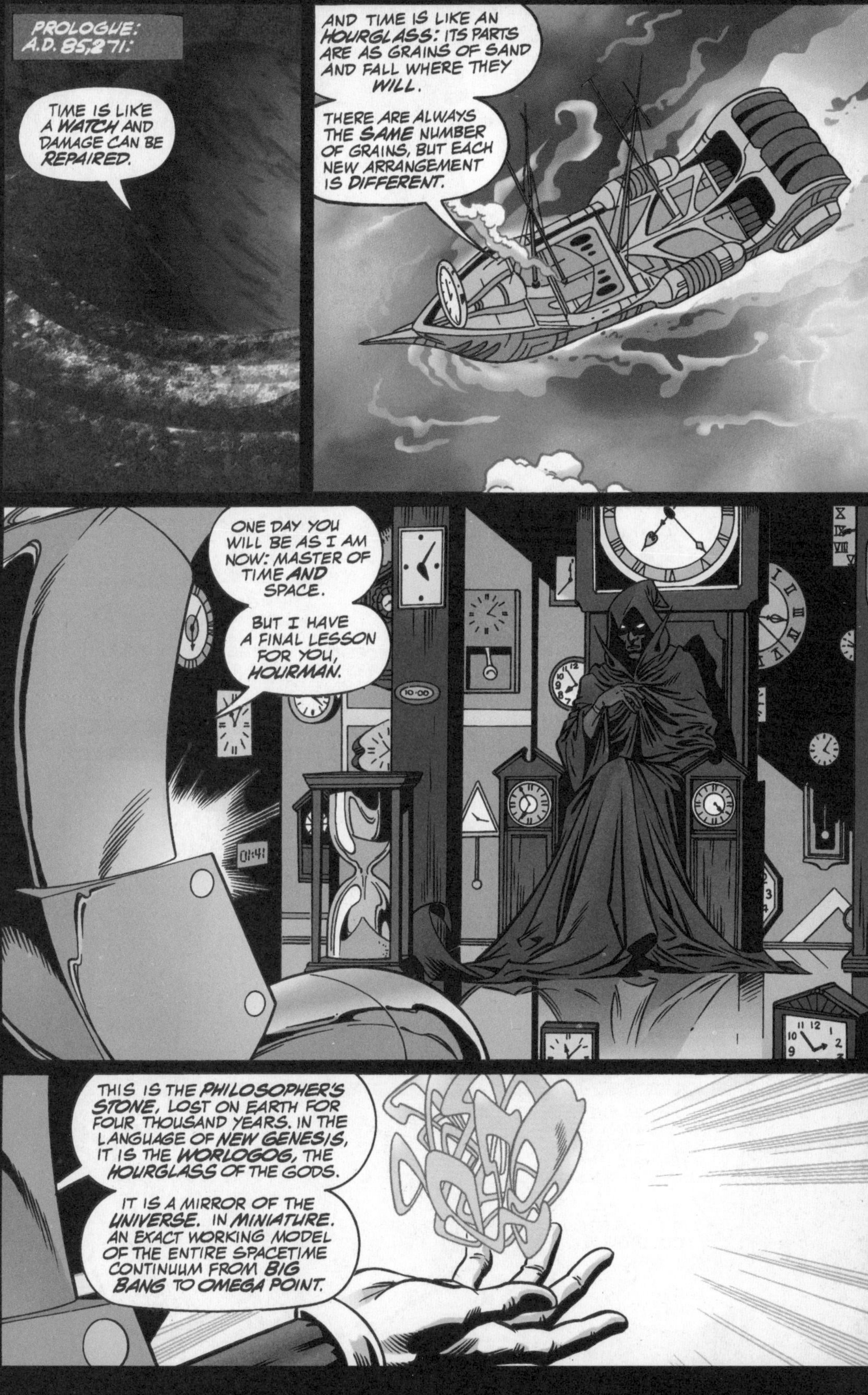
PROLOGUE: A.D. 85,271:
TIME IS LIKE A WATCH AND DAMAGE CAN BE REPAIRED.
AND TIME IS LIKE AN HOURGLASS: ITS PARTS ARE AS GRAINS OF SAND AND FALL WHERE THEY WILL.
THERE ARE ALWAYS THE SAME NUMBER OF GRAINS, BUT EACH NEW ARRANGEMENT IS DIFFERENT.
ONE DAY YOU WILL BE AS I AM NOW: MASTER OF TIME AND SPACE.
BUT I HAVE A FINAL LESSON FOR YOU, HOURMAN.
THIS IS THE PHILOSOPHER'S STONE, LOST ON EARTH FOR FOUR THOUSAND YEARS. IN THE LANGUAGE OF NEW GENESIS, IT IS THE WORLOGOG, THE HOURGLASS OF THE GODS.
IT IS A MIRROR OF THE UNIVERSE. IN MINIATURE. AN EXACT WORKING MODEL OF THE ENTIRE SPACETIME CONTINUUM FROM BIG BANG TO OMEGA POINT.

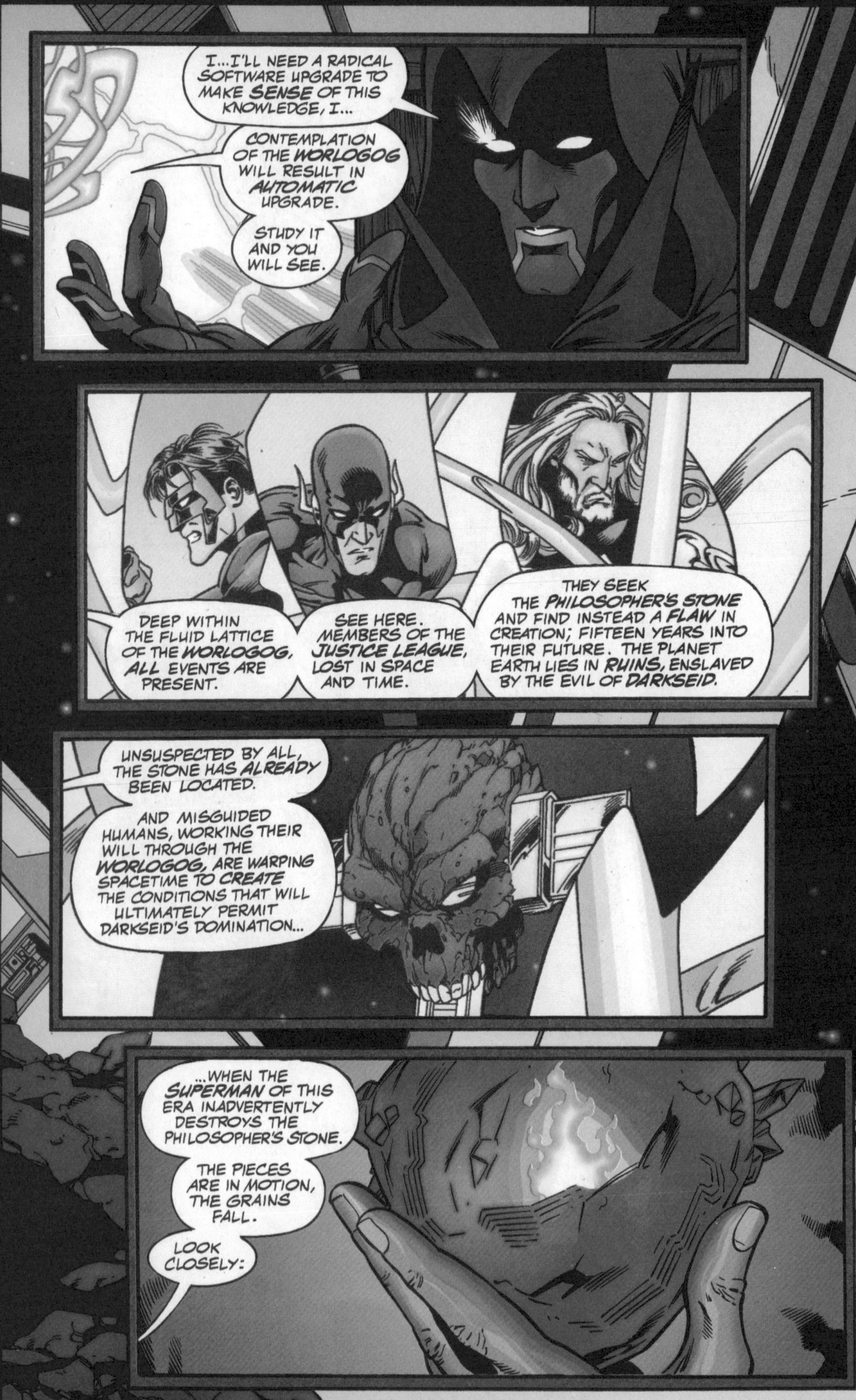

I...I'LL NEED A RADICAL SOFTWARE UPGRADE TO MAKE SENSE OF THIS KNOWLEDGE, I...
CONTEMPLATION OF THE WORLOGOG WILL RESULT IN AUTOMATIC UPGRADE.
STUDY IT AND YOU WILL SEE.
DEEP WITHIN THE FLUID LATTICE OF THE WORLOGOG, ALL EVENTS ARE PRESENT.
SEE HERE. MEMBERS OF THE JUSTICE LEAGUE, LOST IN SPACE AND TIME.
THEY SEEK THE PHILOSOPHER'S STONE AND FIND INSTEAD A FLAW IN CREATION; FIFTEEN YEARS INTO THEIR FUTURE. THE PLANET EARTH LIES IN RUINS, ENSLAVED BY THE EVIL OF DARKSEID.
UNSUSPECTED BY ALL, THE STONE HAS ALREADY BEEN LOCATED.
AND MISGUIDED HUMANS, WORKING THEIR WILL THROUGH THE WORLOGOG, ARE WARPING SPACETIME TO CREATE THE CONDITIONS THAT WILL ULTIMATELY PERMIT DARKSEID'S DOMINATION...
...WHEN THE SUPERMAN OF THIS ERA INADVERTENTLY DESTROYS THE PHILOSOPHER'S STONE.
THE PIECES ARE IN MOTION, THE GRAINS FALL.
LOOK CLOSELY:

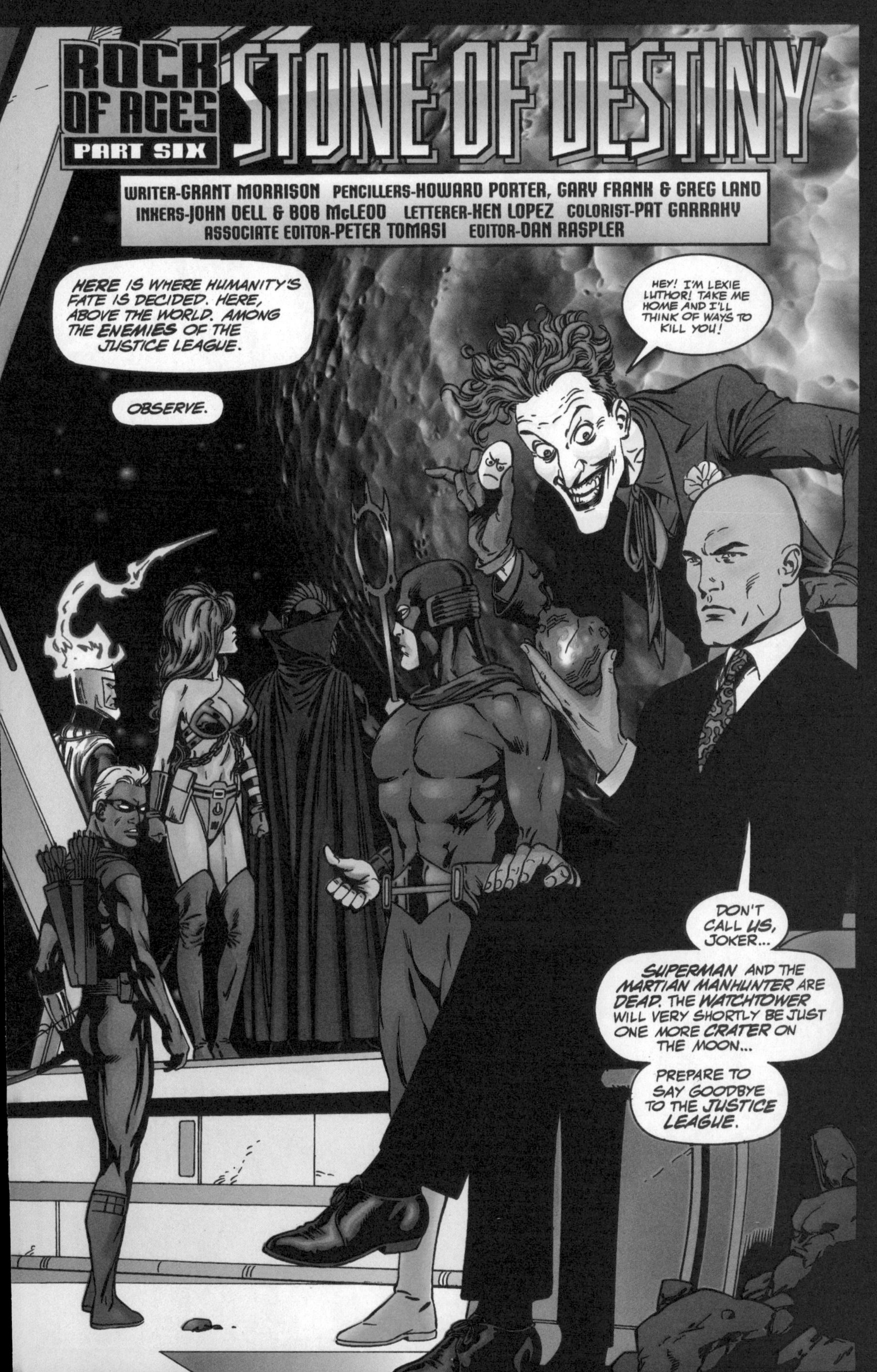
ROCK OF AGES PART SIX
STONE OF DESTINY
WRITER-GRANT MORRISON PENCILLERS-HOWARD PORTER, GARY FRANK & GREG LAND
INKERS-JOHN DELL & BOB McLEOD LETTERER-KEN LOPEZ COLORIST-PAT GARRAHY
ASSOCIATE EDITOR-PETER TOMASI EDITOR-DAN RASPLER
HERE IS WHERE HUMANITY'S FATE IS DECIDED. HERE, ABOVE THE WORLD. AMONG THE ENEMIES OF THE JUSTICE LEAGUE.
OBSERVE.
HEY! I'M LEXIE LUTHOR! TAKE ME HOME AND I'LL THINK OF WAYS TO KILL YOU!
DON'T CALL US, JOKER...
SUPERMAN AND THE MARTIAN MANHUNTER ARE DEAD. THE WATCHTOWER WILL VERY SHORTLY BE JUST ONE MORE CRATER ON THE MOON...
PREPARE TO SAY GOODBYE TO THE JUSTICE LEAGUE.

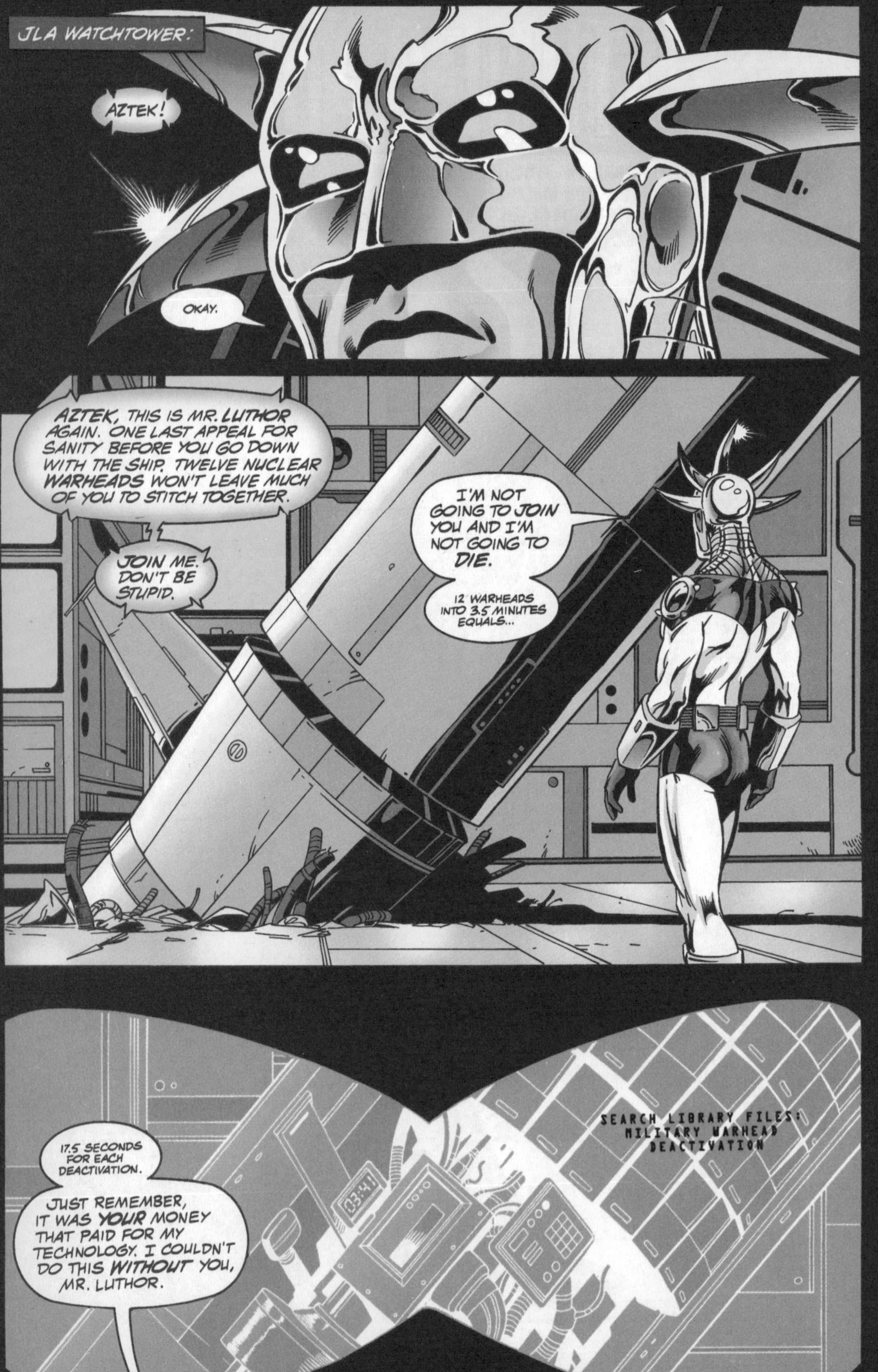
JLA WATCHTOWER:
AZTEK!
OKAY.
AZTEK, THIS IS MR. LUTHOR AGAIN. ONE LAST APPEAL FOR SANITY BEFORE YOU GO DOWN WITH THE SHIP. TWELVE NUCLEAR WARHEADS WON'T LEAVE MUCH OF YOU TO STITCH TOGETHER.
JOIN ME. DON'T BE STUPID.
I'M NOT GOING TO JOIN YOU AND I'M NOT GOING TO DIE.
12 WARHEADS INTO 3.5 MINUTES EQUALS...
SEARCH LIBRARY FILES: MILITARY WARHEAD DEACTIVATION
17.5 SECONDS FOR EACH DEACTIVATION.
JUST REMEMBER, IT WAS YOUR MONEY THAT PAID FOR MY TECHNOLOGY. I COULDN'T DO THIS WITHOUT YOU, MR. LUTHOR.

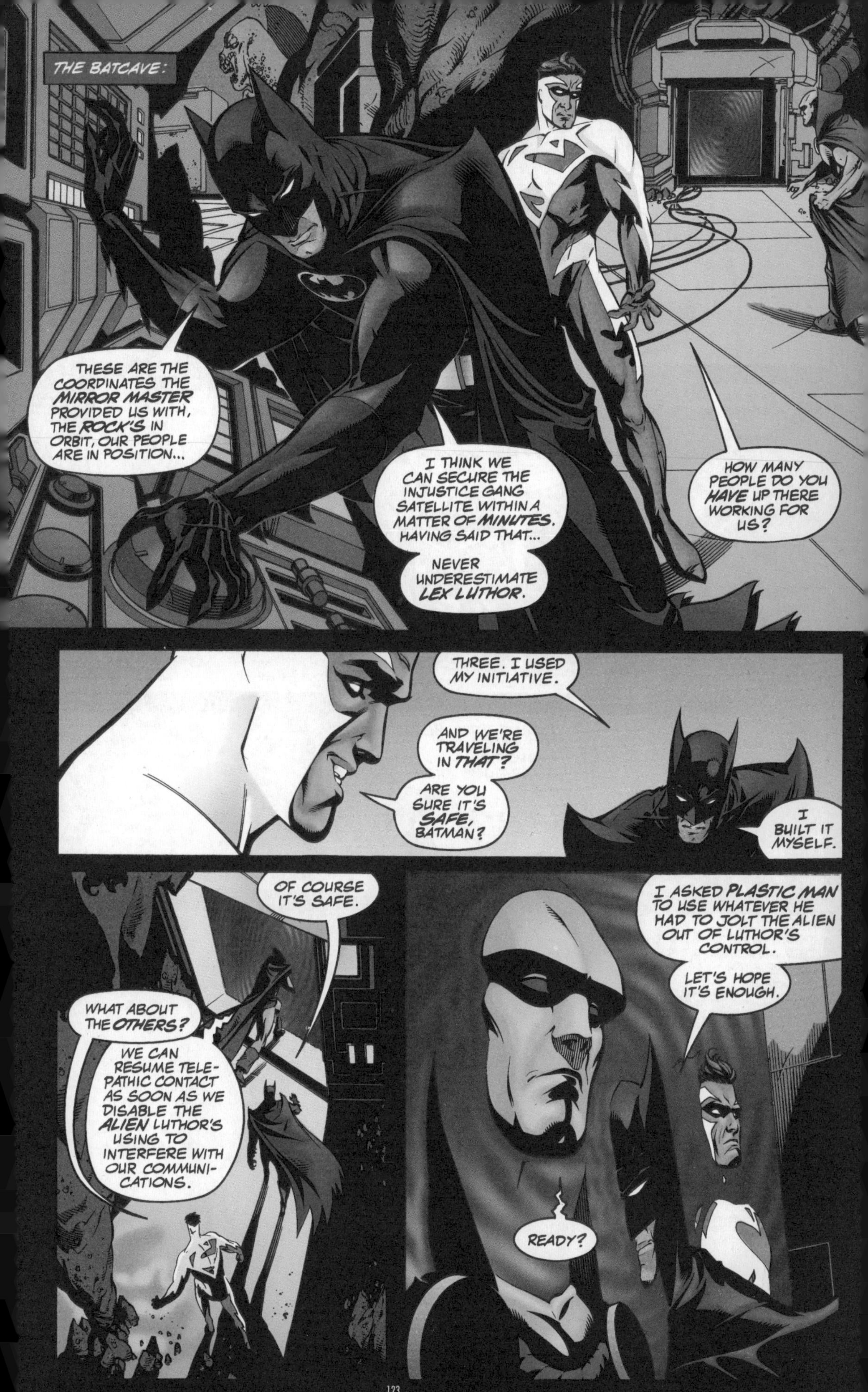

THE BATCAVE:
THESE ARE THE COORDINATES THE MIRROR MASTER PROVIDED US WITH, THE ROCK'S IN ORBIT, OUR PEOPLE ARE IN POSITION...
I THINK WE CAN SECURE THE INJUSTICE GANG SATELLITE WITHIN A MATTER OF MINUTES. HAVING SAID THAT...
NEVER UNDERESTIMATE LEX LUTHOR.
HOW MANY PEOPLE DO YOU HAVE UP THERE WORKING FOR US?
THREE. I USED MY INITIATIVE.
AND WE'RE TRAVELING IN THAT?
ARE YOU SURE IT'S SAFE, BATMAN?
I BUILT IT MYSELF.
OF COURSE IT'S SAFE.
WHAT ABOUT THE OTHERS?
WE CAN RESUME TELE-PATHIC CONTACT AS SOON AS WE DISABLE THE ALIEN LUTHOR'S USING TO INTERFERE WITH OUR COMMUNI-CATIONS.
I ASKED PLASTIC MAN TO USE WHATEVER HE HAD TO JOLT THE ALIEN OUT OF LUTHOR'S CONTROL.
LET'S HOPE IT'S ENOUGH.
READY?

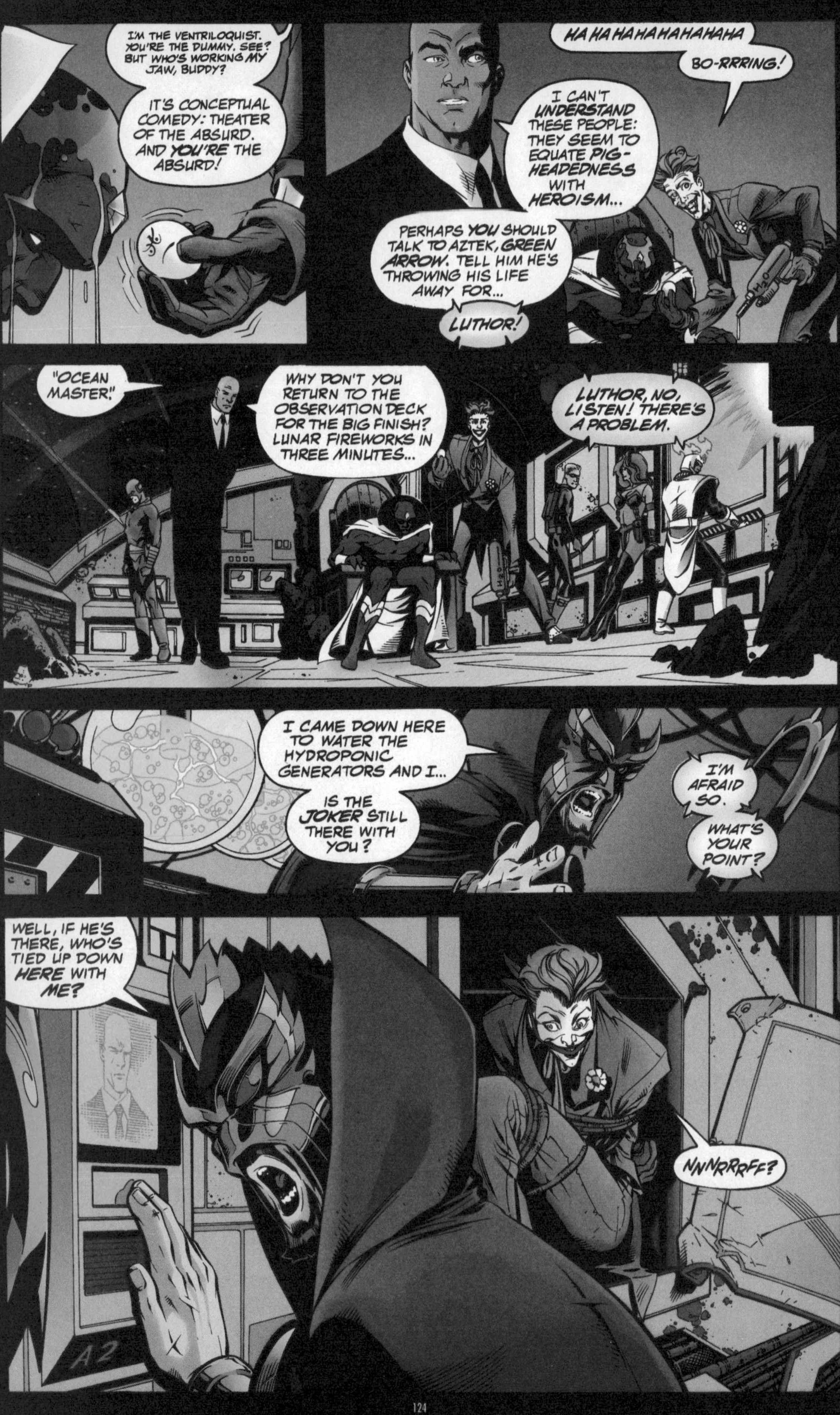
I'M THE VENTRILOQUIST. YOU'RE THE DUMMY. SEE? BUT WHO'S WORKING MY JAW, BUDDY?
IT'S CONCEPTUAL COMEDY: THEATER OF THE ABSURD. AND YOU'RE THE ABSURD!
HA HA HA HA HA HA HA HA HA HA HA
BO-RRRING!
I CAN'T UNDERSTAND THESE PEOPLE: THEY SEEM TO EQUATE PIG-HEADEDNESS WITH HEROISM...
PERHAPS YOU SHOULD TALK TO AZTEK, GREEN ARROW. TELL HIM HE'S THROWING HIS LIFE AWAY FOR...
LUTHOR!
"OCEAN MASTER."
WHY DON'T YOU RETURN TO THE OBSERVATION DECK FOR THE BIG FINISH? LUNAR FIREWORKS IN THREE MINUTES...
LUTHOR, NO, LISTEN! THERE'S A PROBLEM.
I CAME DOWN HERE TO WATER THE HYDROPONIC GENERATORS AND I...
IS THE JOKER STILL THERE WITH YOU?
I'M AFRAID SO.
WHAT'S YOUR POINT?
WELL, IF HE'S THERE, WHO'S TIED UP DOWN HERE WITH ME?
NNNRRRFF?
A2

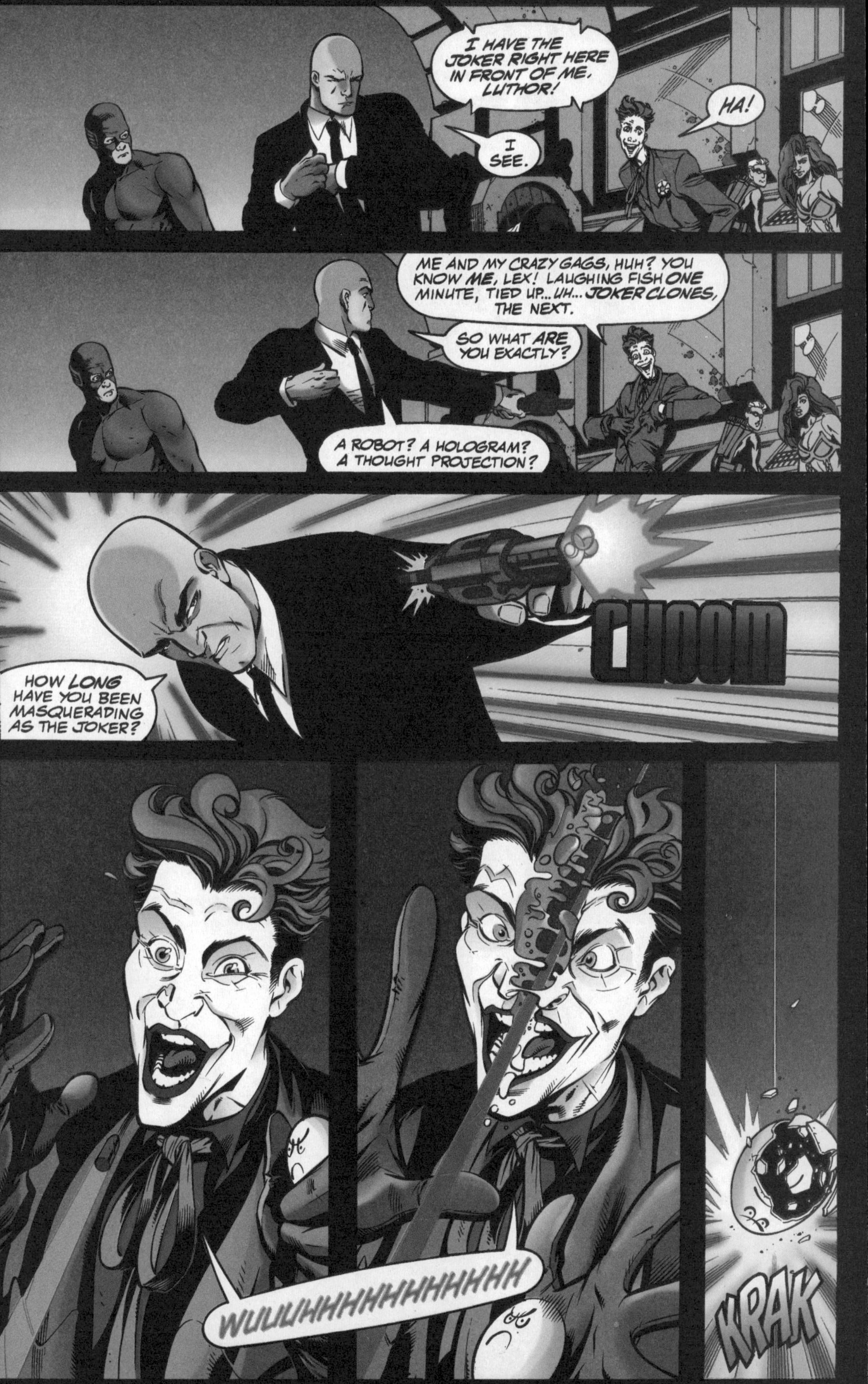

I HAVE THE JOKER RIGHT HERE IN FRONT OF ME, LUTHOR!
HA!
I SEE.
ME AND MY CRAZY GAGS, HUH? YOU KNOW ME, LEX! LAUGHING FISH ONE MINUTE, TIED UP... UH... JOKER CLONES, THE NEXT.
SO WHAT ARE YOU EXACTLY?
A ROBOT? A HOLOGRAM? A THOUGHT PROJECTION?
CHOOM
HOW LONG HAVE YOU BEEN MASQUERADING AS THE JOKER?
WUUUHHHHHHHHHHH
KRAK

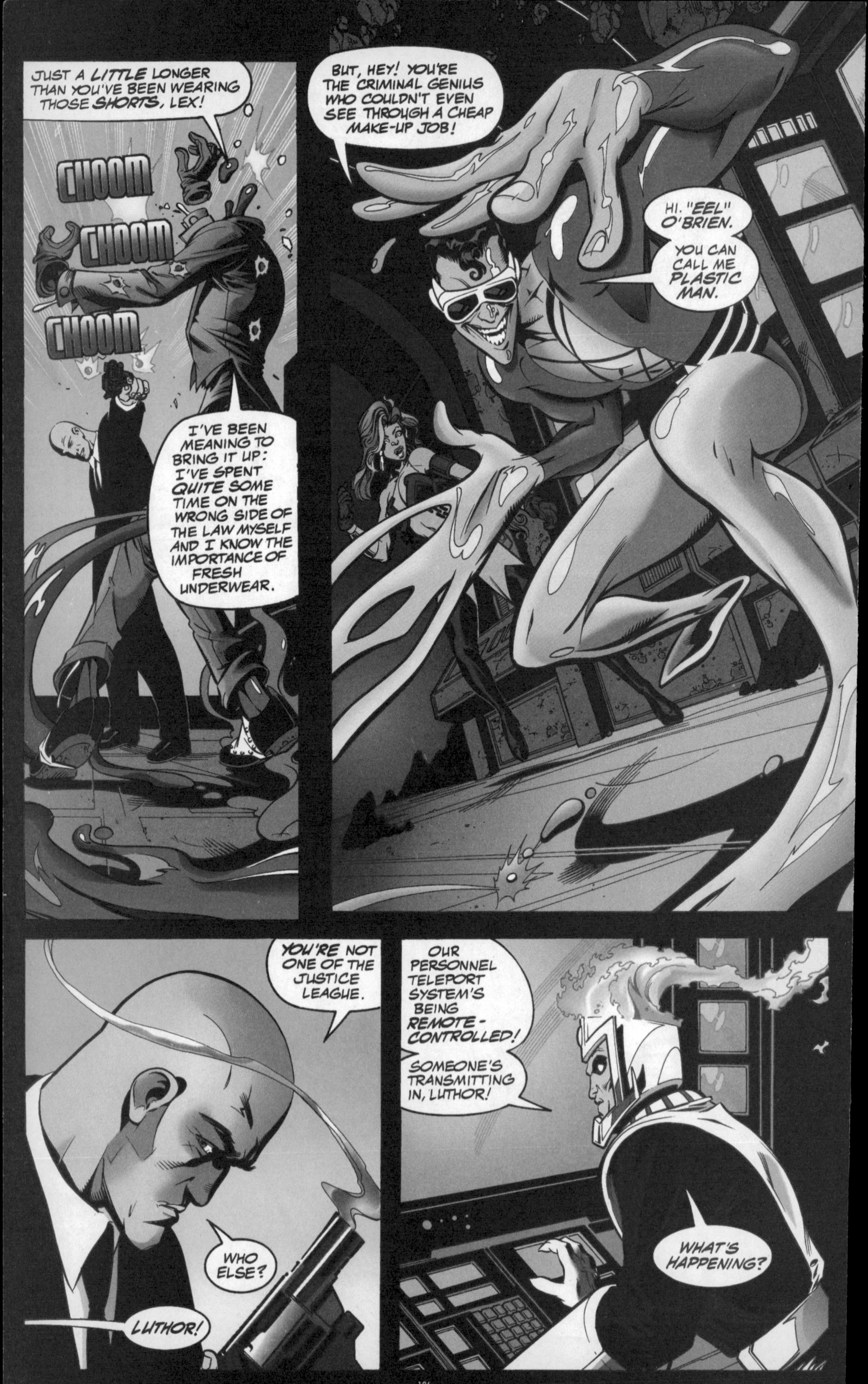

JUST A LITTLE LONGER THAN YOU'VE BEEN WEARING THOSE SHORTS, LEX!
CHOOM
CHOOM
CHOOM
I'VE BEEN MEANING TO BRING IT UP: I'VE SPENT QUITE SOME TIME ON THE WRONG SIDE OF THE LAW MYSELF AND I KNOW THE IMPORTANCE OF FRESH UNDERWEAR.
BUT, HEY! YOU'RE THE CRIMINAL GENIUS WHO COULDN'T EVEN SEE THROUGH A CHEAP MAKE-UP JOB!
HI. "EEL" O'BRIEN.
YOU CAN CALL ME PLASTIC MAN.
YOU'RE NOT ONE OF THE JUSTICE LEAGUE.
WHO ELSE?
LUTHOR!
OUR PERSONNEL TELEPORT SYSTEM'S BEING REMOTE-CONTROLLED!
SOMEONE'S TRANSMITTING IN, LUTHOR!
WHAT'S HAPPENING?

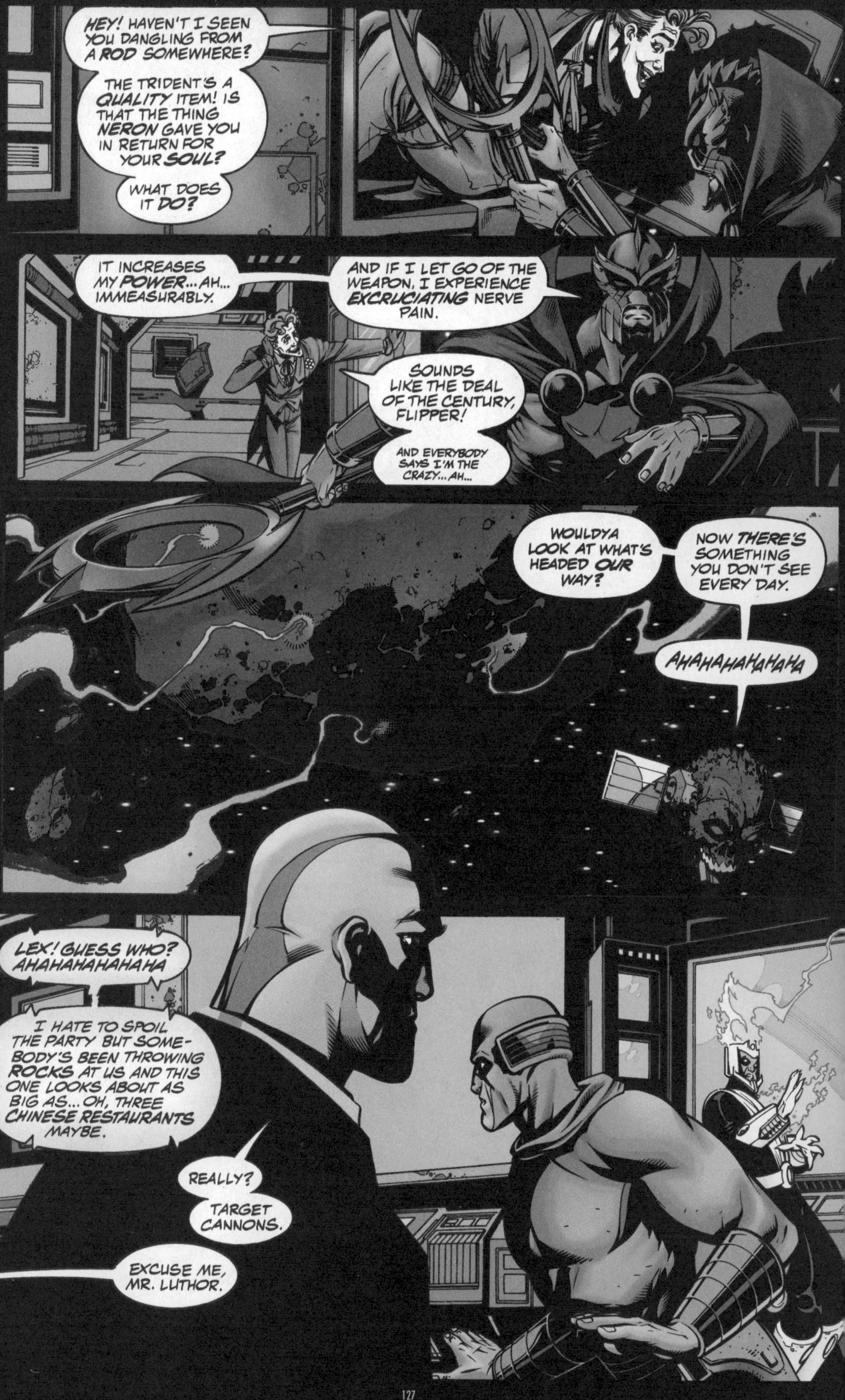
HEY! HAVEN'T I SEEN YOU DANGLING FROM A ROD SOMEWHERE?
THE TRIDENT'S A QUALITY ITEM! IS THAT THE THING NERON GAVE YOU IN RETURN FOR YOUR SOUL?
WHAT DOES IT DO?
IT INCREASES MY POWER... AH... IMMEASURABLY.
AND IF I LET GO OF THE WEAPON, I EXPERIENCE EXCRUCIATING NERVE PAIN.
SOUNDS LIKE THE DEAL OF THE CENTURY, FLIPPER!
AND EVERYBODY SAYS I'M THE CRAZY... AH...
WOULDYA LOOK AT WHAT'S HEADED OUR WAY?
NOW THERE'S SOMETHING YOU DON'T SEE EVERY DAY.
AHAHAHAHAHAHAHA
LEX! GUESS WHO? AHAHAHAHAHAHA
I HATE TO SPOIL THE PARTY BUT SOMEBODY'S BEEN THROWING ROCKS AT US AND THIS ONE LOOKS ABOUT AS BIG AS... OH, THREE CHINESE RESTAURANTS MAYBE.
REALLY?
TARGET CANNONS.
EXCUSE ME, MR. LUTHOR.

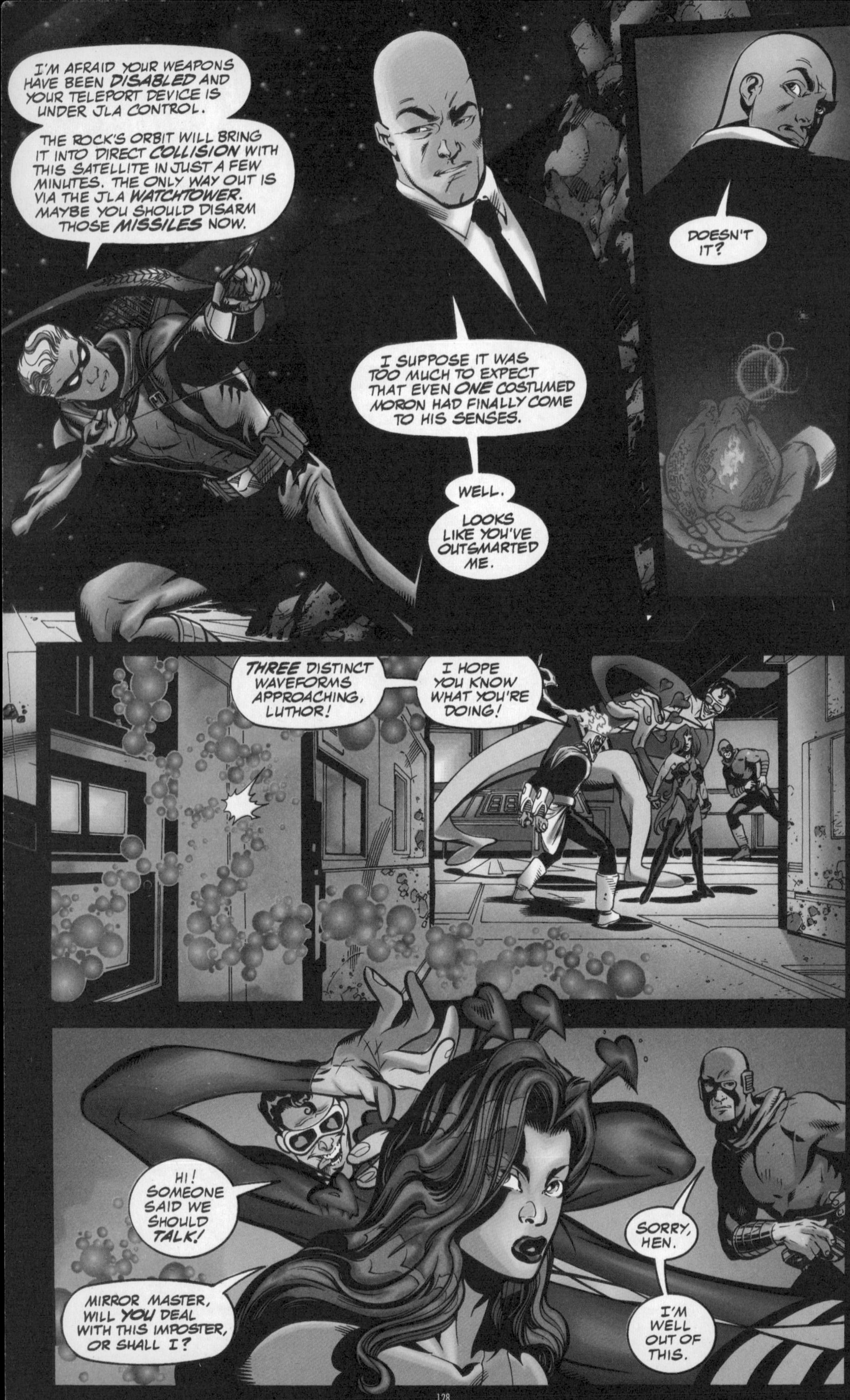
I'M AFRAID YOUR WEAPONS HAVE BEEN DISABLED AND YOUR TELEPORT DEVICE IS UNDER JLA CONTROL.
THE ROCK'S ORBIT WILL BRING IT INTO DIRECT COLLISION WITH THIS SATELLITE IN JUST A FEW MINUTES. THE ONLY WAY OUT IS VIA THE JLA WATCHTOWER. MAYBE YOU SHOULD DISARM THOSE MISSILES NOW.
I SUPPOSE IT WAS TOO MUCH TO EXPECT THAT EVEN ONE COSTUMED MORON HAD FINALLY COME TO HIS SENSES.
WELL.
LOOKS LIKE YOU'VE OUTSMARTED ME.
DOESN'T IT?
THREE DISTINCT WAVEFORMS APPROACHING, LUTHOR!
I HOPE YOU KNOW WHAT YOU'RE DOING!
HI! SOMEONE SAID WE SHOULD TALK!
MIRROR MASTER, WILL YOU DEAL WITH THIS IMPOSTER, OR SHALL I?
SORRY, HEN.
I'M WELL OUT OF THIS.

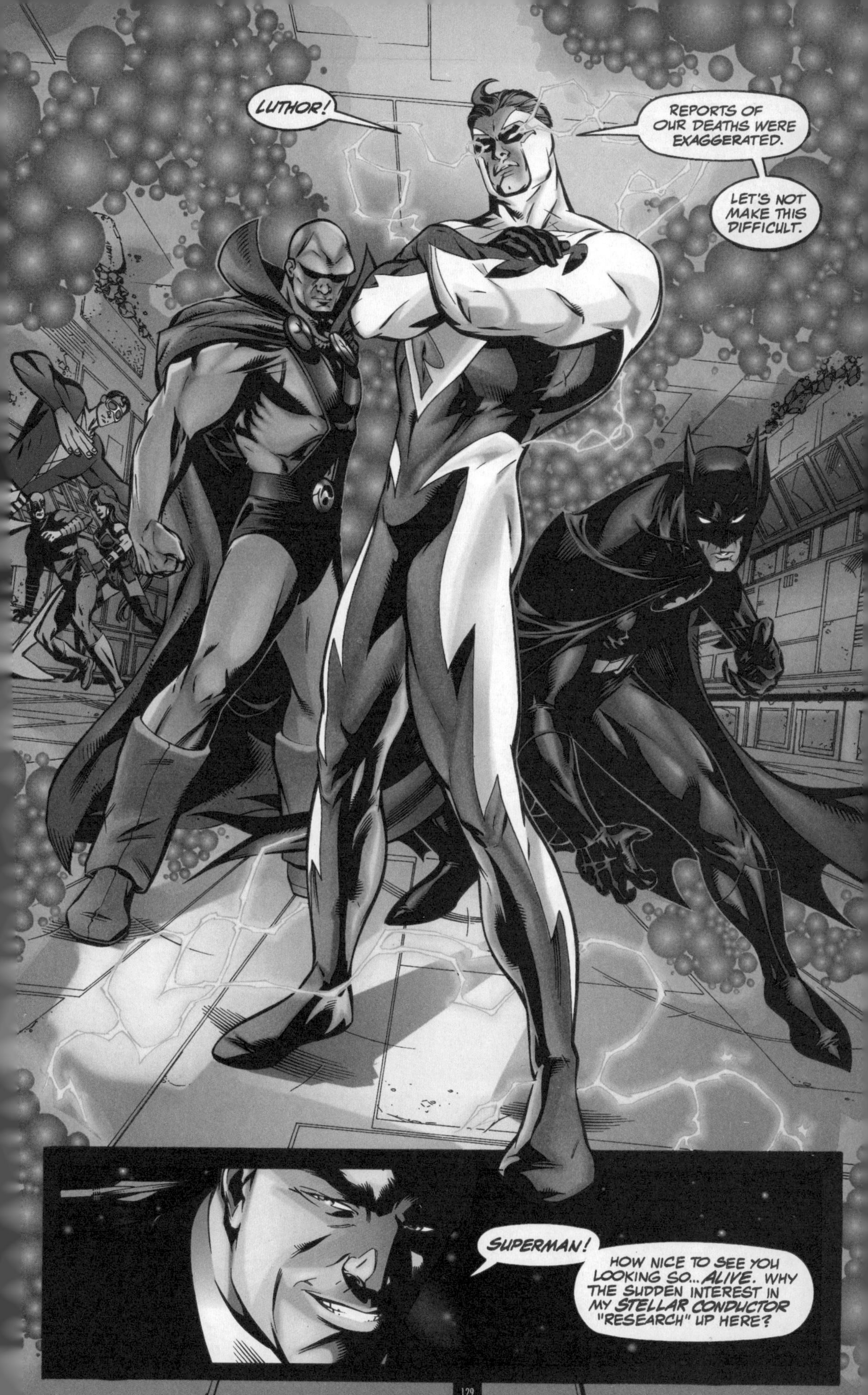
LUTHOR!
REPORTS OF OUR DEATHS WERE EXAGGERATED.
LET'S NOT MAKE THIS DIFFICULT.
SUPERMAN!
HOW NICE TO SEE YOU LOOKING SO...ALIVE. WHY THE SUDDEN INTEREST IN MY STELLAR CONDUCTOR "RESEARCH" UP HERE?

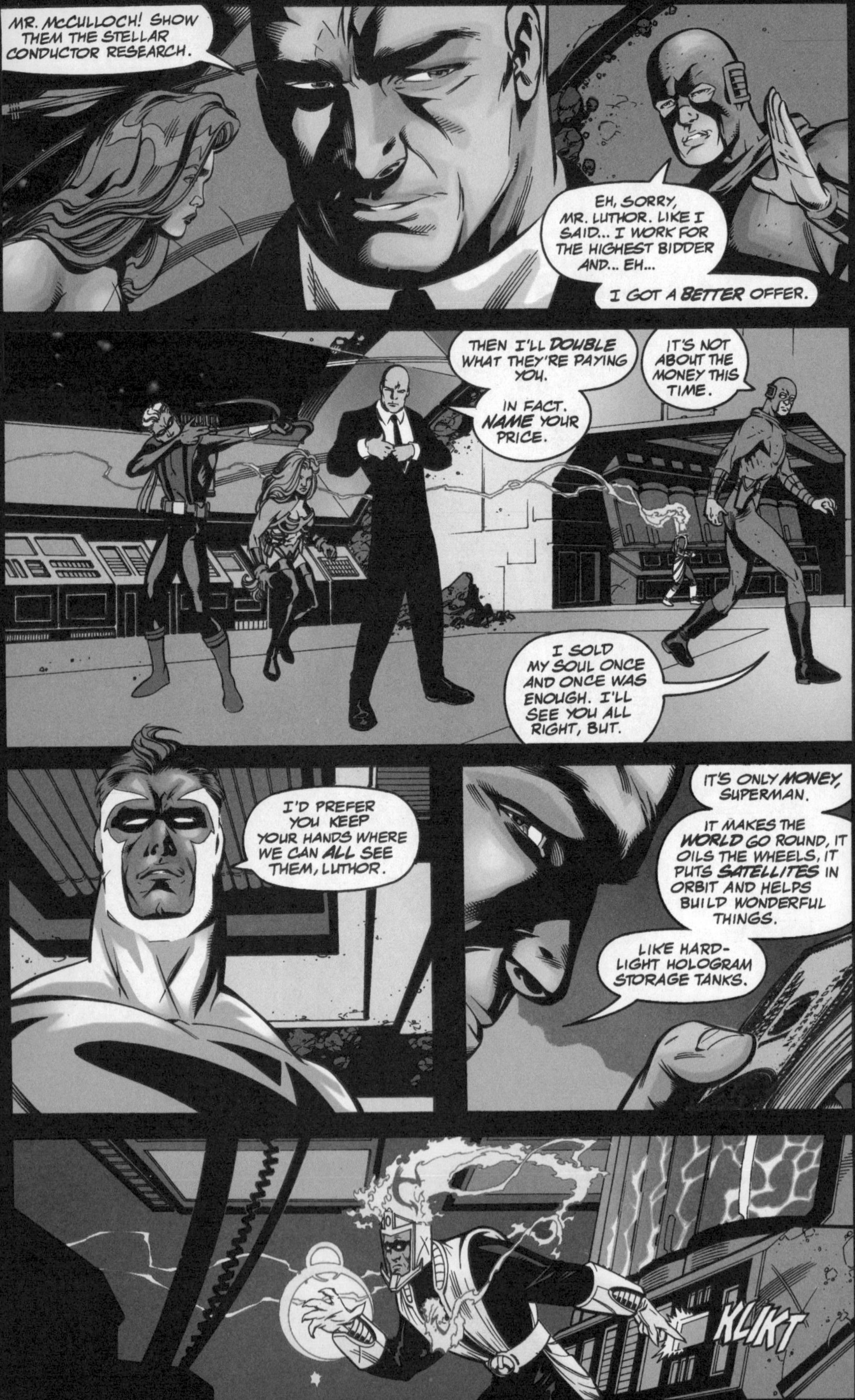

MR. McCULLOCH! SHOW THEM THE STELLAR CONDUCTOR RESEARCH.
EH, SORRY, MR. LUTHOR. LIKE I SAID... I WORK FOR THE HIGHEST BIDDER AND... EH...
I GOT A BETTER OFFER.
THEN I'LL DOUBLE WHAT THEY'RE PAYING YOU.
IN FACT. NAME YOUR PRICE.
IT'S NOT ABOUT THE MONEY THIS TIME.
I SOLD MY SOUL ONCE AND ONCE WAS ENOUGH. I'LL SEE YOU ALL RIGHT, BUT.
I'D PREFER YOU KEEP YOUR HANDS WHERE WE CAN ALL SEE THEM, LUTHOR.
IT'S ONLY MONEY, SUPERMAN.
IT MAKES THE WORLD GO ROUND, IT OILS THE WHEELS, IT PUTS SATELLITES IN ORBIT AND HELPS BUILD WONDERFUL THINGS.
LIKE HARD-LIGHT HOLOGRAM STORAGE TANKS.
KLIKT

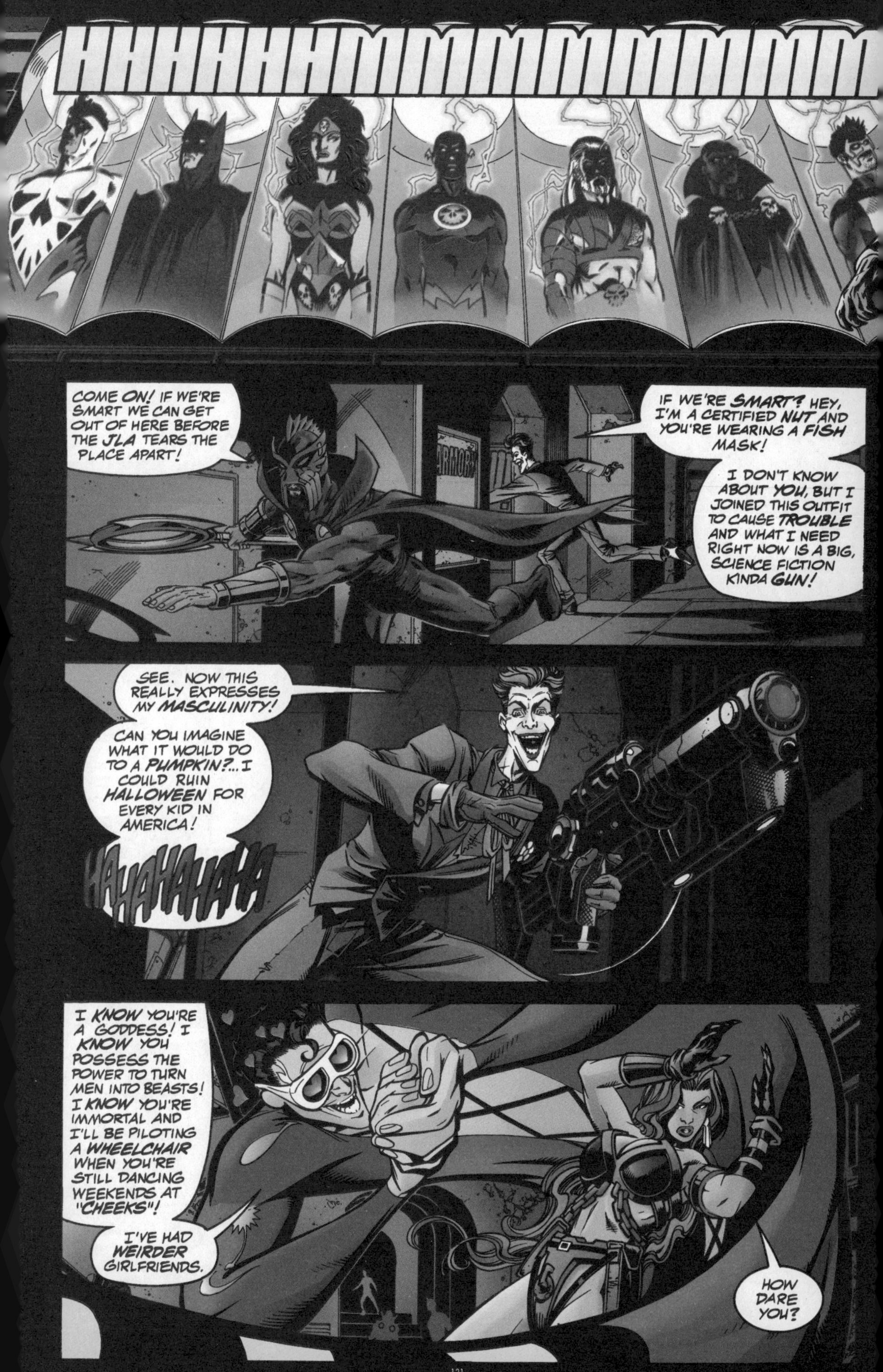
HHHHHHMMMMMMMMMMMMMM
COME ON! IF WE'RE SMART WE CAN GET OUT OF HERE BEFORE THE JLA TEARS THE PLACE APART!
IF WE'RE SMART? HEY, I'M A CERTIFIED NUT AND YOU'RE WEARING A FISH MASK!
I DON'T KNOW ABOUT YOU, BUT I JOINED THIS OUTFIT TO CAUSE TROUBLE AND WHAT I NEED RIGHT NOW IS A BIG, SCIENCE FICTION KINDA GUN!
ARMORY
SEE. NOW THIS REALLY EXPRESSES MY MASCULINITY!
CAN YOU IMAGINE WHAT IT WOULD DO TO A PUMPKIN?...I COULD RUIN HALLOWEEN FOR EVERY KID IN AMERICA!
HAHAHAHAHA
I KNOW YOU'RE A GODDESS! I KNOW YOU POSSESS THE POWER TO TURN MEN INTO BEASTS! I KNOW YOU'RE IMMORTAL AND I'LL BE PILOTING A WHEELCHAIR WHEN YOU'RE STILL DANCING WEEKENDS AT "CHEEKS"!
I'VE HAD WEIRDER GIRLFRIENDS.
HOW DARE YOU?

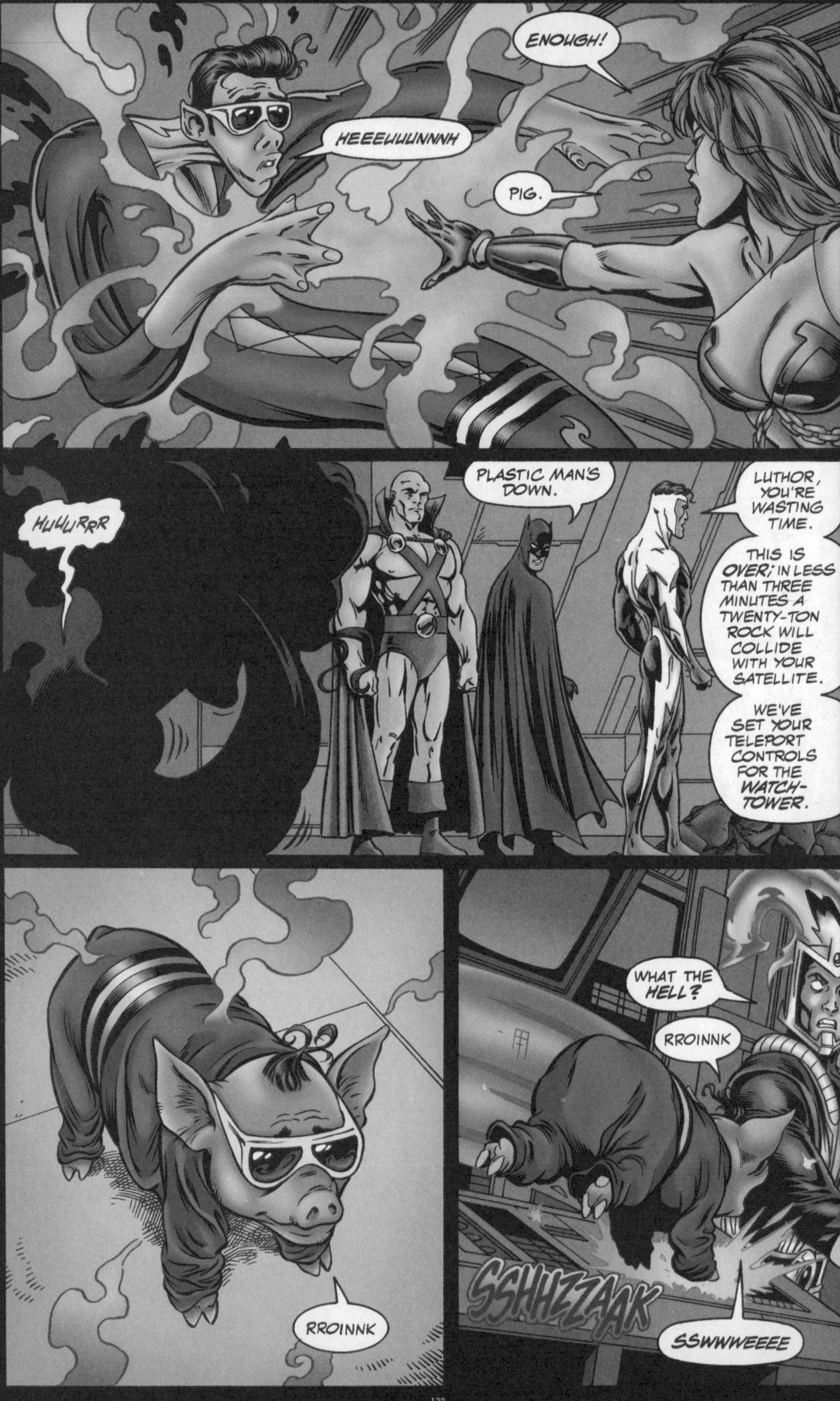
ENOUGH!
HEEEUUUNNNH
PIG.
HUUURRR
PLASTIC MAN'S DOWN.
LUTHOR, YOU'RE WASTING TIME.
THIS IS OVER; IN LESS THAN THREE MINUTES A TWENTY-TON ROCK WILL COLLIDE WITH YOUR SATELLITE.
WE'VE SET YOUR TELEPORT CONTROLS FOR THE WATCH-TOWER.
RROINNK
WHAT THE HELL?
RROINNK
SSHHZZAAK
SSWWWEEEE

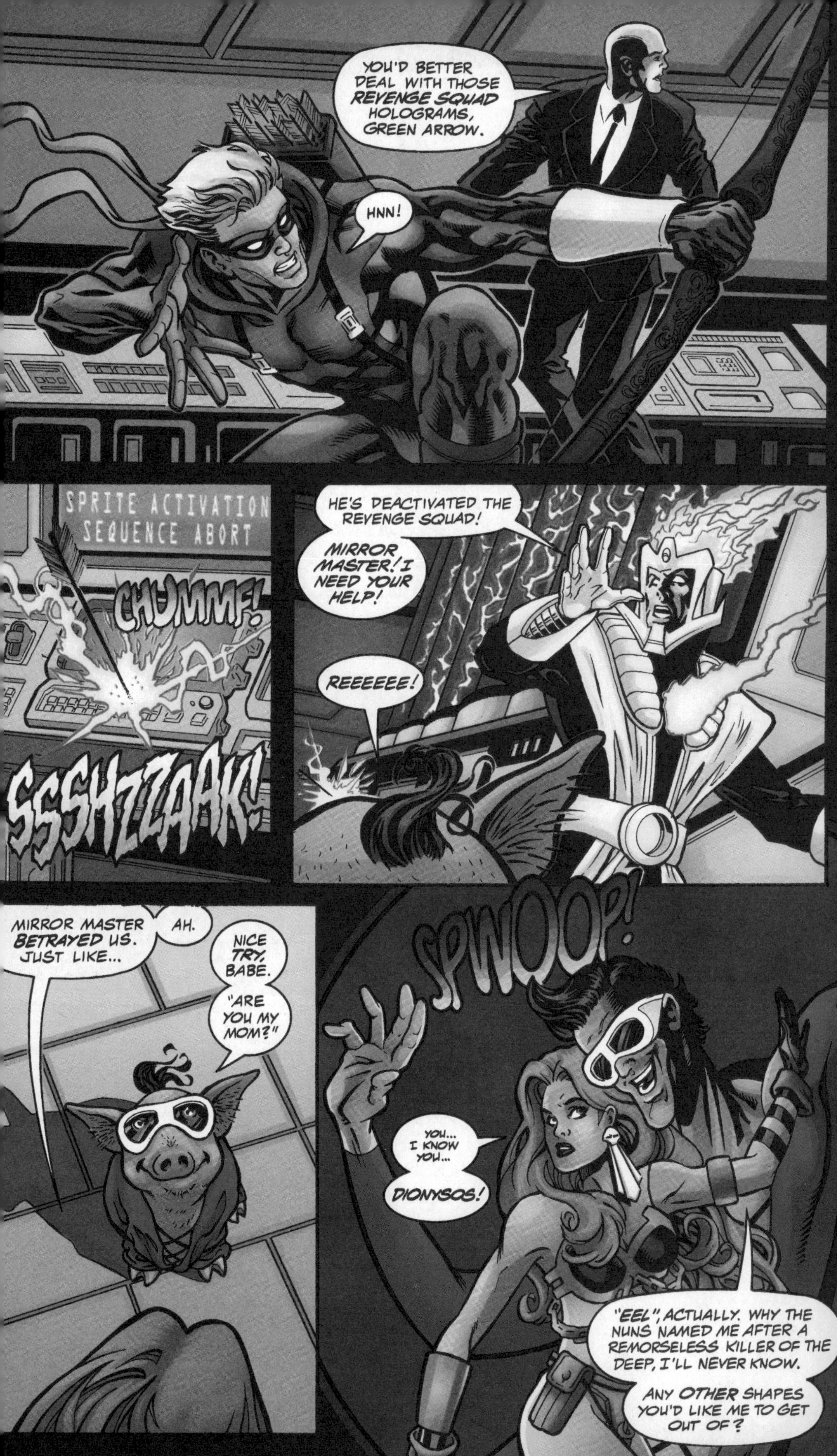
YOU'D BETTER DEAL WITH THOSE REVENGE SQUAD HOLOGRAMS, GREEN ARROW.
HNN!
SPRITE ACTIVATION SEQUENCE ABORT
CHUMMF!
SSSHZZAAK!
HE'S DEACTIVATED THE REVENGE SQUAD!
MIRROR MASTER! I NEED YOUR HELP!
REEEEEE!
MIRROR MASTER BETRAYED US. JUST LIKE...
AH.
NICE TRY, BABE.
"ARE YOU MY MOM?"
SPWOOP!
YOU... I KNOW YOU...
DIONYSOS!
"EEL", ACTUALLY. WHY THE NUNS NAMED ME AFTER A REMORSELESS KILLER OF THE DEEP, I'LL NEVER KNOW.
ANY OTHER SHAPES YOU'D LIKE ME TO GET OUT OF?

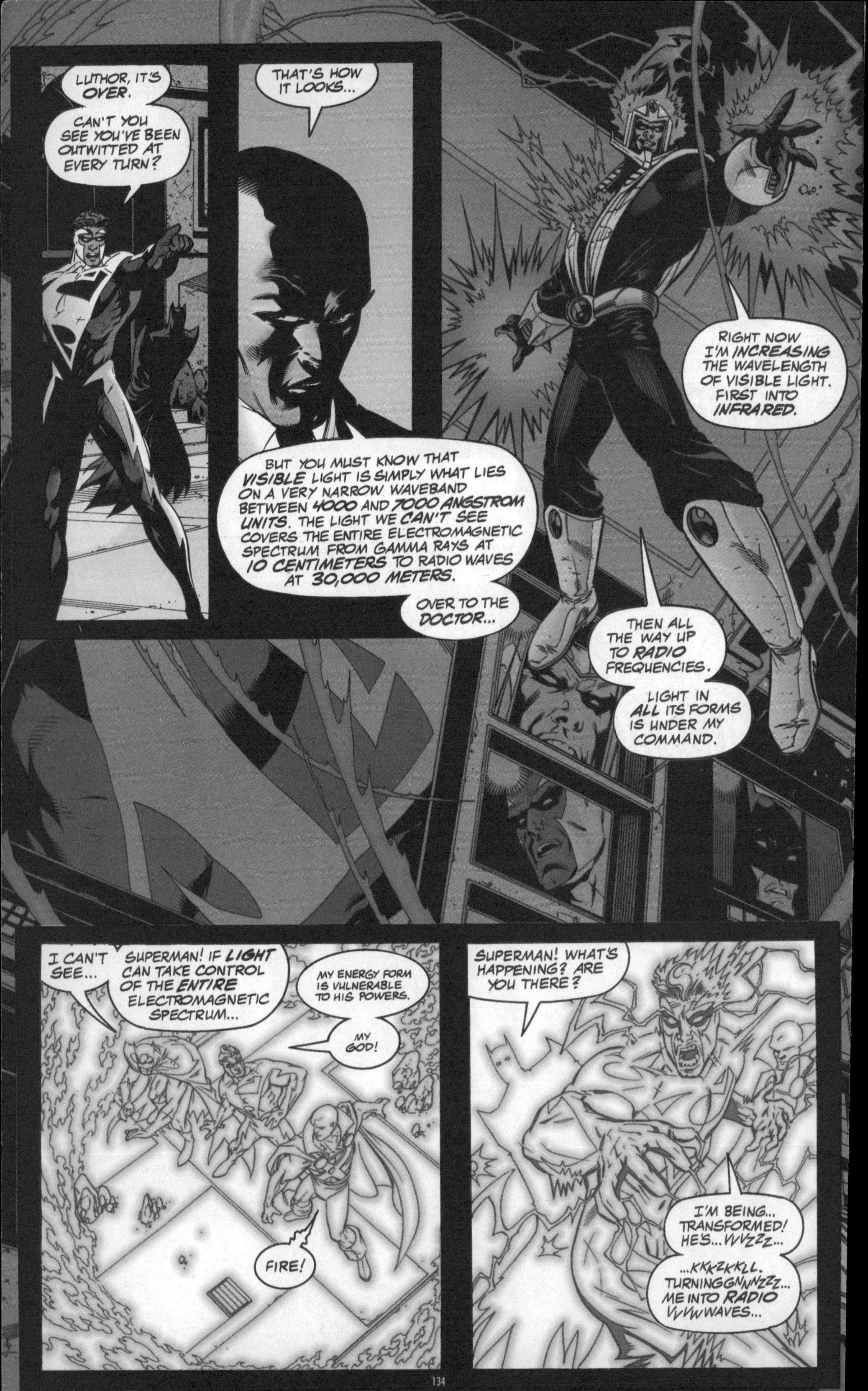
LUTHOR, IT'S OVER.
CAN'T YOU SEE YOU'VE BEEN OUTWITTED AT EVERY TURN?
THAT'S HOW IT LOOKS...
BUT YOU MUST KNOW THAT VISIBLE LIGHT IS SIMPLY WHAT LIES ON A VERY NARROW WAVEBAND BETWEEN 4000 AND 7000 ANGSTROM UNITS. THE LIGHT WE CAN'T SEE COVERS THE ENTIRE ELECTROMAGNETIC SPECTRUM FROM GAMMA RAYS AT 10 CENTIMETERS TO RADIO WAVES AT 30,000 METERS.
OVER TO THE DOCTOR...
RIGHT NOW I'M INCREASING THE WAVELENGTH OF VISIBLE LIGHT. FIRST INTO INFRARED.
THEN ALL THE WAY UP TO RADIO FREQUENCIES.
LIGHT IN ALL ITS FORMS IS UNDER MY COMMAND.
I CAN'T SEE...
SUPERMAN! IF LIGHT CAN TAKE CONTROL OF THE ENTIRE ELECTROMAGNETIC SPECTRUM...
MY ENERGY FORM IS VULNERABLE TO HIS POWERS.
MY GOD!
FIRE!
SUPERMAN! WHAT'S HAPPENING? ARE YOU THERE?
I'M BEING... TRANSFORMED! HE'S... VVVZZZ...
...KKKZKKLL. TURNINGGNNZZZ... ME INTO RADIO VVVWWAVES...

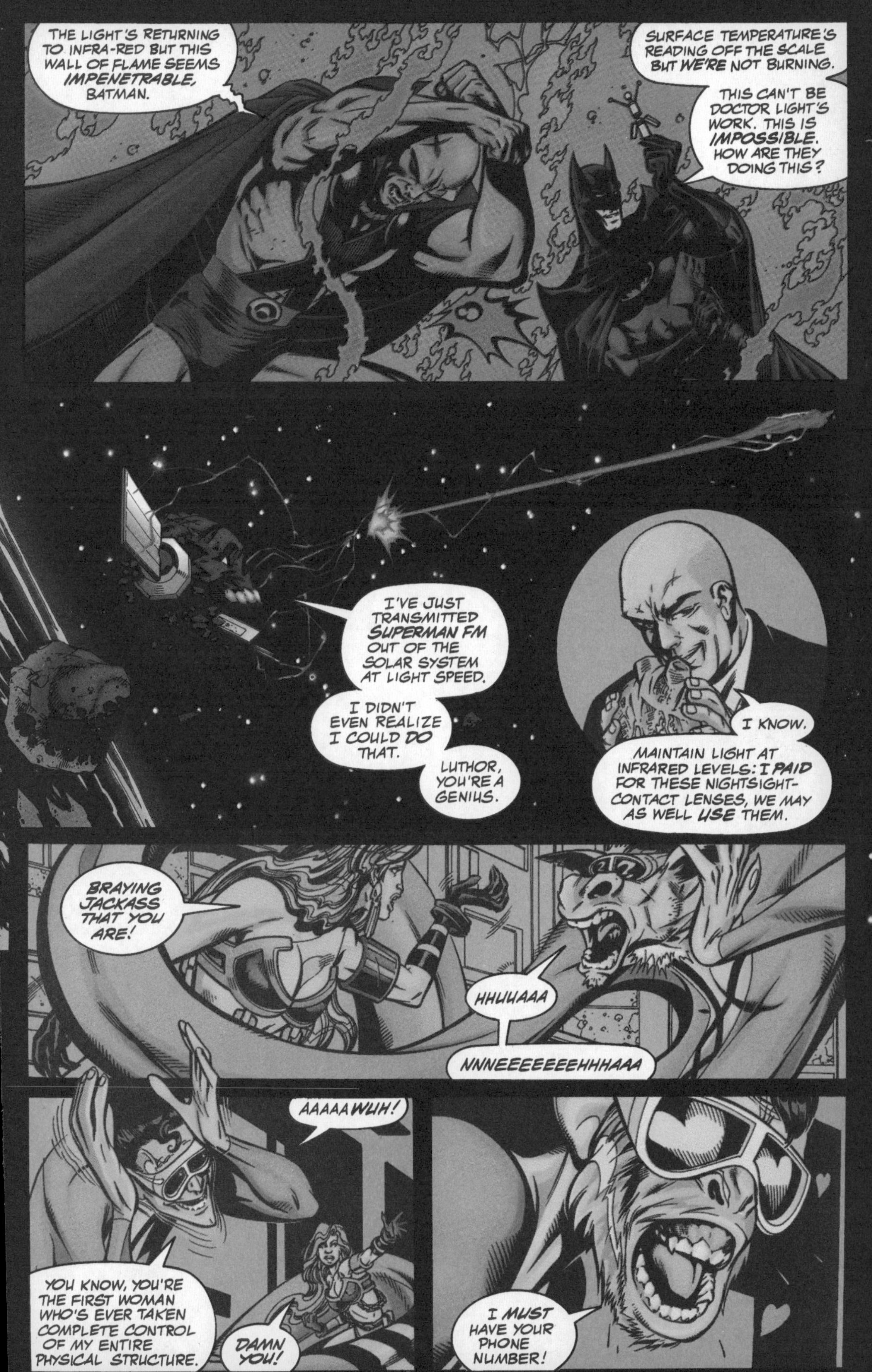
THE LIGHT'S RETURNING TO INFRA-RED BUT THIS WALL OF FLAME SEEMS IMPENETRABLE, BATMAN.
SURFACE TEMPERATURE'S READING OFF THE SCALE BUT WE'RE NOT BURNING.
THIS CAN'T BE DOCTOR LIGHT'S WORK. THIS IS IMPOSSIBLE. HOW ARE THEY DOING THIS?
I'VE JUST TRANSMITTED SUPERMAN FM OUT OF THE SOLAR SYSTEM AT LIGHT SPEED.
I DIDN'T EVEN REALIZE I COULD DO THAT.
LUTHOR, YOU'RE A GENIUS.
I KNOW.
MAINTAIN LIGHT AT INFRARED LEVELS: I PAID FOR THESE NIGHTSIGHT-CONTACT LENSES, WE MAY AS WELL USE THEM.
BRAYING JACKASS THAT YOU ARE!
HHUUAAA
NNNEEEEEEEEHHHAAA
AAAAAWUH!
YOU KNOW, YOU'RE THE FIRST WOMAN WHO'S EVER TAKEN COMPLETE CONTROL OF MY ENTIRE PHYSICAL STRUCTURE.
DAMN YOU!
I MUST HAVE YOUR PHONE NUMBER!

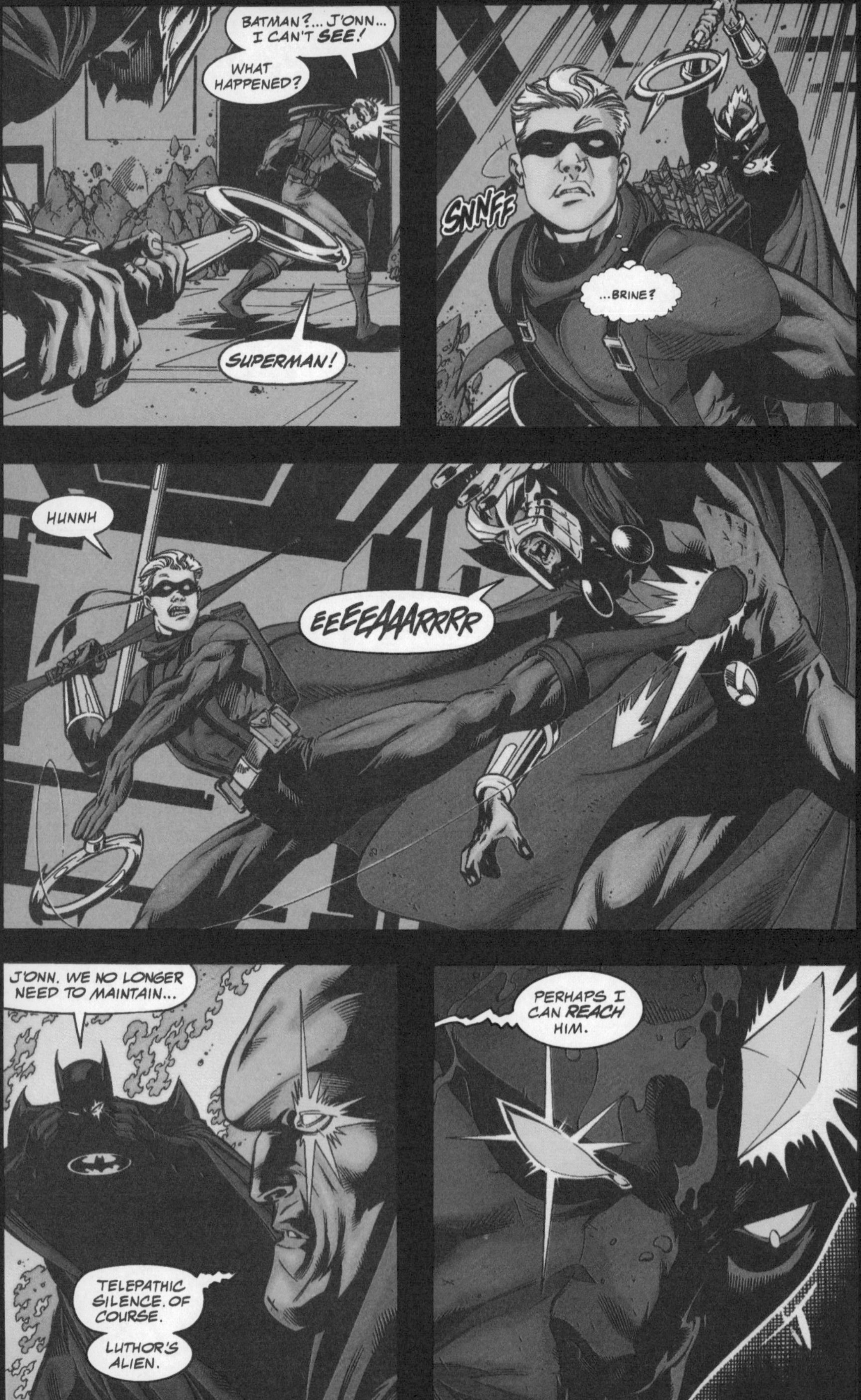
BATMAN?... J'ONN... I CAN'T SEE!
WHAT HAPPENED?
SUPERMAN!
SNNFF
...BRINE?
HUNNH
EEEEAAARRRR
J'ONN. WE NO LONGER NEED TO MAINTAIN...
TELEPATHIC SILENCE. OF COURSE.
LUTHOR'S ALIEN.
PERHAPS I CAN REACH HIM.

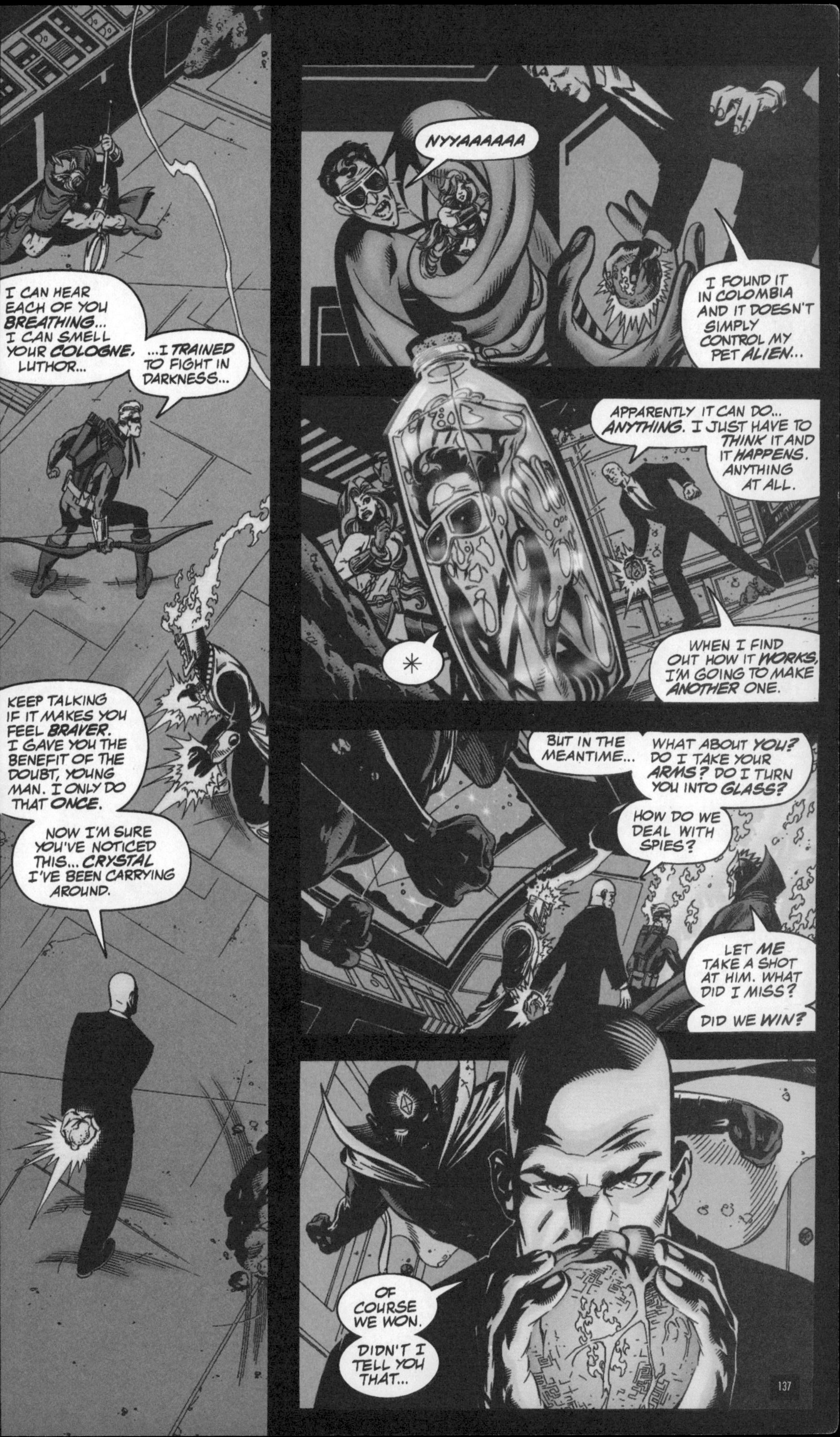

I CAN HEAR EACH OF YOU BREATHING... I CAN SMELL YOUR COLOGNE, LUTHOR...
...I TRAINED TO FIGHT IN DARKNESS...
KEEP TALKING IF IT MAKES YOU FEEL BRAVER. I GAVE YOU THE BENEFIT OF THE DOUBT, YOUNG MAN. I ONLY DO THAT ONCE.
NOW I'M SURE YOU'VE NOTICED THIS... CRYSTAL I'VE BEEN CARRYING AROUND.
NYYAAAAAA
I FOUND IT IN COLOMBIA AND IT DOESN'T SIMPLY CONTROL MY PET ALIEN...
APPARENTLY IT CAN DO... ANYTHING. I JUST HAVE TO THINK IT AND IT HAPPENS. ANYTHING AT ALL.
*
WHEN I FIND OUT HOW IT WORKS, I'M GOING TO MAKE ANOTHER ONE.
BUT IN THE MEANTIME...
WHAT ABOUT YOU? DO I TAKE YOUR ARMS? DO I TURN YOU INTO GLASS?
HOW DO WE DEAL WITH SPIES?
LET ME TAKE A SHOT AT HIM. WHAT DID I MISS?
DID WE WIN?
OF COURSE WE WON.
DIDN'T I TELL YOU THAT...

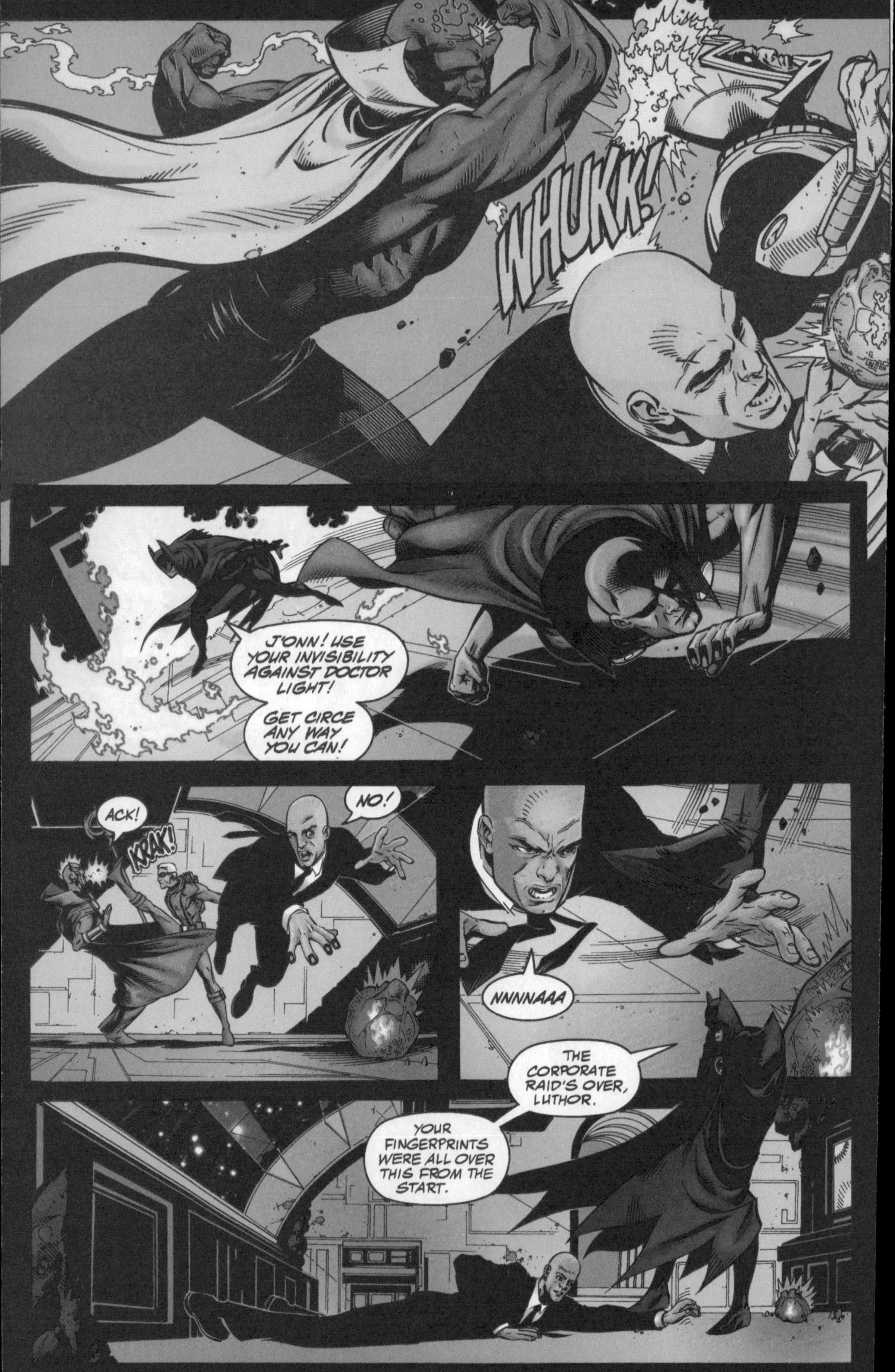
WHUKK!
J'ONN! USE YOUR INVISIBILITY AGAINST DOCTOR LIGHT!
GET CIRCE ANY WAY YOU CAN!
ACK!
KRAK!
NO!
NNNNAAA
THE CORPORATE RAID'S OVER, LUTHOR.
YOUR FINGERPRINTS WERE ALL OVER THIS FROM THE START.

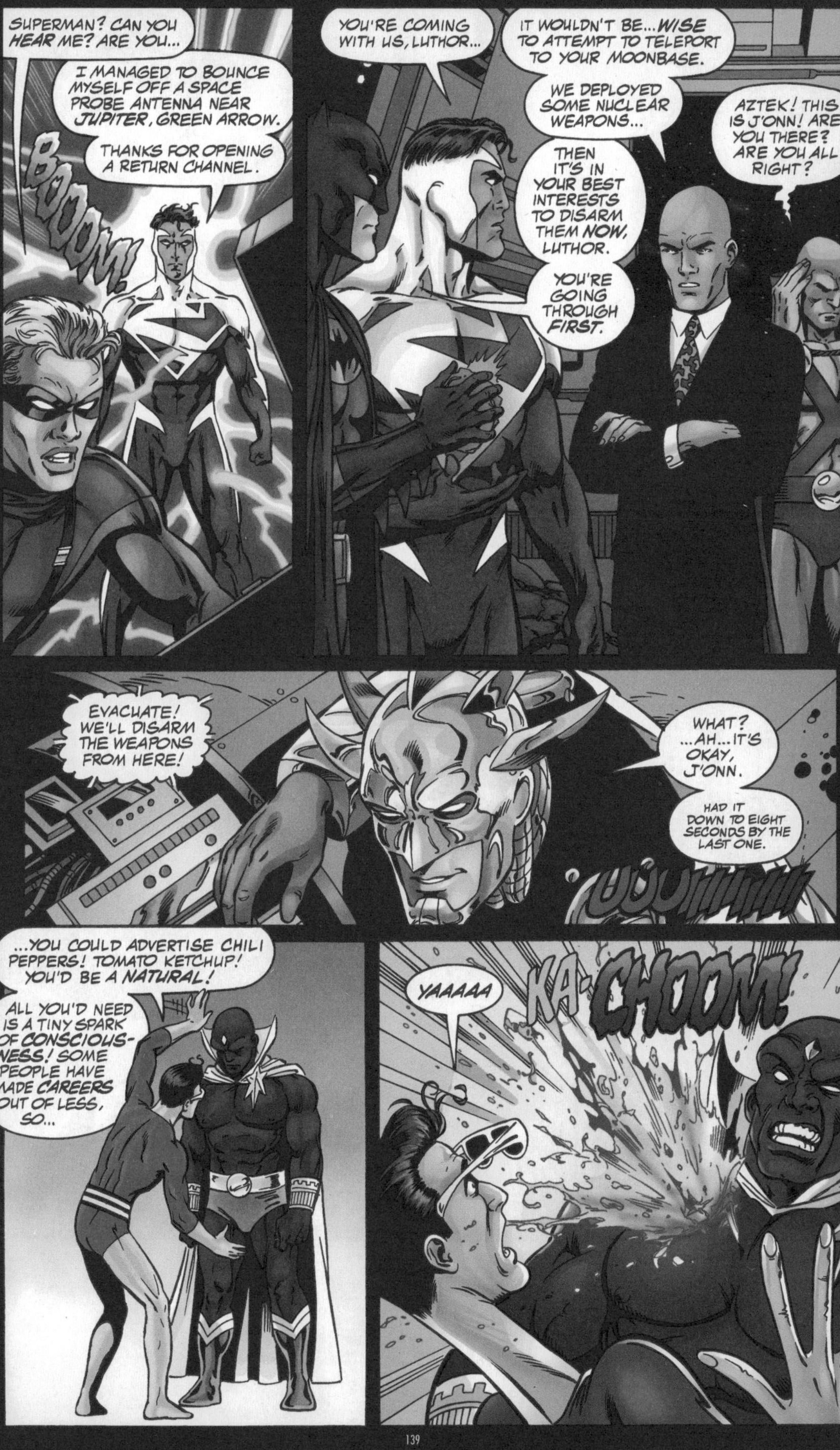
SUPERMAN? CAN YOU HEAR ME? ARE YOU...
I MANAGED TO BOUNCE MYSELF OFF A SPACE PROBE ANTENNA NEAR JUPITER, GREEN ARROW.
THANKS FOR OPENING A RETURN CHANNEL.
BOOOOM!
YOU'RE COMING WITH US, LUTHOR...
IT WOULDN'T BE...WISE TO ATTEMPT TO TELEPORT TO YOUR MOONBASE.
WE DEPLOYED SOME NUCLEAR WEAPONS...
THEN IT'S IN YOUR BEST INTERESTS TO DISARM THEM NOW, LUTHOR.
YOU'RE GOING THROUGH FIRST.
AZTEK! THIS IS J'ONN! ARE YOU THERE? ARE YOU ALL RIGHT?
EVACUATE! WE'LL DISARM THE WEAPONS FROM HERE!
WHAT? ...AH...IT'S OKAY, J'ONN.
HAD IT DOWN TO EIGHT SECONDS BY THE LAST ONE.
...YOU COULD ADVERTISE CHILI PEPPERS! TOMATO KETCHUP! YOU'D BE A NATURAL!
ALL YOU'D NEED IS A TINY SPARK OF CONSCIOUSNESS! SOME PEOPLE HAVE MADE CAREERS OUT OF LESS, SO...
YAAAAA
KA-CHOOM!

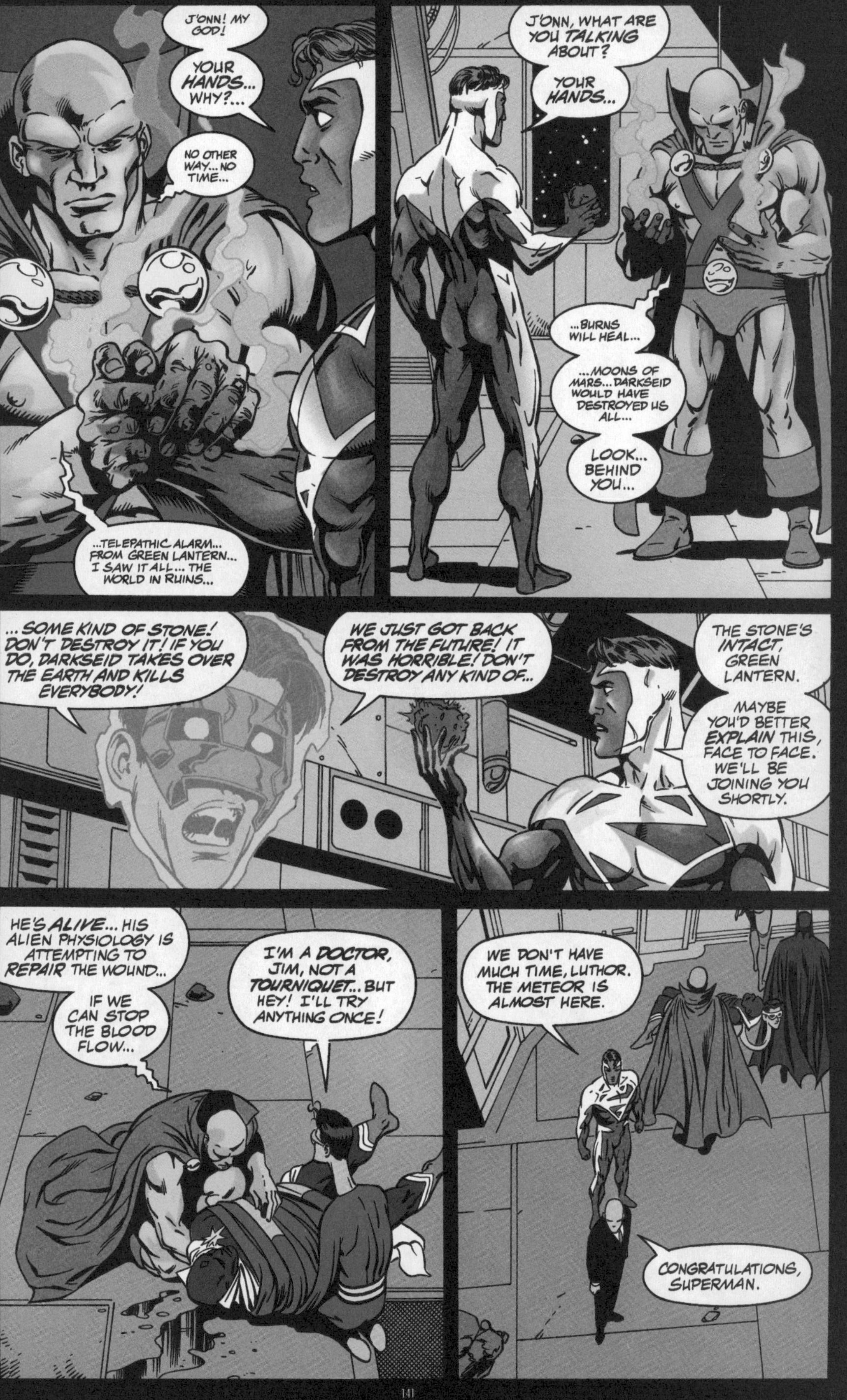
J'ONN! MY GOD!
YOUR HANDS... WHY?...
NO OTHER WAY... NO TIME...
...TELEPATHIC ALARM... FROM GREEN LANTERN... I SAW IT ALL... THE WORLD IN RUINS...
J'ONN, WHAT ARE YOU TALKING ABOUT?
YOUR HANDS...
...BURNS WILL HEAL...
...MOONS OF MARS... DARKSEID WOULD HAVE DESTROYED US ALL...
LOOK... BEHIND YOU...
... SOME KIND OF STONE! DON'T DESTROY IT! IF YOU DO, DARKSEID TAKES OVER THE EARTH AND KILLS EVERYBODY!
WE JUST GOT BACK FROM THE FUTURE! IT WAS HORRIBLE! DON'T DESTROY ANY KIND OF...
THE STONE'S INTACT, GREEN LANTERN.
MAYBE YOU'D BETTER EXPLAIN THIS, FACE TO FACE. WE'LL BE JOINING YOU SHORTLY.
HE'S ALIVE... HIS ALIEN PHYSIOLOGY IS ATTEMPTING TO REPAIR THE WOUND...
IF WE CAN STOP THE BLOOD FLOW...
I'M A DOCTOR, JIM, NOT A TOURNIQUET... BUT HEY! I'LL TRY ANYTHING ONCE!
WE DON'T HAVE MUCH TIME, LUTHOR. THE METEOR IS ALMOST HERE.
CONGRATULATIONS, SUPERMAN.

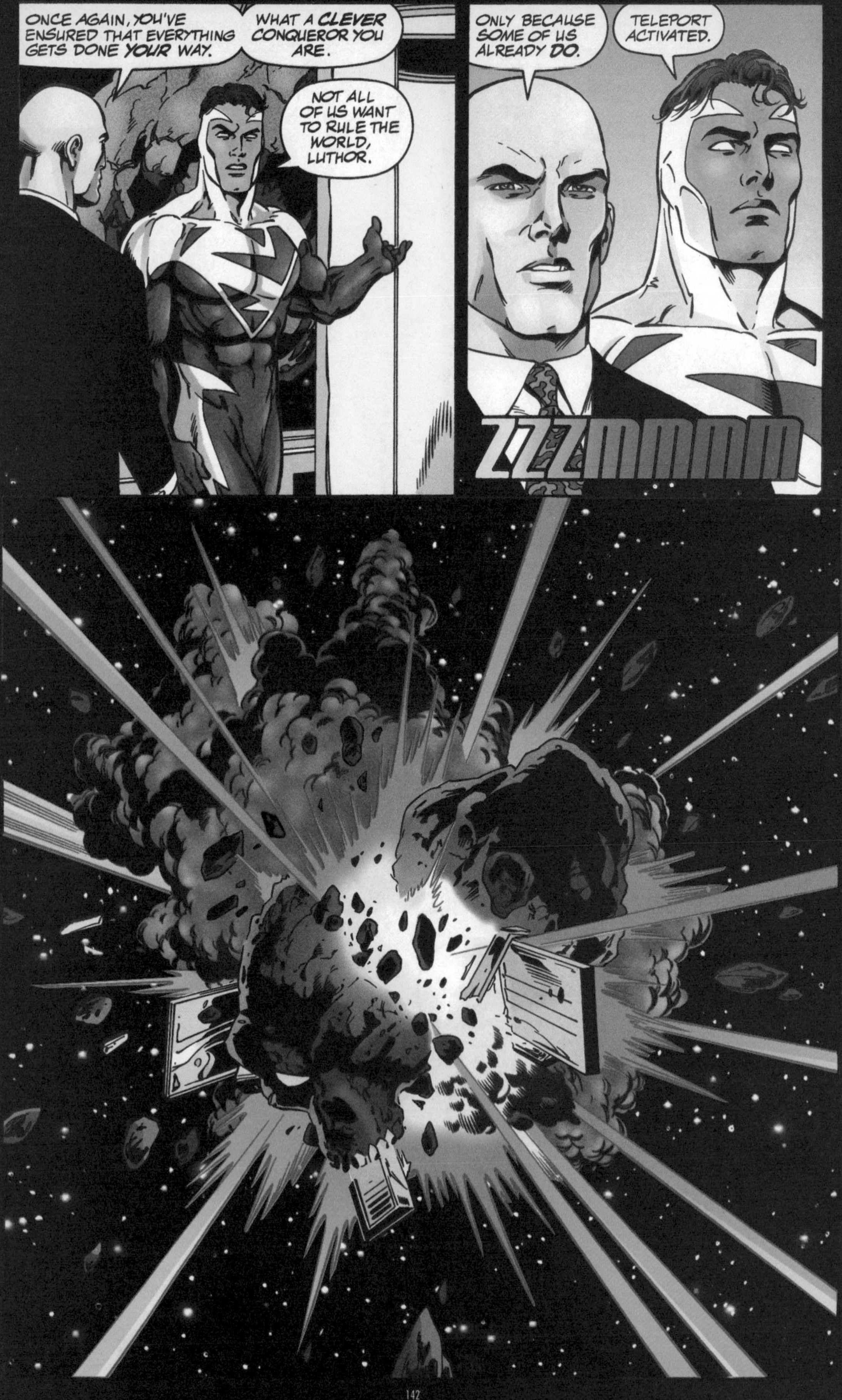
ONCE AGAIN, YOU'VE ENSURED THAT EVERYTHING GETS DONE YOUR WAY.
WHAT A CLEVER CONQUEROR YOU ARE.
NOT ALL OF US WANT TO RULE THE WORLD, LUTHOR.
ONLY BECAUSE SOME OF US ALREADY DO.
TELEPORT ACTIVATED.
ZZZMMMMM

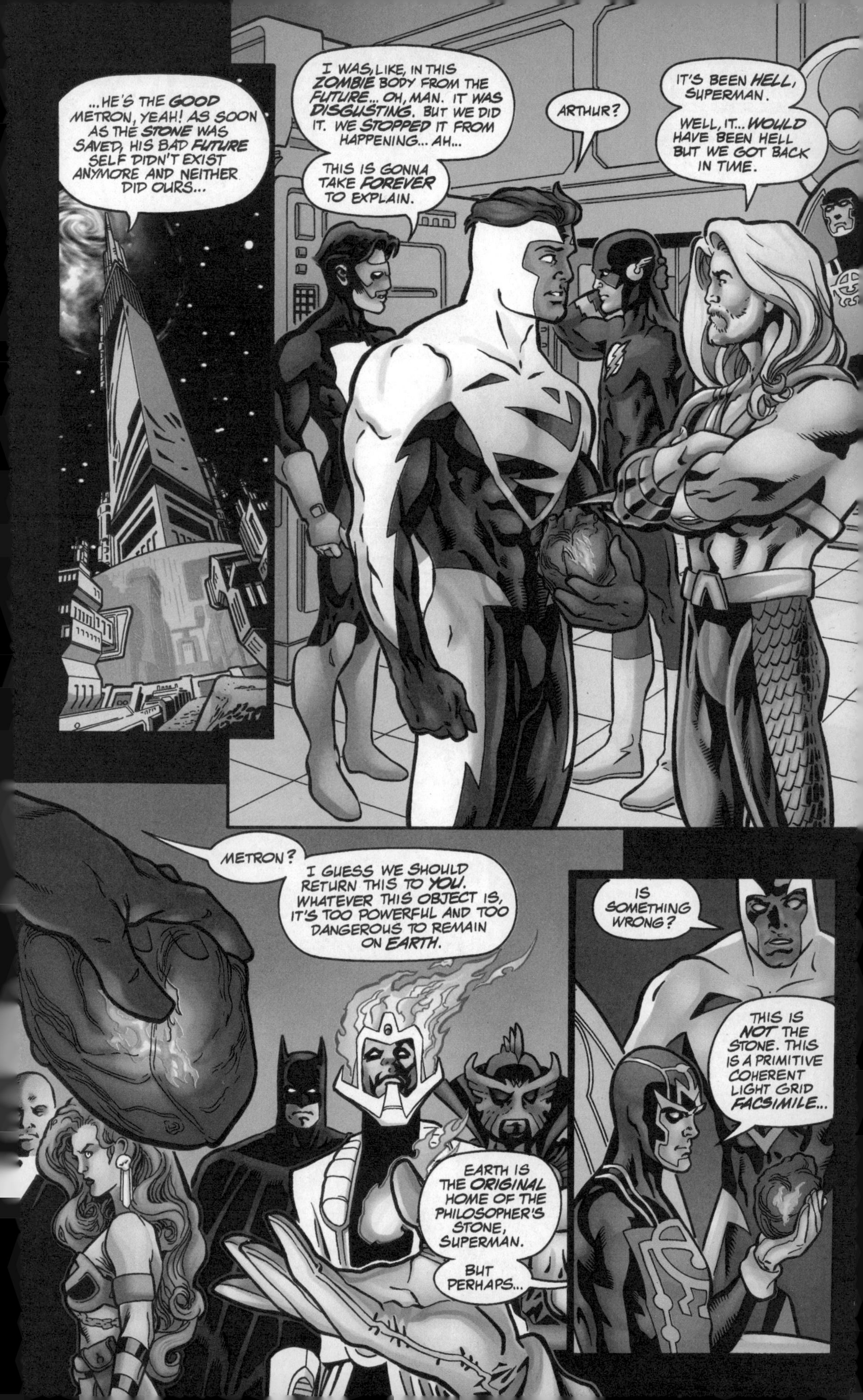
...HE'S THE GOOD METRON, YEAH! AS SOON AS THE STONE WAS SAVED, HIS BAD FUTURE SELF DIDN'T EXIST ANYMORE AND NEITHER DID OURS...
I WAS, LIKE, IN THIS ZOMBIE BODY FROM THE FUTURE... OH, MAN. IT WAS DISGUSTING. BUT WE DID IT. WE STOPPED IT FROM HAPPENING... AH...
THIS IS GONNA TAKE FOREVER TO EXPLAIN.
ARTHUR?
IT'S BEEN HELL, SUPERMAN.
WELL, IT... WOULD HAVE BEEN HELL BUT WE GOT BACK IN TIME.
METRON?
I GUESS WE SHOULD RETURN THIS TO YOU. WHATEVER THIS OBJECT IS, IT'S TOO POWERFUL AND TOO DANGEROUS TO REMAIN ON EARTH.
EARTH IS THE ORIGINAL HOME OF THE PHILOSOPHER'S STONE, SUPERMAN.
BUT PERHAPS...
IS SOMETHING WRONG?
THIS IS NOT THE STONE. THIS IS A PRIMITIVE COHERENT LIGHT GRID FACSIMILE...

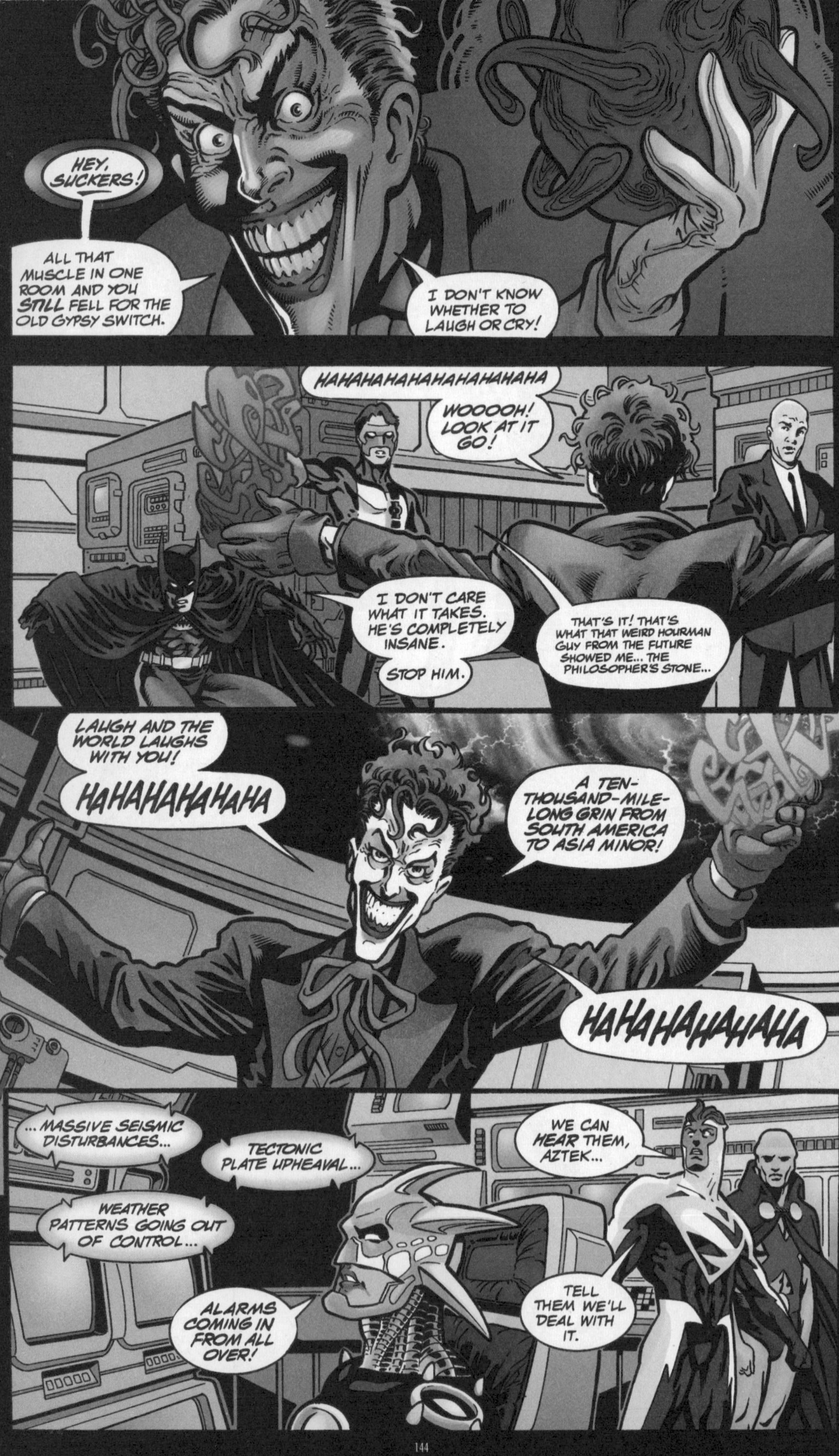
HEY, SUCKERS!
ALL THAT MUSCLE IN ONE ROOM AND YOU STILL FELL FOR THE OLD GYPSY SWITCH.
I DON'T KNOW WHETHER TO LAUGH OR CRY!
HAHAHAHAHAHAHAHAHAHAHA
WOOOOH! LOOK AT IT GO!
I DON'T CARE WHAT IT TAKES. HE'S COMPLETELY INSANE.
STOP HIM.
THAT'S IT! THAT'S WHAT THAT WEIRD HOURMAN GUY FROM THE FUTURE SHOWED ME... THE PHILOSOPHER'S STONE...
LAUGH AND THE WORLD LAUGHS WITH YOU!
HAHAHAHAHAHAHA
A TEN-THOUSAND-MILE-LONG GRIN FROM SOUTH AMERICA TO ASIA MINOR!
HAHAHAHAHAHAHA
...MASSIVE SEISMIC DISTURBANCES...
TECTONIC PLATE UPHEAVAL...
WEATHER PATTERNS GOING OUT OF CONTROL...
ALARMS COMING IN FROM ALL OVER!
WE CAN HEAR THEM, AZTEK...
TELL THEM WE'LL DEAL WITH IT.

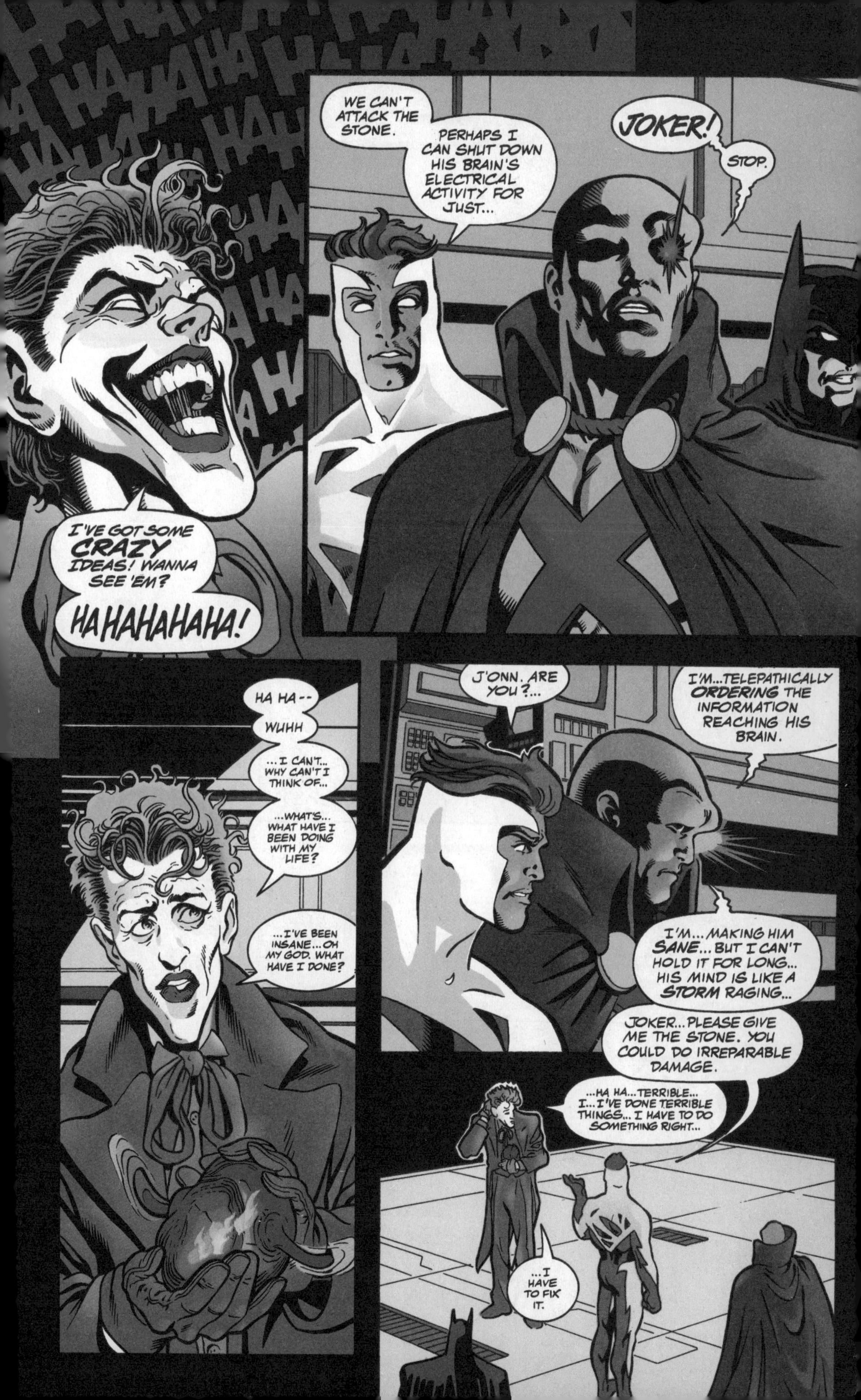
HAHAHAHAHA
I'VE GOT SOME CRAZY IDEAS! WANNA SEE 'EM?
HAHAHAHAHA!
WE CAN'T ATTACK THE STONE.
PERHAPS I CAN SHUT DOWN HIS BRAIN'S ELECTRICAL ACTIVITY FOR JUST...
JOKER!
STOP.
HA HA --
WUHH
...I CAN'T... WHY CAN'T I THINK OF...
...WHAT'S... WHAT HAVE I BEEN DOING WITH MY LIFE?
...I'VE BEEN INSANE... OH MY GOD. WHAT HAVE I DONE?
J'ONN. ARE YOU?...
I'M...TELEPATHICALLY ORDERING THE INFORMATION REACHING HIS BRAIN.
I'M... MAKING HIM SANE... BUT I CAN'T HOLD IT FOR LONG... HIS MIND IS LIKE A STORM RAGING...
JOKER... PLEASE GIVE ME THE STONE. YOU COULD DO IRREPARABLE DAMAGE.
...HA HA...TERRIBLE... I...I'VE DONE TERRIBLE THINGS... I HAVE TO DO SOMETHING RIGHT...
...I HAVE TO FIX IT.

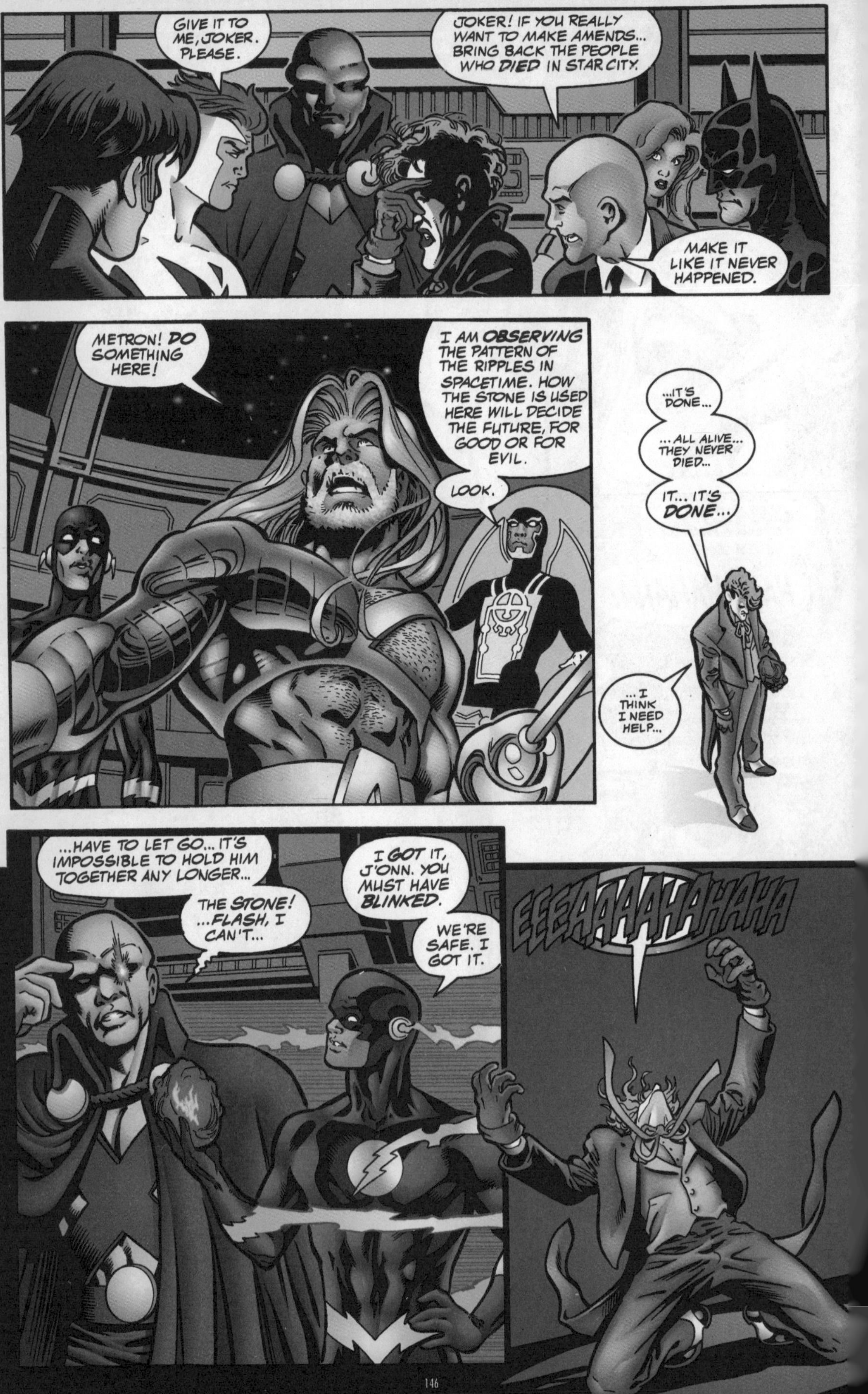
GIVE IT TO ME, JOKER. PLEASE.
JOKER! IF YOU REALLY WANT TO MAKE AMENDS... BRING BACK THE PEOPLE WHO DIED IN STAR CITY.
MAKE IT LIKE IT NEVER HAPPENED.
METRON! DO SOMETHING HERE!
I AM OBSERVING THE PATTERN OF THE RIPPLES IN SPACETIME. HOW THE STONE IS USED HERE WILL DECIDE THE FUTURE, FOR GOOD OR FOR EVIL.
LOOK.
...IT'S DONE...
...ALL ALIVE... THEY NEVER DIED...
IT... IT'S DONE...
...I THINK I NEED HELP...
...HAVE TO LET GO... IT'S IMPOSSIBLE TO HOLD HIM TOGETHER ANY LONGER...
THE STONE! ...FLASH, I CAN'T...
I GOT IT, J'ONN. YOU MUST HAVE BLINKED.
WE'RE SAFE. I GOT IT.
EEEAAAAAHAHAHA

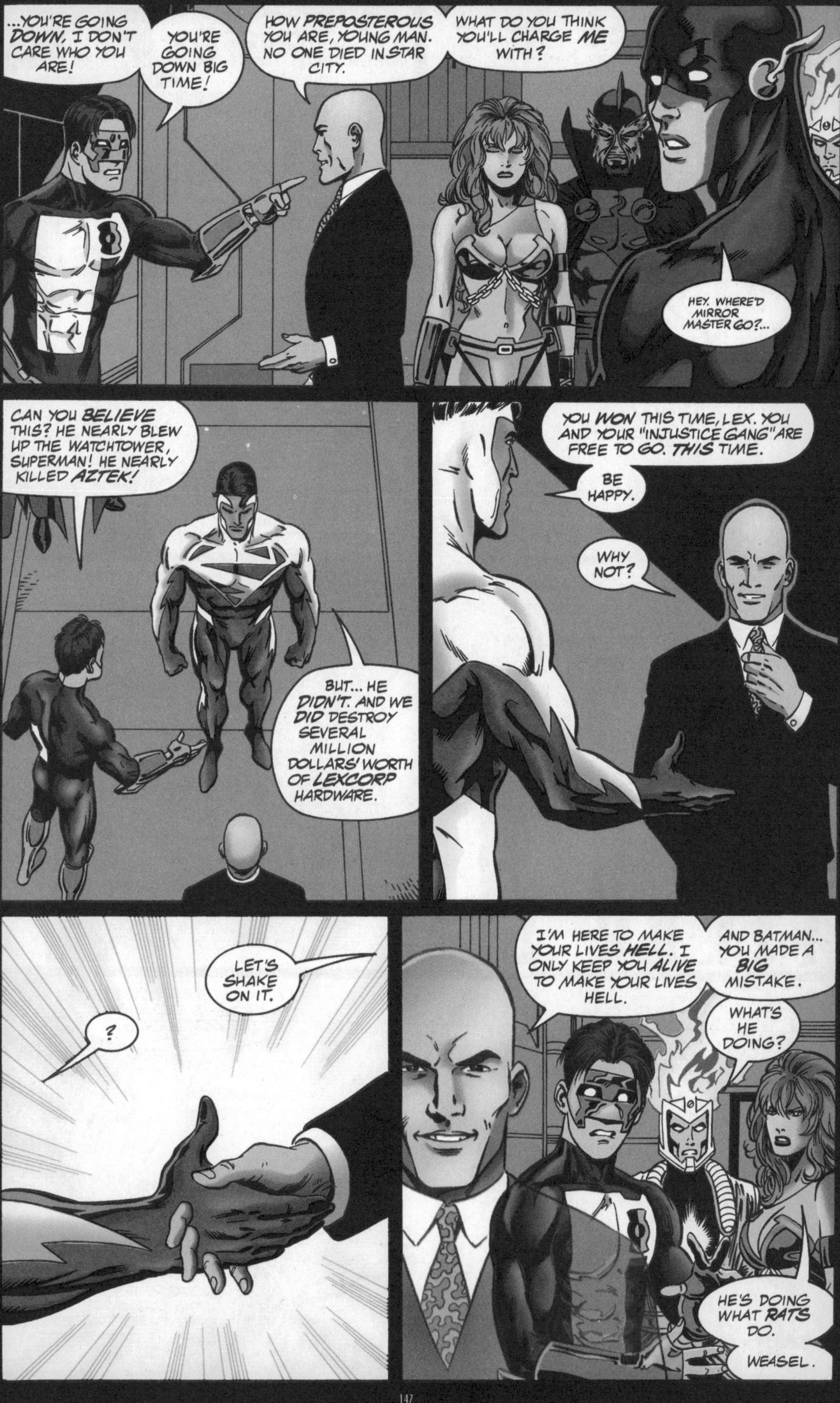
...YOU'RE GOING DOWN. I DON'T CARE WHO YOU ARE!
YOU'RE GOING DOWN BIG TIME!
HOW PREPOSTEROUS YOU ARE, YOUNG MAN. NO ONE DIED IN STAR CITY.
WHAT DO YOU THINK YOU'LL CHARGE ME WITH?
HEY. WHERE'D MIRROR MASTER GO?...
CAN YOU BELIEVE THIS? HE NEARLY BLEW UP THE WATCHTOWER, SUPERMAN! HE NEARLY KILLED AZTEK!
BUT... HE DIDN'T. AND WE DID DESTROY SEVERAL MILLION DOLLARS' WORTH OF LEXCORP HARDWARE.
YOU WON THIS TIME, LEX. YOU AND YOUR "INJUSTICE GANG" ARE FREE TO GO. THIS TIME.
BE HAPPY.
WHY NOT?
LET'S SHAKE ON IT.
?
I'M HERE TO MAKE YOUR LIVES HELL. I ONLY KEEP YOU ALIVE TO MAKE YOUR LIVES HELL.
AND BATMAN... YOU MADE A BIG MISTAKE.
WHAT'S HE DOING?
HE'S DOING WHAT RATS DO.
WEASEL.

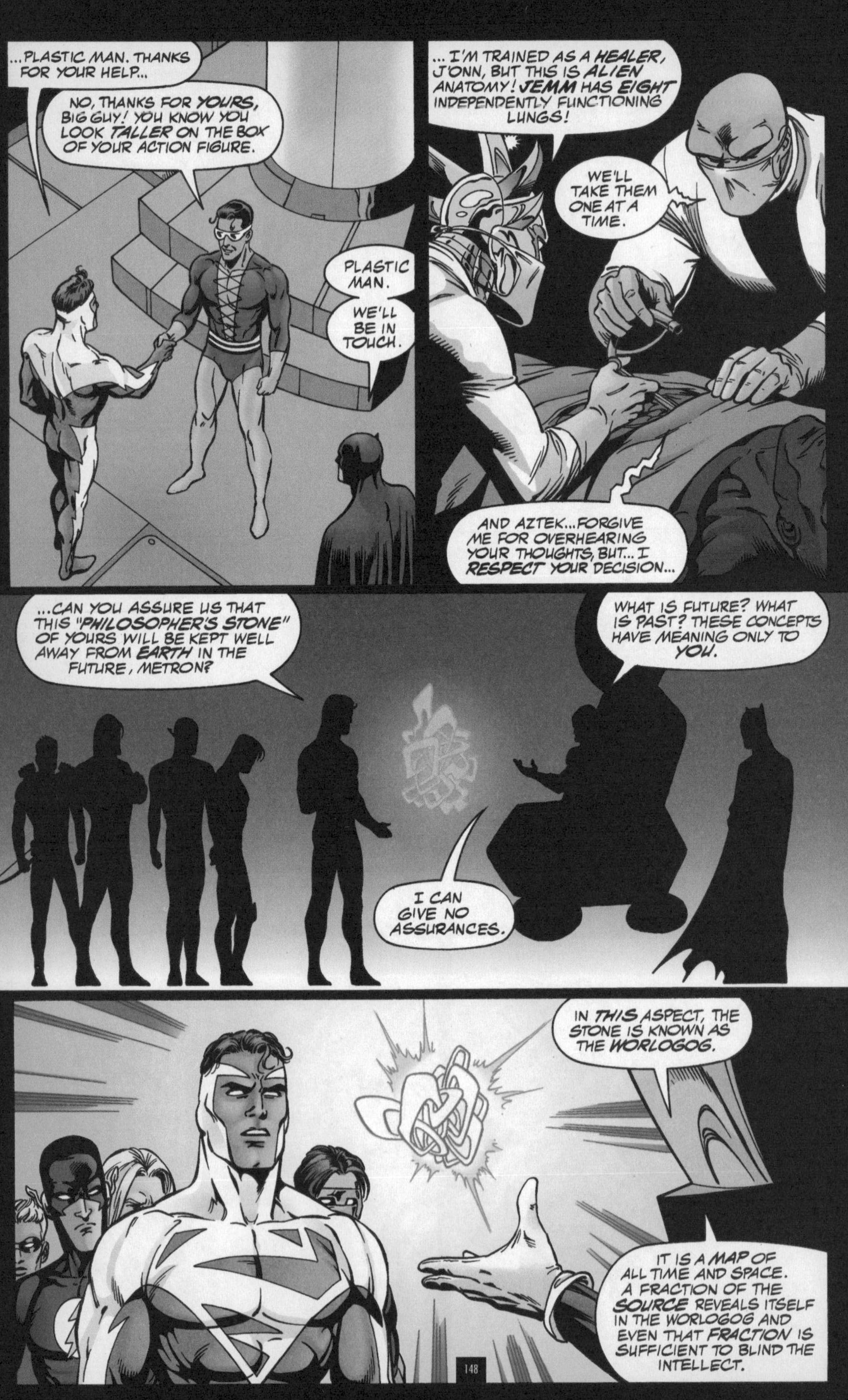

...PLASTIC MAN. THANKS FOR YOUR HELP...
NO, THANKS FOR YOURS, BIG GUY! YOU KNOW YOU LOOK TALLER ON THE BOX OF YOUR ACTION FIGURE.
PLASTIC MAN.
WE'LL BE IN TOUCH.
... I'M TRAINED AS A HEALER, J'ONN, BUT THIS IS ALIEN ANATOMY! JEMM HAS EIGHT INDEPENDENTLY FUNCTIONING LUNGS!
WE'LL TAKE THEM ONE AT A TIME.
AND AZTEK...FORGIVE ME FOR OVERHEARING YOUR THOUGHTS, BUT... I RESPECT YOUR DECISION...
...CAN YOU ASSURE US THAT THIS "PHILOSOPHER'S STONE" OF YOURS WILL BE KEPT WELL AWAY FROM EARTH IN THE FUTURE, METRON?
WHAT IS FUTURE? WHAT IS PAST? THESE CONCEPTS HAVE MEANING ONLY TO YOU.
I CAN GIVE NO ASSURANCES.
IN THIS ASPECT, THE STONE IS KNOWN AS THE WORLOGOG.
IT IS A MAP OF ALL TIME AND SPACE. A FRACTION OF THE SOURCE REVEALS ITSELF IN THE WORLOGOG AND EVEN THAT FRACTION IS SUFFICIENT TO BLIND THE INTELLECT.

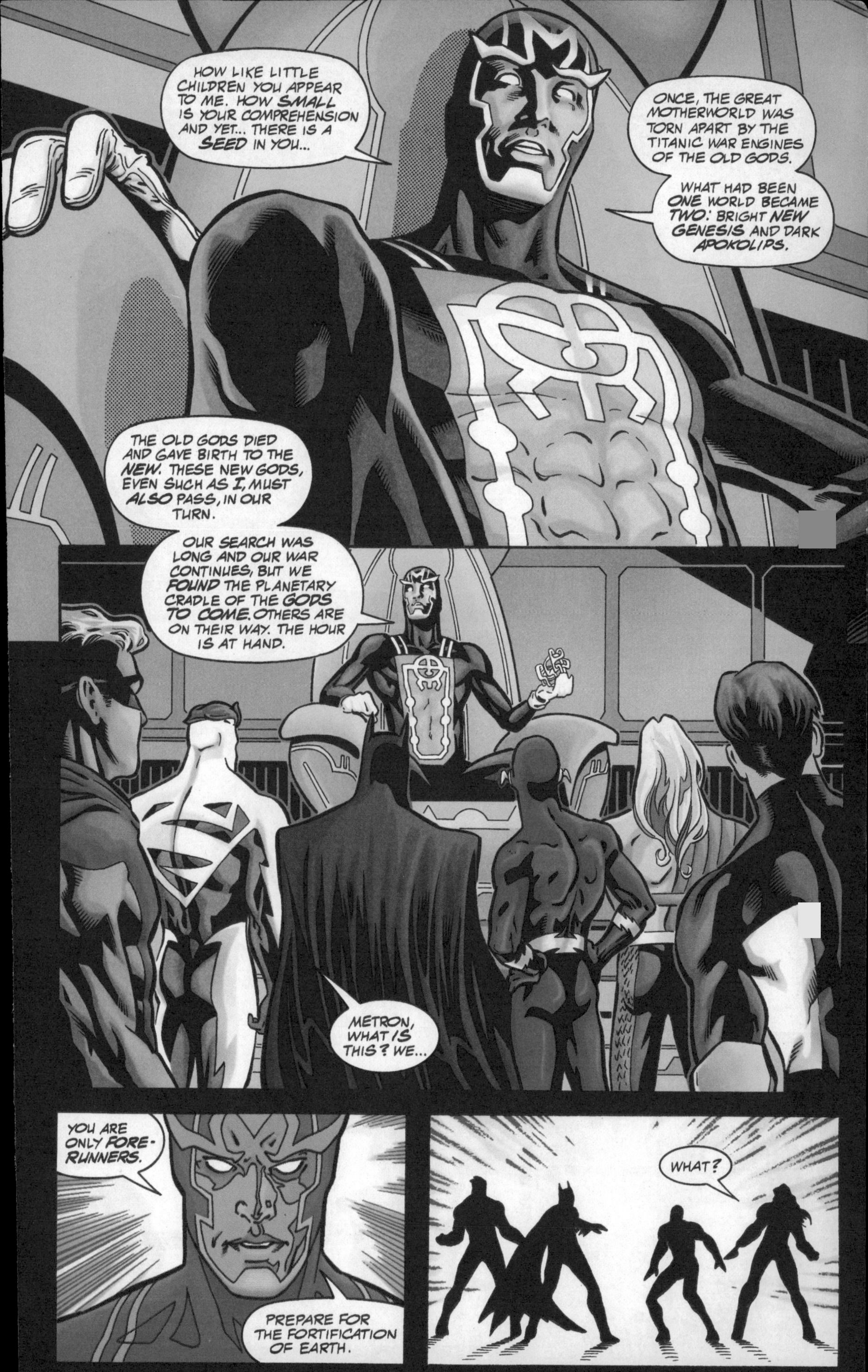
HOW LIKE LITTLE CHILDREN YOU APPEAR TO ME. HOW SMALL IS YOUR COMPREHENSION AND YET... THERE IS A SEED IN YOU...
ONCE, THE GREAT MOTHERWORLD WAS TORN APART BY THE TITANIC WAR ENGINES OF THE OLD GODS.
WHAT HAD BEEN ONE WORLD BECAME TWO: BRIGHT NEW GENESIS AND DARK APOKOLIPS.
THE OLD GODS DIED AND GAVE BIRTH TO THE NEW. THESE NEW GODS, EVEN SUCH AS I, MUST ALSO PASS, IN OUR TURN.
OUR SEARCH WAS LONG AND OUR WAR CONTINUES, BUT WE FOUND THE PLANETARY CRADLE OF THE GODS TO COME. OTHERS ARE ON THEIR WAY. THE HOUR IS AT HAND.
METRON, WHAT IS THIS? WE...
YOU ARE ONLY FORE-RUNNERS.
PREPARE FOR THE FORTIFICATION OF EARTH.
WHAT?

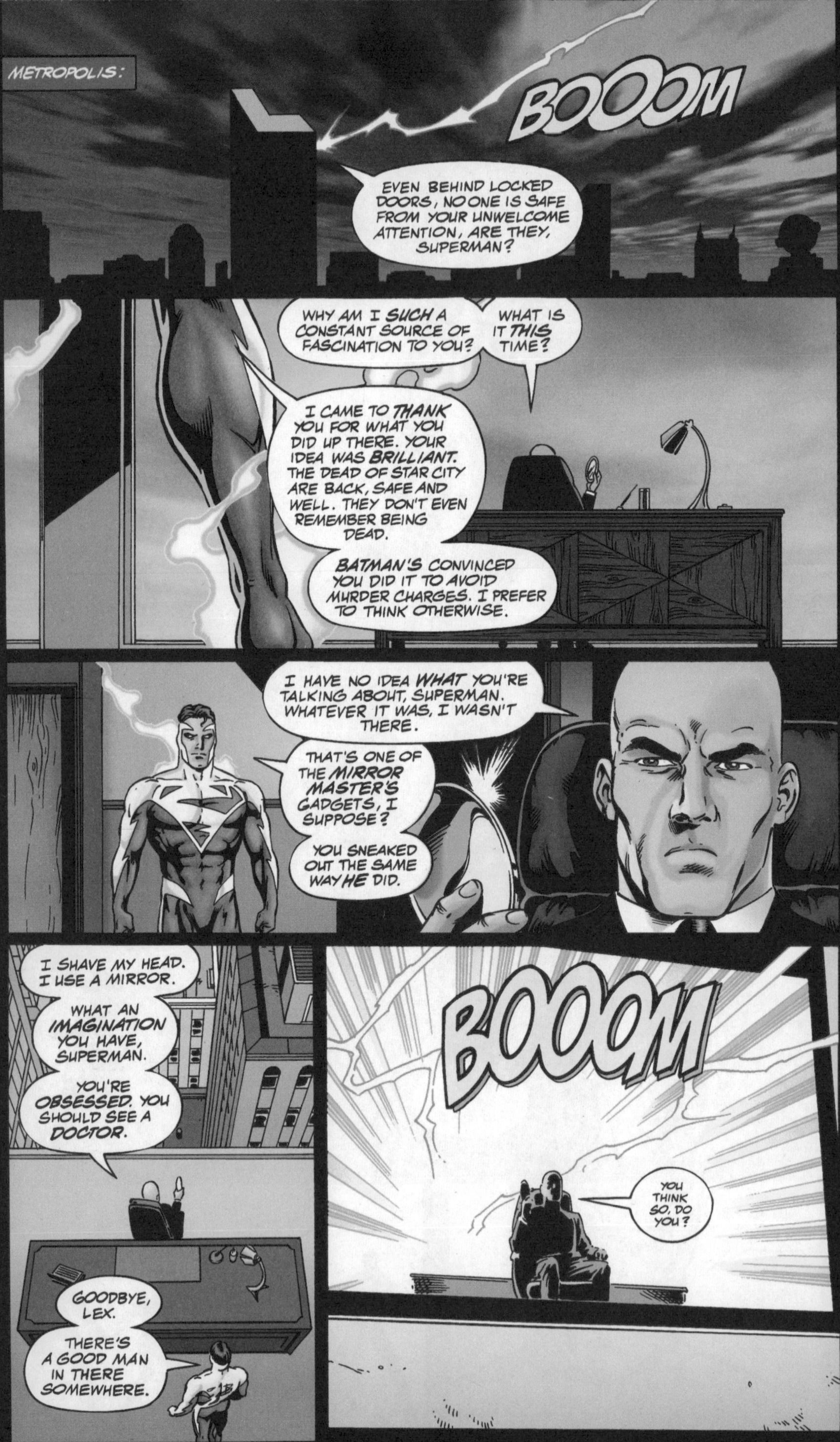
METROPOLIS:
BOOOM
EVEN BEHIND LOCKED DOORS, NO ONE IS SAFE FROM YOUR UNWELCOME ATTENTION, ARE THEY, SUPERMAN?
WHY AM I SUCH A CONSTANT SOURCE OF FASCINATION TO YOU?
WHAT IS IT THIS TIME?
I CAME TO THANK YOU FOR WHAT YOU DID UP THERE. YOUR IDEA WAS BRILLIANT. THE DEAD OF STAR CITY ARE BACK, SAFE AND WELL. THEY DON'T EVEN REMEMBER BEING DEAD.
BATMAN'S CONVINCED YOU DID IT TO AVOID MURDER CHARGES. I PREFER TO THINK OTHERWISE.
I HAVE NO IDEA WHAT YOU'RE TALKING ABOUT, SUPERMAN. WHATEVER IT WAS, I WASN'T THERE.
THAT'S ONE OF THE MIRROR MASTER'S GADGETS, I SUPPOSE?
YOU SNEAKED OUT THE SAME WAY HE DID.
I SHAVE MY HEAD. I USE A MIRROR.
WHAT AN IMAGINATION YOU HAVE, SUPERMAN.
YOU'RE OBSESSED. YOU SHOULD SEE A DOCTOR.
GOODBYE, LEX.
THERE'S A GOOD MAN IN THERE SOMEWHERE.
BOOOM
YOU THINK SO, DO YOU?

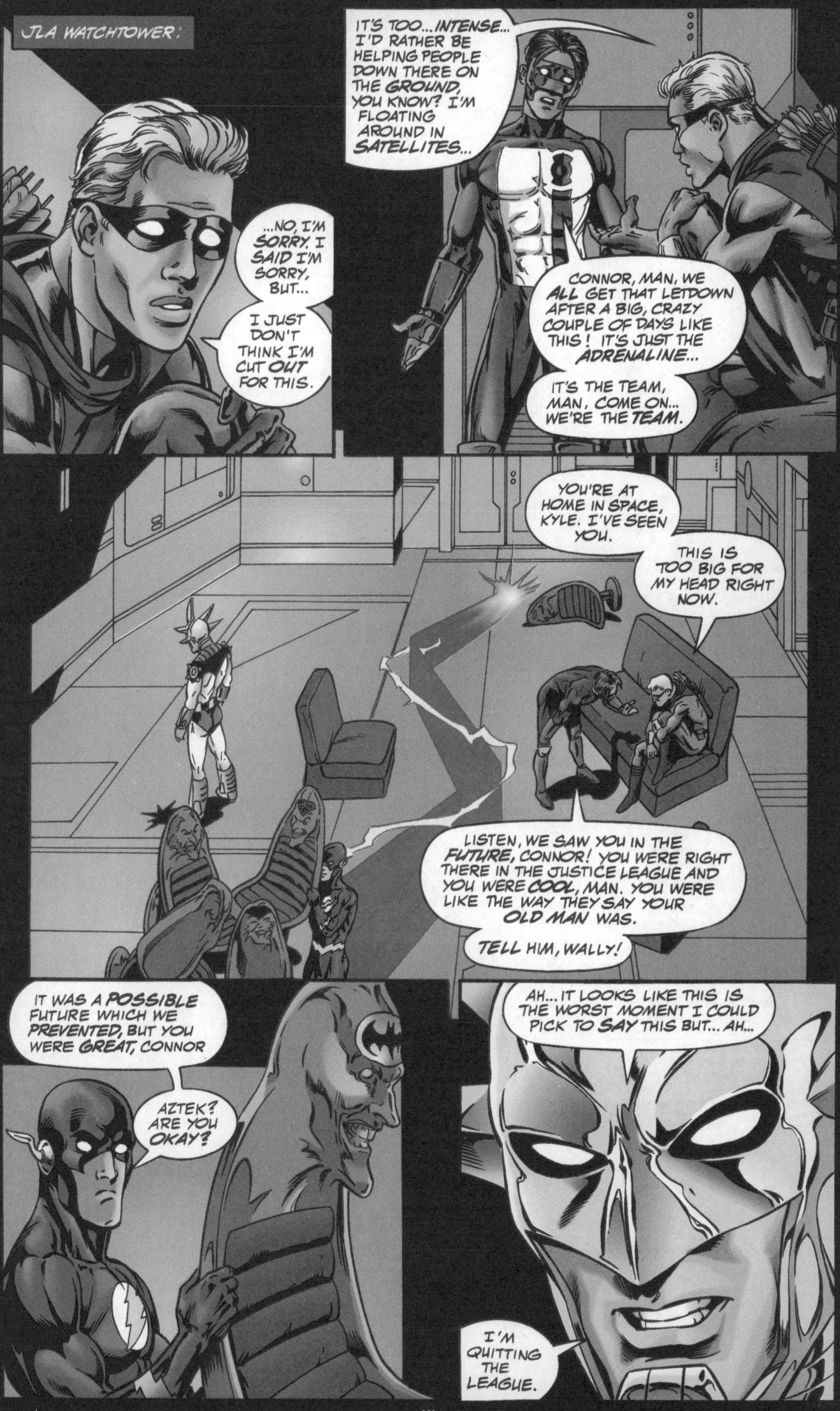
JLA WATCHTOWER:
IT'S TOO... INTENSE... I'D RATHER BE HELPING PEOPLE DOWN THERE ON THE GROUND, YOU KNOW? I'M FLOATING AROUND IN SATELLITES...
...NO, I'M SORRY. I SAID I'M SORRY, BUT...
I JUST DON'T THINK I'M CUT OUT FOR THIS.
CONNOR, MAN, WE ALL GET THAT LETDOWN AFTER A BIG, CRAZY COUPLE OF DAYS LIKE THIS! IT'S JUST THE ADRENALINE...
IT'S THE TEAM, MAN, COME ON... WE'RE THE TEAM.
YOU'RE AT HOME IN SPACE, KYLE. I'VE SEEN YOU.
THIS IS TOO BIG FOR MY HEAD RIGHT NOW.
LISTEN, WE SAW YOU IN THE FUTURE, CONNOR! YOU WERE RIGHT THERE IN THE JUSTICE LEAGUE AND YOU WERE COOL, MAN. YOU WERE LIKE THE WAY THEY SAY YOUR OLD MAN WAS.
TELL HIM, WALLY!
IT WAS A POSSIBLE FUTURE WHICH WE PREVENTED, BUT YOU WERE GREAT, CONNOR
AZTEK? ARE YOU OKAY?
AH... IT LOOKS LIKE THIS IS THE WORST MOMENT I COULD PICK TO SAY THIS BUT... AH...
I'M QUITTING THE LEAGUE.

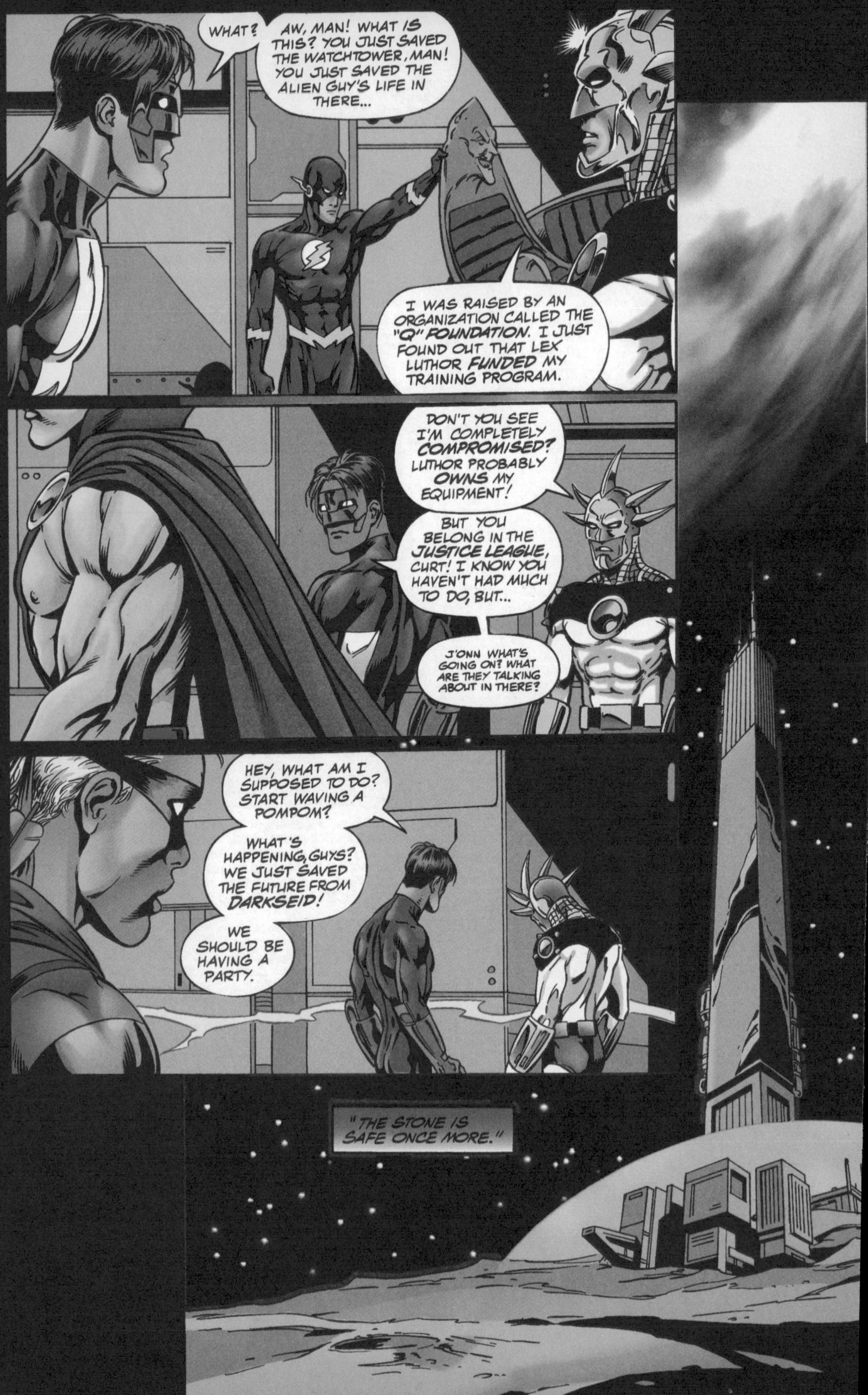
WHAT?
AW, MAN! WHAT IS THIS? YOU JUST SAVED THE WATCHTOWER, MAN! YOU JUST SAVED THE ALIEN GUY'S LIFE IN THERE...
I WAS RAISED BY AN ORGANIZATION CALLED THE "Q" FOUNDATION. I JUST FOUND OUT THAT LEX LUTHOR FUNDED MY TRAINING PROGRAM.
DON'T YOU SEE I'M COMPLETELY COMPROMISED? LUTHOR PROBABLY OWNS MY EQUIPMENT!
BUT YOU BELONG IN THE JUSTICE LEAGUE, CURT! I KNOW YOU HAVEN'T HAD MUCH TO DO, BUT...
J'ONN WHAT'S GOING ON? WHAT ARE THEY TALKING ABOUT IN THERE?
HEY, WHAT AM I SUPPOSED TO DO? START WAVING A POMPOM?
WHAT'S HAPPENING, GUYS? WE JUST SAVED THE FUTURE FROM DARKSEID!
WE SHOULD BE HAVING A PARTY.
"THE STONE IS SAFE ONCE MORE."

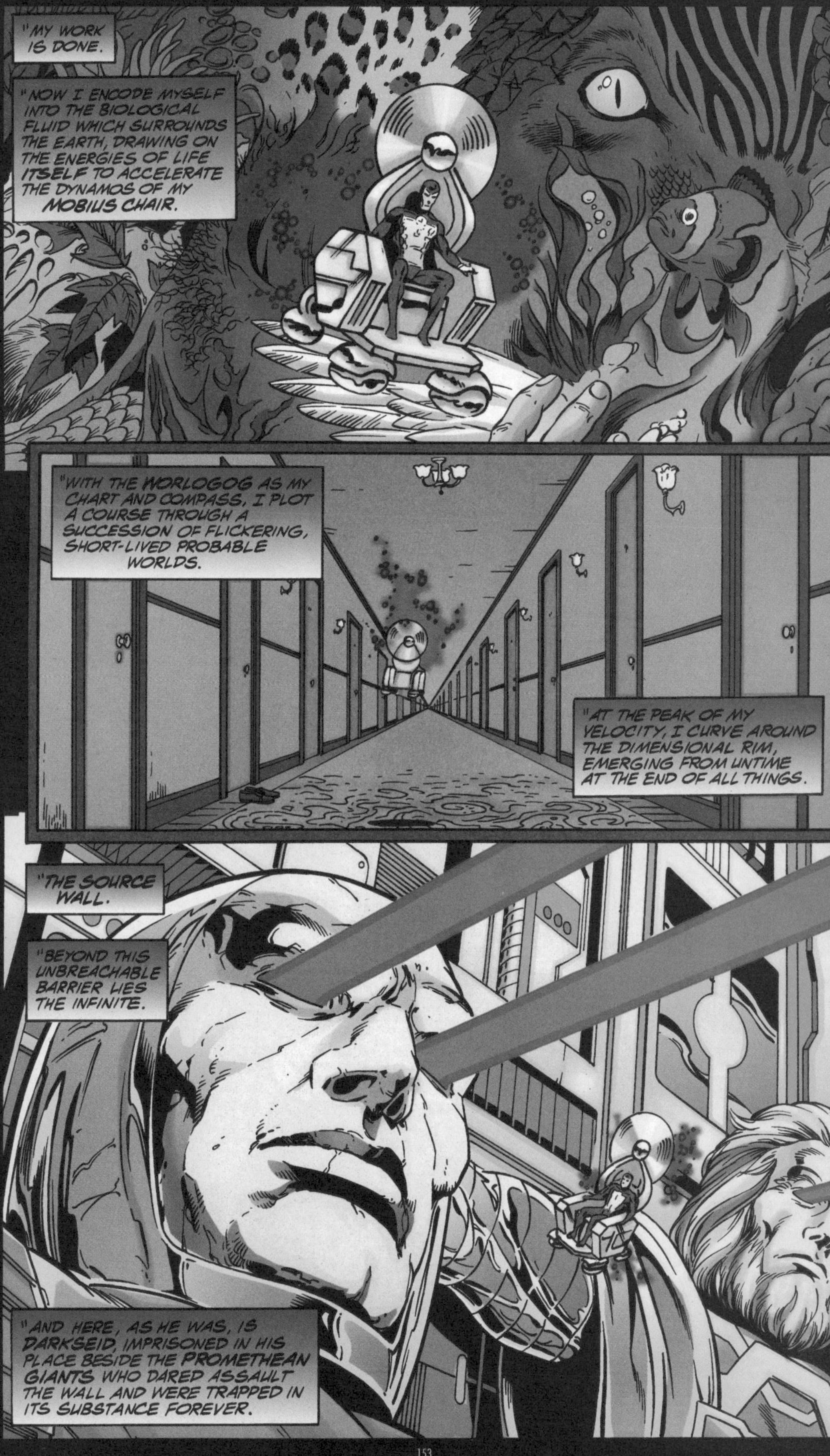
"MY WORK IS DONE.
"NOW I ENCODE MYSELF INTO THE BIOLOGICAL FLUID WHICH SURROUNDS THE EARTH, DRAWING ON THE ENERGIES OF LIFE ITSELF TO ACCELERATE THE DYNAMOS OF MY MOBIUS CHAIR.
"WITH THE WORLOGOG AS MY CHART AND COMPASS, I PLOT A COURSE THROUGH A SUCCESSION OF FLICKERING, SHORT-LIVED PROBABLE WORLDS.
"AT THE PEAK OF MY VELOCITY, I CURVE AROUND THE DIMENSIONAL RIM, EMERGING FROM UNTIME AT THE END OF ALL THINGS.
"THE SOURCE WALL.
"BEYOND THIS UNBREACHABLE BARRIER LIES THE INFINITE.
"AND HERE, AS HE WAS, IS DARKSEID, IMPRISONED IN HIS PLACE BESIDE THE PROMETHEAN GIANTS WHO DARED ASSAULT THE WALL AND WERE TRAPPED IN ITS SUBSTANCE FOREVER.

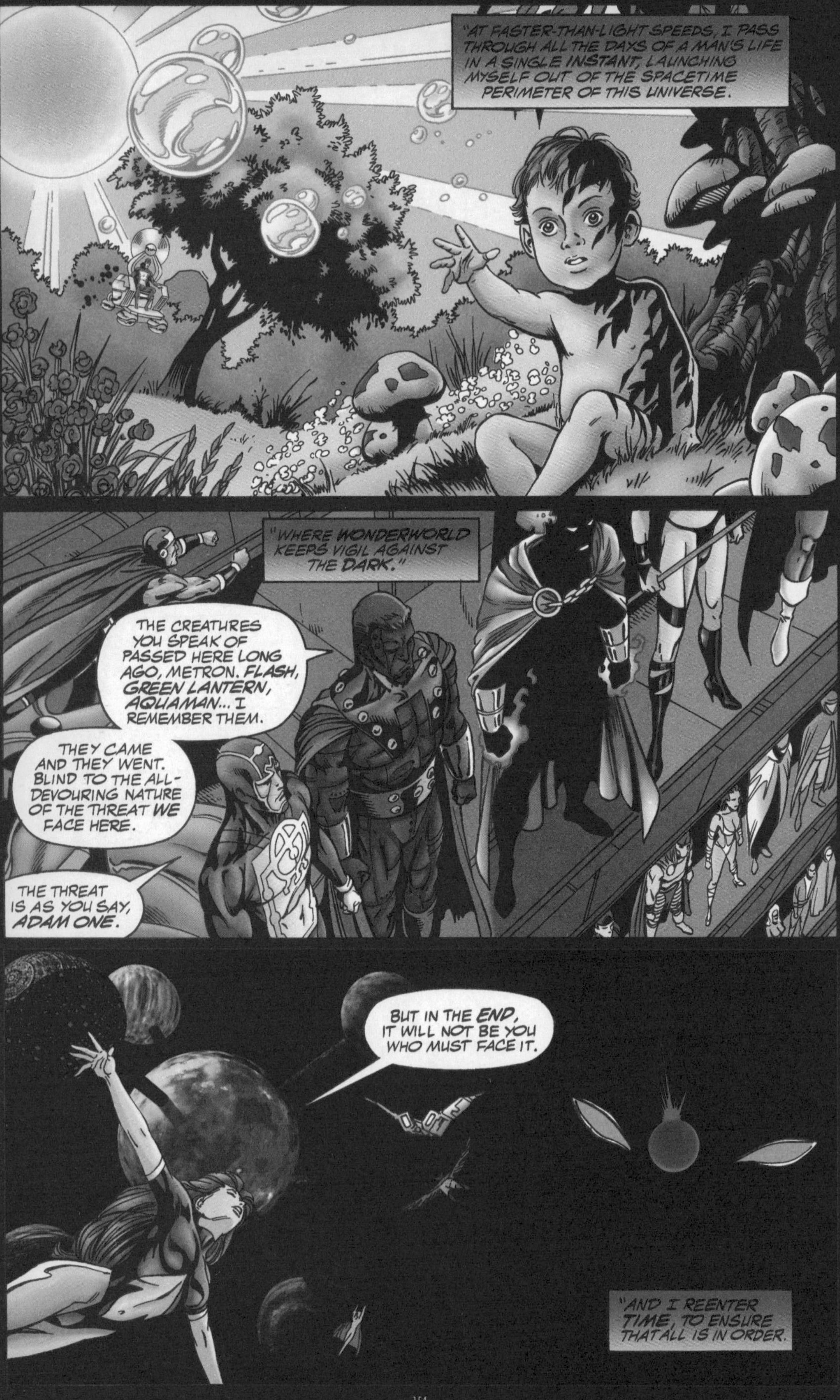
"AT FASTER-THAN-LIGHT SPEEDS, I PASS THROUGH ALL THE DAYS OF A MAN'S LIFE IN A SINGLE INSTANT, LAUNCHING MYSELF OUT OF THE SPACETIME PERIMETER OF THIS UNIVERSE.
"WHERE WONDERWORLD KEEPS VIGIL AGAINST THE DARK."
THE CREATURES YOU SPEAK OF PASSED HERE LONG AGO, METRON. FLASH, GREEN LANTERN, AQUAMAN... I REMEMBER THEM.
THEY CAME AND THEY WENT. BLIND TO THE ALL-DEVOURING NATURE OF THE THREAT WE FACE HERE.
THE THREAT IS AS YOU SAY, ADAM ONE.
BUT IN THE END, IT WILL NOT BE YOU WHO MUST FACE IT.
"AND I REENTER TIME, TO ENSURE THAT ALL IS IN ORDER.

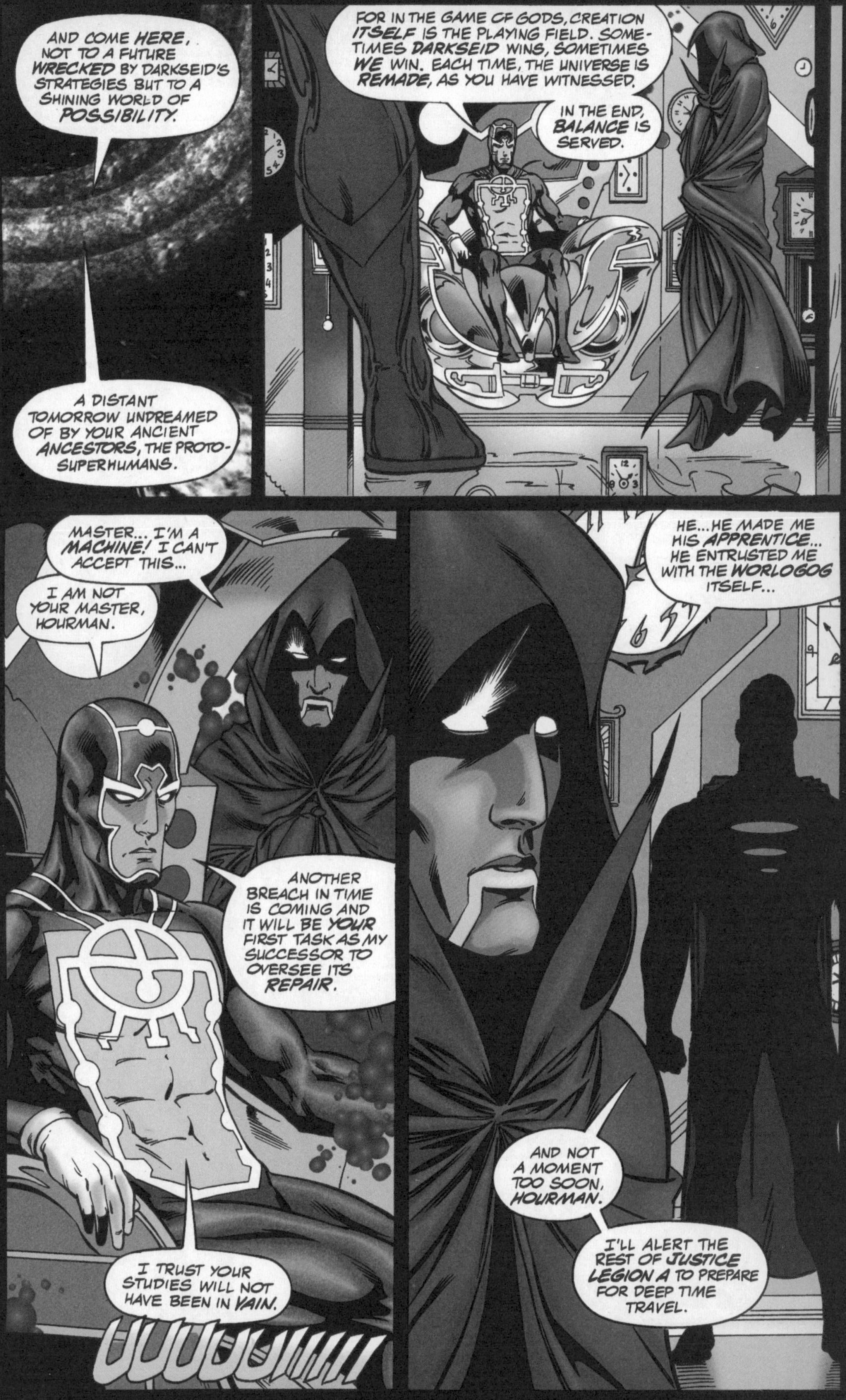
AND COME HERE, NOT TO A FUTURE WRECKED BY DARKSEID'S STRATEGIES BUT TO A SHINING WORLD OF POSSIBILITY.
A DISTANT TOMORROW UNDREAMED OF BY YOUR ANCIENT ANCESTORS, THE PROTO-SUPERHUMANS.
FOR IN THE GAME OF GODS, CREATION ITSELF IS THE PLAYING FIELD. SOMETIMES DARKSEID WINS, SOMETIMES WE WIN. EACH TIME, THE UNIVERSE IS REMADE, AS YOU HAVE WITNESSED.
IN THE END, BALANCE IS SERVED.
MASTER... I'M A MACHINE! I CAN'T ACCEPT THIS...
I AM NOT YOUR MASTER, HOURMAN.
ANOTHER BREACH IN TIME IS COMING AND IT WILL BE YOUR FIRST TASK AS MY SUCCESSOR TO OVERSEE ITS REPAIR.
I TRUST YOUR STUDIES WILL NOT HAVE BEEN IN VAIN.
UUUUUUMMM
HE...HE MADE ME HIS APPRENTICE... HE ENTRUSTED ME WITH THE WORLOGOG ITSELF...
AND NOT A MOMENT TOO SOON, HOURMAN.
I'LL ALERT THE REST OF JUSTICE LEGION A TO PREPARE FOR DEEP TIME TRAVEL.

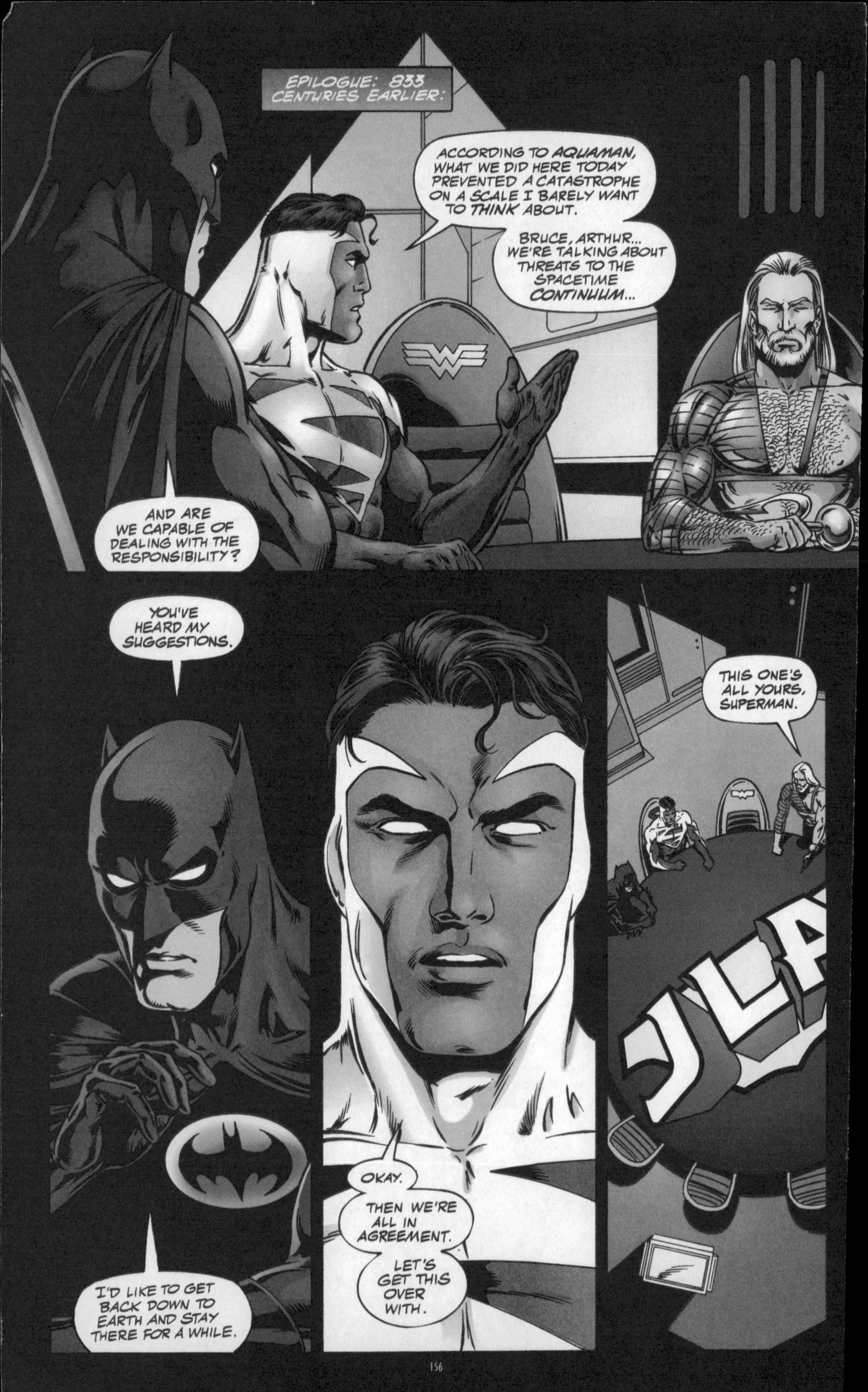
EPILOGUE: 833 CENTURIES EARLIER:
ACCORDING TO AQUAMAN, WHAT WE DID HERE TODAY PREVENTED A CATASTROPHE ON A SCALE I BARELY WANT TO THINK ABOUT.
BRUCE, ARTHUR... WE'RE TALKING ABOUT THREATS TO THE SPACETIME CONTINUUM...
AND ARE WE CAPABLE OF DEALING WITH THE RESPONSIBILITY?
YOU'VE HEARD MY SUGGESTIONS.
I'D LIKE TO GET BACK DOWN TO EARTH AND STAY THERE FOR A WHILE.
OKAY.
THEN WE'RE ALL IN AGREEMENT.
LET'S GET THIS OVER WITH.
THIS ONE'S ALL YOURS, SUPERMAN.
JLA

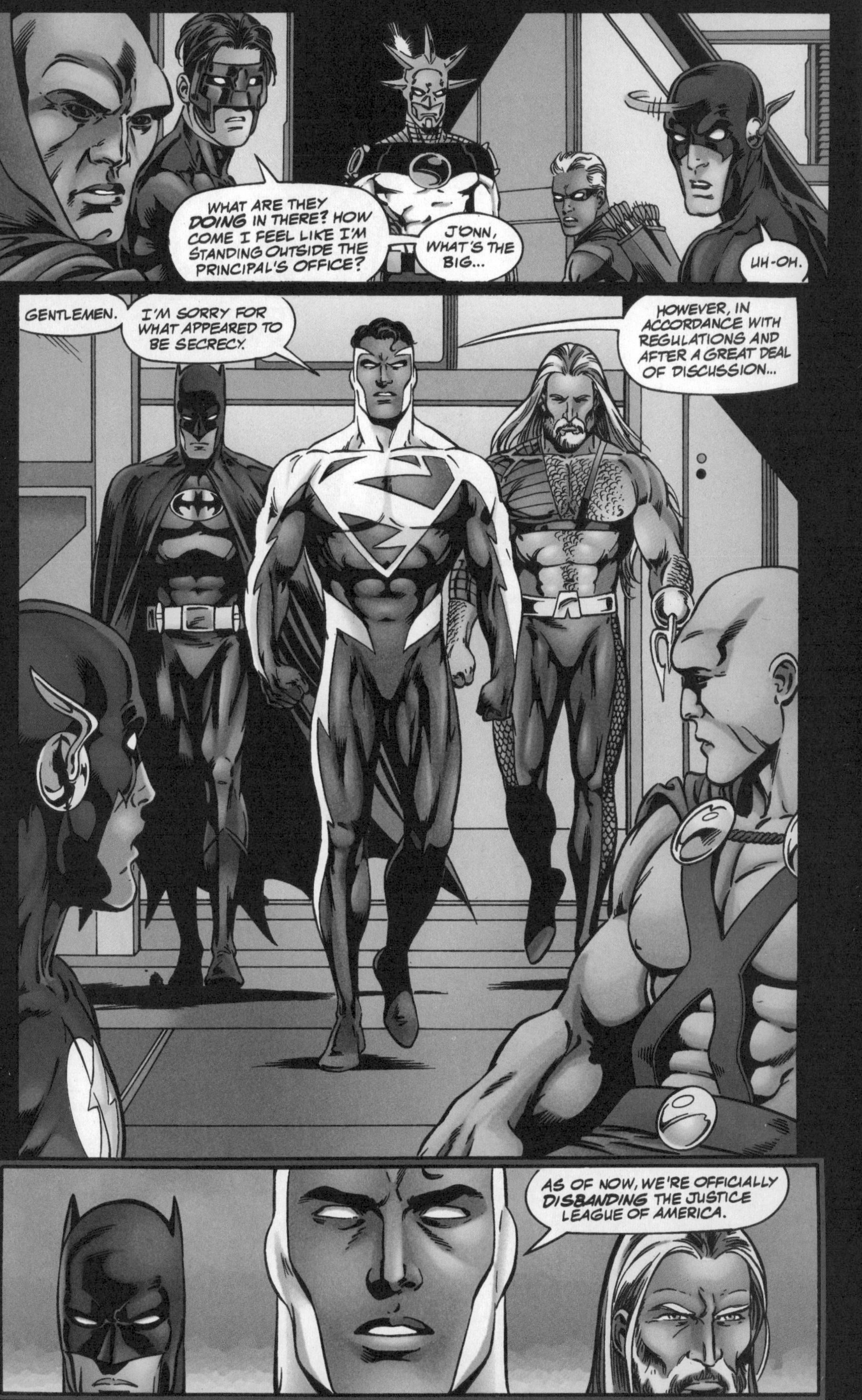
WHAT ARE THEY DOING IN THERE? HOW COME I FEEL LIKE I'M STANDING OUTSIDE THE PRINCIPAL'S OFFICE?
J'ONN, WHAT'S THE BIG...
UH-OH.
GENTLEMEN.
I'M SORRY FOR WHAT APPEARED TO BE SECRECY.
HOWEVER, IN ACCORDANCE WITH REGULATIONS AND AFTER A GREAT DEAL OF DISCUSSION...
AS OF NOW, WE'RE OFFICIALLY DISBANDING THE JUSTICE LEAGUE OF AMERICA.

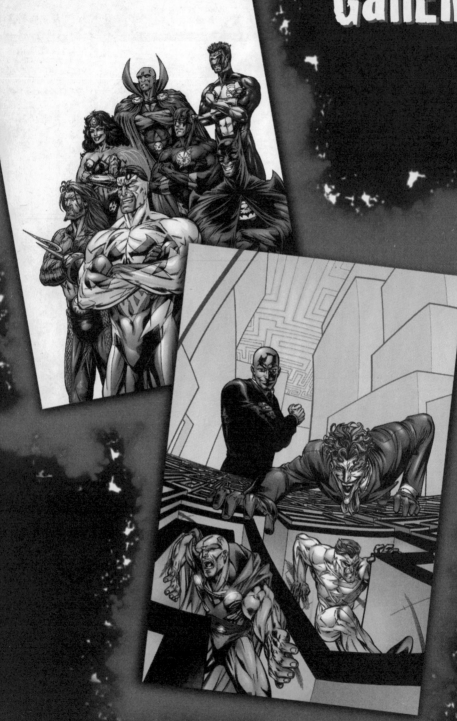

COVER GALLERY

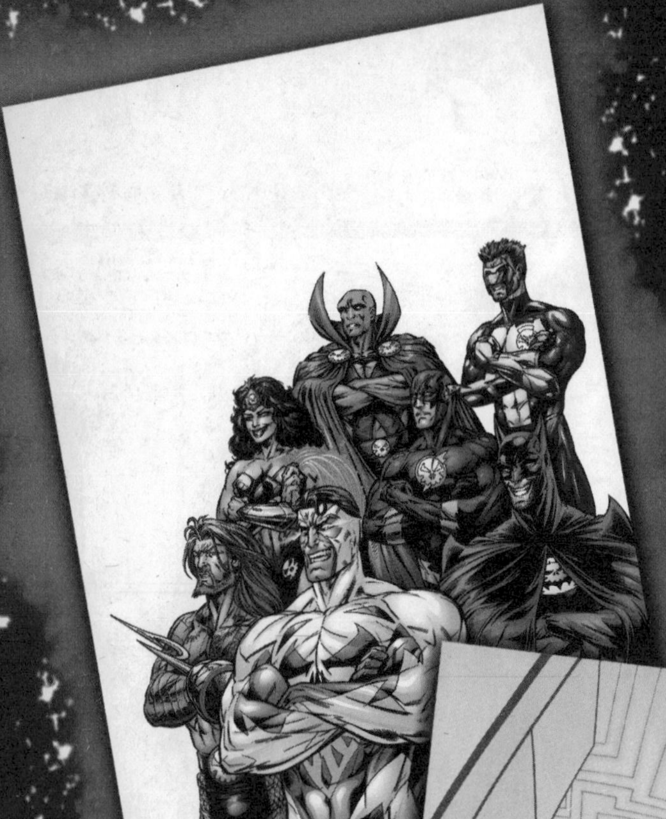

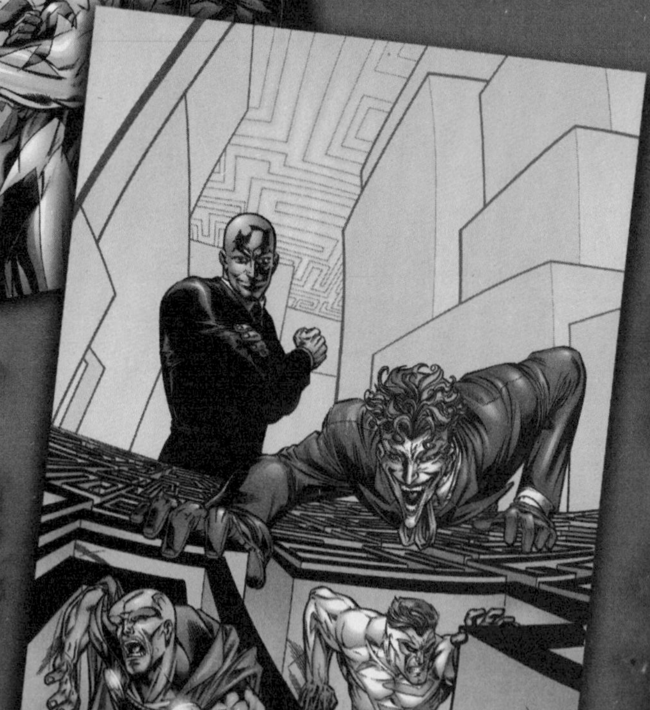

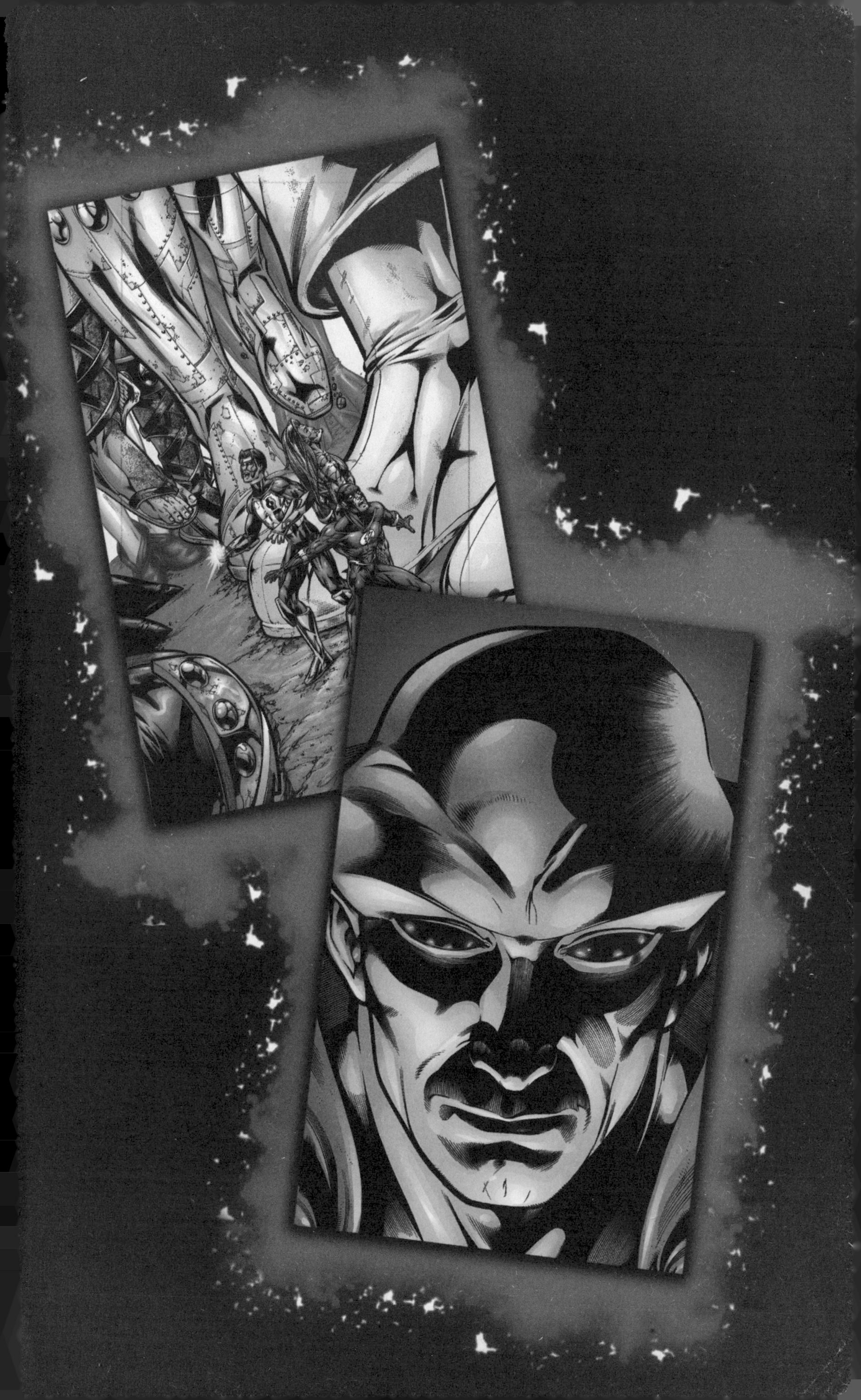

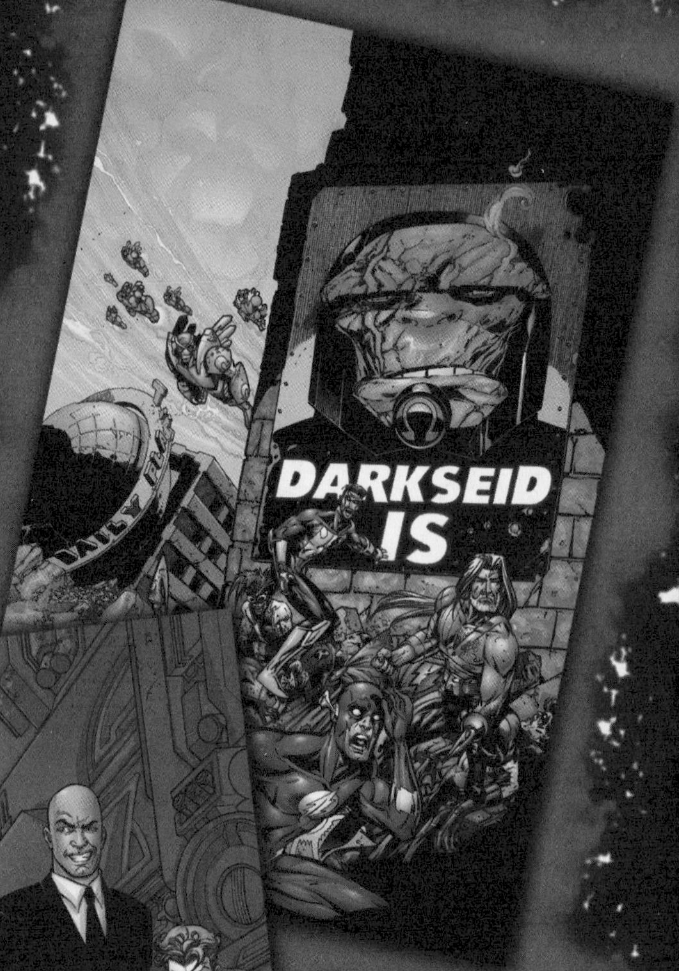
DARKSEID
IS

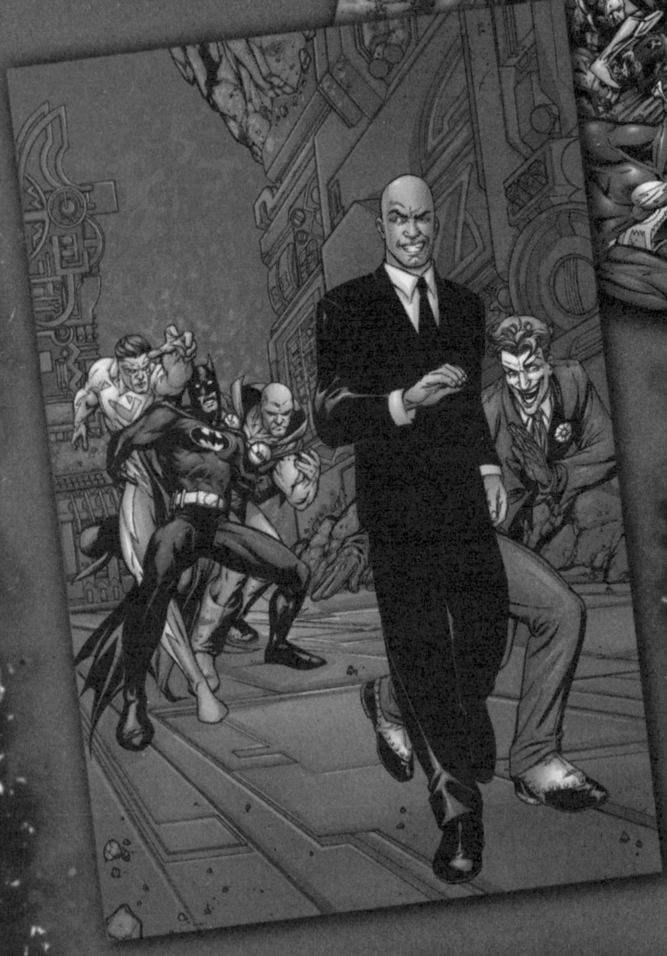